A ROOM OF HIGHLAND HANDICRAFTS

Wall Hanging, Lamp, Candlestick, Copper Plate, Wood Basket, Bellows, Toasting Fork, Rug, and Pottery from North Carolina; Candle, Woodcarving, Coverlet, and Scarf on Chair from Tennessee; Chairs, Broom, Pillow, and Poppets from Kentucky; Bear from Virginia; Table from West Virginia; Yarn from Georgia

Handicrafts of the Southern Highlands

ALLEN H. EATON

With
a new preface by
RALPH RINZLER
DIRECTOR, FESTIVAL OF AMERICAN FOLKLIFE
DIVISION OF PERFORMING ARTS
SMITHSONIAN INSTITUTION

and

a new introduction by
RAYNA GREEN
UNIVERSITY OF MASSACHUSETTS
AMHERST

THIS STUDY
WAS SUPPORTED AND ORIGINALLY PUBLISHED BY
RUSSELL SAGE FOUNDATION.

DOVER PUBLICATIONS, INC.
NEW YORK

Published in Canada by General Publishing
Company, Ltd., 30 Lesmill Road, Don Mills,
Toronto, Ontario.
Published in the United Kingdom by Constable
and Company, Ltd., 10 Orange Street, London
WC 2.

This Dover edition, first published in 1973, is an
unabridged republication of the work originally
published in 1937 by Russell Sage Foundation,
New York.

The 58 photographs by Doris Ulmann (with the
exception of the one facing page 122) have been
reproduced from original prints in the Doris Ulmann
Foundation, Berea College, Berea, Kentucky. The
publisher is grateful to Mr. Harry Segedy, Director
of the Appalachian Museum, Berea College, for
making these rare prints available. (Several of
these photographs are not precisely the same as
those in the original edition.)

The frontispiece and the plates facing pages 180,
186, 246, 260, 278, 310 and 330, here reproduced in
black and white, appeared in color in the original
edition.

A new preface by Ralph Rinzler has been specially
written for the present edition. The new introduction by Rayna Green is an adapted abridgment of
her paper for the 1970 meeting of the American
Folklore Society.

International Standard Book Number: 0-486-22211-X
Library of Congress Catalog Card Number: 72-77661

Manufactured in the United States of America
Dover Publications, Inc.
180 Varick Street
New York, N. Y. 10014

PUBLICATIONS OF
RUSSELL SAGE FOUNDATION

RUSSELL Sage Foundation was established in 1907 by Mrs. Russell Sage for the improvement of social and living conditions in the United States. In carrying out its purpose the Foundation conducts research under the direction of members of the staff or in close collaboration with other institutions, and supports programs designed to develop and demonstrate productive working relations between social scientists and other professional groups. As an integral part of its operations, the Foundation from time to time publishes books or pamphlets resulting from these activities. Publication under the imprint of the Foundation does not necessarily imply agreement by the Foundation, its Trustees, or its staff with the interpretations or conclusions of the authors.

PREFACE
TO THE DOVER EDITION

TWO comprehensive regional surveys of Southern Appalachian folk culture appeared before the Second World War. One dealt with music, the other with material culture. Both authors, Cecil Sharp (*English Folk-Songs from the Southern Appalachians,* Oxford University Press, 1932) and Allen Eaton, were introduced to the cultural riches of the region by Olive Dame Campbell whose husband, John C. Campbell, had established and directed the Southern Highlands Division of the Russell Sage Foundation during the eleven years that it functioned as a distinct operation. Both men used the material they collected in viable, highly successful revival movements—examples of what would today be called applied folklore. Sharp's work has been available since it was first published in 1917; this Dover reissue marks the first reprinting of Eaton's important work since its initial publication in 1937 . . . in the midst of the depression.

During the New Deal era, social concerns on the part of the artist, legislator and the public at large were at a high point. In 1936 ames Agee and Walker Evans spent six weeks in Alabama gathering material which was to appear several years later as the classic *Let Us Now Praise Famous Men.* Farm Security Administration photographers—including such observers as Dorothea Lange and Ben Shahn—were traveling the same roads, capturing the hardships suffered by the rural people and their spirited human response to adversity. Pare Lorentz was creating his motion picture documentaries *The Plow That Broke the Plains* and *The River.* The *Index of American Design* was in preparation, with artists across the nation combing museums and preparing the collection of paintings of the finest examples of American folk art that is now housed at the National Gallery of Art in Washington. Steinbeck's *Grapes of Wrath* brought into sharp focus the era's synthesis of stark social realism and pastoral nostalgia. Allen Eaton's social and aesthetic orientations, as manifested in his *Handicrafts of the Southern Highlands,* were very much in the spirit of these times, although his association with crafts programs, and with the Russell Sage Foundation, had begun long before.

Eaton's father, of New England stock and educated at Dartmouth, had moved to Union, Oregon, where he was operating a hardware business when Allen was born in 1878. Allen, who grew up on a farm, received university training as a sociologist and became a lecturer on art appreciation at the University of Oregon. Then for more than a decade he was a member of the state legislature. His formal involvement with craft exhibitions originated by chance on the occasion of the Panama-Pacific Exposition of 1915. When his proposal for a crafts installation in the Oregon Building was accepted, the task of carrying out the plan fell to him as the only qualified person available.

In 1916 Eaton became acquainted through correspondence with Robert de Forest, who had incorporated the Russell Sage Foundation, and who was then president of the American Federation of Arts and of the Metropolitan Museum of Art in New York. This acquaintance led to Eaton's appointment as first field secretary of the Federation in June 1919. He joined the Surveys and Exhibits Division of the Foundation in June 1920 "to bring into the field of social work a greater appreciation of the vital relation of art and beauty to life" (John M. Glenn *et al., The Russell Sage Foundation, 1907–1946*, p. 369).

Eaton played a key role—which he never reveals in this book—in the establishment of the Southern Highland Handicraft Guild (see Chapter XVI). The plan was first conceived by Mrs. Campbell in 1923 while she was visiting a cooperative crafts shop in Finland during a fourteen-month study of the folk schools of Denmark and neighboring countries. (Earlier, she had worked with her husband while he surveyed the Appalachian region for the Russell Sage Foundation, and then when he became head of the Southern Highlands Division of the Foundation; after his death in 1919 she had edited his papers; subsequently she established the John C. Campbell Folk School at Brasstown, N. C., so often mentioned in the present volume.) Mrs. Campbell and Eaton met by chance in the winter of 1926, and the result of the ensuing discussion was Eaton's first trip to Appalachia, at her invitation, to participate in the annual Conference of Southern

Mountain Workers. His address at that conference sowed the seeds for the establishment of the Guild, and in the years that followed he worked closely with Mrs. Campbell and her friends to develop and crystallize that plan, which was finally realized in December 1929.

Handicrafts of the Southern Highlands was published in 1937. The following decade saw Eaton working in New England with the Boston Society of Arts and Crafts (founded in 1897 by American friends and admirers of Morris and Ruskin) and with its numerous offspring. He brought to them his concerns for traditional craft and succeeded in stimulating craft production and marketing in New England. In 1941 he became the first director of the newly established Department of Arts and Social Work of the Russell Sage Foundation, and from that time until 1949 he worked regularly on his book *Handicrafts of New England,* the northern counterpart of the present volume. Eaton retired about ten years prior to his death, which occurred in 1962.

During his years with the Foundation, Eaton was involved in an extraordinary number of exhibitions, lectures and other projects. He was a collector concerned not only with amassing and studying material, but also with using it in educational and constructive programs beneficial to society. His social concerns were a vital and integral part of his philosophical approach to his work and to his life.

RALPH RINZLER

INTRODUCTION
TO THE DOVER EDITION

IT is particularly appropriate that Allen Eaton's study of crafts
in the Upland South should be reissued at a time when craft revival is once again a live force in the Highlands and elsewhere.
This new revival manifests itself in the suburbs, where adults turn
to hobby-craft as an alternative to boredom; in the cities, where
the young turn to leatherwork, pottery and print and jewelry-
making as alternatives to life and jobs in the Establishment. And
the revival manifests itself once again in rural areas like the
Highlands, where once-traditional peoples, regional and ethnic
groups, return to the craft way as an alternative to poverty.

The reissue of this book is also important because academic and
popular interest in American folklore and folklife is now at an
appreciative peak. Two different periods of postwar nostalgia for
rural America at the popular level, and several different periods
of academic attention, sparked by interpreters of the American
experience like Constance Rourke and Henry Nash Smith and by
regional enthusiasts like the Lomaxes, Vance Randolph, J. Phillips
Barry and J. Frank Dobie, have provided the structure for this
interest. On the popular level, the interest has continued to mani-
fest itself in the revival and support of American traditional music
and of American and foreign traditional craft.[1] On the academic
level—which often merges with or obtains its inspiration from the
popular level and vice versa—the growth of interest in the social
sciences and humanities in ethnic, regional and immigrant groups,
combined with an academic discovery of the various strands of
European folk tradition, has forced American scholars to consider
American traditions in their formal studies.[2]

The reissue of Eaton's book, then, will provide a broadly
based structure for academic and popular interest in the traditional
crafts, the craftsmen who produce them and the cultures which
produce the craftsmen. For the folklife researcher, the cultural
historian and anthropologist in particular, Eaton's book offers
much in the neglected area of folklife studies and specifically in

the area of material culture studies in the United States. Until the last fifteen years, the history of folklore studies in the United States was a spotty one, and the burden of research was borne by scholars who could only devote time to folklore apart from their duties as professors of English, history, classics or anthropology. A good deal of collection was done by the regionalists, but rigorous scholarly attention to the collections was slow in arriving. Even now, with two Ph.D. programs, five M.A. programs and a large number of single courses taught in other departments around the country, folklore as a discipline is still in the formative stages.[3] Moreover, the general area of folklife in America has been thus far slighted in favor of studies which concentrate on the verbal arts rather than on those aspects of expressive behavior which are embodied in ritual, belief, folk medicine, foodways, gesture, speech and material culture.[4]

In the last few years, however, a number of folklore scholars, in appreciation of the depth and breadth of European folklife studies,[5] and in growing appreciation of the richness of folklife in America, have begun to devote more attention to folklife, and in particular to material culture.[6] A new group of folklorists, ones trained in anthropology, rural sociology and cultural geography, as well as those trained in folklore and in the decorative arts, have turned to analysis of the theoretical and real aspects of craft, food, architecture, agriculture, medicine and technology as well as to gesture, speech, ritual and the verbal arts. In the last few years, several important contributions to the history and study of folklife in America have been made by folklorists and by cultural geographers. Work theoretical and descriptive has been undertaken, and it has been done with imagination and rigor.[7] Yet for all the recent interest, we have only begun to cover the field. Theoretical frameworks must still be explored, and those frameworks must be based on thorough descriptive studies of folklife in ethnic groups and regions over periods of time. Historical reconstructions as well as descriptions of current activity must be made, and they must be made in every region, with every group, before we can really begin to understand the forces that form and move cultures.

For these reasons, and because Eaton's book, so long unavailable, was such a remarkably fine early contribution on the scholarly *and* popular level, the reissue will be welcomed. *Handicrafts of the Southern Highlands* stands as one of the few early attempts at an inclusive study of an aspect of regional folklife. Put into perspective, both as subject and study, it can serve as a basic guide to the study of folk culture in the Upland South as well as a guide to traditional craft, craft activity and craftsmen as they are found in the United States. Eaton's study made major contributions to the scholarly study of handicrafts and material culture in America and to the study of folklife in the Upland South. Further, the study offered to the popular audience some framework for their consumption of and interest in traditional craft, in addition to a framework for understanding the structure, context and potential effects of social action programs for the economically depressed. Finally, Eaton's study made some significant contributions to an understanding of the kinds of directions traditional practices may take when exposed to the forces of urbanization, industrialization and mechanization.

First, as to the crafts themselves, the book is a compendium of information on basic technology, design, pattern and form in craft. In spite of Eaton's primary goals for the study, which had more to do with the outsider's appreciation of the craft and culture of the Highlands than with the technology of the crafts, he became interested in the details. Thus he provided descriptions of the basic technology for each craft: the tools, materials and methods of construction, the patterns and basic variations to be found within regions, the important social, cultural, economic and technological influences on each craft, and the basic alterations resulting from the pressures of those influences. One is apprised at every turn of the kind of support, financial and cultural, that any particular craft had, and a core of information about the possibilities and realities of craft marketing is always given. Eaton offers, in almost every case, some indications of the working vocabulary of craftsmen with regard to form, tools, pattern, materials and processes, and defines some of the basic aesthetic criteria used by the craftsmen and acted upon by the community and the outside consumer. He gives, in effect, working typologies recognized for many crafts though he makes no attempt at rigorous typing.[8] He indicates the strength or weakness of particular crafts at the time he studied them, and thus provides information for further inquiry into retention and maintenance of specific crafts, their potential for and actual deviations from the traditional norm as they respond to economic and technological influences. In essence, what he provides is a finding list or handbook for the fieldworker who wants to look further into craft.[9] By implication, if not by direct statement, we can begin to comprehend the fundamental body of information about craft and craft activity in the Upland South.

But beyond the sense of the craft way which Eaton brings to the Highlands, a sense informed by an understanding of the radical historical and technological changes in the community as well as by the knowledge of the craft itself, there is a sense of the multi-textured community. To put it more conventionally, the craft is in context, and it is the craft-in-context which makes the book particularly rich for the student of folklore and folklife, to the student of cultural history.

A rigorous ethnography of the Highland culture cannot be derived from Eaton's study, and yet by implication and by description, a picture of life in the Highlands is there. His understanding and presentation of the culture is often impressionistic, yet it does not lack accuracy. In many ways, the work has some aspects of a contemporary oral history.[10] The craftsmen and the members of the community are allowed and encouraged to speak for themselves, and the sense of the craft and the community comes as much from them as it does from the sympathetic outsider.[11] Even the samplings of speech in fairly accurate transcriptions of mountain dialect lend fullness to the ethnographic picture. We are made to feel that the language, like the craft, the religious and aesthetic stances, the folk beliefs and practices, is poetically and ethnographically expressive of the culture. Eaton allowed his interest to wander widely into the culture of the Upland South, and the substance of that interest is accessible to us in his account.

Perhaps the most remarkable thing about Eaton's work, in terms of ethnography, is that he was so unselective about his attentions to the subject. He *did* belong to the school of thought which insisted that tradition is dying out, and should be collected quickly before it disappeared entirely or was altered beyond recognition. Yet when he looked at the culture, he did not seek only those things that were old, only those things which were representative of a dead and dying way of life. Unlike the early ballad scholars, who for so long ignored other forms which coexisted with the old ballads, Eaton studied and presented the culture of the Highlands as it lived rather than as it "survived." He admired and treasured the old, but also valued the new since he saw it as a part of, a continuation of, the old. He feared the new, it is true, and yet he was willing to deal with it in order that it be put into the most useful perspective. Even though he does try to differentiate between traditional and nontraditional crafts and elements in the crafts, he does not disregard or exclude any. Though he offered no formal theoretical positions on the dynamics of the culture he observed, he clearly never intended to seek out and describe the "golden age" of folk culture in the Highlands. The old and the new merge in his work as they do in actuality, and the movement, the exchange, is valued. Even though the old is valued, Eaton does not allow his feeling for it to obscure and overwhelm the living craft, the moving tradition.

There are, however, failures and limitations in Eaton's book, and these should be acknowledged and remedied by later researchers. Some have already been corrected by time, if not by attention paid to them, for as time moves, stylistic and emotional perspectives move with it. The first problem which stands out in Eaton's work, that of a perspective completely reversed by later writers, is his tendency to romanticize the Highlanders, their craft and their life.[12] The book often reads like a travelogue in which the narrator describes things seen at the side of a road at sunset. Oddly enough, however, the romanticization takes place alongside a presentation (admittedly modified) of the grim circumstances under which most Highlanders live. The juxtaposition of the poverty-ridden life of the mountaineers with their romantic aspects is nowhere better represented than in the photographs by Doris Ulmann which accompany the text. The mountaineers are presented in their archaic, shabby clothes by their rundown shacks, but they are photographed so that the edges are blurred, dimmed out, and the light is altered so that a warm glow is cast on the eyes and hands of the craftsmen.[13] The picture of the Highlanders is not only altered slightly by the text and the photographs, but certain factors are omitted entirely from the account. References to moonshining, for example, as important and prominent a folk practice as craft activity, folk medicine or traditional music, are completely removed from Eaton's narrative.

The failure to present a completely realistic picture of Highland life may be attributed to several factors. Eaton's picture of the Highlands and its craftsmen belongs to the post-Depression period, a period when rural nostalgia and attention to the "little man" was at its peak. And yet, as the country built itself up again, the nostalgia had to be institutionalized into social action on the most fundamental levels. Eaton felt the urgency of speeding attention to the plight of the Highlanders because he knew that the mountaineers were misunderstood, unappreciated and even scorned by the largest segment of American society. He knew that the economic needs of the Highlands would remain critical as long as the outsider viewed the mountaineers as crude, illiterate and lazy people incapable of worthwhile action. He felt that they were an admirable people, and that their richly textured culture existed in spite of the poverty they faced. He felt that their culture, as expressed through the craft, ought to be presented positively to the outside world. Thus, he refused to include anything, any tone, any picture, any description in the book which would speak to negative stereotypes.[14] He conceived of the book as a description, a tribute and a plea. It was all of those, and the distortions caused by the romanticization are not so serious if we keep the reasons and the results in mind. If the tendency to romanticize was perhaps a failure of Eaton's time, the tendency to dwell on pathology is perhaps a failure of ours.

Most of the debilities in the book are due, however, in so far as folklife research is concerned, to the limitations on Eaton's goals for the book.[15] The restricted goals in turn limited his interest and knowledge. For the folklorist and fieldworker who wants to understand the craft-in-context, Eaton's too heavy stress on the social aspects of craft, particularly on the extensions of craft into therapeutic and recreational aspects of life, is irritating. His purpose seems too tied up with demonstrating the "rewards"—economic, social, recreational, therapeutic—of craft rather than demonstrating the crafts themselves. There seems to be too heavy a stress on the public relations aspects, the promotional aspects of crafts and craft activity, though a tremendous amount of descriptive information about the handicrafts creeps in in spite of the stress in the book. Yet, beyond the problem set by his emphasis on the "rewards" of craft, it was impossible for Eaton, within the scope of either his competence or interests, within the bounds he set for the book as he considered its purposes and audience, to deal with theoretical questions. He gives the rudimentary information necessary for further study of craft, and includes much about the culture in relation to the craft, but does not attempt much speculation about origin, aesthetics, transmission, type, pattern, form and change. When he does speculate about such matters, he offers the current popular opinion because he had little reason to doubt such theory, and because he had little reason to pursue theory to suit the needs of his book. Eaton's definition of art, for example ("the best way of doing a thing that needs to be done"), leaves much to be desired as a base for aesthetic judgment. It suits the purposes of his book, but may have been more wishful than real or operative as a principle upon which craftsmen act. The "best" way may have less to do with pragmatic, utilitarian decisions than he thought. But unfortunately, we are left to infer much of what he might have thought about the things he saw, what questions he asked, what he discarded and what he included in his discussion. His field methods, all too often catch-as-catch-can, and his goals leave us with many questions. His errors, though, merely point out the need for further, extensive, rigorous, systematic research.

The real problems in theory do not belong to Eaton's study. He provided us with information, with questions and problems on which to build theory if we want to pursue the difficult problems. The real problems belong not to Eaton, but to craft and the craft way itself and to the study of tradition-in-craft. The problems arise from the multifaceted nature of craft and craft activity. Analysis and description, theory building about indigenous traditions within a region, is as difficult a problem as the definition of the geographic and cultural boundaries of region itself. The problems of definition of a region, cultural traits and the movements of traits embodied in the expressive life of ethnic and regional groups mix with problems (with respect to craft) such as the distinctions and connections between folk, popular and elite elements in culture (the combination and synthesis of folk and nonfolk elements), between distant and recent innovations in technology and operative aesthetic principles, between culturally and individually inspired aspects, between innovations wrought by factors extraneous or new to the producing community and innovations that would occur naturally within tradition, between functional and traditional elements.[16] Though some major steps have been taken to remedy the gaps in our knowlege of these matters, all of these issues are still primary to the agenda of research in folklife studies.

Eaton's book provides for us one kind of structure, one kind of model for one region—one that might be put to use in other regions, one that forms a kind of base study for reference. Yet Eaton did leave too many questions unanswered, ones that, admittedly, we now know how to ask because of work such as his. His predictions and misgivings about the future of craft in the Highlands and elsewhere need reexamination in the contemporary community. With the exception of Ralph Rinzler's study and film on Cheever Meaders, the Georgia potter, and his family, I am not aware of any follow-up studies on Eaton's informants, their children or their communities, even though the book left us with a catalogue of operative craftsmen and craft activity on which to base such further study.[17] If scholars did nothing but go back over Eaton's trail, many resolutions to the problems listed above would be forthcoming. In the Highlands once again, the revival of traditional craft offers us the opportunity for study. Serious attention now needs to be paid to the effects of a long period of successful guild and government activity and to the increase of government activity in support of the crafts. The extensions of craft into urban centers, therapeutic and recreational areas needs examination. The internal and external pressures, the economic, social and cultural forces at work in the craft communities, need examination. And the dynamics of tradition made visible in response to the various pressures and forces deserve scrutiny.

Eaton, and men like him, set a tradition of involvement in what they studied which was remarkable and valuable. Hopefully, this particular tradition will continue to be honored.

RAYNA GREEN

NOTES

[1]The most important popular manifestations of the revival of traditional expression was the growth in interest in the 60's in Bluegrass,
Country and Western music and in the 40's and 60's in folksong and
blues. Presently, there is a tremendous popular interest in traditional
clothing and craft from all over the world, particularly from Eastern
Europe and the Balkans. Folk dancing has continued to attract a good
deal of interest in the universities in the East and Midwest. This all
filters down to affect true traditional expression, both economically
and aesthetically, just as traditional expression has provided the
impetus and base for the revival.

[2]See George Lyman Kittredge's study, *Witchcraft in Old and New
England* (Cambridge, Mass., 1929; New York, 1956), and Francis
James Child's *The English and Scottish Ballads*. Later, Cecil Sharp's
studies of the "Child" ballads in Appalachia are exemplary of the
merging of American interests with European ones, and really mark
the beginning of studies in American tradition.

[3]Indiana University and the University of Pennsylvania grant
Ph.D's in Folklore. U.C.L.A., Texas, Berkeley, Bowling Green
(Ohio), Wayne State (Detroit) and Cooperstown offer M.A.'s and
many single courses are offered in universities throughout the country.
There are many regional journals of folklore as well as the journal
of the American Folklore Society, the *Journal of American Folklore*.

[4]The exception has been American anthropologists who have devoted
attention to the material culture and art of the American Indians,
and the Pennsylvania folklorists who have studied the decorative
traditions of the Pennsylvania Germans.

[5]In Europe, the Scandinavian school of regional ethnologists, as
well as the Welsh, Irish, English and Scottish folklorists and cultural
geographers, have always devoted themselves to the widest spectrum
of behavior in folk culture, including a great deal of attention to
material culture. See Holger Rasmussen, ed., *Dansk Folkemuseum
und Frilandsmuseet: History and Activities* (Copenhagen, 1966);
Sigurd Erixon, "Regional European Ethnology," *Folkliv* 2/3 (1937),
89–108, 2 (1938), 137–177; E. Estyn Evans, "Folklife Studies in
Northern Ireland," *Journal of the Folklore Institute* II (Dec. 1965),
355–363; Alexander Fenton, "Material Culture as an Aid to Local
History Studies in Scotland," *JFI* II (Dec. 1965), 326–329.

[6]When material culture has been studied in America, students have
devoted themselves largely to groups whose decorative traditions and
general material culture are highly visible and prominent in the

culture (to the Pennsylvania Dutch and the Shakers, for example), or to items which represented important movements or aspects of American life such as the log cabin or the Kentucky rifle. Most of this work has been descriptive rather than theoretical.

[7]Such work includes: Don Yoder, "The Folklife Studies Movement," *Pennsylvania Folklore* XII:3 (July 1963), 43–56; the following three articles by Michael Owen Jones: "Folk Art Production and the Artist's Obligation," *The Journal of Popular Culture* IV:1 (Summer 1970), 194–212; "The Study of Traditional Furniture: Review and Preview," *Keystone Folklore Quarterly* XII:4 (Winter 1967), 233–245; "A Traditional Chairmaker at Work," *Mountain Life and Work* XLIII:1 (Spring 1967), 10–13; and the following works by Henry H. Glassie: "The Appalachian Log Cabin," *MLW* XXXIX:4 (Winter 1963), 5–14; "The Old Barns of Appalachia," *MLW* XL:2 (Summer 1965), 21–30; *Pattern in the Material Folk Culture of the Eastern United States* (Philadelphia, 1968); "The Smaller Outbuildings of the Southern Mountains," *MLW* XL:1 (Spring 1964); 21–25; "Types of the Southern Mountain Cabin," in Jan Harold Brunvand, *The Study of American Folklore* (N. Y., 1968); "William Houck, Maker of Pounded Ash Adirondack Pack Baskets," *KFQ* XII:1 (Spring 1967), footnote 69; and (with Fred Kniffen as co-author) "Building in Wood in the Eastern U.S.: A Time-Place Perspective," *The Geographical Review* LVI:1 (Jan. 1966), 40–66.

Glassie's fine study *Pattern in the Material Folk Culture of the Eastern United States,* which devoted itself largely to theoretical questions about material culture, is also descriptive of many aspects of folklife. His book sets up a framework for dealing with the transmission, spread and persistence of items in their cultural contexts.

[8]See Glassie, "Types of the Southern Mountain Cabin."

[9]Examples of other such finding lists would be the *Frank C. Brown Collection of North Carolina Folklore* (Durham, 1951–1962) for the Southeastern United States, Sean O'Sulleabhain's *Handbook of Irish Folklore* (Hatboro, Pa., 1963) and Vance Randolph's *Ozark Folksongs* (Columbia, Missouri, 1946–50).

[10]For a fine recent oral history of a traditional community, see Lynwood Montell's *The Saga of Coe Ridge* (Tennessee, 1970).

[11]Eaton almost moves toward ethnohistory, partly because of his lack of a "scientific method." He simply lets the narrative happen.

[12]Eaton's picture of Highland life differs widely from Horace Kephart's *Our Southern Highlanders* (N. Y., 1913 and 1926), which was a more romantic portrayal of Highland life, and from Harry Caudill's recent *Night Comes to the Cumberlands* (Boston, 1963) and Jack Weller's *Yesterday's People* (Lexington, 1966), both of which

stress the deprivation and grim poverty of the Highlanders. In all of these books, however, the intent is to inspire the outsider's interest in the richly textured culture (as well as the needs) of the mountaineers. Contemporary students may find Caudill's and Weller's accounts more realistic than the earlier two because contemporary tastes demand less sentimentality, and because their stress is heaviest on social action.

[13]For contrast, see Walker Evan's photos which accompany James Agee's text in *Now Let Us Praise Famous Men* (N. Y., 1941 and 1969), done in the same period as the Ulmann photographs.

[14]See Erskine Caldwell's novels of the poor-white South for negative stereotypic presentations of rural, traditional types.

[15]There are some problems with organization of the book, which cause no serious misunderstandings or theoretical problems. The repetitiveness and inclusion of what seem to be random bits of information (the list of herbal cures, for example), reflect the often shaky methodology Eaton used in putting the book together and in conducting interviews in the field. Information is bound to get repetitive when interviewing is being done on one subject and different methods of obtaining information are used.

[16]See Glassie, *Pattern,* for a discussion throughout of these issues. See also Rayna Green, unpublished ms. read before the 1970 annual meeting of the American Folklore Society, "Tradition and the O.E.O.: Craft Revival and the Culture of Poverty."

[17]There has been some attention on a popular level to material culture in the Upland South. The Southern Highlands Handicrafts Guild has offered some publications of its own about the various activities the guild sponsors and about the items produced under its auspices. Since the beginning of publication, both *Mountain Life and Work* and *Foxfire* have printed articles on material culture. For the most part, however, these articles have been descriptive rather than theoretical and have been aimed at a wide popular audience.

MARYLAND

WEST VIRGINIA

VIRGINIA

NORTH CAROLINA

INDEX

Drawn by Martha Eaton

Art when really understood is the province of every human being. It is simply a question of doing things, anything well. It is not an outside extra thing. . . . He does not have to be a painter or sculptor to be an artist. He can work in any medium. He simply has to find the gain in the work itself, not outside it.

ROBERT HENRI

Weaving, hit's the prettiest work I ever done. It's asettin' and trampin' the treadles and watchin' the pretty blossoms come out and smile at ye in the kiverlet.

AUNT SAL CREECH
of Pine Mountain, Kentucky

We have lately become convinced that accurate work with carpenters' tools, or lathe, or hammer and anvil, or violin, or piano, or pencil, or crayon, or camel's hair brush, trains well the same nerves and ganglia with which we do what is ordinarily called thinking.

CHARLES ELIOT

Hit's better for folkses characters to larn 'em to do things with their hands.

WILLIAM CREECH
of Pine Mountain, Kentucky

The pleasure which ought to go with the making of every piece of handicraft has for its basis the keen interest which every healthy man takes in healthy life, and is compounded chiefly of three elements: variety, hope of creation, and the self-respect which comes of a sense of usefulness, to which must be added that mysterious bodily pleasure which goes with the deft exercise of bodily powers.

WILLIAM MORRIS

We of the United States are amazingly rich in the elements from which we weave a culture. We have the best of man's past on which to draw, brought to us by our native folk and folk from all parts of the world. In binding these elements into a national fabric of beauty and strength, let us keep the original fibers so intact that the fineness of each will show in the completed handiwork.

FRANKLIN D. ROOSEVELT

TABLE OF CONTENTS

PART I

MOUNTAIN HANDICRAFTS OF PIONEER DAYS

CHAPTER I

CHAPTER II

PART II

REVIVAL OF THE HANDICRAFTS AND THEIR PRESENT-DAY PRACTICE

Chapter V

Spinning and Weaving for Home and Market . 92

Chapter VI

Coverlets and Counterpanes . . . 111

PART III

THE RURAL HANDICRAFT MOVEMENT AND THE WIDER USE OF HANDICRAFTS

CHAPTER XX

THE HANDICRAFT MOVEMENT IN RURAL AMERICA . 291

CHAPTER XXI

ADULT EDUCATION THROUGH HANDICRAFTS . . 303

CHAPTER XXII

RECREATION THROUGH HANDICRAFTS . . 316

CHAPTER XXIII

IN CONCLUSION 327

APPENDICES

LIST OF ILLUSTRATIONS

LIST OF ILLUSTRATIONS

THE DORIS ULMANN PHOTOGRAPHS

EVERYONE who examines this book will wish to know something of the remarkable photographs which Doris Ulmann has made for it. I believe that no one has ever done a series of photographs of rural people in relation to their handicrafts which in scope, sympathetic interpretation, and artistic treatment equals the collection from which 58 of the subjects in this volume have been chosen. In one sense this book is a memorial to her, not alone because it brings together studies of many people for whom she cared and who cared for her, but also because it represents the endeavors of friends to carry out her wishes in the use of these photographs.

"I am of course glad to have people interested in my pictures as examples of the art of photography," Mrs. Ulmann once said to me, "but my great wish is that these human records shall serve some social purpose." It was something of a coincidence that about this time I had outlined for the Russell Sage Foundation a plan for bringing into closer relation the fields of art and of social work, believing that both would gain much by the association. I ventured to suggest that the artist is one of our most valuable assets in the social field and I felt sure that some, perhaps many, would welcome the opportunity to be identified with this work.

It also happened that I had begun a study of the handicrafts in the Southern Highlands and had established friendly contacts throughout the region. Some years earlier Mrs. Ulmann had herself gone into the mountains of southwestern Virginia and eastern Kentucky, securing a few fine studies of native people. She told me of her desire to make a photographic record of many of these, some types of which were disappearing. Unforgettable is the eagerness with which she responded to an offer to help her continue her journeys into the Highlands under more favorable conditions than she could alone command. "If you will make the contacts for me," she said, "I will be able to get the subjects that I want most and I will photograph the people working with handicrafts that you want," adding that she would do this at her own expense.

Since the workers in handicrafts were as important to Mrs. Ulmann's plan as any other subjects, I felt free to enter into the arrangement she suggested, although I could not obligate the Russell Sage Foundation in advance to use the photographs. Mrs. Ulmann spent much time in the mountains in 1933 and 1934. When in the late summer of 1934 illness compelled her to return to her home in New York, where she died on August 28, over 2,000 plates which she had exposed remained undeveloped. Among these were more than half of the photographs taken by her that have been included in this book.

Few persons have ever undertaken a work and pursued it with clearer purpose and stronger will. Always frail, never enjoying good health, she continued to push on despite the entreaties of friends to rest awhile, until she had covered most of the territory included in the joint plan and had secured many more subjects than had appeared possible. The quality of her work speaks for itself. To those closely associated with her it seemed that she was racing against time and that, measured in terms of achievement, she clearly won the race. Although she did not live to see the images on some of her finest negatives she knew what was there, for few photographers have been surer of what their undeveloped plates contained. She also had the satisfaction of making provision for their care and use.

While to many her portraits of the Southern Highlanders will always be Doris Ulmann's most outstanding achievement, they constitute only a portion of her work. In addition to studies of eminent world figures, including Tagore, Einstein, Galsworthy, and other visitors to America, and many authors, artists, musicians, and other personalities, three books of her portraits were published. These are: Twenty-four Portraits of the Faculty of Physicians and Surgeons of Columbia University; A Book of Portraits of the Medical Department of the Johns Hopkins University; and A Portrait Gallery of American Editors. Perhaps the work with which the public is most familiar is the group of illustrations in Roll, Jordan, Roll, undertaken in collaboration with Julia Peterkin, the limited edition of which is one of the most distinguished examples of photographic illustration done by any American. Prints of these and all other important subjects, selected from upward of ten thousand negatives, she bequeathed to Berea College, Berea, Kentucky, to be preserved in a special wing of the Art Museum. This is to be built by funds which she provided.

The Doris Ulmann Foundation, which is entrusted with the care of this extensive collection, has given the fullest co-operation in getting the subjects into shape for this book on the Handicrafts of the Southern Highlands, even making a grant that has permitted the inclusion of more illustrations than the Russell Sage Foundation would have felt it could afford in a publication to be sold within its accustomed low-price range. The members of the Doris Ulmann Foundation are Mrs. Olive D. Campbell, Helen H. Dingman, Henry L. Necarsulmer, John Jacob Niles, and Allen H. Eaton. They hope that this publication will in a degree carry out Mrs. Ulmann's wish to put her photographic studies to a social use.

It is not possible for me to express my sense of gratitude and admiration for the work that Doris Ulmann has done in the Southern Highlands and the privilege it has been to have had some part in such an undertaking. But I must try to express for my associates and myself a brief word of appreciation of two persons whose co-operation in connection with these illustrations has been indispensable. First to Mr. Niles, who assisted Mrs. Ulmann in the field, and whose notes and many days of work on records of the trips have provided information and data of great importance. Mr. Niles, a native of Kentucky, collected folk music in the Highlands while assisting Mrs. Ulmann with her photographing, but during the last year gave up most of his own plans in order to further her work. Second, too much credit cannot be given to Samuel H. Lifshey, who developed the 2,000 exposed plates and who has made the fine prints that have gone into the Berea collection as well as those in this book. He did more than a perfect technician's job. No one could have treated the plates and made the prints with greater fidelity to the subjects.

Limitation of space prevents further acknowledgment to others who have helped in many ways to bring these illustrations into their present form; but it is gratifying to feel that each one has paid a tribute to an American artist of ability and devotion who found in the people of her country, regardless of their station and circumstances, inspiration and hope which she has interpreted through a medium that we all can understand.

A. H. E.

PREFACE

THE time will come when every kind of work will be judged by two measurements: one by the product itself, as is now done, the other by the effect of the work on the producer. When that time comes the handicrafts will be given a much more important place in our plan of living than they now have, for unquestionably they possess values which are not generally recognized.

The handicrafts suffer from two extreme points of view: one, that we have long since abandoned them in our scheme of life and to advocate handwork for anything that a machine can do is a step backward; the other, that there is an unlimited market for handwork and that almost anyone can do it.

Erroneous as these views are, each contains a measure of truth. Beyond a doubt we are passing out of a handicraft culture into one dominated by the machine. People in cities buy with wages or other income most of the objects and services which they enjoy; but there are still a considerable number of industrial articles made wholly or in part by hand, and in agriculture handicrafts still play an important part. One can hardly accept the view, therefore, that they are entirely of the past; but there is no doubt that we are now in process of deciding the place that they shall have in our daily work and life.

There is, on the other hand, no greater error than the assumption that anyone can make salable objects for the market. The facts are that the demand for hand-made things is contracting rather than expanding, and that it requires both skill and taste and often wide experience to succeed in this field.

A common belief is that the value of a handicraft can be determined entirely by the income which it produces. Certainly the income is a prime consideration, but it is not the only one. Often there is a satisfaction growing out of the practice of a handicraft which exceeds that of its economic return. Therefore to confine our estimate of handicrafts to the market possibilities is to overlook some of their most important values.

The report presented here has to do with people whose chief concern with handicrafts is the income they will bring, for to thousands they offer the only means by which to earn money to pay taxes and buy the few necessities required to support a tolerable standard of life. One purpose, therefore, is to show how indispensable handicrafts are in the economy of countless families throughout the Southern Highlands; a second is to show the other rewards they bring to these same people, what they add to the social and recreational life of the communities in which they are carried on, their educational and cultural significance, the esthetic enjoyment they foster, their help in the field of therapeutics, and the sense of emotional security they give. If these values are not brought out, then the report will fall far short of its purpose. And it will fall short on two main counts: first, instead of being an inclusive fact-finding study upon which the people of the Highlands may safely act, it would be only a partial study with some of the vital factors omitted. Second, because of these omissions the report would be lacking in important experiences which the Southern Highlands are in a position to contribute to the movement throughout our country.

The word "handicraft," as used in the report, is a broad term including all those things which people make with their hands either for their own use or for that of others. The article may be fashioned entirely by hand, including the preparation of all the materials even to the shaping of the tools employed, or it may be made in part by machinery as in the preparation of woods for fine cabinet work, or as in the machine spinning of thread and yarn to be woven on the hand loom; but if the final product, the character of the thing itself, is shaped by hand it is an object of handicraft.

If this definition seems too simple or too obvious, it may be justified on the ground that the dictionaries give no adequate definition of the word. To many people the term handicraft brings up a rather hazy picture of things made for sale, or of "busy work" in school or camp devised too often simply to fill in spare time. These comprise only a small part of handicrafts, which in reality include, besides many fine objects in museums and galleries, countless things in the market. They are the main components of our houses, and the definition admits at once the great number of articles which people make for themselves, especially in rural areas where the practice is still an important part of the daily work.

Indispensable as handicrafts have been in the economic life of our country, it must be apparent to all that they now occupy a very secondary place. The gradual displacement of handwork, in which man was originally often both the machine and the engine, by modern mechanisms that require fewer and fewer attendants, is bringing about one of the most fundamental changes in the history of mankind. This transition, of which we of this generation are in the midst, or more likely at the beginning, is a shift from what an authority in this field has called "an economy of scarcity" to "an economy of abundance."[1] These terms seem to be appropriate designations for the two periods, in the first of which was the universal worry and fear that as population increased, starvation and other suffering would follow; and the second in which we of the present day are faced with the startling fact, so economists tell us, that less than four-fifths of our population could produce all the things needed to support our present standard of life. The great question is of course whether or not we shall have the desire, the ability, and other qualities to adapt ourselves to this unparalleled situation.

Handicrafts are becoming increasingly important in this transition period to large numbers of people throughout our country whom we may think of as belonging to two main groups. First is the group to which the economic returns from handicrafts is the primary incentive; and second, the group in which the cultural and other satisfactions predominate. This is not an entirely satisfactory statement. The terms economic and cultural as used here are not intended to be mutually exclusive but rather as supplementing each other, and there are innumerable instances, as exemplified in this report, in which handicrafts bring both economic and cultural satisfactions to the same person or to the same group.

This gets us back to the statement made earlier that work in handicrafts should be judged by two measurements—by the product itself and by what the making of it means to the producer. Obviously to those who are in what we shall term the economic group the product is most important; it is the vendable thing, counted upon to bring in the economic return. To measure a craft

[1] Chase, Stuart, The Economy of Abundance. By permission of The Macmillan Co., publishers, New York, 1934, p. 51.

by the product is both easy and comparatively exact; we might, if we are thinking of the commercial aspect, call it the consumer's measurement, or, if thinking of the psychological aspect, the objective measurement. For the other group, which we shall call the cultural, the measurement is subjective and it is not so easy to make, but it may be just as important to the individual and in some instances even more so.

The effort, therefore, to keep these two groups distinct, even though we know that strictly speaking we cannot do so, will help us to understand all the values derived from them. What should be kept clear is the fact that one group depends upon the income obtained to help procure the material necessities of life, and to this group everything naturally revolves around the product, especially the marketing of it. The other group may not be dependent upon the income derived, nor even sell the product, but may count upon the health and happiness secured. The workers in both groups may include only a minority of our people, but the importance of the work to most of them cannot be overstated.

One economic contribution now being offered by the handicrafts which deserves wide acclaim is the making of articles for their own use by persons who have no money with which to buy them. Thousands of families have recently learned that on a small tract of land they can raise vegetables and fruit which could not be graded for market, yet which provide them with fresh food to eat at the time or to preserve for winter; likewise that they can fashion with their hands things to serve the family but which for obvious reasons would not be marketable. An example of this may be found in the southern states, where in the past few years hundreds of men and women have grown their own cotton and made excellent mattresses which they could not afford to buy. When people without money produce commodities they can use, they do not deprive manufacturers of sales but create new material wealth and often bring to themselves satisfactions which even the ability to purchase cannot match.

Turning now from the economic to what we have called the cultural group, we see immediately one marked difference. The former group will be found largely in handicraft communities in certain sections of the Southern Highlands, in the more or less related handicraft centers of New Hampshire, in the Indian communities of the Southwest, and so forth; while some of the workers whose end is mainly cultural are identified with these localities, yet many are scattered far and wide throughout the country, a number of them in small groups, but more often they are working alone.

Roughly speaking, the cultural groups work for what we might term a social, educational, esthetic, or therapeutic value. Often a handicraft will bring social opportunities not only to the individual practicing it but to his family; and the educational values will include the advantages of learning that attach to the work itself. The esthetic or the therapeutic value is entirely individual and subjective. While it is probable that most of those so engaged are impelled by more than one motive and sometimes by all of them, an exception might be noted in respect to the therapeutic value around which a very large practice has been built up, especially in hospitals and sanatoriums for the treatment of both physical and mental ailments. But even in these cases the educational and esthetic aspects are vital, and often the social and economic as well.

In all gains to society, especially material gains, there are bound to be certain losses. Part of the price paid for our present civilization is a loss of the creative element in much of the world's work. In the processes of production, which have brought to the average consumer a wealth of creature comforts transcending the dreams of even his own parents, methods have been developed by which the average worker is often but a small cog in the big wheel of a machine over which he has little or no control. The benefits which he receives as a consumer of goods purchased with wages paid him often seem worth the sacrifice he has made in individual initiative, in the ownership of tools, and the use of his hands. This balance of benefits appears acceptable until through unemployment his power as a consumer is greatly reduced and he faces the tragedy of the absence of any resource to which he can turn.

He who does creative work, whether he dwell in a palace or in a hut, has in his house a window through which he may look out upon some of life's finest scenes. If his work be a handicraft he will be especially happy, for it will help him not only to perceive much of the beauty of the world about him but, what is man's greatest privilege, to identify himself with it. If it enables him to earn his daily bread then he should rejoice, for blessed is the man who has found his work; but if, as will be the case of many in our day, his handicraft is not a way of making a living, but through self-expression a help toward a fuller life, he too will rejoice, for he has all the privileges of his fellow-craftsmen without the need of fitting his product to the market.

Each handicraft has its own special reward, but there are a few compensations which all handicrafts bring to him who works at this open window. First, and perhaps greatest, as has been said, is the opportunity for self-expression which much of life's work with its modern advantages does not give. The need of an outlet for the creative impulse is universal, a feeling well expressed by an old-time weaver of North Carolina who, when someone brought her a draft of a new coverlet, said to a neighbor, "I'm rarin' to string up the loom and work it out. Ain't it wonderful what things there is to see and do?" Another compensation is a growing appreciation of beauty in the things of everyday life. The effort to make a useful object pleasing to the eye or touch gives the craftsman an understanding of the age-long struggle to bestow on objects of daily use that quality that renders their ownership one of life's little events. And recognizing beauty in things that he had not noticed before, or looking at had regarded as commonplace, he feels himself a joint possessor with those who have designed them and with all others who enjoy them.

To the worker in handicrafts, perhaps more than to the worker in other arts, the way is open to the enjoyment and appreciation of nature. The lumber with which he builds a house or the small block on which he carves a design opens his window upon the trees of grove and forest; through weaving on his loom he sees the flocks, the flax and cotton fields; or through his pottery he comes to know the many clays and kaolins from which ceramics, porcelains, or building bricks are formed; or in substances for coloring he finds extending over the earth's surface and deep within its crust a hundred hues to stain and dye his handiwork; through the countless forms of massive structures to that of fine jewelry he learns the minerals, metals, precious stones, corals, ambers, and other materials suitable for an infinite variety of work. Thus to his appreciation of man's work, art, is added an appreciation of the source of all the arts, nature.

From such personal experience the worker in handicrafts will wish for others the privileges which have meant so much to him; and he will ask himself if there are not ways by which the sense of beauty could be extended from the somewhat narrow fields of art to the broader field of human relations. And he comes to see that to ask the question is in part to answer it.

He longs to have all share in this larger world. Recalling instances in which some of the lowliest tasks have been done beautifully, he revises the definition of art to meet his new concept. It becomes clear to him that it is not what one does that determines a work of art but the manner in which it is done. An object of art may be a painting on canvas; a cathedral in stone; but it may also be a well-printed and beautifully bound book, a loaf of bread, or a kitchen garden. To restate it, he realizes that art is just the best way of doing a thing that needs to be done—the expression of beauty within limitations. These limitations are the use it is to serve, the materials of which it is made, the place it is to occupy.

That America is coming to this point of view concerning art and is perceiving the need for more beauty in daily life there is much evidence; the growing interest in the folk arts is one, the awakened concern for the rare artifacts of the American Indian another, the widening practice of the handicrafts throughout our country another; and still another is the making available to all for study and enjoyment the treasures of our great art galleries and museums. Perhaps one of the strongest influences is the improvement in form, color, and texture of our industrial arts which include countless objects, large and small, turned out by the help of machines in quantity for the daily use and consumption of millions of people at prices within their reach.

These are indications of the struggle which America is making to bring to all the experience of beauty both in creative work and in appreciation. They are indications too of the need to find beauty, not only in the things we make and use but in the relations we sustain one to another. Nor is this need America's alone—it is felt everywhere. No one has expressed it better than a great English artist and craftsman in writing, John Galsworthy, who has left this message for his fellowmen:

In these unsuperstitious days no other ideal seems worthy of us, or indeed possible to us, save beauty—or call it, if you will, the dignity of human life . . . the teaching of what beauty is, to all . . . so that we wish and work and dream that not only ourselves but everybody may be healthy and happy; and, above all, the fostering of the habit of doing things and making things well, for the joy of the work and the pleasure of achievement.[1]

[1] Candelabra: Selected Essays and Poems. Charles Scribner's Sons, New York, 1933, pp. 116, 118.

INTRODUCTION

THE handicrafts are an integral part of the culture of the Southern Highlands, that vast and for so long isolated region of the Appalachian Mountains which begins with the Virginias and extends into northern Georgia and Alabama. Many parts of it are still difficult of access. The territory includes within its boundaries the western strip of Maryland, the Blue Ridge and Alleghany Ridge counties of Virginia, nearly all of West Virginia, eastern Kentucky and eastern Tennessee, western North Carolina, the counties of northwestern South Carolina, northern Georgia, and northeastern Alabama.

The name "Southern Highlands" was given to the region by John C. Campbell, who registered the reason for his choice in a delightful statement in his study of this section.

The traveler who follows the trails of this far country, fords its rushing streams, and forces his way through thickets of rhododendron and laurel to rest upon some beech-shaded bank of moss, and who toward sunset checks his horse upon the ridge to trace the thread of smoke which signals welcome, may yet be at a loss for a name to describe the land; but when at dawn he wakes with mist rising from every cove and valley, and echoes still sounding of half-remembered traditions, folk-lore, and folk-songs, recited or sung before the fire by "granny" or "grandpap," he knows there is but one name that will do it justice—the Southern Highlands.[1]

Here large numbers of people still carry on life in much the same way as did their forefathers. Thousands of them who had never, until the coming of good roads, visited town or city have in recent years had this experience, and to many others who have not traveled far from home the mail-order catalogues of Sears-Roebuck and Montgomery Ward, known in the mountains as "the wish books," have given real glimpses of modern life, especially to the younger people, and have affected profoundly, though sometimes artificially, their surroundings, their dress, and their mode of living.

The handicrafts have been referred to as an integral part of

[1] The Southern Highlander and His Homeland. Russell Sage Foundation, New York, 1921, p. 12.

the culture of the mountain people. To some it may seem that the word "culture" should not be applied to these disadvantaged people, many of whom live remote from what are usually termed centers of culture, and have very limited contacts with the sophisticated world that most of us know. But if we accept as our concept the definition from Webster's dictionary which reads: "The list of all the items of the general life of a people represents that whole which we call culture," it would then seem that the Southern Highlander has not only a distinctive culture, due to his long sequestered life with its unusual environment, but also that he has sterling qualities of resourcefulness and independence, marked by a high degree of individuality with appreciations and expressions both sensitive and beautiful.

The handicrafts are not the only distinguishing element in the culture of these mountaineers. They have their music—their ballads, carols, old-time hymns, and folk songs, mostly retained from an older day but often adapted to present need, a music until recently unwritten but through use kept in mind and heart. Now, fortunately, much of it is being preserved in written form and on phonographic records. They have also their instrumental melodies, simple and not extensive, and like much of the peasant music of the Old World dependent upon a single instrument, the fiddle, the banjo, or the quaint, plaintive dulcimer.[1] They have their old-time dances too, punctuated at times, as in the running sets, with gems of originality by both dancer and "caller." Although writing was not common in the early days, nor is it now among adults, there is a limited literature laboriously set down and preserved exactly as written. Only a few diaries were kept, but story-telling, always an important feature of mountain life, especially among the men, and passed from one generation to another, has saved many legends, some of which have been recorded by writers about these Highland people. There is still, however, a mine of folklore which it is hoped will be collected before it is too late.

The Southern Highlander and his family are probably as nearly self-sustaining as any group of our population. This is far from saying that his economic standard of living is to be compared with that in other parts of our country; it does indicate, however, that

[1] For a full description of this instrument see p. 199.

he gets along with a minimum of outside help and that his wants are few and simple. That this is so is due in part to the fact that many things, which most of us think we should have, mean little to him, partly because his point of view, often religious, makes him feel that material possessions are an encumbrance to the soul, and mainly, perhaps, because there is really nothing much that can be done about it. These men and women have literally wrung their living from the soil, and usually it is scant soil and of low fertility. To the proverbial "patch of ground" have sometimes been added a few domestic animals, the cow, ox, mule, sheep, chickens, and occasionally a horse, none until quite recently of a high strain.

Their houses, the older ones invariably log cabins, they have made themselves and furnished largely with things shaped from native materials. Practically everything, their construction, their furnishings, and their functions, is done with the hands—man's work and woman's work.

There is no large area in the United States with such a variety of handicrafts today as the Southern Highlands, first, because as a part of daily life they have persisted longer here than in any other section of our country. In fact there are places today where life still goes on in a very primitive way, where plowing is done with oxen, where the family water supply comes from the old spring with the gourd dipper always in reach, where carding and spinning are done by hand and weaving on looms of ancient type, where herbs are gathered for medicine, and barks, roots, and flowers for dyeing yarn, where honey is stored in beegums made by hollowing out a log, where planting is done according to the light or dark of the moon and where grain is cut with the cradle. Second, although handicrafts were first built upon the needs of the people, there later came a period of revival in which many new types of articles were made to sell. The effort to supply outside markets has added greatly to their variety and includes some things of beauty that give them a place in the field of art.

While good craftsmanship will always be a prime factor in any handicraft, there are other considerations which determine its acceptability. The utility of the object is one of the first tests; then come the choice of material, the color, form, and texture, all of which combine to give pleasure and satisfaction to maker and to user. These elements of hand and mind, whether represented in the simplest objects of the home or in the choicest possessions of a museum, are indeed expressions of true culture.

GENERAL SCOPE

This report will include observations of the work of the mountaineer in the building and furnishing of his home, the making of equipment by which he works and lives, the articles which he fashions for barter or for sale, and especially those that find their way into outside markets. Reference will also be made to work done in schools and in other handicraft centers of the territory.

An adequate picture of the handicrafts of the region must include not only the work of the mountaineers but of all who live and work there—the later comers, teachers, settlement workers, nurses, and even some of the visitors who go there usually in the summer with regularity because of their desire to take part in the handwork of this beautiful country. It will consist of all things made, whether done by native or newcomer, from the building of a cabin or a primitive water wheel to fine examples of modern weavings and skilful wood carvings; the baskets, boxes, brooms, candlesticks, chairs, counterpanes, coverlets, decorated panels, dolls, dulcimers, fans, furniture, lamps, mats, pewter and other metal work, poppets, pottery, quilts, rugs, sconces, stools, tables, towels, toys, trays and other receptacles, whittling and wood carving, weaving of baby robes, breakfast and luncheon sets, coats, curtains, dresses, handbags, scarfs, smocks, table and pillow covers, wall hangings, and many other objects in a constantly increasing list.

The main body of the book, Parts I and II, deals almost entirely with the handicrafts of the area, Part I describing the Mountain Handicrafts of Pioneer Days out of which the later developments grew; Part II, Revival of the Handicrafts and Their Present-Day Practice, tracing this development which began about forty years ago, down to the present time, and concluding with a chapter on the Future of the Handicrafts in the Highlands.

Part III, The Rural Handicraft Movement and the Wider Use of Handicrafts, deals with the growth of the movement throughout rural America, including references to some of the agencies which are sponsoring or otherwise encouraging this development. There are many groups outside the Highlands, in both country and city, deeply concerned with the values derived from handwork, and several government agencies are now earnestly engaged in making them serve as instruments to solve human problems. Therefore, although the report is marked throughout with instances which might be applied to effort in the broad fields of education and recreation, it has seemed worthwhile to include a discussion on Adult Education through Handicrafts, and on Recreation through Handicrafts, and finally to suggest the value of handicrafts to the user.

METHODS USED IN MAKING THE STUDY

The Southern Highland region is so vast, the character of the country so varied, and much of it so difficult of access that it has not been possible to visit every part. The effort has been made however, to secure data from each of the 235 counties where handicrafts are now practiced.

The information obtained by the writer ranges from early impressions of this mountain handwork, gained years before he had any thought of making a study of the subject, to later personal knowledge of individuals, families, and environment, and intensive field work that has included examination of local materials, processes, products, markets, and so forth. This information has been further augmented by attendance at meetings and conferences of workers and other interested groups; by planning and arranging exhibitions of handicrafts; by correspondence; and by reading and other research.

Data have been gathered on the following points from the handicraft centers: history of the center, including date of organization, directorship, number of staff members, number of persons engaged in handicrafts in the community; types of articles made; whether in home, school or shop; relative use of native and imported materials; degree of skill required in making the articles; how workers are trained; extent to which machinery is used, also water or other power; use of original designs and standards of workmanship; methods of marketing; and opinions as to the economic, social, educational, esthetic, and other significance of the practice of handicrafts.

33

A Bibliography has been compiled including a list of publications on the general literature of the region, and one on its handicrafts. It includes also a selected list of works on some of the subjects covered in the text, especially those of importance to the Highlands, and a few on which information is not easily available. These are basketry, coverlets, dyes (natural), quilting and patchwork, rug making, spinning and weaving, and whittling. In addition to bibliographies on the literature and on the handicrafts of the region, a reference is made to the Bibliography on Occupational Therapy, issued by the American Occupational Therapy Association, in which the student will find lists of books and articles on the therapeutic value of handicrafts. In short, the effort has been made to point the way toward significant publications on the region, on its handicrafts, and on handicrafts in general so that the student may easily find the printed matter that he needs.

PURPOSE OF THE STUDY

The purpose of this study is threefold: first, to make available information which it is believed will be helpful to the Highland people in solving their handicraft problem and the placing of their work on a better and more permanent basis; second, to acquaint those outside the region with this great reservoir of handwork, to enlist their interest in its continuation, and to encourage a wider use of these products; and third, so to present the findings of the study that they may contribute to the development of the handicraft movement which is today engaging the serious interest of many individuals and organizations throughout the country.

SOME REASONS FOR CONTINUING HANDICRAFT WORK

Living conditions today favor a continuation of the practice of handicrafts in the Southern Highlands. The revival of this work was brought about largely by schools, teachers, social workers, and outside persons in co-operation with the native people who had seen the old crafts disappearing and who sought to re-establish them and to build up new ones.

During this period of revival many things have been made especially for sale, because these "fireside industries" often afford the only opportunity for meager earnings. It is this economic pressure which forms the natural basis for the continuation of handicrafts both in the homes and in the schools of the Highlands.

The economic is not, however, the only motive—there is the social incentive. It is difficult for us who live in towns where numberless occasions bring people together, to realize how lacking the mountains are in opportunities for people to mingle socially. In many communities the church service is the only event that calls neighbors together, and that sometimes only once or twice a year when an itinerant minister may come in. Often the annual revival meetings afford the best opportunity for social gatherings. Of course in some communities services are more or less regular, and these are quite as much appreciated for their social opportunities as for their religious influences. Understanding this, it is easy to realize how significant is such an organization as the Penland Weavers and Potters which affects about 40 widely separated homes in the region of Penland, North Carolina, and which meets regularly at the Weavers' Cabin, a community house that workers built co-operatively in a place fairly accessible to all.[1] Here they gather to discuss questions of supplies, weaving instructions, and shipping and marketing the finished work; but equally important is the social aspect where friends and relatives who had not come together over long periods, sometimes years, meet now more or less regularly.

The educational significance of handicrafts in the Highlands can hardly be overestimated, for there are many instances in which children have been able to go through school, often college, from the earnings gained by their own or their parents' work at a fireside industry. Berea College, Berea, Kentucky, has had many such students. Nor are all the educational benefits indirect. For instance, the knowledge and skill required to prepare the materials for weaving, the warping of the loom, the actual weaving operation, and the taking of the webs from the loom and finishing them are all processes of high educational value both to those who do the work and to those who carefully observe it.

Handicrafts are coming to play a very significant part in the field of adult education. A good example is furnished by a group of mountain women at the Spinning Wheel, Asheville, North Caro-

[1] For additional information see p. 237.

lina, who, beginning with the craft they were following as a means of increasing their meager earnings, made excursions into the fields of geography, history, sociology, science, and art, and found interests which lifted their daily work to a high and important plane.[1]

The esthetic experience is often too a direct return. In many a home the making of simple furniture, the weaving of a coverlet, the converting of local clay into household pottery, and the shaping of a dulcimer are cultural influences for all its members. And to the one actually undertaking the task there is provided an outlet for creative expression as compelling for the mountain dweller as for any other worker.

Not the least important aspect of the work is its therapeutic value. There are many disadvantaged people in this region as elsewhere. Perhaps one of the commonest is that of a child in a large family who, lacking the wit of the other children, is not only neglected but by a cruel though natural attitude of elders and playmates comes to be one marked by failure. Everything seems to contribute to the feeling of inferiority which begun by nature is aggravated on every hand. Then someone may find that this child has a special aptitude which if encouraged will enable him to attain something like a normal position among his playmates.[2]

Next in importance to that of encouraging the Highlanders to continue their handicrafts, and in itself an indispensable factor in that encouragement, is the need to acquaint people outside the mountain regions with these useful and beautiful articles. In 1933 the most comprehensive exhibition of handicrafts of this region ever assembled was circulated throughout the United States by the American Federation of Arts. This exhibition, described in Chapter XVI, The Southern Highland Handicraft Guild, was outstanding as an interpreter of rural handicrafts, but on account of the size, space requirements, and cost of transportation it could be exhibited in only a limited number of places. Even smaller exhibits are difficult to organize, route, and display; therefore it seems that since exhibits cannot be made available generally, a practical and effective way to bring information to the public is through a book

[1] See Chapter XXI, Adult Education through Handicrafts, p. 307.
[2] See Chapter V, Spinning and Weaving for Home and Market, p. 109.

for general circulation, written and illustrated on lines roughly indicated in this chapter, a book that can go into countless communities that may not otherwise be reached. The benefits of such a book should not be limited to people of the Highlands. It should prove valuable to those elsewhere who are contemplating handicrafts as a means of livelihood, as an educational, a recreational, or a leisure-time interest.

The pioneer handicrafts are rapidly disappearing from the mountains, and it is hoped that calling attention to them will create an interest both in the craftsmen and in their products and thus extend the life of these practices. It is also hoped that this record will encourage the preservation of good handicraft traditions not only in the region we are studying but in the remainder of the country as well. The Appalachian pioneers carried into these mountains the tools, the skills, and the ways of living of the people of the Atlantic seaboard which in turn had come directly or indirectly from the homelands of Europe. It has been interesting to trace the shaving horse, used by the mountain basket and chairmakers of North Carolina, Tennessee, Kentucky, and West Virginia to cut out their splints, or "splits," as they are commonly called in the Southern Highlands, and rungs, back to Shropshire County, England, where in its original form it is still used, or was until recently, to make "spelks" and "trugs" for local baskets. The old boom-and-treadle lathe, described and illustrated in Chapter IX, Furniture and Other Woodwork, is said to have disappeared entirely from England, but can be seen working today by those who know where to search in the mountain sections of Kentucky, North Carolina, Tennessee, and Georgia. Is it not interesting to find in this mountain area some of the baskets, chairs, and other handicraft forms which have disappeared entirely in European homelands, just as research has revealed ballads and folk music, which our forebears brought across the sea, that have been saved to the race through the prolonged isolation of the Southern Highlands?[1]

To discover the extent to which old handicrafts are carried on even now is surprising. There are still many old-time craftsmen in the Highlands, and they are getting along in these difficult days

[1] See Chapter XIII, Mountain Music and Hand-Made Instruments, p. 197.

when less resourceful neighbors are suffering or are on public relief. It was supposed that not more than 30 or 40 old chairmakers could be found working in the region, but incomplete reports in connection with this study estimate their number as more than 200. Some of their products are excellent in appearance, have lasting qualities, and can be purchased at very low prices.

It has been pointed out that the Highlanders have retained longer than any other group in our country the primitive ways of living with a maximum dependence on the labor of their hands, which many would insist is a sign of backwardness. But it is just as true that they have retained some of the country traits and graces, some of the amenities which seem to disappear with the coming of extensive machinery and other forms of sophistication associated with material progress. There come to mind pictures of mountain homes and mountain schools in every state of the region to which handicrafts have given character and fascination far beyond what would have been possible had their furnishings been "store-bought." But the important fact is that there are often no funds available for factory-made articles, and, after all, the good country life depends largely upon extracting values from the immediate environment. The handicrafts of the Southern Highlands make this possible through a happy economic and cultural combination.

PART I

MOUNTAIN HANDICRAFTS OF PIONEER DAYS

CHAPTER I

THE BEGINNING OF THE HANDICRAFTS IN THE HIGHLANDS

WHEN the first settlers from the hills of Pennsylvania and the lower lands of Virginia and North Carolina penetrated the Southern Highlands they carried with them the handicraft culture then characteristic of our whole country. Like the pioneers who crossed from the Atlantic seaboard to the Middle States and later over the Oregon Trail and the Santa Fé Trail to the Far West, those who went into the Southern Appalachians were compelled to travel with light equipment, although some took along with them an occasional fine piece of furniture or a favorite household article of comfort or beauty which for generations was kept in a cherished place in the crude log cabin as evidence of the civilization to which they once belonged.

Except for the comparatively few old things that were brought through, and there must have been many more precious possessions left by the way, all the furnishings for the new home were literally wrought by hand out of the great wilderness. This to some extent is still true, although the coming of modern highways and the shift of industries from North to South as well as the development of new ones within reach of some mountain sections have in recent years brought about great changes.

OLD METHODS CONTINUE

Nor are the pioneer crafts which still persist found always in remote or isolated places. In the spring of 1935 a short way off a modern highway in Tennessee settlers on subsistence homesteads were discovered riving boards by hand for long shingles, or "shakes" as they are called in the West, for the roofs of their new houses just as had been done in the Highland country since the earliest settlers came. Not far away a portable shingle mill tended by two men and operated by a gasoline engine was going full blast. It was

41

interesting to see these contrasting methods of work, to hear the nervous hum of the power-driven saw cutting swiftly through the white oak blocks and at the same time the leisurely pounding of the home-made hickory knot maul against the ancient froe, splitting off new boards at a rate comparable to the speed of an ox-drawn prairie schooner with a modern automobile. To state it statistically, the two men with the mill were turning out about 7,000 shingles a day, the homesteader about 1,000.

But there were good reasons for bringing into operation this slow old-time method of work, requiring a skill still possessed by many families in the Southern Highlands. The men who were splitting boards by hand did not own a shingle mill, nor had they money to rent one and thus take advantage of its time- and labor-saving operations. In fact these men had long been out of work due largely to labor-saving machinery in the coal-mining industry which they had well learned was also labor displacing. And while they had no funds with which to buy or hire machines, they did have hands and time aplenty which, coupled with a supply of white oak secured in clearing their land, enabled them to make enough shingles in a few days to cover the new houses into which they would soon bring their families.

When these new houses were finished—their small barns had already been built and the men were living in them—they could set up their new homesteads where countless other things were waiting to be done with hands and simple tools. The Division of Subsistence Homesteads of the United States Department of the Interior was helping these economically stranded people toward a better way of living and toward what it is hoped will be a measure of security which many of them have never known.

However, all the work on this homestead development was not being done by hand. In addition to the shingle mill there was a portable lumber mill, tractors for felling trees, pulling stumps, plowing, and other heavy work which was more economical to have done in part by machines. The farmers could not as individuals afford to buy or to maintain machines, but through co-operation as a group with the government they were able to use them collectively. But great care was taken to permit the individual homesteader to do his own work whenever possible, even though the process was a slow one, for by it he would be creating new values for himself and experiencing the satisfactions which can come from carefully done handwork. The self-reliant attitude of the men is expressed by one who said:

If I had a portable shingle mill and a gasoline engine, and gasoline to run it, and a helper, a horse to draw it about, feed for my horse, a place to keep my mill when idle, some attachments for other kinds of work, and a little money for keeping up repairs I could make as many shingles in a day as I can by rivin' in a week.

And just as he seemed to be making out a strong case for the busy machine he continued: "But when it comes to lastin', a roof of properly hand-rived boards will last four times as long as them cut with a saw." And picking up a clean white oak board from the neat pile he had made and inhaling its fragrance, he explained how every one was split with the grain and would not curl when properly placed, and that he knew of roofs where hand-rived shingles had lasted for fifty and sixty years, and had heard of two which lasted over a hundred years. "But even if you had plenty of money to buy machinery," he concluded, "there still is a satisfaction in making a thing for yourself with your own hands that nobody can deny you."

ANCESTRY OF THE HIGHLANDER

It is generally agreed by Campbell,[1] Kephart,[2] Thompson,[3] and others named in the Bibliography that the early and largest migrations to this region were from southern Pennsylvania, eastern Virginia, and eastern North Carolina. While many families in the mountain sections of Virginia and West Virginia are of German descent, or Pennsylvania Dutch, as they were commonly called, the large majority are of English, Scotch and Irish ancestry, and here, together with the mountain regions of North Carolina, Tennessee, Kentucky, Georgia, Alabama, and South Carolina, is

[1] Campbell, John C., The Southern Highlander and His Homeland. Russell Sage Foundation, New York, 1921.

[2] Kephart, Horace, Our Southern Highlanders. The Macmillan Co., New York, 1929.

[3] Thompson, Samuel H., The Highlanders of the South. Eaton and Mains, New York, Jennings and Graham, Cincinnati, 1910.

to be found the highest percentage of "pure" American or Anglo-Saxon stock in any part of the United States. The Highland sections of each state according to the figures of John C. Campbell, based upon the 1910 census, contained a population of less than 1 per cent foreign born. Of a total of 5,330,111 persons in the whole area, 84.3 per cent were native white of native parentage. It is here, too, that we have a continuation of folkways often more easily traced to England, Scotland, and Ireland than to America, where the many and rapid changes in modes of living and the extensive intercourse with great numbers of European immigrants have developed a culture of many strands.

It is true that the culture of the Highlanders was due to the fact that from the time they entered this great mountain region until recently they were practically lost to outside influence. For generations people of the Highlands and the Lowlands mingled with one another as little as though they belonged to different countries, and until quite recently it was customary to refer to anyone outside the region as a foreigner. However, in the early 1860's, mountain men came out of their coves and valleys 150,000 strong as volunteers in the Union army, where they proved themselves among the ablest of fighting men, and their response in the World War is one of the traditions not only of the mountain region but of the nation.

CONTRASTS WITHIN THE REGION

Inasmuch as the Southern Highlands covers a vast area, it will be well here to clarify what may seem an inconsistency to the reader when he recalls that it includes several modern cosmopolitan cities and towns—Knoxville, Johnson City, Asheville, Roanoke, Lexington, Staunton, Harrisonburg, Marion, Morgantown, and others. These technically lie within the area defined, but most of their inhabitants are not of it in any special sense. While there are in these places, as this report will indicate, handicraft activities in which mountain and city folk work together, especially in the marketing of products, city inhabitants have until recently had little contact with people of the mountains.

If we turn back to the late 1700's and the early 1800's, when the first settlers went into the Southern Appalachians, we will recall that at that period our whole country was so distinctly marked by a handicraft way of living that in the rural sections of the eastern seaboard the country people were about 95 per cent self-sustaining. The diary of a Connecticut family written about that time shows that this percentage of what they had to eat and wear was home grown or home produced.[1] The situation in New England was not very different from that in the Highlands, except for the fact that the list of products in the northern states was larger, and that in many instances the mountaineer had no access to city markets or village stores where he might get tea, coffee, sugar, and other staples. He often made his tea from wild herbs, his coffee from parched corn, and his sugar from wild honey, sugarcane, or from the sap of the native sugar-maple tree.

To leave the impression that all the Highlanders fared alike would be inaccurate, but it is not an overstatement to say that no other group of Americans has lived through generations so meagerly. But if this lean existence seems, as it undoubtedly does, an indication of a low standard, it must in justice be said that the ability of the average Highlander to extract from his surroundings the essential elements of life is no small tribute to his strength, ingenuity, and endurance. He has under circumstances that would have discouraged many another maintained a faith that is one of his outstanding characteristics.

INFLUENCES FROM THE OUTSIDE

That great penalties have been paid by many mountain families for the privations they have endured and that heavy toll has been taken in both physical and mental debilities, are grim facts which those who know the situation admit. Nevertheless these secluded people have won the devotion of persons who in one capacity or another are lending aid to the various enterprises in the region, primarily because Highlanders crave above everything the opportunity to develop their own potentialities and carry their own responsibilities. There have been many instances in which under urgent economic need they have shown pride in being able to resist aid from the Red Cross or other outside agencies, feeling

[1] Chase, Stuart, The Economy of Abundance. By permission of The Macmillan Co., publishers, New York, 1934, pp. 53–60.

that to accept it would strike at the very root of their traditional independence.

The associations which have been most beneficial in recognizing the values inherent in the life of this extensive area have been the teachers, doctors, nurses, and church and social workers who have chosen to live and labor there. They have gone into the mountains zealous to assist with the always present social and economic problems. Confident that they had much to contribute, they did not at first always realize that they had also much to learn, much to gain from the simplicity and dignity about them. But with longer associations they were deeply stirred by the strength and independence of those whom they had thought to help. Therefore they were among the first to encourage a continuation of the fine elements that characterize mountain life and culture.

CHAPTER II

THE LOG CABIN AND ITS FURNISHINGS

O F ALL the handicraft expressions in the Southern Highlands the log cabin, or folk house, is the oldest and to this day one of the most important. Although the log cabin is a symbol of the American frontier associated with every advance of our pioneers into the wilderness, there is no section of the country where so many old log houses are still standing nor where so many new ones are being constructed. The continued interest in this form of building is due to several reasons: in many sections of the Highlands to build with logs is even now less expensive than with sawed timber; there are persons who feel that for the wooded areas and natural outlines of the mountains the log cabin is the most appropriate type of architecture; and finally, in many hearts there is a strong sentiment for its traditions.

It is doubtful if any experience in house building can exceed in satisfaction that which the pioneer felt in literally hewing his home out of the virgin forest. He secured all his materials near the site and worked them by hand, often supplying every item of construction himself, including the wooden or leather hinges, latches, and fasteners for doors and windows carefully whittled out with his pocketknife.

No one traveling through the country can fail to note the harmonious relation of this type of architecture to its environment, and the good judgment and taste generally shown by the builders in the selection of sites. There are tiny cabins nestling in little coves as inconspicuous as a bird's nest, and there are strongly built log houses exposed to wind and sun on top of a mountain ridge commanding what must have seemed a complete view of the universe. And what a variety of scenes the Appalachian region affords with its wealth of contours which no other can excel, its rich flora not surpassed in any part of our country, with every variety of water form, from mountain torrent, cataract, and cascade to placid lake and spring, so abundant that in many places no other domestic water supply is required. The relation of the cabin to the spring which is utilized for drinking water, washing, and as a summer refrigerator is one of the most important problems; the solution is usually practical and often beautiful.

The homemaker of the Highlands is surrounded with natural beauty from the coming of the wildflowers in early spring, including red bud, serviceberry, dogwood, silver bell, and many other flowering trees and shrubs, through the summer with rhododendrons and mountain azaleas, called "honeysuckle" by the natives, until the autumn foliage which in brilliance and gradation of hue, due mainly to the number and variety of hardwoods growing in the Southern Appalachians, is hardly equaled elsewhere in America.

TYPES OF MOUNTAIN CABINS

The log cabin has a number of variants. The early shelter was a crude structure of one room, often without a single window. Then came the more adequate but still simple form of two rooms with a loft over each, the rooms separated by a covered passageway from three to eight feet wide, called a "dog-trot." This type of cabin is known as a "but-and-ben," a term used in Scotland. The most elaborate cabin was that with new rooms or "new houses," as they are called by old inhabitants, built on from time to time. These resulted in combinations of T's and L's or sometimes complete crosses with fireplaces in each of the four gables. Some of the windowless cabins had two doors, one that opened to the east to get the "sun ball" early in the morning, the other opening to the west so that it might receive the evening rays of the setting sun. There are still to be found in the mountains today cabins which have no windows; those with but one are not uncommon.

As late as thirty years ago the introduction of glass windows became a momentous issue in Knott County, Kentucky. This arose over the offer of some outsiders to give windows to those who would use them. Objections were made by oldtimers against installing them. Both moral and religious scruples were raised and a prospective window became a serious bone of contention. There stands now on the grounds of the Hindman Settlement School the old cabin in which Uncle Solomon Everidge, one of the founders of the School, lived to the end of his days. It

A TYPICAL MOUNTAIN CABIN

This Log House in the Mountains of North Carolina Was Built Sixty Years Ago of Hand-Hewn Logs Dressed with a Broadax, Almost as Smooth as If by Plane. The Log Second from the Bottom, of Poplar, Is 22 Inches Wide

A HOME OF HANDICRAFTS

Mrs. Zachariah Field of Russellville, Tennessee, Sitting on a Mountain Chair, Is Churning in a Home-made Piggin. The Stoneware Jar Covered with a Hand-made Linen Towel Is a Local Product, as Is the Coverlet Mrs. Field Wove on the Old Family Loom

contains one window, one of the first, it is said, of the gift windows to be placed in the cabins about Hindman. Much strategy was required and the able persuasion of Uncle Solomon's wife (now Mrs. Cord Ritchie) to bring it about. She is the basket maker shown opposite page 111.

The simplest of these typical old-time log cabins was made of hewn logs in the form of a parallelogram with a roof of split oak boards. A chimney at one end was built usually of stone with clay for mortar, although when stones were hard to get, sticks and clay served for the upper part. The single door was swung on heavy wooden hinges or leather straps made usually from the hide of a wild animal. In the early days the aperture of the window, when there was one, was not covered with glass, but with split boards swung on hand-made hinges which, when opened, let in not only the light but whatever kind of weather happened to be outside. The usual light for the interior of the house would be firelight from the hearth, supplemented in fair weather by daylight from the opened door or in rare cases from the so-called window.

In certain instances a narrow, sometimes vertical, sometimes horizontal opening, would be made in the wall to the right or left of the fireplace, a small space the height of one or two logs and varying in width from a peephole to about two feet. This would afford a lookout and also let in a shaft of light. In this combination of an open fire and a primitive window, the mountain family had two sources of beauty and comfort that many city dwellers would envy—a wood fire and a clear glimpse of the starry heavens.

Such a scene was presented to the writer one evening in a virgin forest in the mountains of North Carolina. Seated before a glowing fire of oak and hickory knots in a one-room cabin with a single small window to the right of the fireplace, an opening about 15 inches high and three feet long gave a perfect view of the evening star sparkling in the deep-blue sky near the sickle moon. Later other stars and constellations came into view, and it seemed that there might not be anywhere greater beauty or a more satisfying combination of evening lights than in a mountain cabin with an open fire on the hearth and the distant stars seen through a small window. It must have been in such a cabin on such a night that a pioneer mother of this region long ago caught the vision of the heavens that she recorded for her children and grandchildren in the Moon and Star patchwork quilt which is described in Chapter VII, Quilting and Patchwork.

BUILDING THE CABIN

An important contribution to the type of architecture which marks the mountain area has been the great variety and large supply of native trees. Among those that have been used are oak, ash, walnut, hickory, chestnut, cherry, maple, and poplar among the deciduous trees; pine, spruce, and hemlock among the evergreens; the hemlock is called "spruce pine" by the natives. The deciduous trees have usually been preferred, and in the evolution of the cabin the logs have been made smoother and smoother with the great broadax until in many a wall, both inside and outside, close examination is often required to determine whether the logs, sometimes 20 feet long, have been hand hewn or sawed out.

Not only in the logs for the walls is the mountain carpenter's skill apparent, but in the structural timbers for the loft floor and the roof frame, the "boards" or shingles for covering the roof, and in the older cabins the boards for the door frames and the doors themselves. The logs, or poles, as they are sometimes called, used as joists to support the floor of the loft, were of carefully selected small tree trunks, oak, hickory, walnut, poplar, or maple, ofttimes smoothed with the broadax on all sides but always on one side to bring them to uniform plane, and these and the rafters would in special instances be further smoothed with the drawing knife, an old but very useful tool in the mountains. After the strong log walls were completed and the framework in place, three more essentials were required to complete the cabin—the floors, roof, and doors. The "puncheon" floors were either hewn as smooth as possible with the broadax or cut with an adz from timbers split out of the log. The boards that covered the roof were thin, narrow, split strips about half an inch thick, four to eight inches wide, two to three feet long, and laid on the roof. These were made usually of oak or hickory and were split with a froe, a long-bladed tool with a handle on one end, the blade driven into the wood by the stroke of a hardwood maul on the back edge, when the board splits off or is pried off. The craft of board making is illustrated opposite page 60.

The doors of the earliest cabins were made of hickory, oak, and ash, which yield the best of the longer dimension boards. There are also records that timbers for both house and bridge construction were cut by hand with a two-man ripsaw, or "pit saw," just as is done today in parts of India, China, and until recently in Japan, one of the sawyers standing on top of the log and the other in a pit below. But this method was used more frequently for commercial than for individual building purposes, although at times floor and other boards were made in this way; later, the lumber for doors and floors was brought from sawmills.

THE FIREPLACE AND THE CHIMNEY

Mountain cabins, as has been said, have been built without windows, many with but one door, and earth has frequently taken the place of wood for the floor; but every cabin, however simple and bare, has its fireplace. It was usually made of rough, native stone in dimensions as found, though there are in a considerable number of the well-finished houses examples of stone cut to regular shapes and sizes, with careful masonry used in the construction. The typical fireplace and chimney, however, are of stone, found in its native state; a picture of such a chimney is shown opposite page 48. The firebox is often too shallow to be of practical use in a town or a country house because the breast of the chimney and the fireboard are very easily smoked, but this narrow construction throws the heat out into the room, although it often throws out also a good supply of smoke. The requirements of living, however, were not so exact in pioneer cabins as they are in more modern houses, but even today some quite prefer the shallow firebox. Whatever the dimensions, the fireplace is the dominant feature of the log cabin, serving as the heating system, as a place for cooking, as a forge, a ventilator, often an illuminating plant as well, and as a center of sociability for which there is no substitute. Only one who has been brought up beside such a hearth can understand the hold it has.

Comfortable, cheerful, and attractive as the fireplace usually is, sometimes a more esthetic feature from an architectural point of view is the chimney, which in its relation to the main lines and mass of the cabin offers great beauty. What scene is more appealing to a wayfarer than the gray-blue smoke of a hardwood fire as it rises from a cabin chimney in the early morning or in the evening of a cool day?

Riding along mountain roads one who is at all interested in domestic architecture will have ample opportunity to enjoy the outside chimneys of the cabins of which they are so conspicuous a part. Perhaps the keenest appreciator of their fine forms and appropriateness will be one who has tried to design a chimney for any kind of house. To him, whether he be professional or amateur, the stone chimney of the Highlands will appeal for its mass, its line, its texture, and often its color. In these combinations many an unknown mountaineer has wrought a masterpiece.

The most common materials, as stated above, are native stone with a mortar of native clay. In order to make a generous opening inside for the firebox, unless it is a very shallow oven, the chimney has a foreordained bulk which gives it massiveness and scale. Then the wide throat of the fireplace and the long, narrow draught further determine the form which relates itself perfectly to the low mass of the cabin, the attractiveness of which is enhanced by a gently sloping roof line that helps to tie the whole structure to the earth out of which it has grown. The chimney rests firmly upon the ground, and the ascent of its stone and mud masonry seems as natural and as beautiful as the growth of a symmetrical tree. Its generally harmonious outline is always pleasantly broken by the varying sizes of the stones used, so that the eye follows, not swiftly but in leisurely fashion, the outside angles of the mass with its horizontal lines equally pleasing. The stone is laid as nearly as may be in courses with the thinner flat ones at the top, but quite irregular because of different thicknesses. No two faces of the stones are exactly alike, some are broken and rough, others smooth; but all, combined with the coarse, lumpy mortar of native clay, give a most satisfying, even beautiful, texture when seen in combination with hewn logs or rough boards in rain, snow, or sunshine.

But it is the color of these native stones and clay mortars as much as the form and texture which often provide unforgettable harmonies. Perhaps the most beautiful range of clay colors in our country is to be seen in the Carolinas; but throughout the Highland regions are similar colors—gray, tan, yellow, brown, rose, black, or red—and sometimes the rocks of the neighborhood seem

THE OLD SPRING HOUSE

This Is Tom Barnett's Spring House at Peachtree, North Carolina. There Are
Hundreds of These Mountain Refrigerators in the Highlands

AN OLD-TIME HIGHLAND CORN MILL

Granddaughters of Uncle William Creech of Pine Mountain, Harlan County, Kentucky, with a Quern or Home-Made Hand-Power Grinding Mill Used by Pioneers for Preparing Corn Meal and Hominy Grits

to take on similar shades. A traveler riding one evening along a country road near Brasstown, North Carolina, saw the sun rays break through the clouds and fall on the dark-gray gable end of a log cabin with a brick-red stone and clay chimney. It was early summer and the tender green of the Virginia creeper was climbing up the chimney side. The scene was too impressive to go unnoted, so he knocked at the door. The mother, who was holding one of the children in her arms, asked him in while other members of the family were busy getting supper. He said he had just stopped to tell them how much he liked their beautiful chimney. "Thank you for 'lightin','" replied the mother, "if it's worth your comin' in for, maybe we can keep it that way. They've been after me to whitewash it. Well, whitewash is nice, but I don't think it's as pretty as the red against the house and with the vines on it." The traveler thought so too and was glad on his journey the next year to note that no "improvements" had been made.

NOTABLE LOG CABINS

The Fireside Industries at Berea College, Kentucky, are carried on in two log houses. One, planned by Mrs. Anna Ernberg, director of the Industries at the College, is built on old cabin lines with all the structural material, both wood and stone, obtained from the immediate neighborhood. The other is of more modern design but beautiful in mass and line and a perfect workshop. Probably the most artistic group of mountain log houses in designs and appropriate setting can be seen at the Pine Mountain Settlement School, also in Kentucky. These cabins, planned by Katherine Pettit, its founder, present a harmony of construction and arrangement that is a worthy tribute to the pioneer undertakings in which the cabin had its origin. At Crossnore, North Carolina, two historic log houses have been transported to the grounds of the Crossnore School and placed together, where they furnish an excellent and spacious workshop for the weavers and rug makers. For the John C. Campbell Folk School at Brasstown, North Carolina, neighbors secured two abandoned cabins in the community from which they selected the best logs for "raisin'" a typical mountain cabin with stone chimney at one end and a chimney of sticks and mud at the other. This building serves as a local museum of pioneer handicrafts.

53

A fine old cabin is used by the Dougherty family at Russellville, Tennessee, for a weaving and display room in connection with the Shuttle-Crafters; the Spinning Wheel at Asheville, North Carolina, has a mountain cabin with the original fireplace which was transplanted from Democrat, North Carolina, for a show- and workroom. Lula Hale has built at Ary, Kentucky, entirely of new material, one of the most attractive log houses in the Highlands, called Homeplace and patterned after one built in Letcher County, Kentucky, by her father fifty-five years earlier. Rev. Hannah Powell had a historic cabin over a hundred years old moved to the grounds of the mission at Pigeon River, North Carolina, maintained by the Woman's National Missionary Association, where it serves as a community recreation center. A new crafts building made of logs has just been completed at Penland, North Carolina, for the work of Penland Weavers and to serve the needs of the Institute held there each summer. All these buildings are connected with handicraft work or are at centers where handicrafts are carried on. It was in the mountain cabins that leaders met for the counsel and co-operation which enabled them to continue the old crafts and to lay the foundation for the new ones they were to develop, and it is fitting that this work which has been carried on largely within the mountain homes should come to be known as "fireside industries."

THE FURNISHING OF THE CABIN

Just as primitive and as simple as the cabin was the furniture for it, and usually of the same materials. The selection of wood, however, was not determined alone by what grew in the vicinity, but often by the tools a Highlander possessed for working the trees into lumber. If he had only an ax and a pocketknife, he would be limited to those woods which would chop and split readily, for it was many years before there was any ripsaw or lumber mill in the region where smooth boards were made; instead, as already explained, boards were split out with ax and froe and then smoothed with plane or drawing knife.

If the settler owned a cross-cut saw he could smooth the legs of a table or a bedstead on the bottom, as well as trim the ends of the logs on the outside corners of his cabin and make his doorframes true. If he owned a broadax he could smooth large timbers almost as though they had been planed. Then if he could construct a turning lathe there would be hardly any limit to what he could do. With all these tools he could cut wood horizontally and vertically, square it, and smooth it for his heavy furniture, tables, bedsteads, benches, and his wife's weaving loom. With his lathe he could make chair posts and rungs, fancy bedstead posts, or complete spool bedsteads. Not often were such elaborations indulged in, but sometimes they were found, especially among the families that came down from the German settlements in Pennsylvania which often had an excellent carpenter or cabinetmaker along who discovered in the Highland forests ideal wood to work.

In addition to tables, chairs, benches, bedsteads, small in number to begin with and increasing with the family growth, were the few essentials for making cloth and clothing, the spinning wheel, the loom, the cotton-gin, the break and hackle for flax, reels, and other spinning and weaving apparatus for wool, cotton, or flax. All these were usually made in the home, although from the earliest days neighborhood chairmakers, basket makers, and carpenters were drawn upon for special furniture and furnishings.

The family textiles, including coverlets, blankets, table covers, linsey-woolseys, jeans, and a variety of weavings, most of which are still made, are referred to in detail in the following section of this report. These fabrics were almost always made in the home, although there were some exchanges and bartering among neighbors. But pottery was not a household craft, rather a neighborhood industry which, although more flourishing in the Piedmont and the lower lying sections, had its makers of jugs, crocks, churns, pots, plates, cups, saucers, and so forth, scattered all through the Highlands, where some of the pioneer kilns still survive.

With wooden trenchers, noggins, piggins, spoons and forks, gourd dippers, skimmers, pottery churns, crocks, baking pots, and common dishes, most of local manufacture, and an occasional "fotched on" pot or pan for the fireplace, where for so long all the cooking was done, the kitchen and eating equipment was complete. The furnishings of the cabin were severely plain, hardly ever being marked by a surface design or decoration. Of many old weaving looms that survive, some well constructed, only one is recalled which had even a few decorations cut into the wood with a chisel, and hand carving on furniture was almost unknown. Even less frequent was the use of paint or stain, although now and then there is an instance in which the dye of some native plant was used to adorn a piece of furniture. The things the men made were about as plain as they could be, except perhaps an occasional dulcimer or a beautifully whittled out weaving shuttle. But the women in their weaving of clothes and especially of bed coverings, seldom missed an opportunity to make the textile beautiful as they saw it. And this use of color, referred to more fully in later chapters, was not easily achieved; it furnishes us with a most convincing proof of the universal love of color and the persistent urge to create beauty under as difficult and discouraging circumstances as could be found anywhere.

SLEDS TAKE THE PLACE OF WAGONS
ON MANY A HIGHLAND FARM THE ONLY VEHICLE OF TRANSPORTATION IS THE HOME-
MADE SLED, USED MORE IN SUMMER THAN IN WINTER

A MILL RUN BY WATER POWER

Throughout the Highlands Are Small Water-Power Mills for Grinding Corn and Sometimes for Cutting Lumber Similar to This One at Pinelog, North Carolina

PART II

REVIVAL OF THE HANDICRAFTS AND THEIR
PRESENT-DAY PRACTICE

CHAPTER III

REVIVAL OF THE HANDICRAFTS IN THE HIGHLANDS

ALTHOUGH there are many instances in which some of the handicrafts of the Highlands have been continued without interruption from pioneer times to the present, yet by about 1890 much of the old work was rapidly disappearing, particularly weaving, which had always marked the home life of the country. But a few years before the turn of the century came influences largely from outside the region which gave impetus to what may be called the beginning of a revival of handicrafts, a movement which though faint at first, grew persistently until today it seems destined to extend itself far into the future.

The revival was not marked by a sudden turning of large numbers of workers to handwork, but rather by a gradual renewing of interest and activity in the old-time arts in different parts of the mountains quite independently of one another. The earliest stirrings centered around Berea, Kentucky, and Asheville, North Carolina, then remotely situated from each other, for the era of good roads in the Highlands did not come until much later. From these two pioneer centers shoots were sent out, taking root in homes far from the parent stock, some of which could be reached only by foot or on muleback. In time other centers were begun in much the same way until eventually every state in the Highlands made a contribution to the handicraft development of that region.

Some early traces of the revival have been lost, but fortunately there are still living a number of people who were closely identified with it and from whom it has been possible to gather the main threads. One of the privileges of the writer has been association with several who were active in the progress of that early work. A brief record, more or less chronological, will be made here of those first steps, some of which are now quite dim. Exact dates are not always available, for few written records were made, but it has been possible to follow the most important strands of development which, although widely separated at first, do finally converge into the groups and centers with which we are familiar today.

BEREA COLLEGE AND THE REVIVAL

The first efforts to revive the handicrafts in the Highlands of which there is any clear account was in the fall of 1893 when Dr. William Goodell Frost, who in that year had been called to the presidency of Berea College, began his long "extension" tours in the mountains and at once noted the attractive homespun bed coverings in many cabins. He purchased several to show to his donors, some of whom wanted to buy them, and it was not long until coverlets became part of the medium of exchange for tuition, some of the students bringing them in to help pay their expenses.

Later a number of the coverlets "bartered for larnin'" were shown in Cincinnati, New York, and Boston, and the designs were found to be similar to those woven by women in New England many years before. Dr. Frost was elated over what he thought Berea College could accomplish not only in gathering and preserving the handwork of earlier periods, but in finding a new market for the products of mountain looms. A visit from Mrs. Candace Wheeler of New York, a well-known and influential authority on the textile arts, in one of these years gave great encouragement.

When, however, weavers undertook to make duplicates of the older work difficulties began to appear. It was found that in many instances the quality of the newly woven "kivers" did not compare well with the older specimens, the former skill in weaving was lacking, the patterns failed to "hit in the seam," the "brung on' cotton warp and woolen yarn were inferior to the old homespun and aniline dyes proved less permanent and attractive than the old-time indigo, madder, and other vegetable colors. The whole situation was pointedly summed up by a weaver who had moved down from the mountains to Berea to educate her family. Dr Frost had inquired whether she thought orders could be filled in a month or two for a half-dozen duplicates of certain coverlets made up to standard. He later referred to her answer as his "first lesson in weaving." She had replied:

President Frost, in order to make so many kivers we will have to raise more sheep, shear them, pick and wash the wool, card it and spin it,

A GOOD BOARD MAKER

This Boy Is Riving Boards or Shingles with Froe and Maul from White Oak and Hickory, as His Ancestors Have Done for Generations

MOUNTAIN PEOPLE LOVE FLOWERS

THERE IS LITTLE MONEY IN THE HIGHLANDS FOR LUXURIES, YET IN ALMOST EVERY HOME
FLOWERS ARE NURTURED, AND MANY A CABIN PORCH LIKE THIS ONE ON TOP-OF-TURKEY
IN BUNCOMBE COUNTY, NORTH CAROLINA, IS FILLED WITH GROWING PLANTS

hen collect the bark and sich to color it. Then we will have to have the
oom all set up, fix the warp and beam it, then get a draft and thread the
varp for the pattern we want, then tie up the loom, and then we will be
eady for the weaving. . . It would take we'uns nigh one year or more
fore we could have that many kivers wove. It's no child's play to
veave a kiver, President.

Dr. Frost, by now convinced that the weaving of a coverlet
required time, skill, and conscientious work, realized the necessity
of keeping up the newly awakened interest in hand-woven articles
and at the same time of stimulating a desire to perfect the processes
n order to reach the high quality attained by earlier workers.
Beginning in 1896, he encouraged the holding of homespun fairs
during commencement week at Berea College. Modest premiums
were offered for the best coverlets, blankets, linsey-woolseys, and
other products of the loom. Competition among the recently made
woven articles and comparison with the older coverlets shown at
each annual fair exerted a marked influence on the quality of the
weaving, color, and design. Likewise the opportunity to negotiate
sales was a further inducement for both exhibitors and those who
came from miles around Berea to see the objects made by old
methods and perhaps to obtain some of them. No commission
was charged on the sales and many exchanges were made. The
fairs continued for several years, hand-made furniture and other
woodwork being added later to the list of exhibits.

These activities brought to notice some of the best of the earlier
workers who still wove for their families back in the mountains and
others who had abandoned the practice but who were glad to pick
it up again as opportunity came. Among those closely linked
with Berea College was Mrs. Mary Anderson, who learned to
weave at the age of fourteen at her home near Tyner, Jackson
County, Kentucky. She was visited by one of the college workers
about 1897 and began sending in her weavings as ordered by
Josephine A. Robinson, then dean of women at Berea. Mrs.
Anderson rode on horseback 25 miles with her baby in her arms
to get supplies for her work. Later she moved to Berea and set
up a house with several looms where she carried on work to order.
Miss Robinson, now Mrs. Edward Drake Roe, Jr., of Syracuse,
New York, has written that Mrs. Anderson was her best weaver

back in those years of the revival, and as far as is known the first woman in the mountains to make a weaving with a border design. Dr. Frost, in speaking of her work and the revival at Berea, called her one of the "old strands." She still weaves at her home in Berea.

Mrs. Susan B. Hayes, who still lives at Berea, told the writer that President Frost came to her home one evening and said that he wanted her to help him get the weaving started at the College. Since she had woven so long ago she had some doubt about being able to do it, but President Frost assured her that she could and her husband said, "Of course you can do it." Thinking this would help to pay the expenses of some of her daughters through school she said she would try. She recalls that President Frost turned to her husband and said, "I was afraid she'd deny me, but I knew you would help." So they got 175 pounds of wool, washed it up and took it over to Waco in the sourwoods where there was a carding machine, and had it carded. Mrs. Hayes spun it and it was woven into coverlets. The colors used, as she remembers them, were indigo, madder, hickory bark, and copperas. They got the indigo at the store, but Mrs. Hayes said, "My grandmother grew indigo in her garden." Mrs. Hayes also brought to this work her practical knowledge of spinning and weaving linen, and in relating her recollections of those active days referred to the fact that Dr. Frost planted some 12 acres of flax to provide the fiber for linen thread, a sufficient supply for many years.

By 1899 the requirements for filling orders, marketing the coverlets, and responding to requests for information about weaving had reached such proportions that Miss Robinson was obliged to give much time to the work. Her contributions to the revival were discouraging the use of aniline dyes; emphasizing desirability to match the design in the seams of the coverlets; and in order to keep in touch with the weavers, assisting in the publication of a leaflet entitled, Repair That Loom.

An article in the Berea Quarterly of February, 1900, describes a number of the new students and the extent to which they carried on spinning and weaving in their homes. The following extracts are taken from this article:

Eliza Hurley . . . can spin and weave and break flax. She is wearing a homespun "linsey-woolsey" dress and the woolen mitts which

A LOG HOUSE ROADSIDE SHELTER

ALONG THE HIGHWAYS OF NORTH CAROLINA ARE LITTLE SHELTER HOUSES BUILT IN THE
PIONEER TRADITION. RESTING IN THE DOORWAY IS FRANCES L. GOODRICH WHO FOUNDED
ALLANSTAND COTTAGE INDUSTRIES

CARDING WOOL BY HAND IN KENTUCKY

CARDING, THE FIRST OPERATION IN MAKING YARN AFTER SHEARING AND CLEANING THE
WOOL, IS STILL PRACTICED IN DIFFERENT PARTS OF THE HIGHLANDS

stand for gentility in the mountains . . . James Combs is twenty-five years of age, and a little more than six feet in height. He is wearing a suit of "Kentucky jeans" of a sheep's-gray color . . . Rachel Bales . . . can both spin and weave . . . Nellie Ambrose . . . is now in her second year at Berea, and earning a large part of her expenses by domestic labor . . . Can spin and weave . . . Martha Beard . . . cannot only spin and weave, but also drive oxen at the plough or in "logging." . . . Her parents . . . have contributed three sheep toward her education.

Berea continued to be a strong influence in the revival of these mountain handicrafts to which Dr. Frost had given the poetic and appropriate name "fireside industries." It soon saw the need for providing careful instruction and of preparing teachers in the arts. It established the earliest school for these purposes in the Highlands, and in 1902 it called Mrs. Hettie Wright Graham to direct its student work. She was the first person to devote her whole time to handicrafts. Mrs. Graham's office was in a log cabin furnished with chairs and tables made by the woodworking class at the College; its decorations were of hand-woven textiles. The looms where spinning and weaving were taught to the college girls and where village women came to weave were set up in another log cabin; by this time 20 women in the town were spinning and weaving.

Mrs. Jennie Lester Hill followed Mrs. Graham as director and distributor of student work in 1903. Under her management sales from the fireside industries reached a new high mark of about $1,500 a year. Also a Berea coverlet won a medal at the Paris Exposition in 1900.

In 1911 Dr. Frost invited Mrs. Anna Ernberg, a native of Sweden, who a few years before had come to New York City to teach hand weaving, to take charge of the Fireside Industries at Berea College. The need of an experienced teacher of handicrafts was recognized, and Dr. Frost found in Mrs. Ernberg the gifts and ability to carry the work to fuller culmination. Under her direction the weaving products at the College have achieved an eminent place among the hand industries of our country. From two to three hundred girls are taught each year, and the school markets the handwork of many homes in the region of the College.

Mrs. Ernberg has designed a small hand loom for use in the schoolroom and homes where the old type of mountain loom might prove too cumbersome to operate or inadequate for the lighter fabrics. She has also restored many of the old coverlet patterns which had been lost or changed in the process of transmission down the generations. Berea College is one of the few schools that make hand looms for weavers.

ALLANSTAND AND THE REVIVAL

At about the same time that the handicraft revival was getting under way in the Kentucky mountains, indications of renewed interest in hand-made things appeared in the Highlands of North Carolina. The movement here centered in the hills of Madison and Buncombe Counties and found root under the able leadership of Frances L. Goodrich, then a social worker in the schools of the Women's Board of Home Missions of the Presbyterian Church in that region. In 1895 Miss Goodrich was living at Brittain's Cove, 12 miles from Asheville, when she and her associate undertook to revive there some of the old crafts, especially weaving, as she said, to make less dull and monotonous the lives of her women neighbors. The story of this experience is so important in the revival of handicrafts that a brief digest of her account of its early stages is given here.[1]

The men and older boys of the mountains made the trip to the neighboring town of Asheville occasionally with tobacco and other produce, and the children were kept busy during the school months of the year, "but for the women life had less color; for them there were few or no outings and many of them were shut in to monotony. One woman who had once been to the nearest railroad station five miles away used to relate with excitement how a freight and a passenger had passed while she was there."

While Miss Goodrich was "pondering the resources at hand for bringing healthful excitement" into the lives of these solitary women, one of them "out of pure good will and affection" presented her with a forty-year-old coverlet, the Double Bowknot pattern, golden brown on a cream-colored background. With it

[1] Goodrich, Frances Louisa, Mountain Homespun. Yale University Press, New Haven, 1931.

came the "draft" from which it was woven—a long strip of paper covered with mysterious figures. Miss Goodrich was "put to her studies" to interpret it. She believed that here was a "fine craft dying out and desirable to revive." Did she in receiving this gift "hold the clue to her puzzle in her very hand"?

The two basic questions confronting her were: Could coverlets be produced at a moderate cost? And if so could a market be found for them? Soon the admiration bestowed on one sent to a friend in the North reaffirmed her belief that a market could be developed. She continues:

We were meeting one afternoon each week at the cottage for sewing and chatting and for a short religious service, closing in time for all to get home for the evening milking and other chores. Few women could come to the Sunday School or preaching services after getting the children "fixed to go" and with the dinner to prepare, so that this mid-week meeting was valued both socially and religiously. Consulting together we found that there was one loom in the Cove, stored away in a barn loft, and Aunt Jane knew how to weave "plain cloth." The loom was set up in our library with much talk of "harness" and "gears" and "sleys" and "rakes" and "temples."[1]

Another who assisted in the revival was "the wise-hearted woman, Mrs. Elmeda McHargue Walker, master weaver of coverlets." Mrs. Walker lived a few miles over the state line in Tennessee and of her and her sisters Miss Goodrich writes:

It was always a pleasure to go there. One rode by the short-cut through a hollow where rhododendrons met over the rider's head, then up a path a few inches wide to the top of the ridge and so along until one came to the tiny farm nestled in the fold of the hill, with the barn and the barn-lot and the house with its paled-in yard where beautiful things grew, March flowers, or Easters, red honeysuckle, flags, dahlias, all sorts of old-time flowers. But the best of it was the welcome of the three sisters of Highland blood who . . . had woven more webs than they could count, of coverlets and counterpanes and plain cloth; most of them being done on shares for their neighbors. Their market, however, had sadly dwindled as "store goods" came in fashion. . . . Mrs. Walker's work hereafter set the standard for our Industries. To follow weaving was her delight and she followed it, producing for us beautiful webs, till she was long past eighty years of age.

[1] *Ibid.*, p. 22.

It was Mrs. Walker who wove the fabric for upholstering the furniture in the Mountain Room of the White House planned by Mrs. Woodrow Wilson in 1913.

As weaving progressed under fresh stimulation old patterns came to light, and soon workers set out to gather as many drafts as could be found. The collection of coverlet drafts at Allanstand now contains about 70 different designs.

When it was realized that a business was being developed a name, Allanstand Cottage Industries, was given to the undertaking. Early residents had known the hamlet as Allan's Old Stand, a place owned by a man named Allan, where in pioneer days the "drovers" coming through from Tennessee to South Carolina were accommodated for the night with yards for the mules and hogs and a log house for themselves.

The threefold purpose of the Allanstand Cottage Industries was set forth in a leaflet by Miss Goodrich as follows:

. . . to bring money into communities far from market and to give paying work to women in homes too isolated to permit them to find it for themselves; to give to these women a new interest, the pleasure of producing beautiful things, the delight of the skilled worker and artist of feeling themselves sharers in the work of the world; to save from extinction the old-time crafts while producing things of value and beauty.

In the beginning, in addition to marketing the products of the mountain homes at Allanstand, an annual exhibition and sale was held in Asheville. But in 1908 a permanent salesroom was opened in Asheville and in 1917 the business was incorporated, the bylaws providing that beyond a small dividend to the stockholder "all surplus should be turned into the business or used for the benefit of the craftspeople of the mountains." The Allanstand Cottage Industries still thrive in Asheville today, but since 193 the enterprise has been conducted under the auspices of the Southern Highland Handicraft Guild, to which Miss Goodrich gave it outright in the spring of that year.

OTHER WORKERS IN THE REVIVAL

No record could be compiled that would adequately describe all the persons and influences lending support to the handicraft re vival. These forces included both small groups banded together to bring about a quickening of sentiment and individuals working independently in isolated localities throughout the region. In the vicinity of Russellville, Tennessee, for instance, the revival did not culminate in organized efforts until some time after the movement had taken shape in Berea and Allanstand. Nevertheless the devotion of a few individuals kept the work going and eventually restored the older home arts and added new ones in this section where in recent years very skilful and artistic work has been done.

The Dougherty family of Russellville, which takes pride in six consecutive generations of weavers and holds a record of accomplishment in vegetable dyes and other pioneer crafts, never surrendered entirely to brought-in things. Traditions were too strongly entrenched in its members to be laid aside, and there has never been a time when carding, spinning, and weaving were not carried on in their household. They possess many rare examples of weaving and their home is a veritable museum of the pioneer crafts.

When the effort to re-establish the old practices was undertaken they assumed a place in the vanguard. Weaving was taken up vigorously not only in the big family house where a number of looms were in continuous use, but in the country about Russellville and farther back in the mountains. Sarah Dougherty developed an outlet for these products, all of which she supervised. This enterprise known as the Shuttle-Crafters is an active handicraft center today.

Mrs. Zachariah Field, also of Russellville and identified with the revival in this section of Tennessee, was an expert in coverlets and she wove almost continuously for twenty-five years. Mrs. Nancy Osborne Greer, who lived in one of the remote mountain homes near Trade, Johnson County, Tennessee, kept at her spinning long after it had gone out in the surrounding country, and her record of the spinning of woolen yarn to be made up into blankets, coverlets, and clothing is perhaps the longest of any known. As she grew older she taught her grandson how to weave, but continued to spin for his loom until her death in the autumn of 1934 at the age of a hundred and one years.

Force was lent to the revival by persons whose homes were outside the mountains. Mrs. Gretchen Bayne spent her summers at Russellville, and while there became interested in the old coverlets found in the region, especially in the many varieties of patterns. Her collection comprised some of the oldest drafts in the Highlands. She herself learned to dye with indigo and established a blue pot which was started from one that is said to have been in continuous use for over eighty years.

In North Carolina, somewhat removed from the Allanstand group, lived a weaver of unusual ability, Mrs. Finley Mast of Valle Crucis, Watauga County, one of the best known in the Highlands. Until her death in 1936 Mrs. Mast carded and spun, and wove coverlets, rugs, and other textiles. She lived with her sister, Mrs. Robert Mast, in the old cabin on the Mast homestead which was built in 1812. Together they worked on two looms even older than the cabin. Mrs. Mast held many exhibitions, gave demonstrations in different parts of the country, and was one of the women who during the first term of President Wilson's administration wove articles for the Mountain Room in the White House.

Aunt Cumi Woody was another versatile worker who could turn her hand to any of the various operations incident to producing woven fabric from the shearing of the sheep to the completed web. She was an expert in the use of vegetable dyes and for many years kept her blue pot going. Although she lived 40 miles from Penland, North Carolina, she gave a good deal of information concerning indigo and other vegetable dyes to the weavers in that center.

In this report it would be impossible to include the threads of all the early efforts to revive handicrafts in this section of the country. Some workers continued to labor alone, others became identified with groups, but all made up the homely and enduring warp of the movement upon which the patterns of today are being woven.

THE HIGH SPINNING WHEEL

WILMA CREECH OF PINE MOUNTAIN, HARLAN COUNTY, KENTUCKY, SPINNING WOOL ON
A HIGH WHEEL, THE WHEEL MOST USED IN THE HIGHLANDS

SPINNING YARN ON THE HIGH WHEEL

An Old Spinner of Grassy Valley, Tennessee, Spinning Woolen Yarn on the High
Wheel Used for Both Cotton and Wool. She Also Makes Lace

CHAPTER IV

THE HANDICRAFTS CONTINUE TO GROW

THE vitality engendered by the several groups and individuals who sponsored the revival of handicrafts, together with the natural aptitude of the mountain people to work with their hands and the encouragement which came from increased demand, carried the movement along, and about 1900 handicraft activities had begun in several sections of the Highlands. Some, as has been indicated, found sufficient foothold to become permanent centers or to assume important places in agencies already established, and these today make up the main body that has brought the Highland crafts to the present stage of progress. Because there is little printed information showing the historical development of these various centers, a chronological list is given here with brief accounts of some of them.

WORK FROM 1901 TO 1913

THE BILTMORE INDUSTRIES

Up to about 1900, endeavors to revive handicrafts were founded primarily on an interest in hand weaving, other types of work being added as weaving progressed. In 1901 Eleanor P. Vance, a wood carver, and Charlotte L. Yale took a cottage on the Biltmore Estate, just outside Asheville, North Carolina, and soon a number of young boys of the neighborhood showed enthusiastic interest in watching Miss Vance work. Encouraged by their eagerness, she organized a boys' class, beginning with four members, and taught them wood carving in the kitchen of her small cottage, "little realizing that she was making history" by bringing this handicraft to a community where later it was to become an important home industry.

Mrs. George W. Vanderbilt's interest was aroused in these small undertakings and wood-carving classes were soon opened also to the girls living on Biltmore Estate. The superintendent of public schools in Asheville invited the two young women to extend their classes to the high school there, but this was not possible because of demands on their time by those already existing at Biltmore. The enthusiasm on the part of the superintendent led later to a course of manual training in the Asheville schools.

From these modest classes in wood carving, cabinet making was the natural result and a skilled cabinetmaker was soon engaged. The abundant woods in the Biltmore forest furnished constant encouragement and Miss Vance evolved original designs with motifs of plants and shrubs growing in the region. Metal work was later introduced. These and other industries which developed through the stimulation and supervision of the early period were later taken over by F. L. Seely and are now carried on with modification under his direction. These are known as the Biltmore Industries.

Mrs. Vanderbilt's participation in the work led her to a desire to introduce weaving. Sheep were brought in to provide the wool, and a number of women on the estate learned to spin and weave. She then turned her attention to the production of all-wool fabrics for clothing fashioned somewhat after the homespun made in Scotland and Ireland. Miss Yale and Miss Vance made several trips to the British Isles to perfect their weaving methods and an old loom over a hundred years old was imported from Scotland. Out of these early experiments came the popular textiles now produced with more modern equipment on the grounds of Grove Park Inn in Asheville. In 1915 Miss Yale and Miss Vance went to Tryon, North Carolina, where they founded the Tryon Toy-Makers and Wood-Carvers described later in this chapter.

HINDMAN SETTLEMENT SCHOOL

In 1898 the Kentucky Federation of Women's Clubs organized a traveling library service in the vicinity of Hindman, Knott County, Kentucky. By 1899 this temporary service seemed to justify more permanent social plans and one of the librarians sent out an appeal for "gentlewomen" to work among the mountain families. Soon afterward a rural settlement was founded on a mountainside far back from the main routes of travel. Song meetings were held, kindergarten subjects taught, and sewing and cooking classes conducted, while visits, often providing entertainment, were made to remote mountain homes in the counties of Knott, Letcher, and Perry. On these visits workers found "much dignity, intelligence, and gentleness of manner." During the summer Uncle Solomon Everidge, then eighty years of age, walked 20 miles to ask the settlement women to give his children and grandchildren an opportunity to partake of the knowledge of the world.

After three successive summers of experimenting, beneficial to both mountain families and workers at the settlement, in 1902 a school was established at Hindman, Kentucky, on what is known as Troublesome Creek. Katherine Pettit and May Stone, who had carried out the program of this rural experiment together, guided the new school from its inception until 1912, when Miss Pettit left to found Pine Mountain Settlement School in Harlan County. From the beginning both encouraged a revival of old handicrafts in mountain homes, and a Department of Fireside Industries was established at Hindman Settlement School "to encourage the native arts of basketry, home spinning and weaving, and to find a market for these products." One of the successful activities of this school has been the exhibitions sent outside the Highlands to acquaint people with its work.

THE BERRY SCHOOLS

In 1902 the first unit of the Berry Schools was established by Martha Berry near Rome, Floyd County, Georgia, and in 1903 it was incorporated. As a part of the plan in which all manual labor at the school is performed by students, handicrafts have had an important place. Among the school buildings constructed by the students is Sunshine Cottage, which contains classrooms for instruction in arts and crafts. Here cotton, wool, and flax are spun and the girls are "taught hand-weaving, designing, combination of colors, the making of feather fans, and all phases of home arts." Other buildings constructed from stone found on the school farm contain shops for carpentry and leather and metal work.

TALLULAH FALLS INDUSTRIAL SCHOOL

In organizing Tallulah Falls Industrial School, on the line of Habersham and Rabun Counties, Georgia, in 1909 the Georgia

Federation of Women's Clubs stressed "training for the hand" as one of its primary aims. Consequently a crafts department was established and the handicrafts have been a regular part of the courses.

Weaving, dyeing, and basketry are the principal activities among the girl students, and they have accomplished excellent results with experiments outside the traditional Highland types. Landscape tapestry for walls and screens, designed from scenes in the neighborhood, are made by a process of combining certain technical methods used in other countries with those of our own. The students also weave many of the old designs—Whig Rose, Tennessee Trouble, and other patterns on the 35 looms in the School.

A shop for working in wood is provided for the boy students and many practical articles for everyday use are produced each year.

Pi Beta Phi Settlement School

The Pi Beta Phi Settlement School was founded at Gatlinburg, Sevier County, Tennessee, in 1912. Situated in a community of sparse educational facilities and meager opportunity for earning, this School "strove to develop initiative and independence among the mountain people and to foster home industries which might become a means of livelihood." Through the active chapters of Pi Beta Phi and the alumnae clubs, markets have been greatly extended for the handicraft products of the School.

One building, known as the Arrow Craft Shop, serves as an exhibition and salesroom, while another presented by L. E. Voorheis is used entirely for handicraft work. In addition to that done at the School, products are made in homes under its guidance by women on new or reconstructed looms where the grandmothers half a century ago had prepared all their own materials and worked undirected. An expert weaver supervises more than 40 looms among these mountain workers, many of whom visit the School to receive further instruction, watch the students at work, or to use the modern appliances. Evelyn Bishop, who was the first head resident, writes that linen weaving, wool and part-wool weaving for dress patterns, and tapestry weaving have been done by the students; that a number of homes have hand-woven

AN OLD-TIME SPINNER AND WEAVER

AUNT LOU KITCHEN OF SHOOTIN' CREEK, NORTH CAROLINA, SPINNING YARN ON THE LOW WHEEL. SHE HAS WOVEN MANY A MOUNTAIN COVERLET SIMILAR TO THE ONE IN THE BACKGROUND

AN OLD HOME-MADE MOUNTAIN LOOM
The Mountain Loom Was Large, Strong, and Took Up Considerable Room, but It
Often Lasted for Generations

curtains, table runners, and towels; and that several women have woven attractive cloth for dresses for their children, coming to the School for evening classes to make them up.

Working with the craft department at Pi Beta Phi School in its earliest years was one of the most famous all-round craftswomen and basket makers of the Highlands, Aunt Lydia Whaley, who died in 1926 at the age of eighty-six. She produced many types of baskets in her lifetime and has the distinction of inventing one that bears her name. It is described in Chapter X, Mountain Baskets.

When the School was opened there had been no spinning in the region for thirty-five years. To Aunt Lizzie Regan, now over seventy-eight years old, much credit is due for bringing back to life this age-old practice. She taught her neighbors how to spin as well as how to operate an old-time loom. In a garret was found one of the ancient swinging batten looms, which was dragged down and she began weaving the type of cloth used a generation ago, jeans for clothing made on three sets of harness. She still weaves cloth in old-fashioned stripes which is now used for modern apparel and accessories.

At the time of the revival Mrs. W. H. McCarter was the only person found weaving cloth in this part of the Highlands. She uses the Gentlemen's Fancy design which is partly original with her; a similar design is said to have been made by English weavers centuries ago.

Otto J. Mattil revived furniture making in the Smokies, establishing the Woodcrafters and Carvers shop at Gatlinburg, which has given considerable employment to men and boys in the community. The practice of weaving corn shucks into chair bottoms is a Smoky Mountain heritage and is used extensively in this neighborhood. "A bottom of shucks'll last sixty-five years," declared Charles Huskey, whose father and grandfather both made them for their own use and for sale or barter.

PINE MOUNTAIN SETTLEMENT SCHOOL

As has been stated, after Miss Pettit and Miss Stone had successfully launched Hindman Settlement School, Miss Pettit turned her attention to another rugged section of the Kentucky Highlands where the need of a school seemed quite as urgent, in 1913 establishing Pine Mountain Settlement School in Harlan County.

William Creech, who had always lived far back in the Kentucky mountains, had ever been concerned about the welfare of young people, and although unschooled himself had developed his own philosophy of education. Uncle William, as he was known to the country around, besought Miss Pettit to build a school on "yon side of Pine Mountain." To support his faith in the influence of education he gave 136 acres for the project. In a letter dated October, 1913, he said, "I have deeded my land to the Pine Mountain Settlement School to be used for school purposes as long as the Constitution of the United States stands. Hopin' it may make a bright and intelligent people after I'm dead and gone."[1]

Handicrafts were made a basic part of the plan at Pine Mountain, and one of the impressive features was the building of log cabins for student and teacher homes. Old Log House and Big Log House remain among the most attractive structures on the grounds. The small, primitive cabin occupied by Uncle William and Aunt Sal Creech has been moved to the School and contains many of their personal belongings, including Aunt Sal's old loom on which she wove the family clothes and many mountain coverlets. One of her granddaughters has recently woven duplicates of some of them.

At a recent gathering of mountain folk from Whitley County a man who happened by picked up a book in which was inscribed the name of Katherine Pettit. "I've always wanted to see her," he exclaimed. "Forty years ago she sent me a circulating library which I carried on horseback sixty-five miles to my country school."[2] Thereupon all those assembled began talking of the schools Miss Pettit had built, the libraries she had furnished, the stumps in paths, both literal and figurative, that she had dug up, the mud holes in roads that she had filled in. "Long after she's dead," said one woman, "she will be remembered by the blossoms she has scattered all over this mountain world."

[1] McVey, Frances Jewell, The Blossom Woman. *In* Mountain Life and Work, Berea, Kentucky, April, 1934, p. 2.

[2] *Ibid.*, p. 1.

WORK FROM 1913 TO 1920

From the well-directed beginnings about 1895 and the continuous progress extending over the period through 1913, the wave of production in handicrafts brought the home arts to a higher place and the question of survival was no longer so pressing. It was this period that restored the old-time blankets and coverlets, revived the natural dyes for weaving and knitting, developed reproductions of old colonial furniture, and the newer decorative carvings, and brought into varied uses the picturesque mountain basket. New types of handwork inspired by buyers outside the Highlands and numerous articles for practical use were undertaken. It is significant that the agencies established in these early days are among the leaders in the handicraft movement of today.

The period immediately following 1913, while characterized by a steady holding of the gains accomplished, was not marked by many new ventures in the handicraft field.

Tryon Toy-Makers and Wood-Carvers

It was in 1915 that Miss Yale and Miss Vance, who had established the industries at Biltmore, turned their attention to the new location 40 miles south of Asheville, where they opened the Tryon wood-carving and toy-making shop. Setting up their benches, they gathered the children of the vicinity around them and began with simple designs. In addition to wood carving they experimented with hand-made toys. The work grew rapidly, and in order to accommodate the increasing trade and to have a place in which to display their unusual wood carving and their articles of original design, the little "custard colored house" with red roof and green trimmings was built against the side of the hill at the edge of Tryon, where today visitors may find many charming toys displayed on beautifully carved and perfectly joined tables and shelves.

One may also find old Florentine, as well as modern and indigenous designs in picture frames, book-ends, nut bowls, fireside benches, tea trays, footstools, bellows, hearth brushes, and so forth. Massive Gothic benches as well are made by these young workers who will also fill special orders in wood carving to meet specific needs. Through the succeeding years the Tryon Toy-Makers and

Wood-Carvers have remained one of the steady and reliable land-marks of the Highland area.

ASHEVILLE NORMAL AND ASSOCIATED SCHOOLS

In 1916 the Asheville Normal and Associated Schools introduced the teaching of handicrafts into their curriculum which had been outlined earlier. In 1935 the schools reported 60 weavers at work on a great variety of articles. Out of native wood they also made tables, chairs, desks, and many smaller objects.

WORK FROM 1920 TO 1930

About 1920 a new surge of enthusiasm for handicrafts was felt throughout the Southern Highlands, and during the decade following a number of groups working at one form or another sprang up. Some were organized within settlements, schools, and missions, while others represented entirely new alignments, a number not connected with organizations engaged in social or educational work. The independent handicraft center developed during this period and justified its existence through several new undertakings sponsored by a few individuals on their own responsibility. These organizations demonstrated the important place handicrafts had attained, for they proved that some of them could under favorable circumstances be sustained without subsidy.

The Carr Creek Community Center founded in Knott County, Kentucky, was the only enterprise organized in 1920 that included handicrafts. Weaving and woodwork were taken up and carried on at the center until 1935, when they were temporarily discontinued.

ROSEMONT INDUSTRIES

In 1920 the Farm Bureau at Marion, Smyth County, Virginia, at the suggestion of Mrs. Laura Copenhaver, who at the time was a member of the Bureau, organized an industry to utilize the surplus wool resulting from a depressed market following the World War. The wool was bought for cash from the farmers, and on two old discarded hand looms was woven into coverlets from old patterns that had been preserved as precious possessions. These coverlets were sold through women's clubs and parent-teacher associations.

The Farm Bureau was later moved from Marion but the coverlet weaving was left there in charge of Mrs. Copenhaver. The demand was so great that an old blanket mill was found which reproduced colonial patterns on a power loom. By this time many women were urging Mrs. Copenhaver to give them work, offering to weave, to hand-tie, to hook, and so forth. She responded by assuming personal responsibility for the undertaking and became deeply interested in reviving the old hand crafts for the women of the mountains. She organized these women into a group giving them the name of her home "Rosemont," then more than one hundred years old, in which the work was carried on. They became interested in collecting patterns of coverlets, quilts, and rugs and in experimenting with dyes for the reproduction of colonial hues and in working for fastness of color. Thus from a beginning in weaving coverlets to consume unsold wool, the endeavor came to include hand-tying for spreads, canopies, fringes, and the hooking of rugs. Rugs have become the principal product of Rosemont and are done entirely by hand; many of the designs which are unique are a special invention of Mrs. Copenhaver. In every way she encourages originality and her group often find inspiration for their design in the scenes and experiences of the region.

PINE BURR STUDIO

Pine Burr Studio, a center in Apison, Hamilton County, Tennessee, was established in 1921 for the purpose of training mountain women to make hooked rugs. With Mrs. F. D. Huckabee as headworker and teacher, the industry has made rapid strides in producing attractive hooked rugs for market. In writing of this work Mrs. Huckabee states, "I would judge that our products are sold in most of the larger cities since the cash sales from one community in 1930 amounted to around $10,000. We have nothing that savors of factory work. Each piece is made in the home of the worker with a small hook resembling a crochet hook."

THE WEAVING CENTER OF CROSSNORE SCHOOL

A Weaving Department, made possible through the co-operation of representatives of the Smith-Hughes Act of the federal government, to promote vocational education, was added to Crossnore

School, Avery County, North Carolina, in 1922.[1] Its purpose, as indicated in the announcement, is to accomplish two things:

1. To provide a way by which older girls may partly defray their expenses while at school—a healthy, happy occupation that makes possible the development of these young minds and souls without harm to their bodies.

2. To provide a way by which the many mountain mothers may earn money which they need more than you can imagine, and long for, with a longing you have never known. Married as mere girls, with almost no education, they have watched the wonderful development of their younger sisters or their daughters, till their own privations and limitations have loomed large. To these hungry minds the weaving lessons open new fields. When they come to the school house for their lessons they not only learn the management of a loom but they establish between themselves and the school a connection that is a source of mutual benefit. Even after they become proficient enough to take their looms home where they can work between times, this relation remains.

The rug making at Crossnore is mainly of the hooked variety, although braided and rag-carpet types have been made. Many of the hooked rugs are standard designs, but encouragement is given to alter these in both form and color. A number of original patterns have been worked out by rug makers at the School and in the community, many of whom find pleasure in the picture types of design.

No work in handicrafts in the Highlands has brought a more whole-hearted response from mountain women to work at a congenial and constructive task than that carried on at Crossnore under the able leadership of Dr. Mary M. Sloop and the immediate direction of Mrs. N. W. Johnson.

The Blue Ridge Weavers

In 1922 Mr. and Mrs. George A. Cathey established the Blue Ridge Weavers at Tryon, North Carolina. Mrs. Cathey, a mountain-bred woman, became interested in the handwork of her own people

[1] The Smith-Hughes Vocational Education Bill: A bill to provide for the promotion of vocational education; to provide for co-operation with the states in the promotion of such education in agriculture and the trades and industries; to provide for co-operation with the states in the preparation of teachers of vocational subjects; and to appropriate money and regulate its expenditure. Approved February 23, 1917, by the U. S. Congress.

A KENTUCKY SPINNER AND WEAVER

One of the Best Weavers in the Pine Mountain Region Is Red Sol Day, Who, with His Sisters, Makes Coverlets and Other Old-Time Textiles

A LINK BETWEEN THE OLD AND THE NEW

The Record of Weaving in the Dougherty Family of Russellville, Tennessee, Has Never Been Broken. Mrs. Leah Adams Dougherty Learned from Her Mother and Grandmother, Taught Her Children, and They in Turn Taught Theirs

while a student at Hull House, Chicago. Beginning with a small savings account, she organized a group of mountain weavers and has since guided them in the effort to keep up a good quality of work. In addition to weaving, basketry, and quilting, hooked and braided rug making and woodworking are carried on. These products made in mountain homes by over a hundred workers are collected and displayed in a large attractive salesroom where many old objects of early mountain life are exhibited.

MATHENY WEAVERS

While her husband, F. E. Matheny, was a member of the Berea College faculty, Mrs. Edith Matheny became interested in weaving and took up training at the Fireside Industries of the College. For some time she experimented for her own enjoyment without thought of teaching others. One day a young country girl came to her home and said she wanted to work for her and learn to weave. In spite of discouragement on the part of Mrs. Matheny the child persisted, and finally an arrangement was made for her to try. In a short time not only had she learned to weave but through Mrs. Matheny's help her mother and brother also had become weavers.

The interest spread to other homes, and in 1922 a community hand-loom weaving project at Berea, an undertaking independent of the College, was established. About 30 homes were engaged simultaneously in weaving under the direction of Mr. and Mrs. Matheny, with other applicants on the waiting list. In time some of the families were able to support themselves entirely by their weaving.

Mrs. Matheny became an expert weaver, developing excellent color combinations and designs. In addition to the various articles regularly made by the Matheny Weavers, special patterns and color schemes are given attention, including colonial weaving reproduced from photographs. The motto which every weaver follows is "Nothing but my best."

THE SHUTTLE-CRAFTERS

Organized in 1923 by the Dougherty sisters, the Shuttle-Crafters of Russellville, Hamblen County, Tennessee, represents the continued efforts of this family "to perpetuate the old-time crafts which have been handed down through the generations and which have been practiced in the Tennessee mountains since the first settlers came westward across the Blue Ridge."

Sarah Dougherty has directed the Shuttle-Crafters, which includes some workers who come regularly to the old mansion just outside the town and others far back in the mountains whose family demands preclude their leaving home.

The well-standardized designs, the careful use of colors, some of them natural dyes, and the excellent workmanship in weaving are qualities that characterize this handicraft center carried on in an atmosphere of antique charm the products of which are constantly flowing to many parts of the United States. A few years ago an abandoned log house built in 1799, which later became a tavern, was carefully taken down under Miss Dougherty's direction and rebuilt near the old mansion, where it serves as a display and work place.

Penland Weavers and Potters

Although plans were begun in 1913 to include a handicraft department in the Appalachian School at Penland, Mitchell County, North Carolina, they were not realized until 1923 when the Penland Weavers was established. This effort "grew first out of a dream to revive and perpetuate the native arts and crafts of a mountain community, and secondly, out of a desire to provide for the people of this mountain community an opportunity of supplementing the products of their small farms with a little cash income."

From the beginning this was more a community than a school endeavor, for the weaving is done chiefly in homes around the region of Penland. Lucy Morgan, under whose direction the organization was begun and who has been its judicious leader, foresaw the benefit that would come if weaving could be introduced as a means of increasing family income and of varying the daily routine of mountain women by bringing in a new and pleasant interest. The objective and early efforts are well described in a pamphlet about the work from which the following is an extract:

It was hard sledding from the first. There was little money and, although there was enough general interest in the work, each individual

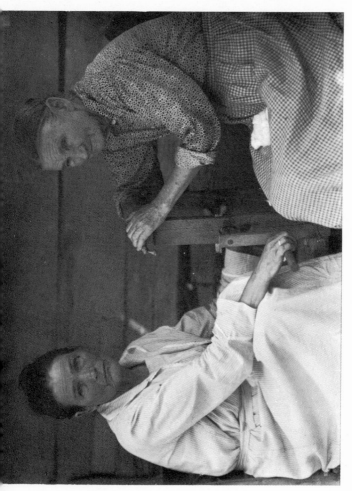

A PRIMITIVE COTTON GIN

COTTON IS STILL GINNED BY HAND IN SOME HOMES OF NORTH CAROLINA. THE MACHINE
USED RESEMBLES A CLOTHES WRINGER AND IS OF A TYPE FOUND TODAY IN INDIA

OLD-TIME WEAVERS HAVE HIGH STANDARDS

AUNT TISH HAYS OF HINDMAN, KENTUCKY, WHO HELPED IN THE REVIVAL OF HANDI-
CRAFTS, IS A WINNER OF MANY PRIZES FOR EXCELLENT COVERLETS SUCH AS THE ONE
IN THE PICTURE

woman had to be shown its advantages before undertaking it in her own household. The roads were bad, and the homes far apart, but Miss Morgan was courageous and utterly believed in the ultimate success of her undertaking. . . . One eventful day in late October, 1923, the first loom was taken in a wagon to the home of Mrs. Henry Willis and the weaving teacher rode down the rough mountain road with it to give her first instructions. The loom had to be set up, and the threads warped, beamed, and threaded through the harness and sley before it was ready for weaving. Miss Morgan spent three days with her pupil and then went away to leave her to finish the warp of "Log Cabin" rugs. The days that followed brought much happiness to Mrs. Willis, taking her back in memory many times to her young girlhood when her own mother had woven the necessary articles of clothing and house-furnishings for a large family, and causing her to look hopefully into the future when perhaps the fruits of her loom might enable her to do the things for her children that she had always dreamed of doing.[1]

And so from home to home in the mountains, instructions were carried, and at the end of the first year nearly a dozen women were ready to weave for the market. As this industry developed, exhibiting its products at county and church fairs, summer hotels, and gift shops, it came to the attention of George W. Coggin of the State Vocational Training Division and was soon included in the list of agencies to receive financial support under the Smith-Hughes Act. Later pottery making and pewter work were introduced. Several of the students in metal work make their own designs, and some boys have been able to earn their way through school by their work in pewter.

PITTMAN COMMUNITY CENTER

The Pittman Community Center, Sevierville, Sevier County, Tennessee, maintained by the Board of Home Missions and Church Extension of the Methodist Episcopal Church, began in 1923 to promote an interest in handicrafts, and the work has been continued as part of the school and community activities. Considerable skill has been shown in whittling and basket making among the workers.

[1] Ford, Bonnie Willis, The Story of the Penland Weavers.

Lincoln Memorial University

In the same year Lincoln Memorial University at Cumberland Gap, Tennessee, one of the older schools of the mountains, initiated a small department of handicrafts in the hope of enlarging the staff for instruction so that more workers could be trained. At the present time weaving of small articles and some woodwork are in progress.

Handicraft Guild of the Diocese of Southwestern Virginia

In 1923 the groups working in the mountains of southwestern Virginia, under the auspices of the Protestant Episcopal Church, established handicraft work in several of their missions and were directed by Mabel R. Mansfield. One of the first experiments was with Italian drawnwork; some of the mountain women, although engaged daily in rough outdoor work, acquired great skill and accuracy in this fine needlecraft. At Dante, Russell County, St. Mark's Mission has worked out several unusual subjects, some furniture, baskets, wood carving, and ingenious figures made of dyed corn husks. Likenesses of George and Martha Washington, a Nativity scene showing Mary, Joseph, and the Infant Child with the Wise Men and animals in the background; and other characteristic figures are among the objects created from the corn plant. Very small split-oak baskets constructed by methods used in the full-sized ones are both dainty and useful.

St. John's-in-the-Mountains the center at Endicott, Franklin County, beginning handicrafts in 1924, has directed work among mountain weavers from which a variety of products is available: coverlets, scarfs, bags, rugs, towels, cushion covers, together with small objects of wood. Some of the missions of the Diocese have old mountain looms in operation.

The Spinning Wheel

One of the most important independent handicraft centers in the region is the Spinning Wheel, at Asheville, North Carolina, established in 1924 by Clementine Douglas and still operating under her direction. In an old log cabin furnished with many of the utensils of a pioneer mountain household, woolens, linens, hooked rugs, and other products are arranged to blend with the setting of by-gone days. In the spacious weaving room of the Douglas home several workers may be found any day figuring out designs, weaving old and new patterns, while outdoors are the kettles for dyeing with hickory bark, walnut hulls, sumac berries, and other native materials. In a folder describing the center and its purpose Miss Douglas writes: "Adapting mountain industries to these changing times is the fascinating occupation of the Spinning Wheel." She has successfully applied guidance in handicraft work with the desire to bring out independence of expression among the workers.

In rug making different families often work out special designs with their own color schemes. Miss Douglas has said that she could tell which family lives in a house by the colors out drying on the fences and trees. The picture designs woven into the borders of towels, lunch cloths, and table covers are so truly interpretations by the workers that they are designated by their names, as Julia's butterfly, Lela's cabin, Ollie's basket, and so forth. Supplementing the work done at the Spinning Wheel, the weavers have interested themselves in learning about the methods and techniques employed in other countries.

WOOTON FIRESIDE INDUSTRIES

Wooton Fireside Industries was established at Wooton, Leslie County, Kentucky, in 1924, under the supervision of Rose McCord for the purpose of promoting the usual mountain crafts. Weaving, basket, broom, and furniture making, wood carving, and rug making are the principal handicrafts engaged in. Spinning is done on both the high and the low wheels, and 16 modern looms and four of the old type constitute the equipment for producing textiles, which include material of good quality for dresses with woven bags to match. Three wood-turning lathes in the community give opportunity for furniture making and a good quality of hickory wood and bark furniture is turned out. Brooms are made from straw grown on the farm of the Industries.

THE WEAVE SHOP

After working successfully for several years with weaving and experimenting with natural dyes, in 1924 Wilmer Stone, now Mrs. Viner, opened the Weave Shop at Saluda, Polk County, North Carolina. Here she has found ample opportunity to carry farther her researches and to add to her knowledge of native plants. She has with her own dye pot achieved distinction as the creator of a range of colors perhaps not equaled by any other dyer in the Highlands.

Mrs. Viner has developed several patterns especially suited to her color palette, which begin with simple stripes and include weaves suitable for scarfs, table runners, couch covers, blankets, dress materials, and tapestry wall hangings. In addition to her own work Mrs. Viner has the co-operation of some of the native weavers of Saluda who have been trained by her.

DRY HILL COMMUNITY CENTER AND CARCASSONNE COMMUNITY CENTER

The Dry Hill Community Center in Dryhill, Leslie County, Kentucky, began work in handicrafts in 1925 with weaving, quilting, and toy making. All activities are carried on at the Center, where at present about 20 workers are engaged.

During the same year handwork was undertaken at Carcassonne Community Center at Gander, Letcher County, Kentucky. Baskets and hooked, woven, and braided rugs are the chief articles made. Most of them are done at the Center. About 25 workers, however, are engaged in handicraft work in their homes.

BLUE RIDGE INDUSTRIAL SCHOOL

Handicraft teaching was introduced into the Blue Ridge Industrial School at Bris, Greene County, Virginia, in 1926, a two years' course being required of each student. The major subject is rug making; among the minor subjects are elementary weaving, decorative needlework, toy and flower making, knitting, crocheting, and some work in novelties.

The aim of this course, as set forth in the Report of the School for the year 1930, is "to perfect the girl in ability to carry on a

A PIONEER WEAVER OF TENNESSEE
DURING THE REVIVAL OF WEAVING IN GATLINBURG, AUNT LIZZIE REGAN SET UP AN OLD
LOOM AND TAUGHT OTHERS HOW TO SPIN AND WEAVE. SHE WEAVES CLOTH BY THE BOLT

A WEAVER AND BALLAD SINGER
WEAVING AND OTHER CRAFTS GO WELL WITH THE OLD-TIME BALLADS AND CAROLS
LEARNED BY THE GIRLS IN THEIR MOUNTAIN HOMES

home industry that is of actual commercial value to herself, her family, and the community she is to enter upon leaving the School; and to encourage the revival and preservation of colonial crafts." An adjunct to this course in craftwork is a neighborhood class in rug making for women under the direction of the School. A ready sale is usually found for rugs in "The Shop-beside-the-Stream," where orders are also taken.

A shop for boys is conducted in connection with vocational agriculture, where training is given in the care and use of tools and instruction in wood and ironwork. Many articles are made in the shop for the School and farm.

Craft Guild of the John C. Campbell Folk School

Founded in part on the principles of the Danish folk schools, the John C. Campbell Folk School at Brasstown, Cherokee County, North Carolina, has ever regarded self-expression through handwork a prime need for every individual. About two years after the School was established, in 1927 a handicraft association was organized, and soon its members and neighbors were busy making hearth brooms, colorful patchwork in chair seats and quilts, black walnut footstools and fireplace benches, mountain chairs, and baskets.

Based mainly on traditional mountain crafts, work at the Folk School has never been bound by any strict set of regulations. In the creation of an object the influence of beauty and good workmanship is held as the paramount guide. A random whittler becomes a carver of farm animals in polished wood. The farm worker turns his scrap-iron into artistic candlesticks, and attractive textiles from the weaving room are shaped to fit wooden bag handles, to adorn the back of a chair, for a table runner, or as a decorative scarf; and in these fabrics are the natural colors which the workers brew in the dye pot in the open and test out for fastness under the North Carolina sun.

Shenandoah Community Workers

The Shenandoah Community Workers, established at Bird Haven, Shenandoah County, Virginia, in 1927, under the direction of William Bernard Clark, state that their purpose is "to help the handicrafts survive." They have banded themselves together in a community undertaking to work out a livelihood for mountain people from the resources around them. Situated on land of sparse yield and recalling the skill of their forefathers in woodwork, they turned to the abundant trees to help solve their economic problems.

A woodworking shop, a dry kiln, and a paint shop were built, and bringing to the shop some of the old furniture from their homes to be used as models, they began as a co-operative group to convert the logs they had cut into lumber, and then into hand-rubbed furniture of the early American type. Toys and garden ware are also made, while the women folk work on hooked rugs.

Dorland-Bell School

In 1928 the Dorland-Bell School at Hot Springs, Madison County, North Carolina, added weaving and basket making to the curriculum. Instruction in these subjects is provided only for the students in the School and the output is therefore limited. All products bear the name of the School. The usual articles of weaving—towels, runners, rugs, curtain material, and bags—are made, and from the sale of these the department is supported. Fifteen looms comprise the equipment. Basket making is entirely a club activity.

WORK FROM 1930 ON

The Home Industries of the Henderson Settlement School at Linda, Bell County, Kentucky, established in 1930, has followed largely the old type of mountain work. Materials are woven on hand looms and colored with home dyes made from local plants. Weaving in the form of towels, breakfast sets, handkerchief cases, table runners, cushion covers, coverlets, and dress materials are some of the products of the looms at the School and in the homes where much of the weaving is done.

The experiment established in 1930 at Ary, Perry County, Kentucky, known as Homeplace, has made handicrafts a part of its threefold activities for the promotion of the agricultural and social program of the community. Effort has been directed primarily toward finding in the region about, all those who have been engaged in handicraft work and in urging them to make the most of their skills and abilities. As far as possible workers avoid taking up a craft that would duplicate objects made in other centers. Mountain furniture, baskets, dulcimers, and the entirely indigenous Kentucky poppets made of buckeye wood and described in Chapter XII, Dolls, Toys, and Miniature Furniture, are among the best known handicrafts of the region.

Pleasant Hill Academy Crafts

Pleasant Hill Academy at Pleasant Hill, Cumberland County, Tennessee, one of the older preparatory schools of the mountains, instituted a crafts department in 1930 under the direction of Margaret B. Campbell. As stated in the announcement concerning handicrafts, "its first aim is to foster a love for creating in order that an art may be developed that is truly an expression of our students and so of this section. It seeks also to develop skill among our students in certain lines of work which will be a source of joy and service to them."

The woodworking industry at Pleasant Hill probably represents the school's most extensive practice in handicrafts. It is divided into three groups: shop workers, whittlers and carvers, and finishing group. In these divisions a student's preference is considered along with his ability to perform the particular type of work.

Whittling, described in Chapter XI, is the most recent and perhaps the most notable achievement in the handicrafts of this mountain school. Boys do most of it, while the girls engage in relief carving. In 1935, 24 students were working out all or part of their school expenses in the woodworking industry.

The Pleasant Hill Community Crafts, an organization working under the direction of Mrs. Mabel Boyce, includes woven rugs, coverlets, table runners, couch and pillow covers, and other textiles.

Mountain Cabin Quilters

The Mountain Cabin Quilters organized at Wooton, Leslie County, Kentucky, in 1931, comprises a group of women who are banded together under the leadership of Mrs. J. K. Stoddard, wife of the community doctor, for the purpose of reproducing old mountain and colonial quilt patterns. The work is done entirely in the homes, some of the quilters often having to walk or ride

10 miles to get the order and instructions for a quilt. Not only do the women who can sew fine stitches and even seams belong to this group, but also those who are able to card the wool or cotton and make the bats that go into the quilts for padding. Some of the best needlework in the Highlands is done by this group of women. During the summer of 1935 the business office for Mountain Cabin Quilters was moved to Cashiers, Jackson County, North Carolina, but the workers under the direction of a local leader continue to work around Wooton.

MOUNTAIN NEIGHBORS

In 1931, Elizabeth J. Winn organized a handicraft center at Oldrag, Madison County, Virginia, known as Mountain Neighbors. Inspired by a desire to revive handwork in this isolated section in order to afford better social and financial opportunities for its inhabitants, Miss Winn reconditioned an old log house in which she set up a few looms and started some of the women weaving rag-carpet rugs of good color and quality. She also opened a class in sewing for the girls, and twice each week rode over the mountain to Corbin Hollow to teach sewing to a group of girls and woodwork to the boys of that community. Exhibits of the products of Mountain Neighbors have been held at the annual fair in Madison County, Virginia, and in Baltimore, Maryland. In addition to weaving, needlework, and woodwork, excellent baskets in the region are marketed through Mountain Neighbors. During the summer of 1935 this center was moved to Kimball, Page County, Virginia, in order to release the land at Oldrag to the Shenandoah National Park.

MOUNTAINEER CRAFTSMEN'S COOPERATIVE ASSOCIATION

In 1932 the American Friends Service Committee organized the Mountaineer Craftsmen's Cooperative Association in the bituminous coal regions of West Virginia. Five communities of destitute miners and their families have been benefited by the opportunity to learn furniture making, weaving, quilting, plain and decorative needlework, basketry, pewter, iron, and other metal work. With the aid of trained and interested people, many of the unemployed

A SPINNER IN HER HUNDREDTH YEAR

Granny Greer of Trade, Tennessee, Spun Woolen Yarn into Her Hundredth and First Year, When She Died in the Mountain Home Where She Had Lived for Eighty Years

MAKING A PATCHWORK QUILT

QUILTING IS STILL A SOCIAL CUSTOM THROUGHOUT THE HIGHLANDS. IN A FEW COMMUNITIES IT IS A HOME INDUSTRY

miners and their families have developed skills by which they are able to produce clothing and furnishings for their homes and objects to sell.

The quality of the handwork found in the products exhibited in the retail shops of the Association bears evidence of excellent supervision and careful training. Some of these articles represent the types and techniques of pioneer handicrafts in West Virginia, while others meet modern demands, often originated by the workers themselves. The later designs in metal work include those made by special teachers brought in from outside for short periods of instruction who have also given help on styling goods for market. The Association has made furniture and furnishings for several of the homes in the federal project known as the Reedsville Experimental Community in Preston County, West Virginia. Some of the woodworking, weaving, and metal shops are now located at the homestead.

John and Mary R. Markle School of Industrial Arts

One of the latest developments to promote handicrafts is the John and Mary R. Markle School of Industrial Arts established in 1932 in Higgins, Yancey County, North Carolina. By 1933 the program for handicrafts was instituted and steady progress has since been made. Practically all the old crafts of the region are encouraged—quilting, dyeing, weaving, and basketry. Native materials are utilized, and two of the outstanding achievements have been baskets made of honeysuckle and the preserving of wild fruits in attractive pottery containers. The School has an exceptionally fine set of buildings constructed of local stone in which ample room has been provided for handicraft experiments and developments.

Lees-McRae College

Although Lees-McRae College at Banners Elk, Avery County, North Carolina, has from its beginning sponsored through the Department of Industrial Arts the making of handicrafts for home and school use, it was not until 1934 that objects were made for sale. The work in shoe cobbling, home sewing, farm tools, and household furniture still continues as part of the college and community program, but the new features comprise weaving, wrought iron, cabinet and general woodworking, including wood turning.

Training in ironwork at the College was organized by Daniel Boone, a descendant of the pioneer. The work of this family is referred to in Chapter XV, Miscellaneous Handicrafts. Original designs by students are used quite extensively, all the processes being done in the college shops. Students at Lees-McRae are required to earn at least part of their expenses, and the schedule of work is arranged so that this is done on alternate days. Provision for compensating them for making objects which the College can sell has enabled many mountain boys and girls to attend.

THE INDUSTRIAL EDUCATIONAL ASSOCIATION
FOR SOUTHERN MOUNTAINEERS

This chapter should not be closed without referring to a pioneer organization which though not a producer of handicrafts has given valuable co-operation in distributing them and otherwise encouraging their development. The Southern Industrial Educational Association was organized in 1905 by Mrs. Martha S. Gielow, a southern woman, for the purpose of promoting industrial education among mountaineers. The Association was able to obtain liberal support for its cause, to establish scholarships, contribute money to erect buildings for industrial work, and to pay salaries to teachers. Auxiliaries of the Association were set up in Philadelphia and New York and an Exchange for mountain crafts was opened in Washington.

In 1925, owing to changed conditions, the Association disbanded but the New York Auxiliary continued the work under the title of Industrial Educational Association for Southern Mountaineers with Mrs. Algernon S. Sullivan, president. Believing that practical home training for the mountain girls, many of whom marry very early, was a primary need, the organization established Practice Homes near some of the schools where the girls gained a knowledge of housekeeping while they continued their school work. Almost all the equipment in these homes was made by hand—carpets, blankets, and toweling; the furniture was constructed by the boys in the school. Gardening, poultry raising, and dairying were also taught.

With Mrs. James E. Pope as president and Mrs. J. Lowrie Bell as first vice-president, the Association for a number of years carried out an active and constructive program. No one outside the Highlands showed a greater devotion to the mountain people and their interests than did Mrs. Bell until her death in 1934. Members of the Board of Directors and friends have held exhibits and sales of mountain crafts from time to time, the entire proceeds going to the workers as there are no administration charges connected with any activities of the Association. This work is being continued under the able leadership of Caroline T. Burkham, now president.

CHAPTER V

SPINNING AND WEAVING FOR HOME AND MARKET

HAND spinning and weaving were at the foundation of the revival of handicrafts in the Southern Highlands, and weaving continues to be the principal home industry there to this day. It was the woven coverlets of homespun that the president of Berea College found as he made his way through the mountains in quest of students that set him to thinking of preserving the skills of these native people and which later led to a department for teaching spinning and weaving in the College. It was a coverlet woven by Mrs. Elmeda McHargue Walker that prompted Frances L. Goodrich to encourage the mountain women to take up again the old art of weaving which resulted in the first enterprise, the Allanstand Cottage Industries, for selling handicrafts in that region. It was a double-woven coverlet made by Mrs. Zachariah Field, a type of home weaving that had almost disappeared, which encouraged Gretchen Bayne and the Dougherty family to seek an outlet for home-made textiles that culminated in the development of the Shuttle-Crafters. And so with most of the schools and other centers of handwork, weaving has been the first craft to be developed, and in many places it remains the most important one.

EARLY SPINNING AND WEAVING

There are two basic processes in the making of any textile: first, the spinning of the thread or yarn, and second, weaving it into a web. These processes have remained the same since the first cloth was made and all the complicated machinery developed and the speed acquired from new power have not changed them. For thousands of years both processes were carried out by hand entirely. Now in our own and other countries both spinning and weaving machines will run for hours at a time without an attendant, producing webs many times as fast as any human hands could work

A SHAVING OR DRAWING HORSE

ᴀsᴏɴ Rᴇᴇᴅ ᴏғ Nᴏʀᴛʜᴇʀɴ Gᴇᴏʀɢɪᴀ ᴀᴛ Hɪs Sʜᴀᴠɪɴɢ Hᴏʀsᴇ, ᴀ Mᴏᴅɪғɪᴄᴀᴛɪᴏɴ ᴏғ ᴀ Fᴏʀᴍ
sᴇᴅ ɪɴ Eɴɢʟᴀɴᴅ, Sᴄᴏᴛʟᴀɴᴅ, Gᴇʀᴍᴀɴʏ, ᴀɴᴅ Oᴛʜᴇʀ Cᴏᴜɴᴛʀɪᴇs ʙʏ Cʜᴀɪʀ-ᴍᴀᴋᴇʀs ᴛᴏ
Hᴏʟᴅ Tʜᴇɪʀ Sᴛɪᴄᴋs ᴀɴᴅ Bᴏᴀʀᴅs Wʜɪᴄʜ Tʜᴇʏ Sʜᴀᴘᴇᴅ ᴡɪᴛʜ ᴀ Dʀᴀᴡɪɴɢ Kɴɪfᴇ

A MOUNTAIN CHAIRMAKER

Peter Ingram of Berea, Kentucky, a Mountain Chairmaker, Is Here Beginning to Make a Seat of White Oak Splits, the Material Most Commonly Used for Chair Bottoms in the Mountains

And yet in as brief a period as a century and a half ago most of the cloth made in America was handspun and hand woven.

There is an interesting comparison to be noted between these two basic processes as carried on in the Southern Highlands and in other parts of our country. In the Highlands, especially in pioneer days, when all weaving was for home use, the two processes went along hand-in-hand, just as they had in other parts of the country in colonial days. So when factory-made goods finally penetrated the mountains the two processes went out together. Later, when the revival of handicrafts came to the mountains and weaving was taken up again, this time to produce articles for sale, involving the use of many varieties of threads and yarns, mill-spun products were purchased and the demand for the homespun yarn grew less and less until for a time hand spinning was discontinued almost entirely, but weaving on the hand loom continued as it has to this day.

Quite the opposite took place outside the mountain region, along the Atlantic seaboard, in Pennsylvania, New England, and other eastern states. Here hand spinning was continued in the home for a considerable period after weaving had been abandoned, and the old loom was stored in the barn or attic or broken up for lumber or firewood. This difference between the relative discontinuance of spinning and weaving in the mountains and the outside country is explained further in Chapter VI, Coverlets and Counterpanes, for it is in these much prized textiles that the record of the change is best preserved. But it may be pointed out here that during a certain period of our history Old World weavers came to America and in the New England and eastern states there developed the trade of the itinerant weaver, who went from place to place to weave the thread and yarn which had been spun during the year awaiting his coming. This division of home spinning and professional weaving continued until about 1860, or until gradually spinning mills were built, and all the processes of manufacturing cloth were transferred from home to factory, which finally absorbed or displaced the itinerant weaver.

In the Highlands, however, the age-old processes of spinning and weaving were carried along together until the end of the last century, and here when a coverlet or the cloth for a garment was woven it was no short-time undertaking, but required the larger part of the year, for the cotton, flax, and wool had to be grown, harvested, and the thread and yarn prepared from the fibers before weaving could begin. Often all this work was performed by the same hands, including the important task of coloring it. Similar methods had characterized the colonies. Many a home had been a miniature manufacturing plant where each operation was performed on the premises.

Mount Vernon possessed all the facilities needed to make fabrics of cotton, linen, or wool, and most of George Washington's clothing was made there. It was a proud day for industrial America when on delivering his first address to Congress, President Washington wore a suit of broadcloth made in the woolen factory of Colonel Jeremiah Wordsworth of Hartford, Connecticut, where all the processes had been performed on the premises except the spinning.[1]

In time even spinning was done in mills, and cloth was supplied first to people to make up at home and then to factories to be converted into clothing and other articles for market. But while the increase of buying power enabled most families gradually to use factory-made textiles, the Highlanders, isolated and poor, continued to make all the cloth for home needs long after hand methods had been superseded by machinery in other parts of the country.

HAND SPINNING

Hand spinning in America has been done almost entirely by wheel, and spinning on a wheel is a magic process. It seems regrettable that such a graceful practice should disappear as completely as it has from many parts of the world. Spinning is one of the vestiges of beauty which the women of the Highlands have helped to keep for us. Even if it had no esthetic appeal, the great contribution it has made to human welfare and to world culture should command the interest of every thoughtful person. The boundless variety of useful and beautiful textiles now within reach of the masses of our people—a wealth beyond the dreams of ancient kings and queens—has come through this age-old hand process

[1] Bowles, Ella Shannon, Homespun Handicrafts. J. B. Lippincott Co., Philadelphia, 1931, p. 71.

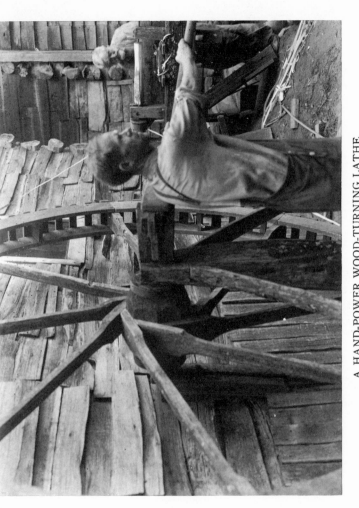

A HAND-POWER WOOD-TURNING LATHE

Jason Reed, at the Lathe, and His Assistant, at the Wheel Which Generates Power, Are Chairmakers in Northern Georgia. This Hand-Powered Lathe Is Common Throughout the Highlands

A KENTUCKY FOOT-POWER WOOD-TURNING LATHE

HENDERSON MULLENS USES THE FOOT-POWER, OR BOOM-AND-TREADLE LATHE, AN ANCIENT CONTRIVANCE EMPLOYED IN EUROPE IN THE FIFTEENTH CENTURY. THE ROPE IS WOUND AROUND THE WOOD TO BE SHAPED, THE FOOT PRESSES DOWN, AND AS THE TENSION OF THE BOOM TURNS THE STICK BACKWARD, THE CHISEL CUTS OFF A SHAVING

Spinning was the basic step upon which the character and quality of every fabric depended.

It seems incredible now that a craft so widely practiced should for so long have remained unprogressive as to the time required for the process. For centuries the preparation of the yarn was the great time problem connected with weaving, and even as late as colonial days practically every woman spun, regardless of her station, because weaving could be done so much faster than the thread could be spun. It is said that eight spinners were necessary to supply one weaver with yarn, and in households where the spinners were also the weavers, they always computed the time for preparing the thread and yarn as several times that required to weave the web.

But if the spinning wheel and the spindle were not noted for speed, as we measure it now, they developed a skill of hand and made a quality of thread or yarn which remains today a source of wonder and admiration. It is recorded that in 1745 a woman of East Dereham, Norfolk, England, spun a single pound of wool into a thread 84,000 yards in length, nearly 48 miles.[1] Since that time, however, it is said that a young English woman of Norwich has spun a pound of combed wool into a thread of 168,000 yards, and that she actually produced from the same weight of cotton a thread of 203,000 yards, equal to upward of 115 miles. This last thread if woven would produce about 20 yards of 36-inch muslin. It would seem that this achievement in England would be sufficient tribute to hand spinning to allow the record to stand, but the Orient offers still more remarkable results.

The yarns for the gossamer-like Dacca muslins of India were so fine that 1 lb. weight of cotton was spun into a thread nearly 253 miles long. This was accomplished with the aid of a bamboo spindle not much bigger than a darning needle, and which was lightly weighted with a pellet of clay. Since such a tender thread could not support even the weight of so slight a spindle, the apparatus was rotated upon a piece of hollow shell.[2]

It was not, therefore, any lack in the quality of the hand product which stimulated the making of textile strands by machinery, but the fact that the operation was comparatively slow.

[1] Chambers, R. (Editor), The Book of Days: A Miscellany of Popular Antiquities. W. and R. Chambers, Edinburgh, 1863, vol. 1, p. 69.
[2] Encyclopaedia Britannica, 14th ed., vol. 21, p. 230. Article on Spinning.

The old, old problem of spinning fast enough to keep up with weaving was ever a Highland problem. Grandma Wilson, now eighty-four years old, living in Macon County, North Carolina, about eight miles from Highlands, tells how her little son had stood on one side of the fireplace spinning in the evening, and her daughter on the other side with another wheel trying to get yarn ahead so that she could continue her weaving the next day. The two children could not, of course, in an evening supply her loom for a full day, but what they did was a great help. This son now raises sheep, the wool from which his wife and daughters spin into yarn to be used at the John C. Campbell Folk School.

TYPES OF SPINNING WHEELS

The Southern Highland women followed the ways of their forebears. In England, Scotland, Ireland, and Germany, whence many had come, spinning was done on two types of wheels, the big high wheel propelled by hand where the spinner stands and walks, which is especially good for cotton and wool; and the smaller low wheel, operated by foot power, used mainly for flax, but also for wool, at which the spinner remains seated.

It would seem that the old high wheel was the more widely used in the Highlands. In addition to the fact that it fitted the people's needs more adequately, it is also probable that the simplicity of its construction made it available to many who could neither make nor buy a low wheel. For its frame any wood can be used, the wheel itself being made of a thin piece of hickory, white oak, or ash bent into a hoop and reinforced with spokes and hub. The only part that any woodsman could not easily construct would be the spindle, which is of metal, and this was sometimes made by a local blacksmith. Many Highlanders were their own blacksmiths. The spindle of the big wheel was too high for a small child to reach, therefore the usual way of adjusting it to the child's height was to cut a hole in the floor and drop the front end of the frame down so that he or she could reach the spindle. An old spinner of Cherokee County, North Carolina, Granny Hatchett, remembers her father fixing the wheel that way so that she could learn.

Both high and low wheels were used throughout our country as long as spinning remained a home industry, and while it has not been possible to trace either type in the Highlands back to the areas in the lowlands whence they came, low-type wheels probably came through German settlers from Pennsylvania. In a narrow little valley about two miles long in southwestern Virginia, originally settled by Germans, seven spinning wheels survive, five of the low type.

In the Highlands the warp for most of the early coverlets was linen thread made from home-grown flax which thrives in many parts of the region. Flax was much used for household fabrics, and combined with wool made the well-known linsey-woolsey, a favorite old-time dress material. Mrs. W. J. Martin, living a few miles from Murphy, North Carolina, uses cotton in her home. It is raised on the homeplace and ginned by her on a primitive handmade machine resembling a clothes wringer. She cards and spins the fiber into thread from which she knits or crochets objects for home use. Cotton was raised in some areas and spun for home use, and even now a little cotton spinning is carried on, but wool has always been and is today the principal spinning fiber.

CARDING THE WOOL

In the old days all the wool for yarn was carded in the home and made into rolls for spinning, and even now most of the carding is still done by that method. The fibers are combed out with hand cards, which resemble the broad currycombs of the stable. There are now, however, mills which clean and card the wool, not in short, soft rolls, but in continuous fluffy ropes which make the spinning operation much simpler and faster. Mill-carded wool is used at Tallulah Falls Industrial School in Georgia, but students are also taught to card by hand so that they may understand the old method.

Besides that used by the school at Tallulah Falls, homespun yarn, most of it from hand-carded wool, is used at Berea College, Pine Mountain Settlement School, and Hindman Settlement School, at Allanstand Cottage Industries, the Spinning Wheel, the Weave Shop, and the John C. Campbell Folk School, at the Shuttle-Crafters, and occasionally at other schools and settlements.

ADVANTAGES OF HAND SPINNING

There are three advantages in connection with hand spinning which, in addition to its economy, commend it: the control that it gives over the coloring process for weaving; the fact that it can be carried on in the rural home with a minimum of equipment and no overhead expense; and that for some it is a very pleasant occupation with special therapeutic value. The control which hand spinning makes possible in the use of color is perhaps more fully appreciated by the tapestry maker than by the weaver of plain cloth. Commercial yarns, though they come in a great variety of colors, are dyed in the skein and are therefore solid in color, while with handspun yarns, by dyeing the wool before it is carded, it is possible to mix the colors in the carding process. This gives the weaver as much command over his palette as a painter could have in oils or in any other mixable pigment, and it is a fascinating process which can be fully appreciated only by one who has mixed colors or has seen them mixed on the cards. Hand carding also makes it possible to get a considerable range of colors through the use of a few dyes.

As has already been indicated, the equipment for spinning is simple and inexpensive, a pair of carding combs and a wheel, both of which with care will last for many years. In the Blue Ridge Mountains of Virginia is a low wheel that, according to the date cut into its frame, was built in 1828. It is still in service. Both carding and spinning can be picked up for a time and dropped again without loss from interruption.

Spinning like knitting is restful and relaxing, and for many people the rhythm of the wheel is distinctly soothing. This applies especially to the low wheel at which the spinner sits propelling the wheel with a treadle, the correlation of action between foot and hand being important. The spinning songs of many peoples pay tribute to both the esthetic and curative values of the work.

One of the most interesting examples of the use of handspun yarn in the Highlands is a red and white coverlet, in the Walls of Jericho design, recently woven by Taft Greer, who lives about four miles off the road from Trade, Johnson County, Tennessee. All the yarn was spun on a low wheel by his grandmother, Nancy Osborne Greer, some of it in her hundredth year. From childhood

ISAAC DAVIS, BROOM MAKER OF BLUE LICK, KENTUCKY

This Sturdy Broom Is Formed by Cutting the Shavings from the Handle, Leaving Them Attached at One End and Folding Them Back, Bunched Neatly. Hickory and White Oak Are Commonly Used for These Brooms

CORN-HUSK CHAIR SEATS

Mrs. Lucy Lakes of Berea, Kentucky, Is an Expert Weaver of Corn Husks. Her Hands Are Shown Here Splicing, Twisting, and Braiding the Corn Husks for a Stool Seat

Mrs. Greer had an excellent knowledge of spinning, weaving, and dyeing, all the processes of making cloth by hand. She taught her grandson how to spin and weave. She died in the autumn of 1934 in the cabin where she had lived since 1853, in an upper room of which was the spinning wheel given to her by her mother-in-law at her marriage eighty years before. Mrs. Greer, seeing how few were the opportunities in the mountains to earn money, had encouraged the working up of a business that could be carried on at home. While the income from it is meager, it provides partial employment for her grandson who weaves a good coverlet, and it kept her busy spinning yarn, as she wished to be, to the end of her days.

To what extent hand spinning will continue in the Highlands is not possible now to predict. From the extensive variety of factory-made yarns of good quality in the market, including excellent imitations of handspun, it would seem that the demand for this yarn would be very limited; but the high prices of much of the factory product make it prohibitive for the use of many mountain people in knitting socks, gloves, mittens, sweaters, and other wearing apparel for the home. Therefore, unless some unexpected interest in it develops elsewhere, it is likely to be restricted to the Highlands.

WEAVING

While the revival of weaving was first identified with coverlets, linsey-woolseys, jeans, and other textiles which a few weavers were still producing for family use, it was not long before many articles planned to meet the needs of outside purchasers were being made. Weaving has increased in both volume and variety until now the output in the mountains far exceeds that of any other industry in this region. How many weavers are at work in homes, schools, and handicraft centers it is difficult to determine because the number is continually shifting. Nor will the incomplete figures gathered on the number of looms found in the region indicate the number of workers, for a loom is often used by several members of a family, even by some of the neighbors, and in the schools by a succession of students.

Nevertheless the list of looms reported by members of the Southern Highland Handicraft Guild is of interest. It is as follows: In Kentucky, Berea College has 50 in the schools with 12 in the surrounding community. In North Carolina, Crossnore School has 40 in the school alone; the Spinning Wheel has eight and there is an equal number in nearby homes; the Penland Weavers have about 40, most of them in homes of the neighborhood. In Tennessee the Shuttle-Crafters have 10 with many more in the country about; the Pi Beta Phi Settlement School, in connection with its work, estimates 150 in the center and in homes of the locality.

TYPES OF LOOMS

The looms now used in the Southern Highlands are of two types: the old mountain loom, a heavy-timbered structure usually made in the home itself; and the lighter modern loom made either in a school or shipped in from a manufacturer outside. The later type far outnumbers the former in the region today.

The old type is usually quite rough in construction, often cumbersome to operate, and heavier than is necessary for much of the weaving that has developed in recent years, such as runners, napkins, towels, scarfs, bag materials, and other small or light-weight textiles. These old looms are also very bulky and often take up more space in schoolroom and home than can easily be spared; they permit little elasticity in operating, and some teachers say that accurate work cannot be done on them. When Mrs. Ernberg went to Berea College to direct the Fireside Industries she introduced the small loom of Swedish type, but expressed surprise and admiration at the quality of weaving which many of the mountain women were able to attain on their old home-made looms. Several of these are still in use at Berea College and some excellent work is being turned out. Mrs. Finley Mast of Valle Crucis, North Carolina, and her sister, Mrs. Robert Mast, worked on looms that have been in almost continuous use for more than one hundred years. The native weavers who gave indispensable help in the early days of the revival of handicrafts in almost every instance worked on the old type of loom. Among these were Mrs. Mary Anderson and Susan B. Hayes of Berea, Mary Pigman of Ivis, and Aunt Sal Creech of Pine Mountain, Elmeda Walker and Granny Jude of Allanstand, Aunt Cumi Woody of Penland, Aunt Lizzie Regan and Aunt Lydia Whaley of Gatlinburg, Mrs. Zachariah Field of Russellville, and many others.

The old looms were of two general types: those in which all the apparatus was swung in the upper part of the frame; and a much less frequently used type called the cradle-rock loom, in which a part of the mechanism, including the beating apparatus, operated on a rocker below. An example of the latter type may be seen in the Museum of Mrs. Edna Lynn Simms at Gatlinburg, Tennessee.

The newer and lighter types of looms that have come into use in the mountains differ somewhat in form, but the principles of design and operation are about the same; they are adequately described in books listed in the Bibliography. A list of loom makers and manufacturers is given below.[1] In his book, Foot-Power Loom Weaving, Edward F. Worst describes thoroughly with drawings and photographs the modern loom and all its parts. He also gives working drawings for the construction of Danish and Swedish looms and instructions for using them.[2]

Mary Meigs Atwater in The Shuttle-Craft Book of American Hand-Weaving[3] deals quite fully with hand looms, especially with the types used in this country, illustrating with photographs an old design of American loom much like many of those in the Highlands, a smaller type such as is widely used in schools and for light weaving at home, and an old loom reconditioned for modern weaving. Mrs. Atwater suggests the main points which an inexperienced weaver should consider in the selection of a loom, and with practical enthusiasm she encourages the hunting out of old ones and reconditioning them for modern work. In the book may also be found full instructions for setting up a loom, dressing it, and for weaving. Both Mr. Worst and Mrs. Atwater offer detailed information about coverlets and other forms of weaving practiced in the Highlands, with drafts and explicit instructions for weaving many of them. Mr. Worst uses the word "counterpane" instead of "coverlets." Miss Goodrich in Mountain Homespun[4] explains the

[1] Sam Clark, Berea College, Berea, Ky.; League of New Hampshire Arts and Crafts, 276 North Main Street, Concord, N. H.; Georgetown College, Georgetown, Ky.; Borsodi-Winborn Domestic Looms, Suffern, N. Y.; Mrs. Marie Ashtrup Kalstad, Norway House, 92 Columbia Heights, Brooklyn, N. Y.; Hartland Looms, Hartland, Mich.; Ely McCarter, Great Smoky Mountains National Park, Gatlinburg, Tenn.

[2] Foot-Power Loom Weaving. Bruce Publishing Co., Milwaukee, 1933.

[3] The Shuttle-Craft Book of American Hand-Weaving. By permission of The Macmillan Co., publishers, New York, 1933.

[4] Yale University Press, New Haven, 1931.

principle and working of the hand loom as used in the Southern Highlands.

The traditional loom of the Highlands is a hand shuttle, or, as it is sometimes called, a finger-shuttle loom. It is distinguished from the fly-shuttle loom by the different way in which the shuttle is propelled. The hand shuttle carrying the thread is passed through the shed of the warp with the hand; the fly shuttle is propelled through the shed by a jerk or slight pull of the arm, and once released travels entirely through the shed to the opposite side when, the warp threads having been crossed into another shed, a jerk sends it back again. In working with a hand shuttle the weaver has a maximum of control, being able to stop the shuttle at any point as, for instance, to lay in a design with the fingers and to pick it up again when desired. With the fly shuttle the weaver has no such opportunity to vary the pattern, for when the shuttle is released it completes the distance across the web mechanically. The fly shuttle provides much speed and a wider web can be readily woven.

Three basic objections have been made to the introduction of fly-shuttle looms into the schools and homes of the Highlands. First, the relatively greater speed of the fly shuttle would enter into serious competition with the hand-shuttle loom. Second, the fly shuttle in its usual form, except some looms designed by D. C. Churchill and used by the Churchill Weavers in Berea, is noisy and hard to operate. Third, there is an advantage in having sufficient elasticity for creative expression in design and for experimentation which the mechanically repetitious effort of the fly-shuttle loom with its objective of speed and quantity production cannot supply. Many vitally interested in the continuation of hand weaving in the mountains feel that it is more important to encourage originality and merit in design and improvement in quality than to strive for larger quantities or a fabric in which the weaver exercises little direction over the character of the output. Other practical objections to the fly-shuttle loom are that it costs more and is difficult to keep in repair.

KINDS OF WEAVING

Much variety has marked the weaving in the Southern Highlands, especially in recent years. The plainest webs are the stripes and plaids used for blankets and the linsey-woolseys dating back to early days. A large number of patterns are made on multiple-harness looms, the jeans or twills used for clothing by the pioneers, the varied designs of coverlets and counterpanes, and the elaborately patterned damask being woven sometimes on 10- and 12-harness looms. The more recently developed types of weaving are the "inlay" or "finger weaving."

The term inlay describes a process in which the design is laid in with the fingers while the shuttle carries on the woven background. It is sometimes called finger weaving. Tapestry weaving is a different process although it is often confused with inlay or finger weaving; but in tapestry weaving the design and background areas are woven separately, the woof thread being carried with the fingers or on a spool or small spindle or shuttle. The technique is much like that employed in some of the tapestries of the Scandinavian countries. Considerable progress is now being made by Highland weavers with this type.

New designs and adaptations are constantly supplementing the long list of weavings. The experiments in the types employed in other countries are features of some of the work in the centers of the South, such as the Finnish rya wall hangings woven at Tallulah Falls Industrial School, the Greek patterns at the Spinning Wheel, the English and Danish webs at Penland Weavers, and the Swedish designs developed at Berea College.

The following list is fairly representative of the various products of the hand loom, and for convenience in checking is arranged alphabetically: afghans, bags, bibs, blankets, counterpanes, coverlets, dress patterns, homespun, jeans, linsey-woolseys, luncheon sets, mufflers, napkins, purses, pillow tops, robes, runners, shawls, scarfs, table covers, towels, tray cloths, and wall hangings.

WEAVING IN THE HIGHLANDS TODAY

Although much of the old-time weaving is still carried on, the more modern work constitutes the bulk of weaving in the Highlands today. Much of it is related to schools and handicraft centers through which instruction, supplies, supervision, marketing, and other co-operation have come.

The Allanstand Cottage Industries was developed on the basis of a weaving interest, and it still includes some of the best coverlet and counterpane weavers in the Highlands. Modern weaving is also done by some of them. All weaving for Allanstand is performed in the homes. The Penland Weavers have from the time of their organization achieved an excellent record. Instruction has come primarily through Lucy Morgan, although neighbors are usually eager to help string up the loom for a beginner and offer first instruction. The type of weaving done is superior and several successful experiments with multiple harness have been worked out, one being a fine damask woven on a 12-harness loom. The Penland Weaving Institute held each summer, referred to in Chapter XVIII, Handicraft Training, Production, and Marketing, represents an outstanding innovation in the progress of weaving. Much of the old type of product has been continued at Crossnore School, especially coverlets, but the School has also developed an extensive variety of small articles for sale. At the Weave Shop in Saluda, North Carolina, Mrs. Wilmer Stone Viner, in addition to plain weaves, employs a type of inlay or finger weaving embracing both naturalized and conventional designs in plant forms and landscapes which, carried out with her vegetable dyeing, has produced textiles distinguished for their interest and beauty. The weaving at the Spinning Wheel, under the direction of Clementine Douglas, ranks second to none in combination of design, color, and good craftsmanship. Both double- and multiple-harness looms are used, and finger weaving in small pieces is artistically produced. Original patterns in plaids and Roman stripes with cheerful use of color for driving robes, blankets, shawls, pocketbooks, purses, and many other small articles, and linsey-woolsey dress and coat patterns have been special products of the Spinning Wheel looms.

Berea College, through its Fireside Industries, has been preeminent in the training of weavers among its students and has sent out a larger number of teachers than all the other Highland schools combined. A wide variety of weaving is done and the students while mastering the technique may make articles for their own use or for sale, and many are able in this way to earn part of their expenses through college. The products of the Matheny Weavers at Berea include blankets and coverlets as well as many other articles of utility. Several regular workers for this industry have been able to build their houses through earnings from the textiles they make. In the vicinity of Hindman Settlement School are several hand weavers who in making coverlets follow largely the fashion of olden times, but in small articles they employ both old and modern designs. At Pine Mountain Settlement School and in the neighborhood are made some of the best old-time blankets and coverlets to be found in the mountains, but much of the present-day weaving has been adapted to modern style such as stripes and plaids for bags, runners, and so forth.

Many of the attractive products of the Churchill Weavers of Berea are made on fly-shuttle looms and the rest on hand or finger-shuttle looms. Two distinctive qualities in the Churchill textiles are due to the designing and styling ability of Mrs. Churchill, who has a fine sense of color harmony, and the practical ability of Mr. Churchill, an outstanding engineer in the textile industry. They employ native help almost exclusively and have trained many excellent weavers from mountain boys and girls.

Gatlinburg, Tennessee, is one of the largest and most important weaving centers in the Southern Highlands. There the Pi Beta Phi Sorority through its school has set a high standard of work, and its looms turn out practically every type of weaving from the crude but attractive linsey-woolsey and striped patterns of the olden times to modern stripes, plaids, and figures in scarfs, shawls, afghans, couch covers, and many other textiles for home and personal uses. The handicrafts of the Pi Beta Phi Settlement School were developed under the general leadership of Evelyn Bishop who was director of the School for many years. The first full-time weaving teacher was Winogene Redding who came in 1926 to supervise the weaving department. Victoria Strand also contributed to its growth during her period as supervisor. The selling organization of the department, under the name of the Arrow Craft Shop, was fostered in the earlier stages by La Delle Allen. Among the weavers who combine distinctive color combinations with a high quality of weaving is Mrs. Georgia M. Duffield, in charge of the Pi Beta Phi showroom in the Mountain View Hotel at Gatlinburg.

Besides the weavers associated with Pi Beta Phi Settlement School there are many about Gatlinburg working independently or in small groups, producing types of weaving for which there is market demand, particularly among the tourist trade of which Gatlinburg is a center, being situated at one of the gateways to the Great Smoky Mountains National Park. Among these outlets for weaving in Gatlinburg at this time are Mary F. Ogle, Wiley's Shop, Smoky Mountain Handicrafts, M and O Tea Room, Bear-skin Craft Shop, Mrs. Amos Trentham, and the LeConte Craft Shop. An interesting experiment in weaving cloth for men's and women's suiting has been carried out on the home looms of Mr. and Mrs. L. E. Voorheis who live near Gatlinburg. Mr. Voorheis employed H. J. Ostenberger, a fine Alsatian craftsman, to make two looms from native cherry and maple, on which Mrs. Voorheis has woven excellent fabrics.

The products of the Shuttle-Crafters represent a faithful combination of both early and modern types. Old mountain coverlet patterns are woven in wool, silk, and other materials for coverlets, crib covers, pillows, and runners. Coverlets are also made in vegetable-dyed yarn with natural color cotton warp identical with those of early days. Much of the weaving at this center is done by women who live back in the hills and who have little opportunity to earn except through the products of their looms marketed by the Shuttle-Crafters.

The quality of weaving and the experiments in different types at Tallulah Falls Industrial School are worthy of note. The girls at the School have woven blankets and small rugs in patterns adapted from Indian and Mexican designs with technical perfection and taste. They have also drawn on other lands for some of their patterns and occasionally copy very intricate and beautiful designs, but usually they adapt both design and technique to their needs, thereby gaining a practical knowledge of the arts and crafts of other peoples. Weaving has always been regarded as a definite part of the work at the Berry Schools near Rome, Floyd County, Georgia, an institution dedicated to rural living. "Hand

A LOOM MAKER AT WORK

Samuel Clark of Berea, Kentucky, Has Made More Hand-Weaving Looms Than
Any Other Man in the History of the Highlands

THE "LASTINGEST" CHAIR BOTTOM

THE HICKORY BARK SEAT FOR THE MOUNTAIN CHAIR, SUCH AS FRANK RITCHIE OF MUD
LICK, MONROE COUNTY, KENTUCKY, IS WEAVING WILL OUTWEAR ANY OTHER

woven linens and wool rugs are made by the girls from flax grown on the farm and from wool clipped from Berry sheep."[1]

Mr. and Mrs. A. E. Barnes of Murl, Wayne County, Kentucky, are among the individual weavers of the Highlands who have acquired a high degree of skill especially in coverlet weaving. Mrs. Barnes had woven as a girl, and her interest was revived when her daughter returned from Berea College eager for hand-made things in the home. These the family were not able to buy and to make them was the happy alternative.

Mrs. Barnes found an old walnut loom of fine workmanship which a very old weaver, who had made many coverlets on such a loom in her time, helped them to put together and to work out a formula for weaving. On this they began their work. They have collected throughout the mountains many old drafts and among their products are textiles in plain weaving, overshot, summer and winter, and double weaving. They now teach weaving in their home.

Mrs. Mast, one of the best exponents of mountain weaving and one of the effective workers in the early part of its revival, had never entirely given up hand weaving and worked regularly at it until her death. Mrs. Anderson of Berea, referred to in connection with the revival of handicrafts, is still a successful teacher of weaving. Coverlets are her specialty but she also weaves many smaller textiles for the market. Elizabeth Johnson of Knoxville, who learned to weave at the Pi Beta Phi Settlement School, is one of the younger weavers who have developed unusual skill and taste in dress fabrics. She produces a herringbone pattern in several combinations of colors that portrays in both design and texture the prevailing trend in dress and suit material, yet it is woven on a mountain-made loom by a technique differing only slightly from that of the homespun of former days.

Several years ago Gertrude Smith, formerly a teacher in the School of Art of the H. Sophie Newcomb Memorial College at New Orleans, undertook to teach some of the women in the little valley around Andrews, North Carolina, to do simple weaving for their own use. In 1932, the need of money became so urgent that she

[1] Byers, Tracy, Martha Berry, The Sunday Lady of Possum Trot. G. P. Putnam's Sons, New York, 1932.

determined to help them work out a product that could be sold. She persuaded them to concentrate on plain weaving of good quality and they have developed a two-harness weave of homespun wool woof of fine texture on a cotton warp, 36 inches wide. This is being sold for lounging robes, sports suits and coats, golf apparel, and combined with hand embroidery which is done in excellent taste for peasant blouses. The weavers are beginning to experiment with colors for this material and have already attained some good results.

These brief references to some of the principal weaving centers and a few individuals in the Southern Highlands it is hoped will suggest the variety, quality, and beauty of the work now in progress. There is, of course, some weaving of mediocre quality, but the average results are reassuring, especially as the quality of both design and workmanship continually improves. In recent years, as has been indicated, many fine examples of mountain weaving have gone into the White House. Mrs. Woodrow Wilson selected rugs, coverlets, and upholstery material. Mrs. Coolidge, Mrs. Hoover and Mrs. Roosevelt have worn dresses of cloth woven on looms in the Highlands. It is, however, the middle-class homes into which most of this weaving has found its way, and it is upon these home makers that the future of American hand weaving largely depends.

REWARDS OF WEAVING

Among the best weavers of the mountain area are women who have long been accustomed to hard, rough work, outdoors and in. An idea of the importance of a gentle way of earning an income by the fireside, as well as one that reflects the skill and adaptability of the mountain folk, is furnished by the following story of a Highland woman. For several years her only means of earning cash had been to go into the timber and, unassisted, fell trees and work them up into railroad ties which she loaded, and with her span of mules hauled to the nearest railroad camp eight to twelve miles away. This was not an occupation from choice, but the only way open to her to bring into the little mountain home some of the necessities for her isolated family. Then came an offer to teach her to weave and to help her secure a loom. In time she became one of the most skilful and dependable home weavers, and her daughter, with the painstaking characteristic of her mother, learned also to do excellent weaving. Now two looms are working in their home.

Admiration for an old-time coverlet of good quality and color, in an exhibition of the Southern Highland Handicraft Guild, brought out the story that it had been woven by a mountain girl, one of 11 children, who was once thought so dull that her family never asked her to do as much as an errand. A teacher at a settlement school offered to distribute a few looms to mountain homes. The family applied for one, but there being no road to their house the teacher explained that it would not be possible to send it. One of the youngsters who had seen a loom in the weaving room of the school said, "Us children can tote it in." Consent was finally given and on the appointed day eight of them came over the mountain and, taking different parts of the loom, more or less according to their sizes and carrying capacities, "toted" it in pieces over the ridge and up the branch to their home where they put it together again. Later the teacher got over to help warp it up, and she left with them instructions for plain weaving. The old grandmother showed them how she used to weave in the old days.

Some time later several of the children appeared at the school bringing rugs that they had made on the new loom, rugs firm and surprisingly well woven. Inquiry revealed the fact that all the family had taken a hand in weaving except the dull girl, who could never remember how to do anything. She was then twenty-three years old. The teacher noticed, however, that she liked the rugs and would hold them in her hands studying their colors. When asked if she would care to come to the school and learn to weave she was delighted, but her expression changed immediately. "It's no use, I can't learn anything," she said.

The teacher encouraged her to try. She came over to the school and with shy eagerness began. At first she would sit at the loom and do only what she was told; when it came to a change, she could not remember and either stopped or continued in the same way. But whatever she completed was well done and her teacher expressed enthusiasm for it. The girl was always on hand before weaving started, always stayed at her loom as long as she could, and little by little she learned how to remember. Finally she could make a simple rug entirely by herself. She was then asked to help beginners. This opened up a new world to her, and stimulated by the hope of showing others how to weave she learned to warp up a loom, and then taught others. All of this, of course, required a long time, more than a year to learn what her bright little sister got in a few lessons. But whatever she learned she retained, and now she weaves several kinds of articles including the old mountain coverlets which she likes best.

All the satisfactions that come from hand weaving are not subject to measurement. Although one of the principal ideas behind the revival of the age-old craft of weaving was to provide some income for those cut off from other avenues of earning, remuneration in terms of money was not the sole return, the only compensation. It became apparent to those who had studied the situation prior to the revival of handicrafts, that something of great value had passed when weaving went out of the home, something which the older women of the mountains missed very definitely. Aunt Lydia Whaley, who had spun all the thread and yarn for her own clothes and for her children's from wool and cotton that she grew, expressed a philosophy of work that revealed a source of genuine satisfaction, a satisfaction which only the worker can know, when she said of her favorite skirt, " I have seen that Balmoral run thru the fields on the back of a lamb, I've seen it heaped up in sheared wool and plucked cotton, I've seen it suck up the color from the juice of mountain herbs and berries." Granny Jude, an old weaver at Allanstand in the early days, in speaking of the weaving of a new coverlet remarked, "That's Pineburr, a mightly sweet draft . . . Delia, here, she brought me one from over the mountain called Philadelphia Pavement. I'm a rarin' to draw it in and see how the spots come out. Shucks, ain't it grand, the things they is to do and to find out about."[1]

[1] Goodrich, Frances Louisa, Mountain Homespun, p. 63.

FINE FURNITURE BY MOUNTAIN BOYS

All the Furniture in the Home of President Hutchins of Berea College Was Made by Students in the Department of Woodworking

A BASKET MAKER OF KENTUCKY

AUNT CORD RITCHIE, WHO LIVES OVER THE MOUNTAIN FROM HINDMAN SETTLEMENT
SCHOOL IN KNOTT COUNTY, KENTUCKY, SPECIALIZES IN WILLOW BASKETS. ALTHOUGH
SELF-TAUGHT MANY OF HER NEIGHBORS HAVE LEARNED FROM HER

CHAPTER VI

COVERLETS AND COUNTERPANES

OF ALL the folk arts of the Southern Highlands, with the exception of the folk house or log cabin, the coverlet has from time immemorial held first place not only in the hearts of the pioneer women to whom it was the happiest outlet for creative expression, but of kinsfolk and friends who in one way or another have felt its many services of use, sentiment, and beauty. Even today, far back in the mountains of every Highland state, are families whose meager incomes do not exceed a few dollars a year, but who treasure the old "kivers" and would never consider selling one of them except "for to get a doctor."

Recently in a remote place in North Carolina where cash income had long since been cut off by the "lean times," a mother explained that she did not see how she could raise the amount necessary to pay the taxes on the old home that year. When asked if she would care to dispose of any of the coverlets in the three cupboards filled with them and with patchwork quilts, she made it clear that these were being kept to pass on to the children and nothing would induce her to part with them, not even to save the old place. Care and affection, similar to that bestowed on the Old World dower chest with its much wider variety of articles, go into the collection of these coverlets which are piled up one by one in the cupboard, if there happens to be one, or if not, which is more often the case, on a shelf in a corner of the living room or in the sleeping loft, against the time when the sons and daughters leave the family home to found their own.

In her book of delightful verse, Kinfolks,[1] Ann Cobb, of the Hindman Settlement School, has given us this charming picture of coverlets or "kivers" as they are usually called by mountain people.

[1] Houghton Mifflin Co., Boston, 1922, pp. 7–8. Reprinted here by permission of the author. Kinfolks is now out of print, but at this writing a few copies are available at Hindman Settlement School, Hindman, Kentucky, and at the Southern Highland Handicraft Guild, Asheville, North Carolina.

Kivers

Yes, I've sev'ral kivers you can see;
'Light and hitch your beastie in the shade!
I don't foller weaving now so free,
And all my purtiest ones my forebears made.
Home-dyed colors kindly meller down
Better than these new fotched-on ones from town.

I ricollect my granny at the loom
Weaving that blue one yonder on the bed.
She put the shuttle by and laid in tomb.
Her word was I could claim hit when I wed.
"Flower of Edinboro" was hits name,
Betokening the land from which she came.

Nary a daughter have I for the boon,
But there's my son's wife from the level land,
She took the night with us at harvest-moon—
A comely, fair young maid, with loving hand.
I gave her three—"Sunrise" and "Trailing Vine"
And "Young Man's Fancy." She admired 'em fine.

That green one mostly wrops around the bread;
"Tennessee Lace" I take to ride behind.
Hither and yon right smart of them have fled.
Inside the chest I keep my choicest kind—
"Pine-Bloom" and "St. Ann's Robe" (of hickory brown),
"Star of the East" (that yaller's fading down!).

The Rose? I wove hit courting, long ago—
Not Simon, though he's proper kind of heart—
His name was Hugh—the fever laid him low—
I allus keep that kiver set apart.
"Rose of the Valley," he would laugh and say,
"The kiver's favoring your face to-day!"

There are three types of coverlets, distinguished by their weaves, which were woven in pioneer days and which are still being made. In addition to the coverlet is another bed covering, the counterpane, a close relative in weaving but different enough to be separately classified. Sometimes the term "counterpane" is applied to the coverlet, but with Highland weavers there is a distinction, and effort will be made here to use their nomenclature.

The three types of mountain coverlets (there is another type found outside the Highlands which will be mentioned later) are the simple overshot weave, the summer-and-winter weave, and the double weave. The first is by far the most representative and was woven in New England and other parts of the eastern country in colonial days and later; the second, the summer-and-winter weave, is believed to be an American invention; the third, the double weave, two webs joined together, while not so common in the southernmost states of the Highlands, was done quite extensively in parts of Virginia and West Virginia, where undoubtedly the migrating Pennsylvania Germans influenced this weave considerably. It has in recent years been revived in several Highland states.

The simple overshot weave in wool on a cotton tab base is the most characteristic coverlet of the region, but some of the oldest ones were on a homespun linen warp and base, although the majority were as now on cotton thread. Nine out of ten of the coverlets done in the mountains of North Carolina, Tennessee, and Kentucky in pioneer days and in the revival are of this first type which is sometimes called the float weave.

The summer-and-winter weave, the origin of which is attributed to America and that some authorities say is not found at all in Europe, is one in which, instead of making the long skips as in the usual overshot type, the pattern thread is closely interwoven with the base. The result is a design that, if blue on a white ground on one side, will on the other be white on a blue ground.

In the double-weave coverlets the colors of the pattern are reversed on the two sides of the fabric, like the summer-and-winter weave, and are usually sharply defined. One can easily distinguish the double-woven fabric by separating with the finger and thumb the two webs which are joined by the pattern-making threads.

The counterpanes or "county-pins," or "dimities," as they were sometimes called, represent a very old form of weaving with fine cotton thread in both warp and weft and are usually in one color. Some women in different parts of the Highlands have always woven these bedcovers and a few continue to do so, but the type has never been common. Many are quite beautiful in pattern and texture. The "honeycomb" design is a special favorite, and there are "huckabucks," "basket weaves," and many others the original names of which have been lost.

COVERLETS OF THE ITINERANT WEAVER

As mentioned before, there is still another and very different type of American coverlet which has seldom been made in the region but which is often shown in exhibitions of mountain coverlets, giving the impression that it is the work of Highland women. This coverlet is distinguished by its elaborate, often naturalistic patterns of flowers, birds, scrolls, emblems, houses, and other pictures. It is a type which could not be woven on a mountain loom, and was done in the lowlands by itinerant weavers, many of whom came from Europe bringing with them Jacquard looms on which it was possible to weave almost any kind of figure. These experts, with looms quite in advance of anything hitherto known in our country, traveled from place to place weaving the yarn and thread which the women of the household had spun.[1] The professional skill and knowledge of the trade learned in the Old Country, where textile weaving had been highly developed, are not to be underestimated, but the indispensable contributor to these elaborate picture patterns was the mechanical equipment of the Jacquard loom.

It is not difficult to understand the importance of the traveling weaver to the people whom he served and the interest and delight which so often attended his visits. Many coverlets made by him have been preserved in museums, private collections, and homes, some in as good condition as on the day they were taken from the loom. These remarkable examples of skill, ingenuity, and technique are a valuable part of our handicraft heritage, yet they often lack the quiet beauty of the simpler weavings, and their color combinations, though usually more standardized, do not always achieve the fine harmony of some of the vegetable-dyed coverlets of the mountain women.

[1] Hall, Eliza Calvert, A Book of Hand-Woven Coverlets. Little, Brown and Co., Boston, 1931. This book includes several illustrations of coverlets woven on Jacquard looms and gives an interesting account of some of these weavers.

A TENNESSEE MOUNTAIN WOODWORKER

Mac McCarter of Gatlinburg, Tennessee, Makes Baskets, Chairs, and Does General Woodwork of Native Timber. His Baskets, Usually of White Oak Splits, Are Sometimes Colored with Vegetable Dyes

HONEYSUCKLE BASKET MAKERS

LENA AND FLORA DYSART, WHO LIVE NEAR RYDAL, BARTOW COUNTY, GEORGIA, MAKE
EXCELLENT BASKETS ENTIRELY FROM THE NATIVE HONEYSUCKLE VINE WHICH GROWS
ABUNDANTLY THERE AS IN MANY OTHER PARTS OF THE HIGHLANDS

INDIVIDUALITY IN MOUNTAIN COVERLETS

As examples of ingenious craftsmanship the Highland coverlet deserves high rank among the handicrafts of our country. Often all the materials were prepared and each operation performed by one person, in some instances the weaver also making her own loom.

It is quite true that all mountain coverlets are not attractive; there are some of uninteresting design, unpleasant color combinations, and very poor craftsmanship, but these are exceptions. The majority have much individuality. The display of the factory-made coverlet in stores where quantities of like designs are offered is unfortunate. There is no textile more inappropriate for quantity production or mass display than this one, and usually the factory-made product is of inferior material, as a little use will reveal. The featuring of "old mountain coverlets" sales in department stores in order to dispose of quantities of poor factory imitations has done much harm to the reputation of the genuine Highland cover. It was designed often to be the only decorative textile in the room. Many of these rooms were somber, and whether deliberately planned or not for the night light, the coverlet is often at its best when seen in the glow from the fireplace.

Those who have traveled in the Southern Highlands have carried away with them recollections of their favorite coverlets often seen in remote places and as vivid in memory as a flower garden of which they are sometimes reminiscent. Not to be forgotten is the soft blue, rose, and white coverlet, probably an old German pattern, seen in a Blue Ridge cabin near White Top, Virginia, in a section where the "Pennsylvania Dutch" had settled; that unusual mixture of glowing red and light gray seen in Breathitt County, Kentucky; the deep blue Charity Wheel design in Wears Valley, Tennessee; the Hickory Leaf motif in golden yellow over on Shooting Creek, North Carolina; and the rose, green, and tan of an unnamed coverlet that came off a load of tobacco on its way out of the mountains of South Carolina. It is a tribute to the mountain coverlet that Mrs. Hall,[1] in choosing some 16 for color reproduction in her book on the subject, included 13 that had been woven in the Southern Highlands on old-time looms.

[1] A Book of Hand-Woven Coverlets.

Mountain coverlets are woven in separate lengths and sewed together when taken from the loom, sometimes with such perfect register and care that only the closest examination reveals the seam, although many are not too accurately matched. A strip wider than about three feet could not be woven on a hand loom. A hand-woven coverlet is therefore always joined, while a full-width one, without a seam down the middle, is factory made. This is one of the obvious and distinguishing marks between the hand and the factory product.

PREPARING THE MATERIALS AND WEAVING

The methods now used in coverlet weaving are practically identical with those employed in the Highlands since the coming of the first settlers. That made at the present time is woven on cotton warp, and the same-sized cotton thread is used in the weft to form a tab. Some of the earlier ones were made on linen warp, a very strong base spun from flax. The flax was grown in the summer months, cut in the fall, and retted usually in the open where it was thoroughly disintegrated by the rains and snows before it was finally scutched, the fiber separated, and made fine enough for spinning, usually on a low wheel. Retting was not often done in streams as in the Old Country, probably because water was not so abundant; but if the rains did not serve, the flax was sprinkled with water and sun-dried until the fibers were thoroughly loosened.

The making of linen thread was a slow, laborious process which was in most places superseded by cotton thread spun on the same high wheel used for wool. Naturally there were thrifty families who raised flax, cotton, and sheep for wool, from which fine materials for excellent clothing were produced. As a rule, however, cotton thread was used and the greater number of old coverlets are wool filled on cotton warp. Preparing the cotton warp required time, hard work, patience, and skill. The mountain woman often planted, hoed, and picked the cotton and then, being too far from a cotton gin, and too poor had she been near enough to take advantage of Eli Whitney's great invention, she would gin the cotton on a small home-made contrivance resembling an ordinary clothes wringer, after which she would card it, spin it on the big wheel, and twist it into strong thread.

Then came the second material, the wool. The mountain weaver often sheared the fleece from the sheep herself; after laboriously picking out the burrs, bark, and tangleweeds gathered by the animal which ran loose in rough country, she washed it and put it by until the time arrived to card it into soft rolls, a long, strenuous, and particular procedure. That being done the wool was ready to spin into yarn, usually on the high wheel, although the low, or flax wheel, could be used. Some old weavers say that spinning is faster on the high wheel than on the low one; others that it is handier to use just one kind of wheel. The high wheel could be built much more easily and cheaply than the low one, an important item in a country with few skilled mechanics. One comes across comparatively few low wheels in the Highlands of Kentucky, Tennessee, and North Carolina, while in remote sections of the Blue Ridge Mountains of Virginia there are more.

Before the cotton warp could be wound upon the loom, the heddles threaded, and the woolen woof shot through, the woolen yarn had to be colored and set. Usually, as has been stated, the white thread of the warp was used in its natural color and occasionally the natural color of the wool was not altered, but in most instances the woolen yarn was dyed before weaving began. Sometimes the wool would be dyed before it was carded, giving opportunity for combining shades and securing mixtures in colors which could not be obtained in any other way.

These various processes did not necessarily follow one another in succession, but all had to precede the weaving. Oftentimes the procedure was to choose the pattern and the color scheme to be carried out long before the cotton flower had blossomed or the sheep been shorn of its fleece. If white and blue were the colors decided upon, a favorite combination, only the blue had to be prepared, but to obtain the old-time color required a knowledge and skill possessed by few dyers of today. Setting the blue pot was an event of great importance fraught with much risk and worry, although a few Highland women who seemed invincible on any occasion thought it no trick at all.

The warp and woof having been dyed as desired, the design or pattern chosen, the loom was threaded up and the weaving, for which such long and patient preparation had been made, was begun. The weaver's guide was a "draft" or pattern, on a slip of paper, a description of which is here quoted from Miss Goodrich's book on the subject.[1]

In the "drawing-in" and in the actual weaving of a coverlet, a design or pattern is necessary and this was called a draft. The good offices of a preacher or lawyer were often called upon to "draw off," that is, to copy, a draft. It was written on a narrow slip of paper, from four inches to half a yard long according to the length of one unit of the pattern, and was fastened on the front of the loom in plain sight of the weaver. Old drafts are often written on the backs of letters or bills or law papers. The draft consists of lines and figures, or—if the reader could not read figures—of lines only, mystifying to the uninitiated. These may be found in many an old house tucked away in trunks and cupboards, rolled up and tied carefully with thread. When spread out they are seen to be marked with multitudinous pin pricks as one worker and another has put in a pin to keep her place in the "drawing in."

What understanding of this small slip of paper upon which so much of the beauty of the mountain home depended! Some of the parallel lines with their carefully laid-in dashes and dots resemble nothing so much as bars of music, the rhythm of which from shuttle and batten beat out harmonies in form and color to such lyrical names as Flowers of Edinboro, Maid of Orleans, Kentucky Snowflakes, Flower of the Mountain, Wonder of the Forest, Sunrise on the Walls of Troy, Morning Star, Lilies of the Valley and of the Meadows, and scores of others which have come down through the years.

PRESERVING OLD MOUNTAIN DRAFTS

Among the meager treasures of many modest Highland homes are to be found little nests of such weaving drafts on old slips of paper browned with age and sometimes quite large collections of these music-like records. The customary way of keeping the drafts is to roll and tie them with thread; black thread seems to have been used most often. Through their cryptic lines color schemes and dates as well as the valued instructions for weaving the pattern are often revealed. There are a few people in the country who are able to translate the drafts, and such ability is considered a scholarly attainment, especially when the translation yields im-

[1] Mountain Homespun. Yale University Press, New Haven, 1931, pp. 8–9.

portant information hitherto unknown or directions that may be put together to fill out some uncompleted pattern in the possession of another person. Countless old drafts have been destroyed on the assumption that they were no longer useful, or because those into whose hands they fell were not able to interpret them and therefore did not comprehend their significance.

Lou Tate Bousman, a weaver of experience and ability who received her training at Berea College, has interested herself in collecting and recording names and other data on the old drafts of her home community in Kentucky. Soon after launching this work in 1928 she visited Nan Owens, an old coverlet weaver who lived in Barren County, Kentucky. Miss Owens, then past eighty, was bedridden and had not woven for many years, but she was delighted to learn that girls and women were still weaving, and she sent to the attic for a cherished box which contained the drafts of five generations. Some were dated; one of Queen Anne's Delight bore the year 1825 and had been used by Susan McGuire of the second generation who also made several drafts for dimities or counterpanes. Mary Higdon of the third generation had used drafts dated 1840 to 1850, after which came the coverlet and dimity drafts of Sarah and Sally Owens, and finally Miss Nan's own drafts. Altogether there were 42 of them, including Miss Higdon's drafts of Green River Beauty, Wonder of the World, dated 1841, The Olive Leaf, Tennessee Flower, and Virginia Barley, all dated 1842, seven unnamed dimity drafts and as many unnamed coverlet drafts, one of these a summer and winter weave. These old designs furnish authentic clues to the history of weaving in Barren County, and interest is greatly increased through the fact that Miss Bousman is able to weave coverlets from them and is doing so as she finds a new and promising draft.

There are several ways of recording drafts, and at least six have been studied and translated by Miss Bousman. While numbers were generally used, other small marks were employed for those who could not read or write Arabic. There was also another quite human feature which the student of weaving drafts will encounter —the tendency to record the instructions so that no one else could read them, although most weavers were generous about sharing their designs.

NAMES OF COVERLET PATTERNS

For an extensive list of the often quaint and sometimes beautiful names of coverlet patterns the reader should consult two books already referred to, Mountain Homespun and A Book of Hand-Woven Coverlets. In the latter one chapter is devoted to coverlet names and more than a hundred, gathered from all parts of the country, are given. Because these names are in themselves so expressive, a selected list is arranged alphabetically in Appendix I. Miss Bousman explains that some patterns she has collected were brought to the section in which she lives by brides from other parts of the Highlands. Several names suggest their origin as being from a neighboring state.

The name, however, is not always an infallible designation. A pattern may have a half-dozen names and the same name may be applied to different patterns, according to locality. Miss Bousman has found for the well-known Snail's Trail and Cat Track 20 different names, among them Blooming Vine, Ocean Wave, Rattlesnake, Vine around the Stump, and Winding Vine. She has found that 15 different ones have been used for the Double Bowknot illustrated on page 186. Some names are very prosaic; for instance, Philadelphia Pavement, which is also called Lovers' Knot. There is Tennessee Trouble, but probably that is not so bad as Tennessee Trouble in North Carolina. Freemason's Walk, Guinea-fowl, Queens' Patch are among the less poetic designations. They have served their purpose, however, by adding to the interest, color, and euphony of many a Highland community.

THE SOUTHERN HIGHLAND COVERLET

There is no handicraft in our country which offers more incentive for research than coverlet making, especially that of the Southern Highlands. The fact that coverlets are still woven on old looms and that many have been preserved as well as the drafts, provides a continuity of interest making it possible to learn much about them. Moreover, there are yet living a number of old weavers who can give invaluable information concerning this craft in their own and in other communities. In not a few mountain neighborhoods a large part of the local history could be written around the coverlets made there. One of the most interesting segments centers about the Sloan family in West Virginia.

In 1780 Richard Sloan at the age of twenty-eight years reached Philadelphia from Ireland and later went to Romney, Hampshire County, Virginia, now West Virginia, where he established a business of custom weaving. He brought nothing with him in the way of history when he came to America, but he undoubtedly belonged to a family of weavers. Ten children were born to him and five of the seven boys followed their father's craft. Together they operated six looms. The daybook which they kept indicates that they gathered trade from as far west as central Ohio. They wove linen and other textiles, but the larger part of their output was coverlets, and some of these are still in the possession of descendants of the Sloan family in West Virginia. They are of many different designs and colors, of which blue and white and red and white predominate, but other combinations were also used. The colors remain bright and fast even today, although many of the coverlets have been subjected to hard usage, some having been employed for saddle blankets and ironing pads before their value as heirlooms was established and their beauty and workmanship appreciated.

Richard Sloan died in 1820 and his sons carried on weaving until about 1835, or until power looms came into use, when they went into other businesses. The family was very conservative by nature and inclined to be clannish. The five weaving brothers agreed that they would all stay together; therefore that it would not be expedient or possible for each to take a wife. They decided that one should marry and the others make their home with him. Lots were cast and it fell to the youngest brother to have a wife. So far as is known the arrangement was entirely satisfactory. All these brothers except one lived to an old age but passed nothing of their weaving experience on to the next generation.[1] Recently two old account books have been discovered in which there are scores of entries showing charges for weaving the two types of coverlets characteristic of that region, the "flote" weave, the most widely made throughout the Highlands, and the double weave, of

[1] This information was furnished by David Arnold of Keyser, West Virginia, one of the many descendants of the Sloan family.

which the Sloan brothers made many. In the back of one of these books are several drafts, the designs of which have not yet been deciphered.

The Colonial Coverlet Guild of America, a national organization incorporated in Chicago, Illinois, in 1924, has done much through its programs, exhibitions, year book, and other literature to promote interest in the home arts of America and especially the coverlet, of which it has its own collection, and 400 photographs of different examples secured through its members.[1] Twenty-two members of the Guild are weavers. Membership is available to anyone owning one coverlet.

The Guild is connected with the Highlands through its support of an annual scholarship in the weaving department of the Pine Mountain Settlement School, and in a more remote but interesting way through coverlets owned by many of its members. The pattern adopted by the Guild as a cover design for its year book is a reproduction of a four-snowball pattern with a pine-tree border on three sides.

There are many forms of hand weaving in America besides the coverlet, but it is doubtful if any other will continue to hold the interest of our people as this pioneer textile does. The opportunity to make a thing of use and beauty is a rare experience at any time, and in the mountain coverlets we have convincing evidence of the persistent quest for beauty in the face of discouragement, penury, and hardship. Some of these experiences suggest how deep is the appreciation of beauty often among untrained and unlettered people. Aunt Sal Creech voiced the joy-giving qualities of creative work with the hands when she exclaimed, "Weaving, hit's the purtiest work I ever done. It's settin' and trompin' the treadles and watchin' the blossoms come out and smile at ye in the kiverlet."

[1] For further information, see Appendix II, p. 339.

A NORTH CAROLINA MOUNTAIN WHITTLER

W. J. Martin, Who Lives Near Murphy, Cherokee County, Likes to Whittle Out Animals Both Domestic and Wild. His First Whittling Was a Wild Turkey. He Is Here Shown with "a Chance of Pigs" Made from Apple Wood

A TENNESSEE MOUNTAIN WHITTLING

This Barnyard Scene Is Typical of the Work of Sam Smith, Who Lives Back in the Mountains from Pittman Community Center, Near Sevierville. He Whittles Mountains from Pittman Community Center, Near Sevierville. He Whittles M the Once we from the Native Poplar

CHAPTER VII

QUILTING AND PATCHWORK

JUST as the coverlet or "kiver" has long been the most distinguished product of the loom in the Southern Highlands, so quilting and patchwork have been the most outstanding expressions in needlework. There is no reason to compare the coverlet with the quilt for honors; both fill an indispensable need and both are old plants that flower in the garden of American folk art. There is this difference, however: most of the hand-woven coverlets now made in the United States are produced in the Southern Highlands, while quilts are still made in every state in the Union. In the National Quilt Contest held at the Eastern States Exposition in Springfield, Massachusetts, in 1932, over 600 entries were listed with all but eight states of the Union participating, and information indicates that quilt making is carried on in all those not represented. Each state in the Highlands took part in this exhibition and in several states, in addition to many women who make quilts for their own use, are groups who do both patchwork and quilting to produce income.

Although we are concerned here only with the making of quilts in the mountain sections of the South, it will be noted in passing that in the neighborhoods of Lexington and Harrodsburg, Kentucky, which lie outside the area of this study, the most extensive quilting industries in America, if not in the world, have been developed. Here rural women have attained a high degree of perfection in workmanship and their products have a nation-wide sale. The industry is quite thoroughly organized, and it and the candlewick bedspread industry of northern Georgia are among the most extensive employers of rural women in the handicrafts of the South.

QUILTING

Quilting is a method of fastening together sometimes two but usually three layers of material by a pattern of all-over stitching. These materials consist of a base which is usually a solid piece of cloth; a filling or a bat, which may be a thin or even fairly thick layer of wool, of cotton flannel or felt cloth, thistledown, or some other soft material; and an upper covering which, with the base, holds the filling in place until it is stitched or quilted into permanent form. The upper covering may be a single piece of cloth or it may be made up of many pieces sewn together, called "patchwork." A bedcover made with a patchwork top is known as a patchwork quilt.

Little imagination is required to picture the development of the quilting process, fastening two or three thicknesses of materials together to secure a covering of more warmth as a garment or bedcover, or to gain softness for a padding, as under a coat-of-mail, or for many other uses. The materials were first fastened together with plain stitches to hold them in place, without thought of design. When this prime need had been met, then followed the effort which has marked the growth of every handicraft since the dawn of history—the beautifying of the work. Even where there was no difference in color between the cloth and thread the stitches were varied to express the fancy of the needleworker. From this simple craft developed an art which has come to be one of the most restrained and beautiful in the whole realm of needlework. Quilting with white thread on white material has come down to us as one of the most satisfying expressions in the long procession of domestic arts. Many early American quilts were made in this way, a very fine example of the type being in Dumbarton House, Washington, D. C., the possession of the National Association of Colonial Dames of America.

Quilting is a very old craft, having been practiced thousands of years ago in Egypt, China, India, and ancient Greece, and among other old civilizations; likewise in the Middle Ages and through to modern times in every country where textiles are in use, not alone for bed quilts but for clothing, upholstery, and many other purposes. Our own traditions in quilting have probably more of their roots in England and in Holland than in any other countries, although it would be an error to suggest that a nation made up of people from so many homelands of Europe as is America has not been influenced to some extent by all of them. But it is likely that the colonists from England and from Holland introduced the first quilting into America, and that it was the English quilts that exerted the greatest influence on the early development in this country. An expert quilter and an authority, writing on the subject, states that the art has never died out among the rural women of England;[1] another authority in a recent work[2] shows some illustrations of beautiful North Country designs which are identical with many stitches that have marked American quilts from colonial times to the present.

The variation from plain quilting, with which we are most familiar, is the patchwork top, a feature which, according to a well-known authority, has been developed in America, both in variety and in beauty, to an extent not equaled in other lands. In a comprehensive book on the subject she says:

As for quilts, the European peasant of whatever country appears always to have employed patchwork, especially pieced patchwork, for the making of bed-clothing.

But nowhere has the quilt played so distinct and characteristic a part as in America. Quilt-making here is an antique art whose tradition has never wholly died. Unusual is the native family that does not possess at least one patchwork quilt, often made by a still living generation.[3]

Quilt making is a pleasant home craft, although somewhat exacting, which requires very simple equipment. While not more than one person can work at a loom at a time, several persons may work together on a quilt. This gives a social value to the craft, and in the Highlands today the quilting party is an important feature of social life. In the summer of 1935 at the log raising of the new Craft House at Penland, North Carolina, which continued through a period of several days, a dozen women quilted on a nearby cabin porch while the men worked on the new building. They were making a quilt for a girl who had recently married. The custom

[1] Scott, Beatrice, The Craft of Quilting in the North Country. The Dryad Press, Leicester, England, Leaflet no. 87. (No date.)

[2] Heynes, Anne, Quilting and Patchwork. The Dryad Press, Leicester, England. 1930.

[3] Finley, Ruth E., Old Patchwork Quilts and the Women Who Made Them. J. B. Lippincott Co., Philadelphia, 1929, p. 22.
For those who may wish to learn how quilts are made Chapter III of Mrs. Finley's book will prove clear and comprehensive. The technical side of the craft is treated quite fully in the publications issued by the Dryad Press, Leicester, England.

of the Penland workers is to present a patchwork quilt to every bride going out from one of their homes; and they were working diligently these days, for they were "behind on quilts for two brides."

But even the lone worker, of whom there are many in the mountains, finds the quilting frame usually better adapted to her needs than the loom would be, and materials for quilts are now easily procurable. Left-overs and unused material sent on from thrifty friends from outside can be worked up into patchwork. If these or trips to the country store do not yield the desired pieces there are always the "wish books," the mail-order catalogues, through which most anything can be had "that a body has the money to buy."

A feature of quilting among Highland women, probably not practiced to such extent in any other section, is the preparation of the filling or "bats" of cotton from plants which they have raised, or of wool from the sheep of the family flock. And this is used not only in quilts made for their own use but in some of the best that go to outside markets. The Mountain Cabin Quilters of Wooton, Leslie County, Kentucky, prepare the filling for all their quilts. A picture of this work and what it means to the workers is given in a letter[1] written by "Doc's woman," Mrs. J. K. Stoddard, wife of the local physician who organized these quilting groups:

Wooton lies in a gap—not a valley—and in every direction the Appalachians surround it, and to the very tip top they are covered with oaks, chestnuts, maples, laurel, rhododendron, and dogwood. Through these trees in unbelievable numbers are scattered the cabins of the mountain people. News is carried by the traditional "little bird" and gets about with the facility peculiar to that active creature. And so was started this organization—the outcome of "Doc's woman" attending a "Quiltin'!"

Many of the mountain women have never before had any money of their own. Now they earn it by doing beautiful work with their own toil-scarred fingers—for it is the women who make the fire, milk the cow, feed the pigs and chickens, cook for the family, do the washing, and have a baby at least every second year. For all that, they do not hesitate to walk or ride ten miles to get their order for a quilt. If one is not equal to the quilting, she can card the wool, from her own sheep, or the cotton that she has grown in her garden, and have a share in the venture.

[1] Reprinted in a leaflet entitled Mountain Cabin Quilters.

A NORTH CAROLINA MOUNTAIN WHITTLER
HADEN HENSLEY, ONE OF THE WHITTLERS AT THE JOHN C. CAMPBELL FOLK SCHOOL

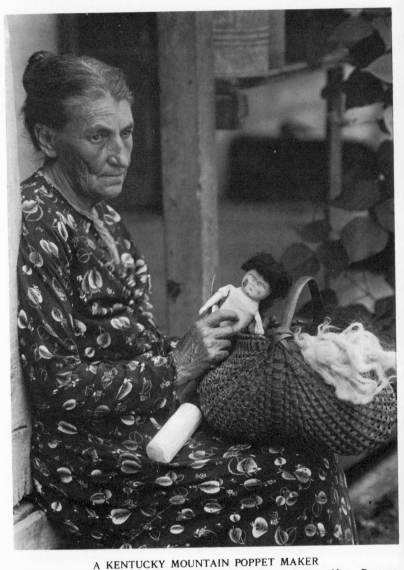

A KENTUCKY MOUNTAIN POPPET MAKER

Mrs. Orlenia Ritchie and Her Sister, Who Live in Perry County, Make Poppets or Mountain Dolls from the Native Buckeye Wood, as Their Mother and Grandmother Did, Shaping Them with a Pocketknife

QUILTING AND PATCHWORK

In the making of a quilt, there are several serious considerations. The "piecing" means perfect points and corners and exact shaping of the pattern. The quilting is exact too, and just as good on the wrong side as it is on the right. It takes from ten days to six weeks to do the quilting alone, and all the time it is in the making it must be kept spotlessly clean. . . . Usually there isn't space enough to have the frame stay hung down in the room, so it is swung up to the ceiling when not being worked on—tightly covered on both sides. The children's fingers may never touch it and above all it must be protected from the soot of the soft coal which these mountaineers get by the sledful from their own hillside.

The names of the patterns belong to their family traditions, and are all delightfully quaint—"Old Maid's Ramble," "Hearts and Gizzards," "Rob Peter to Pay Paul," "Dove at the Window," "Toad in a Puddle," "Fanny's Fan," "Star with Many a Point."

The coloring is selected by the manager and all the work must pass her censorship and that of the committee consisting of four mountain women. The material is sun-fast gingham and will wash perfectly. If one prefers, quilts can be filled with cotton instead of wool. Then they become charming bedspreads for country bedrooms.

When the quilts are made, the money goes straight into the roughened palms. The proceeds go to manifold purposes. One old woman is saving for a set of teeth; another is buying herself a home after years of "staying around"; another, who herself can neither read nor write, is helping to put her boy through school. Another now has a pump in her kitchen so she need no longer carry water from the branch. And so it goes, and they have the splendid experience we all have shared, of spending their windfall in a dozen ways before they really part from it. . . .

PATCHWORK QUILTS

Patchwork quilts are of two kinds: pieced or appliquéd. Sometimes both methods of work are combined in one quilt. In pieced work the sections are all sewed together with a seam, but in the appliqué method a smaller piece of cloth is laid upon a larger one and hemmed down. An interesting combination of both techniques is found in a quilt illustrated on page 196 which was shown in a traveling exhibition of mountain handicrafts assembled by the Southern Highland Handicraft Guild and circulated throughout the country by the American Federation of Arts, 1933–1935. The center design, a delicate wreath, was inlaid—very narrow strips pieced together—while the design for the remainder was of patches set on in appliqué. This quilt was originally designed in 1860 by a mountain woman in Virginia, it was pieced by the granddaughter of the designer in North Carolina in 1932, and was later quilted in Kentucky.

Many old designs known to other parts of the country and some that were used by New England quilters more than a century ago are to be found in the Highland states. Now and then a pattern is discovered that is entirely original. Of these, two will be mentioned: one is a modern quilt that was made in Tennessee; the other an heirloom belonging to a family in Georgia. The modern one was a charming patchwork quilt with flower pattern in a variety of colors on a nicely quilted white background and designed by Mrs. Andy Hatcher of Wears Valley, Tennessee, not far from Gatlinburg. It formed the center piece of the first exhibition held by the Southern Highland Handicraft Guild in Knoxville, Tennessee, in 1930. Mrs. Hatcher learned to quilt from her mother. Although her craftsmanship is always of a high quality, the outstanding feature is the design and the originality of her color combinations. These are inspired by the wildflowers of the mountains or by her own country garden, and she rarely makes a duplicate pattern. The design of the quilt shown at the exhibition, while still a typical example of American needlecraft, reveals the free expression which is characteristic of much of the peasant work in the old countries. One feels the satisfaction the artist experienced in working out her forms in a color scheme especially pleasing. The roses are not red—that would have been the conventional thing to do and less interesting; but blue, pink, yellow, and lavender. As they fill the eye with pleasure one is glad that this needlecraft horticulturist has developed both a blue and a lavender rose, for they are the colors needed to suggest a flower garden in early summer.

Mrs. Hatcher has "quilted" her two eldest children, a boy and a girl, through high school and expects to do equally well by her four younger sons who are still at home. The Hatcher family first settled in Wears Valley in 1795; their land has never been sold but has passed down through five generations to the present one.

The other quilt of original design, known as the Moon and Star pattern, comes "nigh onto being an antique," having the reputation of being "over a hundred years old," as many things in the High-lands are reckoned to be. It was made by the pioneer grandmother of its present owner, Mrs. M. B. Cox of Marietta, Georgia. Grandma Holcomb, who lived far back in the mountains of northern Georgia, if she had any patterns at all, had none equal to those she saw in the beauty of nature about her. So when she designed a quilt it was also a record of her reaction to some wonder of the universe of which she felt herself so vital a part. Another granddaughter has a quilt of an original design, the flower of the tulip tree, which grows to great size and perfection in the mountains of Georgia and from which some of the logs in Grandma Holcomb's cabin were hewn.

The heavens were her inspiration for the Moon and Star quilt. On a certain night, when she was a young woman, she watched through the narrow window by the fireplace in her cabin the new moon and a nearby star in its different phases, noting down their relations at three points, each an hour apart; to be more exact, at six, seven, and eight o'clock in the evening, and recorded them on the quilt. The first position shows the star just within the crescent, in the next it is nearer the lower point of the crescent, and in the third position it is slightly below it. Astronomically the design may not be perfect, but why should not a quilt maker, as well as a poet, have some license in such matters? If the star seems a little too close to the moon for the astronomer, certainly it is none the less effective. Why should she not adapt a favorite spot in the heavens to a favorite piece of patchwork?

The subject of mountain quilts recalls many familiar scenes to the writer. One of them is a cabin where he spent the night; and in the morning, while churning for the hostess with an old dasher churn in the kitchen, in order to have fresh butter with the corn-bread at breakfast, saw through the door of an adjoining bedroom a great stack of quilts and mountain coverlets. There were 22 of them, piled high from a low shelf to the ceiling, which the mother of the household had made for the two unmarried sons when they should "step off." Later in the evening after the younger boy had gone coon hunting and his older brother was "off sparkin'," she unfolded the collection of coverlets she had woven and the quilts she had pieced during her spare time in order to have them ready when the boys needed them. Among the quilts were some original designs and many old ones, including Ocean Wave, Sunflower, Bear's Paw, Napoleon's Wreath, Log Cabin, Bird in a Tree, Solomon's Crown, and Noah's Dove.

A delightful experience with quilts of one traveling a few years ago in the mountains of North Carolina, not far from the Georgia state line, is printed here.

When night overtook me I had not reached my destination, which was a visit to a hand spinner living two or three miles beyond the end of the road in country difficult to reach even in daylight. An old but beautiful cabin stood near the road and here I asked if I might spend the night. After a good supper and a visit around the fireplace, I was directed to my bedroom above the living room, commonly called the loft. When I had climbed the crude stairway the light of my candle revealed the whole sleeping apartment floor covered with beautiful patchwork quilts and, neatly hanging from the roof beams the entire length of the room and on both sides of my bed, were coverlets and quilts to afford additional protection from any drafts, or rain, or snow which might come, and also, it seemed to me, to give splendor to the scene.

These people had no carpets for their floor nor curtains for their windows, but they had a rare collection of home-made quilts, some of which were old and worn, but all I thought very beautiful and arranged in a way to create a royal room for the traveler who might drop in to spend the night. I could not walk over this carpet of quilts to my bed without first removing my shoes and by the candlelight that night I studied the designs and color combinations in perhaps ten or twelve of them. I doubt if I shall ever have the privilege of sleeping in such surroundings again, and if the sight of a patchwork quilt does not stir in me anything more than the recollection of the experience in this lovely scene it does quite enough.

It is not possible to name here more than a small fraction of the quilt makers in the Highlands, as nearly every handicraft center has at least one expert and many have several. The Mountain Cabin Quilters mentioned earlier are probably the most extensive producers. The Women's Club at the John C. Campbell Folk School began work modestly with patchwork for chair seats, table mats, and other small articles which they pieced together with good taste and excellent craftsmanship. Quilts are made by the Mountain Neighbors at Oldrag, at the Hindman Settlement School, the Pine Mountain Settlement School, the John and Mary R. Markle

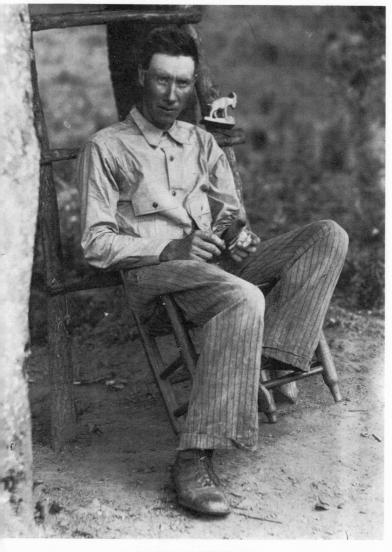

A MOUNTAIN WHITTLER

Floyd Laney, a Skilful Whittler at the John C. Campbell Folk School, Did the Logging Outfit Illustrated Elsewhere

A MUSIC MAKER OF THE HIGHLANDS

THIS MOUNTAIN GIRL OF TENNESSEE PLAYS THE GUITAR AND DULCIMER AND SINGS THE OLD-TIME BALLADS AND CAROLS. THE INSTRUMENT IS A MODERN DULCIMER; ITS SEVERAL FORMS ARE DESCRIBED IN CHAPTER XIII

School of Industrial Arts at Higgins; the Allanstand Cottage Industries, Crossnore School, Berea Fireside Industries, Pi Beta Phi Settlement School, Penland Weavers and Potters, and the Mountaineer Craftsmen's Cooperative Association.

Much of the information on American quilts is scattered through newspapers and periodicals, but the titles of some available books will be found in the Bibliography. An important contribution is in preparation by Dr. William Rush Dunton, Jr., of Catonsville, Maryland, who has made a comprehensive study of the craft and has had extensive experience in its application in the field of therapy.

OLDEST AMERICAN DATED QUILT

There is an old custom with a few makers in America of attaching the date when a quilt is finished or when it has been the center of an important event. It appears that the oldest dated quilt in our country, the Framed Medallion, was made in the Highlands of Virginia and has remained in the mountain section of that state, now become West Virginia, for more than one hundred and forty years.[1] It bears on the homespun back the initials WTG and the date 1795.

The present owner is Mrs. Murray C. Brown, Charlottesville, Virginia, who is the daughter of Mrs. M. L. Coyner of Clover Lick, West Virginia, to whom the quilt descended. The traces of ownership through records of other needlework in a family is a significant example of the relation of needlework to history. In verifying the date and original ownership, a sampler made by Hannah Moffat Gatewood (who was Mrs. Coyner's grandmother) on the occasion of her marriage in 1838 provides evidence. Miss Gatewood's great-grandfather, so the family record discloses, was William Travers Gatewood, the only member of the family whose initials are identical with those on the quilt. It would seem, therefore, that the initials establish the owner as William Travers Gatewood, and the date of the quilt, in relation to the marriage date of his great-granddaughter forty-three years later, is probably correct.

Its foundation is natural color linen on which flowers of lavender, purple, blue, pink, and green are tastefully blended and various

[1] Finley, Ruth E., Old Patchwork Quilts and the Women Who Made Them. For illustration see p. 24.

131

designs of piecework are appliquéd in buttonhole stitch. The elaborate combination of the two kinds of patchwork is striking and represents an individual working out of old methods and designs.

Quilting, as has been said, is an old folk art of the United States which holds an interest for every part of our country not only for its historical and antique value but because it is a home craft widely practiced today.

CHAPTER VIII

NATIVE DYES AND HERBS

THERE is probably no craft in which greater interest exists at the present time than that of coloring with natural, and particularly vegetable dyes; nor one about which there are more erroneous ideas. Here again the Southern Highlands hold a wealth of information for students and craftsmen, because this region is not only the conserver of many very old traditions concerning vegetable dyes, but it is also a present-day laboratory in which new experiments are being worked out.

Parallel to the interest in extracting from the plants of garden, field, and woodland coloring matter for yarns, threads, finished textiles, and baskets is the interest in their use as food, drink, cosmetics, or medicine. Plants for medicine, as in pioneer days, are still common in some places, and a number of men and women give a large part of their time to gathering and vending herbs; many of the older generation possess from a little to much knowledge of their traditional uses.

There is frequently a close affinity between plants which yield dye and those used for other purposes, all of which spring from the same soil. Sometimes plants or trees, as for instance the native nut tree, will supply food, medicine, and beautiful coloring material. One finds occasionally an old inhabitant who knows equally well both the dye and the medicinal properties of trees and smaller plants, but as a rule each branch of knowledge is considered a specialty firmly lodged in the minds of those who "tell it to you" by word of mouth, writing it down only when pressed to do so.

Much understanding of the utility of plants, particularly for medicine, was brought to the mountains by the pioneers, for botany and medicine had come down the centuries in Europe together and the scientific division of the two had not taken place when the Highlands were settled. However, it seems likely that much of the present-day lore is an indigenous development and reflects the ingenuity of the people in employing the properties of the rich flora of the region.

The term "natural dyes" usually comprises the coloring materials obtained directly from plants, animals, insects, or minerals. The majority are of plant origin, so that except for an occasional reference to perhaps the red and pink coloring extracted from the insect cochineal, or to the orange and yellow made from copperas it is to those commonly known as vegetable dyes that attention will be given. Most of those mentioned will be the home dyes of the Highlands; yet, because of the interest in other parts of the country, some of the treatises on the general subject are included in the Bibliography.

COMMERCIAL AND NATURAL DYES COMPARED

Something should perhaps be said at the outset on the relative merits of the home or vegetable dyes as compared to the store-bought dyes of commerce, and some suggestions made in justification of a wider use of home-made dyes, particularly in rural districts, where there is an abundance of dye material available as in the Southern Highlands.

The claim that vegetable dyes are always permanent and commercial dyes are not is a very common error. No general statement can be helpful, for comparison must be made between a specific vegetable dye and a specific commercial dye and must include the operations that attend the process of dyeing. Absolute quality is not alone in the dye itself, but often in the way in which it is prepared and applied. Moreover, fastness is a relative matter; that is, a dye may be comparatively fast when exposed to light but may fade when washed. On the other hand, a dye may be fast when washed but may fade when exposed to light. Also fastness may vary with the material used, whether wool, cotton, silk, or some other fiber. Thus some of the natural dyes may be applied successfully to one kind of material but less so to another.

The best of the commercial dyes are prepared to be used on a specific fiber. The only conclusion therefore at which one can arrive as to relative permanence of vegetable and commercial dyes is that a number of the former are more lasting on certain fibers than are some of the latter, and the reverse is true. The record for fastness, however, is with vegetable dyes which have been in use for centuries, while synthetic dyes are of fairly recent invention.

There is one fact about the fading of the two kinds which seems to give an immense advantage to natural dyes. Usually when they fade they still bear a definite relation to their original color, often becoming softer and more beautiful without losing their character; while a faded synthetic dye usually bears little resemblance to its original tone. Since few colors in any fabric are absolutely fast, the fact that those obtained from natural sources do not usually deteriorate in quality, but sometimes improve, is a definite advantage in their use.

A question often asked by craftsmen wishing to experiment with native dyes is: "Can I get a sufficient color range to insure good results?" A satisfactory answer depends upon two basic things: first, the range desired, and second, the locality. It is true that in choice of colors the synthetic dyes generally far outnumber the natural dyes, even where one has access to a large number of dye-producing plants. But a wide variety is not always the need of the artist. A few carefully chosen colors will usually bring better results than experiments with many; just as in the graphic arts, much of the best printing is achieved with a few well-selected type faces rather than through the endless variety made available by type foundries.

However, a greater variety of colors than is generally known has been developed from plants in the Southern Highlands and experiments to increase them are still in process. As complete a list of colors as it has been possible to secure from plants growing in the region is printed in Appendix III, but it may be that some of those obtained by the pioneers have been lost because of the absence of written records. The list does, however, include the following roughly described colors: black, blue, brown, tan, gray, green, orange, purple, red, yellow, and many shades of some of these. It would therefore seem that a craftsman need feel no great handicap through too limited a variety.

Another question often asked is that concerning the comparative difficulty of using natural and synthetic dyes. The latter are as a rule much simpler because the craftsman merely applies a color that has been manufactured; otherwise he must make it himself.

Yet a craftsman often experiences great satisfaction when he engages in the complete process and has thorough control over his medium.

To many the relative cost of the two kinds is important. For the city dweller synthetic dyes are more economical because they are cheap and easily obtained; native plants are inaccessible. The country dweller too can now purchase synthetic dyes at a low price, but often he has little cash and to make his own dye is therefore an economy.

It is obviously not possible to know all the reasons why a natural dye is chosen. However, some who spin and weave by the old processes will wish to complete the circle of the home textile. They will understand the enthusiasm of the old mountain weaver who said, "I enjoy seeing my petticoat all the way from the sheep's back."

Others who find in vegetable dyes an opportunity to create a color palette of individuality and often of much beauty, consider this a unique experience. There is always a new plant to discover, a new dye to make, and a worker can often trace his methods back to those of the homelands of Europe and to recipes used there for centuries. An herbal of the sixteenth or seventeenth century is likely to contain formulas employed in the Highlands today.

COLORS OBTAINED FROM PLANTS

The most important colors used by pioneer women of the Highlands were indigo and madder; that is, blue and red. Both indigo and madder produce many varying shades, and a majority of the old coverlets and blankets were dyed with one of these, sometimes with both.

Indigo, derived from the plant *indigofera*, was introduced into Europe in the sixteenth century, when it supplanted to a considerable extent a similar dye made from the leaves of woad, an herb of the mustard family. There was much opposition to its introduction into England, and Queen Elizabeth issued orders against its use, declaring it inferior to the blue made from woad.

Some believe that the indigo plant is native to the Southern Appalachians, for it seems to have been used when pioneers did not have access to markets in which to purchase the dye. Mrs.

Wilmer Stone Viner, of the Weave Shop, an authority on natural dyes, says that in colonial days South Carolina became a great producer of indigo, and it is possible that some of that used by mountain women came from there. It was also raised in Louisiana and the dye was manufactured in New Orleans. Mrs. Viner and others, however, feel certain that pioneers used the wild plant. An old mountain dyer told her that the plant, which bears yellow flowers in August, should be gathered in that month and worked while fresh. To prepare the indigo, flowers and plant should be placed in a barrel, covered with a layer of straw, then with a layer of sumac for the tannin; water is poured over all this and it must stand until it decomposes. The combination effected by the mixture and the chemical reaction forms a cake in the bottom of the barrel. This is then ready for the blue pot.

The blue pot, the container for indigo dye, is an iron vessel (kept usually in a shed outside the house because of its disagreeable odor) replenished from time to time and kept going indefinitely, often without cessation over a long period of years. Sarah Dougherty knows of one pot that has been in continuous use for ninety-four years; and it is said that Mrs. Gretchen Bayne started her indigo dye from a pot that had been in use since 1797.[1]

Katherine Pettit states that the seed for the indigo plants that were raised at Pine Mountain as an experiment were secured from Madagascar, that they grew very well in the mountains, but that the time required for planting, harvesting, and preparing the dyes was too long to make the process practical. Zekie Huff, also of Pine Mountain, whose family has raised indigo from the seed, insists that the home-grown indigo yields a brighter dye than that bought at a store. Part of a report of the experience with indigo raising and dye making by a member of the Department of Agriculture[2] is printed in Appendix IV.

Although the preparation of indigo dye is somewhat complicated, one who wishes to work with this interesting color from the ground up will find it practical by following the old dye-pot or dye-vat

[1] West, Max, The Revival of Handicrafts in America. U. S. Dept. of Commerce and Labor, Bureau of Labor, Bulletin 55, Washington, 1904.

[2] Fawcett, Edna H., Typewritten Report on Indigo Experiments, Pine Mountain, Kentucky, September 15–October 1, 1925.

process, which does not require a mordant; that is, the application of a chemical which will remove the natural resistance of a fiber to absorb the dye readily. The important thing is that a dye should "bite," as some say. The process of dyeing with indigo is adequately described in a pamphlet issued by the federal Bureau of Home Economics.[1] Since indigo is a favorite color, as well as one of the most permanent dyes and is susceptible of a great variety of shades for either wool or cotton, further experimenting with it might well be engaged in, especially in the Highlands where it has been one of the traditional colors since the earliest settlements.

Madder, an ancient dye used by the Egyptians, later by the Moors in Spain, and imported probably first into Holland in the sixteenth century where it was developed into a commercial article, is now one of Holland's important contributions to world commerce. It was probably brought to America by the Dutch and by early settlers from the British Isles. It gives a wide range of colors, from a deep turkey-red to a delicate pink. Combined with quercitron the dye produces a bright orange. It works equally well on cotton and wool, but unlike indigo, the material upon which madder is to be used must first be subjected to a mordant before it will take the dye. Even though the process of preparation and dyeing is somewhat long and tedious, madder, because of its many shades of color and its harmonious combination with others, was often first favorite with pioneer women in the Highlands.

The madder plant is both native and cultivated in the Highlands, and while most madder dye now used in that region is from the roots of the plant of commerce, pioneer women undoubtedly used the wild plant and many raised their own supply. Proof of the use of wild madder has been difficult to secure, although many statements support the belief that it was common in the old days. Of the cultivated madder there is abundant evidence. A very old madder bed discovered some years ago by F. E. Matheny of Berea was visited in 1930 by him and the writer. It was found not far from Berea in the middle of a cornfield near what was once a fine log cabin. Although the plants had not been used or tended for a long generation, the roots were quite large; the plants appeared

[1] Furry, Margaret S., and Viemont, Bess M., Home Dyeing with Natural Dyes. U. S. Dept. of Agriculture, Washington, 1934. (Mimeographed.)

FOUR DULCIMER MAKERS OF THE HIGHLANDS
ABOVE: JETHRO AMBURGEY OF HINDMAN, KENTUCKY, AND SAM RUSSELL OF MARION, VIRGINIA. BELOW: BRISTOL TAYLOR OF BEREA, KENTUCKY, AND W. C. SINGLETON OF VIPER, KENTUCKY

STIRRING CLAY FOR MOUNTAIN POTTERY
THIS METHOD OF GRINDING OR STIRRING CLAY FOR POTTERY MAKING IS STILL COMMON
IN THE HIGHLANDS AND THE PIEDMONTS, THE POWER BEING A HORSE OR MULE

to be in excellent condition and were full of color. For information about the bed inquiry was made of Aunt Sweet Davis, seventy-six years of age, who was living alone in a cabin down the road "a piece." She said that her grandmother had planted the madder and used it to color yarn. She herself had often used it. After her parents died she had moved off the old homeplace but had kept the land and farmed it out, and each spring when the men plowed, asked them to leave the madder patch. The plowing had been done none too carefully, and what was probably once a symmetrical garden plot was now a ragged patch from two to six feet wide and perhaps 20 feet long, but the plants seemed to have lost little or none of their virility. This remnant of a once thriving madder bed was reported to the Southern Highland Handicraft Guild and efforts are now being made to preserve it.

Among other natural dye colors were browns, blacks, and grays from walnut and butternut hulls, roots, and bark; grays and tans from sumac berries; pinks and lavenders from pokeberries; yellows from hickory bark; deeper yellow and orange from the dye flower (wild coreopsis); pink-yellow from sedge grass; green from pine needles; and many colors from the cultivated plants and flowers of the garden.

SOME PRINCIPLES OF DYEING

Directions for preparing many of the dyes will be found in the publications listed in the Bibliography, but a few of the processes used in the preparation of all vegetable dyes will be briefly given here. This will include, first, the gathering of the dye-making material; second, the preparation of the dye; third, the preparation of the fiber to receive the dye; and finally the actual immersion of the fiber and the drying of the colored product.

The material of which the dye is made may be from such native plants as sumac berries and hickory bark, or from cultivated plants or trees, as coreopsis flowers or apple bark, or from a plant or tree that is both wild and cultivated, as the black walnut tree. The dye sources may be the roots, barks, leaves, hulls, nuts, flowers, fruits, stems, seeds, or the complete plant. In many cases the time of the year when these are gathered is important. This would be obviously true with flowers and fruits, but it is also true with certain roots and barks. From the sumac blossom and fruit, for instance, a different shade, varying from a light cream to a deep tan, is obtained according to the month. Some materials when gathered must be made up at once; others can be dried and used later. There are dyes which can be kept in liquid form for considerable time without losing their potency, and still others in which a part of the dye solution, for instance, the indigo dye, can be kept for very long periods, although it will require replenishing for each new batch of material.

The fibers dyed in the Southern Highlands are mainly cotton and wool, although in the old days considerable flax for linen and linsey-woolsey was grown. Some dyes will color both wool and cotton without any preliminary preparation, as is true of indigo, but the majority require treatment of the fiber with a mordant. Different agencies, in addition to acting as a mordant, serve to modify the shade. For instance, when madder dye is applied to wool with alum used as a mordant, a rose color will be the result; but if the mordant is muriate of tin, a brick color. The main purpose of the mordant is to prepare the fiber to absorb the dye and give it fastness.

The actual process of dyeing follows treatment with the mordant, if one is required, and calls for great care in respect to proper timing, the right temperature, constant stirring, and careful manipulation of the material so that it will not be crowded in the vessel, lifting and draining it intermittently, and sometimes introducing other ingredients to affect the color or quality of the dye. Also the kind of vessel—tin, brass, copper, or iron—often has a bearing on the color that is obtained. The manner of removing the material from the vessel and drying it is often of great importance in obtaining an even color. It is generally believed that the best results come from dyeing in the open, and anyone who has ever smelled a blue pot will agree that outdoors is the only proper place to work with it.

The processes just described apply to the dyeing of the yarns and threads after the most common methods practiced in the Highlands. There are two other ways in which dyes may be applied: one to the wool before it is carded and spun, the other to the finished piece of woven cloth. Anyone who masters the coloring of yarn or thread with vegetable dyes will be able to apply them with equal success to the unspun wool and the finished fabric.

The use of vegetable dyes in connection with baskets is further considered in Chapter X, Mountain Baskets.

USERS OF VEGETABLE DYES

In experiments which Mrs. Viner has made at the Weave Shop, she has not only worked out most painstakingly tests for washing and exposing to light a great number of natural dyes but has developed a complete color palette. From four of the dye plants native to North Carolina, sumac, dye flower, dye leaf (horse sugar), and black walnut hulls, Mrs. Viner has extracted a remarkable series of colors which she weaves into the stripes of the North Carolina Blanket. Sumac, as indicated, produces a variation of tans; walnut yields light browns to dark browns or black; dye flower gives light yellow to orange, and mixed with the dye leaf produces an orange-red or dark red. By combining these, nine distinct shades are obtained in the blanket. The blending begins with the lighter colors and graduates to the deeper ones, then out into the lighter ones again. The warp, a small wool yarn dyed a light tan, contributes to the color harmony, giving the entire textile a kind of bloom and making the North Carolina Blanket a fine example of the use of local dyes. Mrs. Viner has written a useful treatise on vegetable dyes and dyeing based largely upon her own experiments, which is to be published in the near future.

Allanstand Cottage Industries was a pioneer in encouraging the continuation of native dyes among mountain women, especially for coverlets, some of which the workers still color in the old-time way. It was also probably the first to encourage basket makers to use native dyes, the experiment beginning with a worker at Brittain's Cove about 1896, who made a brown dye from chestnut-oak bark with which he colored some of the splits for his melon-shaped basket, resulting in a brown-and-white combination, the first deviation, in the Highlands, it is believed, from the all-white or natural-toned baskets.

The Shuttle-Crafters is a storehouse of information on dyes and herbs and a present-day laboratory of natural color experiments. Mrs. Leah Adams Dougherty is not at this time active in weaving, but she has continued her long interest in the use and lore of natural dyes and herbs, being an authority on those practiced by the Cherokee Indians as well as by the whites of that region. Her daughter, Sarah, also an expert in this field, who directs the work at the Shuttle-Crafters, writes:

Of the list of ten colors I sent you my mother and I dye all here except the indigo, which is dyed by Mrs. Alice Greer, whose large iron pot has contained blue dye yeast for the last ninety years. This is the very same process used in old England called "blue vat" instead of blue-pot dye. Her materials too are the same, indigo, wheat bran, madder root, and wood ash lye. Our formula for madder was one that was used in England in the fifteenth century, according to an old book on dyes. This formula has been handed down in our family. It calls for ash lye, sour bran water, madder root, and alum. The process is different for different shades. My great-grandmother, Nancy Smith Flannery, was a professional indigo dyer and I have her formula for dyeing blue.

At Pi Beta Phi Settlement School are a number of pioneer families who carry on the old mountain customs in dyeing, especially in its application to wool. An authority on vegetable dyes in the district is Aunt Lizzie Regan, now past seventy-five years of age. There is no record that anyone has ever influenced her ideas of color harmony the least bit. Her textiles, in which she now uses some store-bought dyes, are made into handbags, album covers, and sometimes used locally in yard lengths. As a rule her weavings are in plain narrow stripes quite as uniform as though the threads had been counted off. The colors include reds, blues, greens, yellows, browns and blacks.

Pine Mountain Settlement School has from the beginning been a dependable source of information on vegetable dyes, and nowhere have they been more tastefully applied to native blankets. In the region have long lived pioneer families of resourcefulness and skill who have never abandoned the old processes in handicrafts. A Pine Mountain blanket shows a beautiful combination of indigo, madder, and the natural wool in an original pattern designed by Ophia Jackson Holcomb, who made the blanket entirely, from the shearing of the sheep to the finished product.

Hindman Settlement School uses vegetable dyes in coverlets and other weavings when requested, but they have for a long time

A YOUNG POTTER IN THE GEORGIA HIGHLANDS

Nearly All Mountain Pottery Is Formed on the Ancient Kick-Wheel Where the Potter Himself Generates the Power by Pushing with His Foot a Wheel Parallel to the Turning Table

A FAMILY OF MOUNTAIN POTTERS

The Meaders Family, Father and Seven Children, All Work Together in Their Pottery on the Homeplace Near Cleveland, Georgia

given special attention to the use of old home dyes in basket making. No gray can be found that is superior to the "willer ooze" which Aunt Cord Ritchie makes for some of her baskets, or the red-brown color made from the bark of spruce pine (hemlock) used by the neighborhood basket makers. The gray is obtained from the willow by boiling the bark which has been scraped off in preparing the switches. The spruce pine or hemlock dye is made by boiling the inner bark of the tree, and it is equally successful on willow switches and oak splits. When used on oak the alternate splits are dyed before being woven, the finished basket being brown and white.

At Crossnore School part of the weaving is colored with the dyes of commerce and part with dyes made from hickory bark, madder roots, indigo, laurel leaves, maple, sumac, spruce pine, and onion hulls.

One of the most recent and active experimenters with natural dyes is the John C. Campbell Folk School, where much of the wool used in the weaving is colored by the old process. The dyeing at the school has been developed under the direction of Louise Pitman who has applied her dyes in three ways: to the raw wool, to the yarn before it is woven, and to the finished textile.

Too much credit cannot be given those individuals who have painstakingly recorded the old-time methods of coloring fibers and textiles from the natural dye materials abounding in the Highlands. The old-time dyer was not "a writin' woman"—and it takes more than ordinary persistence to get her to clarify her knowledge so that she can set a recipe down on paper. When the writing is done, however, it is often more than mere directions; it is good literature because it is direct, its meaning is unmistakable, it reflects life, and is full of feeling.

Explanations of how to use these natural colors are given below in the words of Mrs. Sally Gayheart of Knott County, Kentucky, who learned what she knows from her grandmother "who was a Salisbury from that absent and faraway country they call England."[1]

Walnut Dye.—You want to git your roots and sprouts. Git 'em on the new moon in June. Skin 'em from the root up. Bile 'em about two or

[1] Hall, Eliza Calvert, A Book of Hand-Woven Coverlets. Little, Brown and Co., Boston, 1931, pp. 146–149.

three hours. Bile just about one ooze. Put your wool in the ooze and bile it. If it haint dark enough, take out and bile more bark and put it in that. A grain of copperas'll make it darker. If you hang it out in the sun, hit'll turn dark.

Green Dye.—Git hickory bark any time. Better git it when the sap's up. That's heap the easiest time. Bile out your ooze, and put in a little alum. Keep bilin' until it gits strong enough. Put in your wool. You kin tell when hit's green enough. (Just here I asked Aunt Sally to make me a pretty green coverlet. She said, "Hit's right smart botherment to put in just one kiverlet.")

Dye for Cotton.—Just take maple and chestnut bark. (How much? I asked.) I never pay no 'tention to how much. I just throw it in until I git enough. Hit'll either be coal black or purple, when you bile it enough.

Purple or Black.—Git maple bark and bile it. Throw in a grain of copperas and put in your wool. Bile it just about so long, if you want purple, and longer if you want black. The longer you bile it the darker it gits.

Green.—Git black jack or black oak and bile it right good, and put in a little piece of alum. This makes the prettiest green, mighty-nigh, that ever was.

Yellow.—Git brown sage (sedge grass), and bile it and put in a little alum. It makes the prettiest yaller that ever was.

HERBS AND THEIR USES

"Herb for the service of man," to use Frances Goodrich's phrase, is still important in the life of the Highland people. Even in some of the towns and cities of the region are specialists who collect, cure, and sell a great variety of herbs. A list of 52 separate herbs was secured one day from the stock of a local dealer in Tennessee. Some served both as medicine and dye, although the vender was interested primarily in their healing properties. They were susceptible of many combinations, and in certain instances a blend of as many as eight or ten was recommended as being especially efficacious. Some of the items from the list were as follows:

Bloodroot, dried from the year before, a good spring medicine. Hit makes blood. The root keeps three or four years in sacks without losing strength. Is also one of the finest dyes. (A year later the writer came across bloodroot being used as a dye by an old chairmaker near Crossville, Tennessee, to make pretty yellow rings on a child's rocking chair.)

Blacksnake root, good stomach medicine.

144

Black gulver root, used for kidney trouble.

Blackberry root, for checking the bowels.

Black haw bark, for fevers and chills.

Boneset, made into a syrup, good for bad colds.

Burdock, excellent "rheumety" medicine.

Brats vane or wintergreen, good for colds, worms in children, stomach medicine, or good in many other ways.

Butterfly root, is a lady's medicine, good for female and kidney trouble.

Burbine, makes tea for children and is generally good for them.

Buckeye, good for "rheumety," or if the nut is carried in the pocket hit brings good luck, and you can make tea out of hit for cramps but don't take too much of hit.

Crabapple bark, good for asthma and wheezing.

Calamas, good for sour and gassy stomach.

Dewberry root, will check the bowels.

Dandelion root, blood tonic.

Devil's shoestring, will scatter pain and for appendicitis make a tea of hit.

Golden seal is a yaller cast flower, use root for stomach, sore eyes, kidney trouble, and tonsilitis.

Heart leaf, good for weak hearted persons and good for the nerves.

Indian turnip, good for asthma and cramps.

Larkspur tincture, for trouble in the hair.

Lady slipper, good for lady troubles, kind of builds them up.

Mullen, makes good cough syrup.

Prickly ash root, good kidney medicine.

Persimmon bark, makes good salve for just anything.

Pennyroyal, good for bed bugs, also for bad colds. For bed bugs prinkle leaves in straw ticks, will run any bed bug out.

Redroot, called coonroot sometimes, shocks the bowels, good for kidney trouble too.

Red pinkroot, good for worms in children.

Rattlesnake root, good for snake bites, eat it straight and chew it quick.

Sweet apple bark, good for asthma or for physic or for wheezing.

Stone root, good for gravel in the kidneys.

Slippery elm, good for sore eyes, drink the water for stomach trouble.

Wild ginger, good for diarrhea, for bilious stomach cramping.

Wild comfort, a manhood medicine.

Witchhazel bark, makes good salve for burns, sores, eczema.

Red oak bark, good sized with witchhazel boiled down with lard or mutton "taller" (the dealer's mother mixed this with fresh churned butter).

Scaly bark hickory, gives special flavor to maple syrup.

Sticks from the red bud (Judas tree) roots, used to rub on and clean the teeth instead of tooth brushes.

Teas for home use brewed from wild cherry, yellow sarsaparilla, pink root, yellow dock, white horse mint, linden bark, wild raspberry leaves, wild tea leaves, sassafras root, and thyme to mention only a few.

Wild thyme used for flavoring sausages and other meats.

Complete as the above list appears for any emergency to which flesh is heir, the herb specialist recorded in Miss Goodrich's volume already referred to, summarizing her knowledge and reducing her remedies to a minimum, has for brevity and inclusion surpassed any list yet discovered. Her prescription reads: "One herb for the head, one for the back, one for the chest, and one for when you don't feel so good." Another collector of herbs has a formula for carrying their benefit beyond the physical realm; "spignet," she is reported as saying, "is good for the back and balm fortifies the morals."

THE DAUGHTER OF A GEORGIA POTTER

THE MOUNTAIN POTTER OFTEN DEPENDS UPON HIS CHILDREN TO HELP WITH
LIGHTER OPERATIONS IN POTTERY MAKING

A POTTER OF DISTINCTION
O. L. Bachelder of Candler, North Carolina, Established the Well-Known
Omar Khayyam Art Pottery. He Died in 1935

CHAPTER IX

FURNITURE AND OTHER WOODWORK

THERE are few handicrafts in the Southern Highlands in which wood does not play a very significant part. The forests are in the midst of the greatest hardwood region in North America, which once extended east to the Atlantic seaboard, west beyond the Mississippi River, north into the Pennsylvania country, and south as far as the northern part of Georgia and Alabama. In addition the region is enriched by many varieties from what the foresters call the Northern Forest; that is, the trees of Pennsylvania, New York, and New Jersey, and even New England, which come through the elevation that makes up the Appalachian range. This elevation carries many of the northern trees through the high sections of the whole chain. These combining forests include both deciduous trees and evergreens; but the hardwoods predominate, and some writers have said that for variety and quality the hardwood forests of the Appalachian range surpass those of any other region in the world.

Among the trees which the United States Forest Service lists as native to the Highlands are the following: white, black, northern red, scarlet burr, chestnut, and chinquapin oaks; shagbark, southern shagbark, mockernut, pignut, butternut, and big-leaf hickories; white, blue, green, and red ashes; American, rock, and slippery elms; red, sugar, and silver maples; beech; yellow poplar (tulip poplar); sycamore; chestnut; black walnut; cottonwood; hackberry; black cherry; basswood; buckeye; northern white and eastern red cedar; post, southern red, blackjack, shumard red, swamp chestnut, and pin oaks; red and black gum; black locust; dogwood; persimmon; willow; osage orange; red, black, and white spruces; southern balsam and balsam fir; white, red (Norway), jack, pitch, short-leaf, and Virginia pines; hemlock (spruce pine); yellow, black, paper, gray, and river birches; large-toothed aspen and aspen; tamarack; and cucumber-magnolia. These are only a few of the better known trees native to the region of which there are said to be at least 157 varieties. The immense significance of such a wealth of trees to the development of handicrafts is obviously clear.

In America we are accustomed to evaluate our forest resources in terms of the amount of timber that can be cut from them, either as logs or as lumber which go to outside points, and unless the quantity looms large we are likely to think of it as of no great value. But when we estimate its use for handicrafts the supply takes on a different meaning. An amount which would not attract lumbermen, who cut in quantity by modern machinery, may be quite ample to use for handicrafts or even small industries for many years, and a much larger return reverts to the community than would come from lumber alone. Such advantages are well set forth in a recent report on the subject.[1]

TREES USED IN WOODWORK

Among the trees of the Highlands most commonly used in furniture and woodwork are oak, ash, hickory, maple, walnut, cherry, linden, sassafras, and pine. Mention of each variety brings to mind some pleasant thoughts connected with the tree, perhaps its beauty as it stands in the forest, a particular quality of its wood, or the recollection of some object formed from it. But to the worker who lives among these trees they signify much more, for in his simple economy each kind fills a special place, and although the catalogue of their services is diminishing, it will aid one's appreciation of the trees of the region to consider the various uses of one of them—the shagbark hickory, for instance.

Several varieties of hickory grow in the Highlands, all nut-bearing trees, the shagbark yielding an especially good nut for human food. The long, straight grain of the wood, common to all varieties, causes it to split readily. Home-made wooden mauls used by timbermen to split logs are usually made from this tree with a handle easily shaped from the straight grain and a tough knot selected for the head. A hickory knot will stand harder usage as a maul than almost any other mountain wood. It also supplies

[1] Manny, T. B., and Nason, Wayne C., Rural Factory Industries. Division of Farm Population and Rural Life, U. S. Bureau of Agricultural Economics, Circular 312, April, 1934. (Mimeographed.)

excellent ax, hammer, and pick handles, and it is used extensively for basket handles and hoops and for splints in basket making. As a firewood it is extraordinary, burning bright and steady to a soft light-gray ash which is good for home-made soap and as an ingredient of vegetable dyes. When a burning log is covered in the fireplace at night it holds the heat and a firm red-hot coal remains to start the morning fire. The bark when burned alone produces a bright, long, fairly steady flame, and pioneer neighbors of the Lincoln family have said that it was the flame from the shagbark hickory more frequently than from the pine knot that Abraham Lincoln used in the fireplace for a light to study by.

Hickory bark smoothed, stripped, and woven into a seat is the best, most durable, and to many the most attractive for a mountain chair or bench. A good craftsman can weave a smooth and attractive table top from hickory bark. Ropes of the twisted bark laced from the sides and ends of the bedstead were used in early days to support the mattress or filled bedtick in the frame. A sturdy broom for stable, for a stone floor, or for scrubbing is sometimes made from hickory, both handle and broom being of one piece. The broom is formed by cutting the shavings from the handle, which remain attached at one end and are folded back and neatly bunched, as illustrated opposite page 98. A part of the inner bark of the hickory is used to make dye for coloring wool. It produces varied shades of yellow, which will color both hickory and oak splints for baskets. A tea brewed from hickory bark furnishes a medicine, and those who have used it in combination with other herbs assert that it is beneficial for several body ailments. Maple syrup is sometimes flavored with hickory bark, and green hickory limbs produce a fragrant smoke for curing ham and bacon, giving a flavor that nothing else can supply.

There are other uses for the wood, bark, roots, nuts, and leaves of hickory which one can learn from the herbals, and some not found in these books may be learned from the nature lore of the Highlander. To these practical attributes should be added the beauty of the tree growing in the woodland. While walking through the forest on a late October day a boy from Pine Mountain Settlement School pointed out to the writer his favorite autumn bouquet. It was a tree with a gray, ragged trunk, dark branches, and a great mass of glowing yellow leaves, standing out on the top of the mountain against the blue sky, a shagbark hickory, a tree which, in addition to its beauty, provides food, lumber, cordage, fiber, fire, light, dye, a flavor for cooking, a preservative for meat, a medicine for the body.

KINDS OF FURNITURE

Furniture made in the Highlands, may be roughly divided, for the purpose of this chapter, into two classes: old mountain furniture and furniture of modern type. The term "old mountain furniture" will comprise those objects made by people of the region largely for their own homes, utilizing the natural properties of the wood, with little in the way of decoration or finish. Furniture of the modern type will include the many objects made by rather modern processes and finished in accordance with the more conventional methods.

Makers of the old type, particularly chairmakers, are to be found in every Highland state and possibly in every mountain county in some of these states. Many live far back among the hills. Modern furniture, on the other hand, is made in fewer places; up-to-date machinery is employed in the preliminary steps, and the finished article bears the mark of intensive and painstaking handwork. There are instances in which both the old mountain type and the modern type are produced at the same place; the Mountaineer Craftsmen's Cooperative Association at Morgantown, West Virginia, is an example. Its work began with patterns of some of the best known chairs of the West Virginia mountains, and these patterns are still made, but in addition its shops, equipped with present-day facilities for joining and finishing, are turning out modern furniture comparable to the best in the region.

Old mountain furniture includes chairs, stools, tables, benches, settees, bedsteads, and a few other articles of which the chair is a typical example and perhaps a symbol. All engaged in work of this type are called "chairmakers," no matter how wide a variety of objects they may make. There are several kinds of mountain chairs: babies' high chairs and children's high chairs, old folks' rockers, and the type of chair that outnumbers all others, the well-known "settin' chair," made with a curved back for general use in a number of sizes and with slight variation in the pattern.

The settin' chair was made in the old days in every part of the mountains and even today is made much more extensively than is probably known. An inquiry in the 235 counties in the region brought the information that chairmaking is carried on in some 200 places where one or more people are working. Since 50 counties did not report and several chairmakers discovered through other means were not included in these returns, it is probably conservative to say that chairs are made in more than 250 places in the Highlands.

MATERIALS IN OLD MOUNTAIN CHAIRS

Chairmakers usually procure their materials from their own wood lots or from nearby woodlands; some buy materials from neighbors. The woods used principally are sugar maple or ash for the posts, hickory for the rounds, and either white oak splints or hickory bark for the seats. A few chairmakers use other woods such as black walnut, white walnut, mulberry, yellow locust (for rounds), poplar, beech, and birch. Where the supply of white oak has been depleted, splints for the seats are imported from other sections. When the chairmaker gathers his own timber it costs nothing; when he buys it the estimates run from about 20 to 25 cents per chair. The price of settin' chairs ranges from about $1.00 to $2.00 each, depending upon the pattern. Some special chairs—rockers and ladderbacks—bring from $3.00 to $6.00, and an especially heavy rocker or one made of selected woods will sometimes bring a much higher price. Children's chairs cost from 50 cents to $1.50.

TOOLS USED IN CHAIR AND FURNITURE MAKING

In chairmaking, a brace and bit, and a pocketknife some craftsmen find ample, but others also use turning lathes of various kinds, drawing knives, planes, spoke shaves, and chisels. The majority of chairmakers use simple equipment, some having no lathe for turning the posts, but those who make a number of chairs usually have some form of lathe or "lay," as it is often called in the Highlands. The lathe is the nearest approach to a machine which the chairmaker has, and probably in no other place in the world can such a variety be found. There are all types from the primitive boom-and-treadle, sometimes called the pole or foot lathe, to an occasional modern, electrically driven lathe. At present several of the old hand-power types are in use; the turner works at the lathe while another, usually a strong boy or girl, turns the big wheel that furnishes power. Illustrations of both the hand-power and the foot-power or the boom-and-treadle lathes are shown on pages 94 and 95. The latter is so ancient that to encounter it in any place much less in America, makes a brief description appropriate.

This old wood-shaping device, instead of turning the piece of timber to be shaped in rapid revolutions as is done on any other lathe so that a continuous shaving can be taken from the wood, is a contrivance in which the strap, rawhide, or rope is fastened to a sapling, or a pole overhead which forms a tension or spring, and is brought down and wound around the piece of wood to be shaped, and extending toward the ground is attached to a board treadle. The turner pushing down on the treadle with his foot turns the strap around the piece of wood and the tension of the spring above his head unwinds the strap rapidly. As it unwinds, the chisel in his hand cuts the revolving wood. The pressure of his foot on the treadle winds up the belt again, and the spring of the lever above unwinds it as he cuts another shaving. A gouge is used to rough out the wood and a straight chisel to finish it. This ancient process soon turns out a well-formed post. A few old workers prefer it to any other kind of lathe. Such simple equipment requires practically no cash outlay either for purchase or for repairs and offers a good example of resourcefulness which a modern turner cannot but admire. Previous to making this study it was freely stated that no example of a boom-and-treadle lathe remained in the mountains, the only clue to it being an old photograph made by Walter Cline, a pioneer photographer of Chattanooga, Tennessee. Seven such lathes, however, have been discovered in the Highlands.

METHOD OF CONSTRUCTING A MOUNTAIN CHAIR

However simple or elaborate equipment may be, the outstanding feature of the work is the method of putting a chair together, without screws, nails, or glue, but by using the natural properties of the wood to hold the frame firm. The posts for the chair frame, commonly maple, or "sugar tree," as the wood is often called, are cut and worked while green, but the rounds or rungs, usually of hickory, are well seasoned. The rounds are also carefully shaped at the ends with a slight bulge in the tenon, so that when they are driven into the holes bored in the posts the greatest pressure will be exerted against the center and not against the edges of the post, which might split. Correct fitting of the joint is very important, calling for both skill and experience. When the hickory rounds are driven properly into the posts and the frame is put together to season, it is a job that will last, for as the green posts shrink over the ends of the already dry hickory rounds, they grip them in a vise which "will hold till the cows come home," as one old chairmaker put it, "and the only way to get 'em out is to break 'em out." This natural holding quality is not exaggerated, and not an uncommon sight in the mountains is a settin' chair which has been sat back on so many times that the ends of the legs have been literally worn off nearly up to the lower back round, but in which the joints have held firm.

These chairs are usually left without finish or decoration, time, exposure, and smoke being the agents which mellow the wood. There is, however, near Crossville, Tennessee, a chairmaker who has retained some of his father's old-time recipes for decorating chairs. His favorite color is orange made from "coon root," an abbreviation for puccoon, the Indian name for bloodroot. This is especially attractive on light wood. He also uses a more reddish-yellow stain which he calls hemlock, probably made from the bark of the well-known hemlock tree. These colors are applied in bands or rings on children's chairs.

The method described above as used in making a settin' chair is employed for stools, high chairs, rockers (both for children and for adults), benches, settees, and tables. An interesting variation of materials in some of the rocking chairs is that of using walnut for the rockers, "so the chair won't creep." Either maple or hickory gets smooth from rocking and slides about, but there is a quality in walnut that causes it to cling to the floor, usually made of boards. The chair will stay in place no matter how vigorous the rocking.

The settin' chair illustrated opposite page 197 is of maple and hickory with hickory-bark seat. The posts are made on a hand-made lathe run by boy power and the rungs are shaped with a drawing knife. The rear posts which extend above the seat as part of the framework for the back are made pliable by wetting or steaming, and then bent or bowed in a home-made wooden vise. The bending and shaping of the cross-slats to fit the back of the individual, which add greatly to comfort, are also done in a crude wooden vise.

Chairs are usually made in an open shop or shed with a roof to keep out the rain or sun, and in the winter the work is sometimes transferred to the house. One of these primitive outdoor shops without lathe equipment will always be remembered by the writer for its picturesqueness. It was discovered one autumn in a little clearing in the woods of North Carolina with all the materials needed for chairmaking growing close by. In the open space was the drawing horse, a frame contrivance consisting of a long, light log held up at one end by two round stakes spraddled out, and a home-made vise arrangement in which the chairmaker could, by pressing down with his foot, hold the piece of wood in place while he shaped it with his drawing knife. Such a drawing horse is illustrated opposite page 92. Sitting on an old chair he put the frame and rungs together and laced in the substantial seat with oak splints made on the spot. This simply furnished workshop was interesting, but it was the setting of natural beauty which marked it apart. All about the 20-foot circle had fallen brilliant autumn leaves, a few still tumbling down, of that variety of every shade of yellow, brown, and red which only the Appalachian Mountains yield, with the green grass underneath showing through. Around the edges of this golden carpet was a natural border of wild blue gentians in full bloom.

LIFE OF A MOUNTAIN CHAIR

The length of service of mountain chairs varies, it would often seem, with the opinion of the informant. Some declare that they will last a lifetime, some a hundred years, and others say forever. There seems to be evidence to support all claims unless it be the "forever" one, and if that is freely interpreted to imply "as long as a man lasts," that claim could likely be supported too.

A ONE-MAN TANNING WORKS

Covey Odom of Luther, Hamblen County, Tennessee, Makes Excellent Leather by Using the Native Tanning Materials and Old-Time Methods Once Common throughout America

A CRAFTSWOMAN OF GREAT VERSATILITY

MRS. ROSALIE PLESS OF RUSSELLVILLE, TENNESSEE, WHO SPINS, WEAVES, MAKES BASKETS, AND OTHER OBJECTS, IS VERY SKILFUL WITH CORN-HUSK FIGURES

In an old home not far from White Top, Virginia, several chairs known to have been made on the place thirty-seven years ago are in prime condition, only the bottoms of oak splints having been replaced. Bud Godlove of Wardensville, Hardy County, West Virginia, one of the best known mountain craftsmen, whose father and grandfather were chairmakers before him, says his family every day use chairs made over fifty years ago. Edward Loudermilk of Caldwell, Greenbrier County, West Virginia, writes:

I make the life-time split bottom chairs. I use white tough hickory, fire dried rounds, posts of young growth tough white oak. . . . My father taught me to make chairs when I was a boy. I have been making chairs for forty some years. . . . When a man buys chairs from me he gets what he needs and he is done buying chairs as long as he lives. . . . Nothing cross grain.

Mrs. Mabel Brooks of Mannington, Marion County, West Virginia, has two mountain chairs of hickory over one hundred years old which were owned by Dr. Amos Brooks of French Creek, Upshur County, West Virginia, in 1830. At his death in 1855 they were purchased by J. E. Vance, who had a family of 10 children. They are in daily use and are as strong today as when made. They were recently rebottomed in split oak. Photographs of these chairs were made and sent in by A. B. Brooks, naturalist at Oglebay Park, Wheeling, West Virginia. There are two mountain chairs in use at Hindman Settlement School which the donor, a pioneer mountaineer, said were "over a hundred years old" when he gave them to the school over thirty years ago. Mrs. Gordon Boggs of Franklin, West Virginia, owns a chair which is said to have been made in 1781. This is the oldest chair of which we have found record and it is still in use.

"We have nothing in our modest home with more character than our settin' chairs from Kentucky," writes one from outside the mountains. "They are small, but not too small; strong, but not clumsy; light and easily moved around; and above all comfortable for man and beast. Even the cats and our little dog prefer them to the other chairs, perhaps because they are usually to be found before the fireplace."

CHAIRMAKING AS A CRAFT

Chairmaking is rarely a full-time job, most who carry it on being farmers who fill in between the seasons of outdoor work. Often a chairmaker is also a basket maker, and since the same or similar materials are used in each the combination works well. Although supplementary to farming, chairmaking is oftentimes the main source and sometimes the only source of cash income.

Many chairmakers have learned the work from their parents and the craft has been practiced in some families for generations. It is true that a number in the Highlands do rough and sometimes careless work, using nails and short cuts in an effort at cheapness, but usually those who carry on chairmaking as a family tradition take pride in their work.

In the mountains of North Carolina are descendants of craftsmen who came from Buckinghamshire, England. At Zebulon, North Carolina, which is outside the area of this study, it is claimed that chairmaking has continued without a break since about 1750, when a group from Buckinghamshire settled in that part of the country. One turner at least at Zebulon uses the old boom-and-treadle lathe which was common in England in the seventeenth and eighteenth centuries.

Ralph C. Erskine of Tryon, North Carolina, writes about the work of Jim Gosnell, believed to have descended from an English group of chairmakers who worked about twenty-five years ago in the neighborhood of Tryon. He used what he called a "measuring stick" upon which he laid out his chair pattern. He could neither read nor write nor did he use figures, but by marks or notches on the stick he was able to register the lengths for the posts, rungs, the size of the seat, and all other dimensions needed for the complete design, and he made chairs accurately from these marks on a single stick.

MARKETING THE CHAIRS

The making of a mountain chair, to anyone interested in woodworking, is fascinating at every stage, but no operation is more picturesque than some of the means employed in getting the chairs to market. In these days of course many of them can be carried out of the mountains by truck, automobile, and wagon, but others must still be brought from remote places by manback, muleback, and sled. The sled, made entirely of wood, is an invaluable home-made vehicle, which can be pulled over trails not open to wagon or cart even if such luxury of transportation were available. The sleds loaded with chairs, and sometimes baskets, too, for they ride well together, tied on with twisted bark or ropes are pulled and pushed up and down the mountain paths to a main road and then to store or settlement. One of the most spectacular and surprising sights is to meet a mule coming around a mountain trail with chairs piled high on his back and his sides bulging with them, some-times as many as two or three dozen, all of which he has carried from some distant cabin. Nor is it unusual to see the maker him-self trudging along a path with four to six chairs balanced on his back, the load to be lightened as he is able to sell or trade one or more along the way.

Mountain methods of transportation in pioneer days were often very ingenious. D. F. Folger of Crossville, Tennessee, gives an account of the way his family marketed tobacco grown in the moun-tains of South Carolina more than a hundred miles from Augusta, Georgia, the tobacco center. They constructed a hogshead with a pole through the middle fastened at each end. This formed a hub for the hogshead which thus became a broad wheel five or six feet wide. It was then filled with tobacco, and an ox or a pair of oxen rolled it up and down the mountains until it reached its destina-tion. Trips of from 50 to 150 miles and more were made annually by this mode of transportation.

INDIVIDUAL CHAIRMAKERS

One of the most interesting, enlightening and altogether pleasant features of this study has been the correspondence with many re-motely situated chairmakers throughout the region. Replies came promptly from almost all to whom letters were addressed, although in some instances it was necessary to have other persons write the letters for them. It is not possible in the compass of this report to include a reference to all these chairmakers, but a few are men-tioned and brief quotations given from the letters of others. They contain information about old mountain furniture and its making not heretofore available and they cover a wide area of the region of this study. Chairmaking is still a very important occupation in the economy and life of the Highlands.

There is probably no better known chairmaker in all the Highlands than Bud Godlove, already referred to, especially known for his work in connection with the handicrafts and small industries established in the coal-mining region at Morgantown, West Virginia, by the American Friends Service Committee. When the Committee undertook to provide work for the impoverished miners they chose Mr. Godlove to teach them how to make the old Godlove chairs. He went with them into the woods to cut the logs and split them into quarters, and later in a small improvised shop, with a second-hand heating stove for curing the rounds before driving them into the posts, he taught them all the tricks about putting the chairs together. From the patterns he left them this group, now known as the Mountaineer Craftsmen's Cooperative Association, continues to turn out the Godlove chair after the best mountain traditions.

W. N. Stacy of Hindman, Kentucky, makes a variety of mountain chairs, particularly a good substantial settin' chair, using maple posts, hickory rounds, with a durable seat of hickory bark. Mary Ownby, who lives in the Glades near Gatlinburg, Tennessee, one of the few women chairmakers, turns the posts of her chairs on an ancient boom-and-treadle "lay." She prefers it to the new high-speed lathes because she says she can control it better. She writes:

I use maple, cherry, walnut, hickory. I get my timber in the woods, just cut the trees and split my timber out. I do not use glue or nails, rather they are driven together to stay without them. I use a foot lay, run it with my foot, use brace, bits, drawing knife, hand saw, chisel, pocket knife, and axe. I make the chisels. I have made chairs with a pocket knife. My father taught me to make chairs and I have been making them for twenty years.

Henderson Mullins, who lives on Bear Fork, Puncheon Camp Creek, Knott County, Kentucky, also uses the boom-and-treadle lathe. He is past seventy and nearly blind, but he gets out the legs of the chairs and his son joins them together.

Elmer D. Frost of Town Creek, Lawrence County, Alabama, makes all his tools used in chairmaking. Ambrose Sizemore, Erose, Knox County, Kentucky, writes: "We have our own timber, it

MAKING A HOOKED RUG

Mrs. Anderson and Her Son of Saluda, North Carolina. Both the Sliding and the Stationary Hook, the Latter Often Home Made, Are Used in the Mountains

BORING OUT MOUNTAIN RIFLE BARRELS

MARY OWNBY, AN EXCELLENT CRAFTSWOMAN, WHO LIVES IN THE GLADES NEAR GATLIN-
BURG, TENNESSEE, LEARNED FROM HER FATHER HOW TO MAKE AND USE THE BORING
MACHINE FOR CONDITIONING THE BARRELS OF MOUNTAIN RIFLES

groweth here. . . . I sell my chairs right here. . . . We make any size you want . . . good size rocking chair, lace back with hickory bark . . . small rocker for children." Mrs. Theo Begley of Pine Mountain makes chairs in black and white walnut with a pocketknife. John Clinton Cantrell, near Wheelersburg, Magoffin County, Kentucky, writes: "My occupation is mostly farming. I just make chairs a little in the winter time. I haven't much of an outfit. Just a hayrake wheel with an iron crank in it run with a foot treadle. I learned to make chairs when I was a boy." Bird Owsley, Vest, Knott County, Kentucky, makes chairs, baskets, and walking canes. W. T. Pennington, Causey, Leslie County, Kentucky, uses foot power to make his chairs and hauls them to market on a sled.

E. E. Lackey, Hiddenite, Alexander County, North Carolina, writes: "We still have yet in these mountains of North Carolina several old-time chairmakers who use the hand lathe and drawing knife. Some of them have a little overshot water wheel on a tiny stream to pull their lathe which is very crude."

W. R. Crump, Gragg, Avery County, North Carolina, writes:

My grandfather on my mother's side was a chairmaker. When I got big enough to run around the house he had a lathe at the back end of the house under a shed, he tramped with his foot to do his turning with. My father took the chairmaking up and he made chairs with a pocketknife and a drawing knife for several years. Then he put him up a little lathe and went to turning chair posts and run it by foot power. Then I started out making chairs and put up a small water power and have been going ever since.

Charles J. Dobbins, Patterson, Caldwell County, North Carolina, reports: "I have a small mountain shoppe . . . where my boy and myself make chairs, baskets, candleholders . . . in all the depression we have not been out of a job."

Arthur A. Woody, Spruce Pine, Mitchell County, North Carolina, writes: "My father made old style chairs when I was a small boy. He also made spinning wheels, wagons, beds, tables, etc. My first chair was made with a knife and auger . . . we don't make them very fast as we do it by hand. I am now too old to work much, my son mostly runs the shop."

Leander O. Winkler, Shulls Mills, Watauga County, North Carolina, writes:

I turn a little groove in the end of everyone (rung) where they are set in the post and drive them in the post tight before the post is seasoned much, then the post shrinks to them. I flatten two sides of the rounds a little where they are set in the post, so they press more against the ends of the timber than the sides; this prevents it from splitting when you drive them in hard.

Solomon W. Odom, Shell Creek, Carter County, Tennessee, who has been making chairs for twenty years, says that eleven rounds are required to make a sturdy chair, and the back should be curved for comfort. He thinks that with reasonable care mountain chairs will give twenty-five years of satisfaction without any repairs except bottoms; with rebottoming they ought to last seventy-five years.

Ebb Bowman, Greeneville, Greene County, Tennessee, writes: "My rounds are fire dried driven in green posts. They last from now on. Everything about them is split out with the grain of the wood and straightened with a hand axe, nothing sawed out. When one is made better it has got to be made out of something stronger than wood."

Ernest Woods, Newcastle, Craig County, Virginia, says low, swampy land is best for white oak splits for chair bottoms. Joe Stewart, Blackwater, Lee County, Virginia, writes that in addition to chairs he makes plow stocks, cedar pails, and baskets, and that his father made old-fashioned looms, reels, and big spinning wheels. He describes his lathe as follows:

I have a wooden lathe with a spring on each end. It has a small lever. I put a rope to that and tie that rope to a plank to put my foot on, wrap the rope around my chair post, chisel in my hand. I can chisel them out any way I want to. I put my bottoms in of oak splits or hickory bark about three-quarters of an inch wide. Will last anyone forty or fifty years of use.

F. R. Foster, Luray, Page County, Virginia, writes that he makes hand-plaited corn-husk and imitation rush seats. He advocates 10 rounds in a chair and says that the chairs he made twenty years ago are still tight. Frank A. Cain, Glenville, Gilmer County, West

Virginia, gives a full list of the tools he has made, including a froe, mallet, lathe, boring machine, gouges, and chisels. Charles Fulwider, Caldwell, Greenbrier County, West Virginia, prefers white oak but has used white ash and some "sugar tree" for posts. He writes: "I have some chairs my father made which I have used for twenty-three years and they are as strong as they were when made."

Patrick G. Burns, White Sulphur Springs, Greenbrier County, West Virginia, writes:

I have my posts two-thirds seasoned when I set up a chair. The backs and rungs are completely seasoned. I use a machine for boring. Yes, I have made a few chairs with a pocketknife years ago before I learned about the lathe. . . . I have made a few black walnut chairs, but the mountain ash for frames and white oak splits for bottoms give the most satisfaction for the least amount of money.

It is probably true that most of these isolated craftsmen, without investment in machinery and overhead expense, can still make chairs and sell them at a price lower than factory-made chairs. Partly because of this fact mountain-made chairs are still much used in mountain homes. They are also usually preferred to many of the "fotched on" variety because they are more comfortable to sit on and are also more sturdy.

MODERN FURNITURE MADE IN THE MOUNTAINS

Much of the Highland furniture of modern type is made in schools and centers scattered throughout the region and in the several woodworking shops that one finds usually near a handicraft or tourist center. The designs in modern furniture are frequently original, but more often they are exact copies or adaptations of early American or unusual pieces that have been found back in the mountains.

Wood Craft, the woodworking shop of Berea College Student Industries, produces some of the finest modern furniture in the region. J. Edward Davis, director of Wood Craft, has made special searches in the mountains for exceptional designs in bedsteads, chairs, and other objects, and has preserved in the form of well-made furniture many old pieces from Highland homes. The students have formed a Woodworkers Guild through which they study the various woods of the region and carry out special projects. The home of President William J. Hutchins is furnished throughout with pieces constructed by them.

The Woodcrafters and Carvers of Gatlinburg are a group of craftsmen working with unusual care and skill at reproductions as well as in new designs. Under the direction of O. J. Mattil, who has also searched in remote mountain places for old designs, many reproductions of these early pieces as well as modern adaptations are executed with great care and finished with taste and artistry. They also reproduce furniture in miniature.

Among the schools deserving mention for the quality of furniture made in their shops is the Pine Mountain Settlement School. Because of lack of roads it was not possible until recently to bring into this settlement any large pieces of furniture. A woodworking department was developed in the School and most of the furniture now used was made there. One of the finest desks in the Southern Highlands was constructed by students for the office of the director of the School; and the beautiful chapel, a memorial to Charlotte F. Hedges, was furnished entirely by student work.

Probably no body of workers has developed more rapidly in a short time than the Mountaineer Craftsmen's Cooperative Association started by the American Friends Service Committee, mentioned earlier in this chapter. Their pieces have been widely distributed, many of them having gone into the furnishings of the Reedsville Experimental Community in West Virginia. In addition to the wood carvings and toys referred to in a subsequent chapter, the Tryon Toy-Makers and Wood-Carvers have attained high rank in the production of tables and benches made of native walnut slabs with original designs of rare beauty. The workers understand thoroughly the cutting and curing of this wood, which grows abundantly in the Highlands, as well as the principles of constructing it into furniture of fine craftsmanship. The Artisan Shop at Biltmore Forest, Asheville, North Carolina, makes small pieces of excellent furniture under the direction of George G. Arthur, one of the mountain boys trained at the Tryon Toy-Makers and Wood-Carvers school. The furniture turned out by the Shenandoah Community Workers at Bird Haven, Virginia, is done entirely by native men and boys who perform all the proc-

A RURAL COMMUNITY MUSEUM

THIS END OF THE NEIGHBORHOOD MUSEUM AT THE JOHN C. CAMPBELL FOLK SCHOOL IS
A GOOD EXAMPLE OF A WOOD AND CLAY CHIMNEY

A MOUNTAIN MAN AND HIS JENNIES

FRANK HENDERSON OF BRASSTOWN, CHEROKEE COUNTY, NORTH CAROLINA, MAKES HIS OWN HARNESS AND OTHER CONTRAPTIONS FOR HIS MULE EQUIPMENT. HE IS A GREAT STORY TELLER AND IS KNOWN LOCALLY AS THE JENNY MAN

esses of manufacture from the cutting of the lumber from the logs to crating and shipping the finished article. The primary purpose of this organization is to provide work for mountain people in a region known as Happy Valley.

Throughout the Highlands are many men and boys who carry on excellent work in furniture building, repairing, and restoring. A few are mentioned to suggest the wide distribution of workers and the variety of things produced. Two craftsmen, J. R. Nance and John Lucas, encouraged by Rev. Edward W. Hughes of the Associate Missions of Southwest Virginia, have supplied the local market and have shipped to points outside the mountains. In Elkins, West Virginia, F. C. Williams utilizes native woods, especially walnut, in the making of chairs and tables for local use and in repairing old furniture. At Blowing Rock, North Carolina, C. W. Moody has had a shop for several years where he makes furniture largely to supply the tourist market in that section. At Wooton, Kentucky, Frank Gayhart operates a mill and also makes furniture, and here one may see all the processes from the sawing of the log to the finished product. He also makes most of the tools he uses in his mill and his one-man factory. In northern Georgia a number of cabinetmakers and woodworkers do a great deal of repairing and restoring for that portion of the Highlands.

OTHER USES OF WOOD

There are innumerable objects other than furniture made from the abundant woods of the Highlands. For many of these almost any wood will suffice, but for others special wood is particularly suitable. Bowls for fruit, nuts, candy, and other purposes are made of walnut, maple, cherry, or cedar. Boxes are made of the same woods and also of holly, a close-grained evergreen, a very white wood which is also excellent for turning or carving candlesticks and lamp bases. The small trunks of the sourwood tree, twisted by the honeysuckle vine, have been used attractively for lamp and candle bases. Bag tops are usually made of walnut, cherry, or holly, while the animals, birds, and other carved figures are made from apple and other close-grained woods. Ax, hammer, and pick handles are made from ash, hickory, and maple; bobbins are made from any of the hardwoods, but dogwood and persimmon are especially good. The Cherokee Indians make blow-guns from the native cane, a member of the bamboo family. The spoons, canes, forks, napkin rings made by Standing Deer of the Cherokee Reservation are carved of mountain laurel.

Tom Mann of Bear Wallow, North Carolina, makes trays, bowls, and other receptacles from a variety of native woods glued together in small squares or diamonds, the several shades of the wood emphasizing the variety of the forest resources of that section. A large map of West Virginia has been made by a native of that state who has used a different West Virginia wood for inlaying each of the 55 counties. Picturesque wooden pumps may be seen in the country about Madison, Virginia, and all the way up the valley to Oldrag. These are made by a Negro, Beedle Row, who cuts the pine trees in the woods, hollows out the logs, and puts the parts together in a very practical and attractive way. A somewhat new experiment in wood has developed in several centers in the whittling out of quite delightful small animals, birds, and other figures with a pocketknife or a carving chisel. This will be described in some detail in Chapter XI, Whittling and Carving in Wood.

There are any number of wood utilities which the Highlander knows and practices in his own daily life that do not present themselves in those objects which he makes for sale. One of these is mentioned here because of its unusual interest and because it has not been found anywhere else. A traveler reports a recent experience as follows:

One evening as I entered the home of a pioneer family in the mountains of North Carolina, not far from the Georgia line, I was impressed by a beautiful pile of fine shavings on the floor of the living room near the fireplace. My first thought was that they had been used in shipping some object from a mail order house. But I could not recall ever having seen packing material as fresh looking as these shavings were.

Upon inquiry the grandmother who was sitting by the fireplace said, "This is my feather bed," and picking up from the hearth a witchhazel limb perhaps three inches through and twenty inches long she proceeded to peel off with her pocket knife the fine curly shavings, which when she had a sufficient quantity would be put into a bedtick for filling.

I had been familiar with corn husks, wheat straw, and some other materials used in country districts, but never before had I seen anyone make a mattress of wood shavings. She assured me that they were quite preferable to any other filling of which she knew, having unusual resiliency and lasting for a long time. It has been a practice in their household for many years. I had the opportunity that night to test out the good qualities of a witchhazel shaving mattress and discovered it excellent. She thought that this custom was practiced by many mountain people, but I have made wide inquiries and have never been able to find anyone who had used or had known of others using witchhazel shavings in this way.

The visitor to the more remote sections of the Highlands is continually surprised by examples of ingenuity in the use of natural resources, especially the woods, to meet daily needs.

CHAPTER X

MOUNTAIN BASKETS

IN NO part of America can one find such a wide and interesting variety of good home-made baskets as in the handicraft centers, village shops, and mountain cabins along the winding highways of the Southern Highlands. This is due largely to the fact that baskets have always been an important part of the home equipment of the people, and during the long period of isolation many practical and satisfying forms were worked out of materials near at hand. The best of these have been continued to this day and many new designs which have come in from outside through the handicraft revival have been added, and still others have been invented within the region. All the old and most of the new types have been made possible through an abundance of good material growing wild throughout the area.

Basketry, which is almost a universal craft, is probably the oldest of the handicrafts, although archaeologists are divided on the relative antiquity of basket making and pottery making. The oldest examples of these crafts to which approximate dates can be fixed are pottery fragments; but baskets have always been made of vegetable fibers and subject to decay. Evidence furnished by surviving examples is not therefore conclusive proof of the relative antiquity of the two crafts. Primitive weaving, or the intertwining of branches and stems of plants, was a much simpler and more direct process than making pottery, which required forming, drying, and firing. Basketry in some of its crudest forms undoubtedly came as soon as man laced together a few twigs or limbs for a carrier, or fashioned a framework of branches or saplings for a shelter. In many parts of the earth and at about the same time, although quite independently, it has reached very high development. Ethnologists have observed that frequently its best expression has been attained by primitive people, and there is general agreement that the American Indian has created the finest baskets in history.

The extent to which Indian culture may have influenced the later settlers in the mountains has not been determined, nor have any of the baskets of that region been traced to their original sources. Some of the patterns are undoubtedly indigenous; others correspond to types belonging to countries to which the Highlanders seem to have had no relation.

One of these puzzling coincidences is furnished by the illustration opposite page 206 which old-timers call a "bread raisin' basket," that is, one in which the dough was placed, wrapped in a coverlet or blanket, and set in a corner by the fireplace to warm and rise. A basket recently recovered from an old house in Virginia is filled between the coils by what is unmistakably dried dough. Such baskets were used in Pennsylvania and are to be found in old collections in New England. But the point to be made here is that baskets of similar design and of similar material and construction were placed in the tombs of Egypt three and four thousand years ago. This coincidence is probably not due to any relation between ancient Egypt and America, but to the fact that similar plants grow in each country and in forming baskets from these plants shapes resembling each other have naturally been developed.

Basket making represents an ideal home craft which can be carried on with the simple implements found in the average mountain household; it has survived because of the extent to which baskets are employed there in the absence of the numerous containers found outside this section. They are used for gathering, measuring, storing, and carrying or "toting," as the Highlander often puts it; and because of profuse wood and plant resources and the development of skill, they can be produced at less cost than any other container. Stores and other trading places, where the mountaineer goes for family supplies, have accepted baskets in trade, and in certain localities in the old days they seem to have been almost legal tender. Often today one may see in country stores hanging from the ceiling, on the shelves, or piled about the floor, baskets of assorted types and sizes for sale made by local craftsmen.

The satisfactory quality of many of the hand-made baskets is due to the primary fact that the entire process is controlled by one individual throughout. The experienced basket maker knows where to find the tree and when the rising of the sap makes the time right to assure the best quality of strips and thongs to which he must reduce it; he has learned how to quarter the wood and subdivide the quarters to break right with the grain, and with simple tools to work it into narrow, pliable but durable strips. These, by methods as old as history, he bends and weaves into shape, and with notches, splices, pegs, and thongs produces a basket that will hold together for years of hard use. This intimate association endows the maker with a feeling for quality and a pride of workmanship not experienced by one who does only a small part of the entire process.

MATERIALS AND DYEING

Among the materials from which baskets are made are broom sedge, corn husks, corn stalks, wheat and rye straw, oziers (willows), both branch and twigs, rushes, cane, honeysuckle vine, inner bark of pine, hickory bark, peeled willow bark, pine needles, and oftenest of all splints of oak, hickory, and ash. All these grow throughout the Highlands except the long-leaf pine needles, which usually come from the lower lands of North Carolina, Georgia, and Alabama. In a few instances baskets are made of raffia and reed, articles of commerce imported from other countries. White oak or basket oak, as it is commonly known in the mountains, and hickory are the materials generally used in baskets made of splints.

Mountain baskets classified by the materials going into them may conveniently fall into two groups. One includes those constructed of material which undergoes little or no change of form in preparing it for use, such as willow switches, honeysuckle vine, sedge grass, pine needles, and certain other growths. The other group comprises baskets made of material that requires considerable treatment, such as the splitting and shaping of hickory, oak, and other wood before the strips are in condition for weaving. The baskets most characteristic of the mountains are of the latter class. They are produced in great numbers, the ratio being perhaps six of the splint, or prepared wood variety, to one of the other kind.

The old baskets of the mountains were scarcely ever dyed, but woven and left in the natural color to season and mature. The practice of dyeing came with the revival of handicrafts, the first experiments having been made at Allanstand in the early years of this century, when some of the vegetable dyes used by the textile weavers were tried out on the oak splints with such satisfactory results that Allanstand Cottage Industries now at Asheville has continued to produce baskets of dyed materials. In time similar experiments were conducted in other places. Now many baskets are colored either by treating the material before it is woven, in which a part is colored while the remainder is left natural, or by dyeing the basket one solid color. This latter result may be accomplished by dyeing all the material before it is woven, or by applying the dye to the finished article with a brush or by dipping it in the dye bath. Both vegetable and commercial dyes are used but generally the former, which are sometimes extracted from the wood of which the basket is woven.

NAMES AND TYPES OF MOUNTAIN BASKETS

Names of mountain baskets are derived in most instances from their shape or their use. Among names designating shape are: round, flat, square, triangular, cylindrical, oval, oblong, melon or hip, boat, and jug. Among names designating use are: egg basket, measuring, tea, trinket, clover seed, charcoal, lady basket, market basket, wall, work, flower, fruit, and lunch baskets. New types are named in conformity with the purpose they serve, such as automobile, bassinet, book holder, bobbin holder, hampers, favor, plant, garden, knitting, needlework, letter holder, magazine, nut, picnic, arrow quiver or carrier, spindle holder, sandwich, shopping, storage, wall pocket, waste basket, and so forth.

Sometimes a basket will bear the name of the family making it. An abstract from an interesting article on the subject written by a teacher of domestic arts at Berea College reads:

The Rector basket is a round one woven of round splints. The Purvis basket is of flat splints and is melon-shaped. The Moore basket has been made in the family for at least three generations. It is also a melon-shaped basket but is made of round splints. The splints are of "basket oak," a variety of white oak. . . . No better farm baskets were ever made than are these same melon-shaped mountain baskets, balancing as they do on the hip, or across the neck of a horse in front of the rider. It is the boast of some of the most skilful old basket-makers that their baskets will hold water, and it is an actual fact that they are sometimes so closely woven that meal can be carried in them.[1]

A Tennessee basket that still retains the name of its inventor is the Aunt Lydia basket, which originated with Mrs. Lydia Whaley of Gatlinburg many years ago. Mrs. Whaley is perhaps the best remembered of the pioneers of Gatlinburg. Her basket, which is one of the handsomest in the mountains, is round and made of strips of willow bark worked over unpeeled, smooth willow with a handle of a larger switch. It is noted for its exceptional design and the soft reddish-brown color of the inside bark of the willow splint. None of its kind has been found elsewhere. The harmony between the bowl of the basket and the handle is not accidental, but is a consistent working out of bark and branch in combination.

Mrs. J. V. Huskey, a daughter of Mrs. Whaley, living at Seymour, Tennessee, the successor to her art, is the only person now making Aunt Lydia baskets. She describes the process as follows:

The bark is gathered in the summer when there is a nice smooth sap on it. It is skinned from the willow tree, the hard outside part of the bark is removed before it is left to dry. When dry the rough side is smoothed with a knife—the side which is seen on the inside of the basket—and the bark is then cut in splits and woven into the basket.

The Kentucky egg basket is one of the oldest designs in the Highlands and one of the most attractive as well as useful. It was devised to carry eggs and other articles on horseback, or more often on muleback, and no basket could be more convenient for the purpose, the long, flat side fitting snugly against the animal's body. The shape, larger at the bottom and sloping toward the top, was designed to hold the eggs in place, and there is a legend that in the early days this basket was made in standard sizes to hold even dozens of eggs, making counting unnecessary, as filling the basket performed this service. In the vicinity of Pine Mountain Settlement School it is made today in several attractive colors—browns

---

[1] Hill, Jennie Lester, Fireside Industries in the Kentucky Mountains. *In the* Southern Workman, April, 1903, p. 212.

PIONEER CABIN OF WILLIAM AND AUNT SAL CREECH
THIS LOG HOUSE BUILT BY UNCLE WILLIAM, WHO GAVE THE LAND FOR THE PINE MOUN-
TAIN SETTLEMENT SCHOOL, IS NOW A LOCAL MUSEUM

A MOUNTAIN BLACKSMITH TURNED CRAFTSMAN
CHARLES WESLEY ALLEN OF BEREA, KENTUCKY, ONCE A BLACKSMITH, IS PROBABLY THE
OLDEST ORNAMENTAL IRON WORKER IN THE HIGHLANDS

blacks, yellows, and tans—all dyes from native trees and shrubs. Because of its shape it is sometimes also known as the jug basket. The best type of Kentucky egg basket is made of hickory ribs and handle with split oak cross-pieces. The one illustrated opposite page 325 is of this material, an excellent example of design and craftsmanship.

Other baskets notable for originality of design have no names at all. For instance, the round bowl-like willow basket with three spiral handles which Aunt Cord Ritchie, who lives across the mountain a few miles from Hindman Settlement School, "just made up," has a classic form combined with good color from a natural dye which she also "made up." Mrs. Ritchie is one of the best basket makers in the Highlands. She uses willow, oak splints, hickory splints, and other materials, but willow is her favorite. Feeling for her material marks her as a true craftsman. She once said that she could not live where willows did not grow. The "willer ooze" with which she dyes the peeled switches is made by boiling down the bark of the tree, which produces a beautiful gray tone not seen in any other basket. An almost equally beautiful brown dye is made by peeling the bark from spruce pine (hemlock) and boiling it until it is red, and after straining, adding soda. The basket is then dipped into this solution until it acquires a dark-brown color. Both the gray and the brown hues are very lasting. Although the three-handled basket is perhaps her outstanding creation, her favorite is a golden willow flower basket. This is a native yellow variety which she weaves without stripping the bark. After a time the golden yellow turns to brown, but the loss in color is partly compensated on foggy and rainy days when the moisture-laden air brings out a delightfully pungent fragrance from this favorite basket.

Aunt Cord is self-taught. Years ago she examined a basket which someone had brought from "over the mountains," took it apart, experimented with local materials, and worked out a method of constructing similar baskets and also created new designs. It is said that she taught all the willow basket weavers in Knott County. A portrait of her appears opposite page 111.

Hindman Settlement School is deservedly famous for its baskets, having encouraged this craft through all the years of its existence. Their baskets, some of which are shown in the illustration opposite page 207, are woven and dyed with great care. In a report on the handicrafts in Knott County[1] appears the merited statement that no center has done more to raise and keep high the standards of mountain basketry.

Among the excellent makers in the vicinity of Hindman, mention should also be made of Bird Owsley of Vest, Kentucky, who has been deaf from birth and who has made baskets for thirty-five years chiefly out of split oak. Mr. Owsley takes special pains with his splints, sandpapering them and then dyeing some with extract from walnut bark, others from spruce pine bark. He uses an old melon-shaped mountain design, but has modified it somewhat with original touches which give the baskets a distinctive appearance. He also makes good mountain chairs.

Pine Mountain Settlement School is another center near which some of the old-time baskets are made and, as at Hindman, natural dyes are used for coloring. Most outstanding of them, perhaps, is the Kentucky egg basket already referred to.

Jean Thomas of Ashland, Boyd County, Kentucky, owns a basket of a type once common in parts of Kentucky. It was used extensively for carrying charcoal atop the head when charcoal was used to make iron in that part of the country. Browned by use and age, it was accepted as payment for medical service rendered to a mountaineer by an old physician who gave it to Miss Thomas for the collection of old-time articles she has assembled in her cabin home.

The baskets of Mrs. Nannie B. Sego, living near Macon, Hart County, Kentucky, sold through Berea College Fireside Industries, are extraordinary combinations of delicacy and strength. They are made of oak, which is first split from the tree with an ax, cut with a pocketknife, and then made finer with a pair of scissors. The basket illustrated on page 209 is one recently made of fresh white oak. The handle is constructed of heavier material, but, desiring to have the several parts harmonize, she has woven over the heavy handle a simple braided design of fine splints. Mrs. Sego learned basketry from her father. She makes many shapes but

[1] Nason, Wayne C., Rural Industries in Knott County, Kentucky. U. S. Department of Agriculture, Bureau of Agricultural Economics, in Co-operation with Kentucky Agricultural Experiment Station, Washington, December, 1932. (Mimeographed.)

likes best a square-top one with round bottom which she says is very hard to make.

In the neighborhood of Oldrag, Virginia, can be seen types of interesting and very practical mountain baskets that have been used in that part of the country for several generations. One of the best of these the writer discovered in the village store at Syria, Madison County, as it was brought in filled with eggs by a local farmer. The basket, which had been used for carrying eggs to the store for forty years, was round, ten inches across by six inches deep, with a strong handle and about as black in color as any basket could be, but a beautiful contrast to the white eggs which filled it to the brim. It was an ancient type that had been made by several branches of the Nicholson family who, as far as they recollect, have always lived in this section.

There are perhaps a dozen basket makers in the mountains near Oldrag, of whom Silas Nicholson is one of the best. He takes great pride in preparing his oak splints and in making the baskets in convenient sizes, often nesting them one within the other for convenience in shipping. His principal baskets are round, although he makes other types. He learned basket making when a small boy from his father, who had learned it from his father. He is also a good stone-mason and has built most of the stone chimneys in the log cabins of his neighborhood. One of Silas Nicholson's baskets is shown opposite page 208. Elizabeth J. Winn, who organized and directs the center in Madison County, has done much to promote the handicrafts in that part of Virginia, securing many orders and encouraging workers to keep their standards high.

Basket makers are also to be found throughout the hills and mountains of West Virginia. At the annual Forest Festival held at Elkins, Randolph County, in the autumn of 1933, baskets made by native workers were used in an exceptional way. The culminating feature of the Harvest Festival pageant celebrating the bounty of the state was a procession of young women who carried to the throne of the symbolical figure of Mother Nature the products of forest, farm, and home. The carriers and containers used by these gift bearers were baskets, trays, and other receptacles made from native woods by the mountain people. This pageant, an outstanding expression in the arts of rural life, was written and directed by Betty Eckhardt of Oglebay Park, Wheeling, West Virginia.

A basket maker of the region, Mrs. Susan Killingsworth, uses to advantage a part of the young white oak tree which is often discarded, the heart somewhat darker in color and probably not so easily worked as the clearer white wood which grows nearer the bark. The natural color of this inner wood, an attractive deep tan, is much like the dye of sumac. Mrs. Killingsworth sometimes makes of this heart wood her lady basket, a graceful elliptical form from eight to ten inches high, the cover fastened to the top with a wooden thong hinge.

Mrs. Gordon Boggs of Franklin, West Virginia, member of the West Virginia Farm Women's Bureau, has furnished information about Levi Eye, a famous basket maker of Pendleton County who died in 1926. She writes:

Mr. Eye had a family of sixteen, including parents, which he maintained by making and selling baskets. . . . He would barter his baskets for lard, meat, flour, or whatever was needed. . . . I asked him how many baskets he had made in his long life time and he said, "Well I was just figuring the other day on the number and I made it a little over 7000. I began when a small lad, working with my father . . . and then I have kept an account for a long time."

His baskets were of the split-oak variety. Several of his sons followed his trade.

A worker of West Virginia, perhaps known to more people outside the mountains than any other, is Carrie Lyon who, in her Bedroom Factory at Elk Garden, Mineral County, creates several types of flower baskets, work baskets, shopping and fruit baskets, trays and coasters, most of them constructed of imported reeds. Miss Lyon's baskets are interesting not only because of their utility and workmanship but because they furnish an outstanding example of the therapeutic value of the handicrafts to one who has had to battle both illness and poverty.

Miss Lyon had been a school teacher. She was stricken with arthritis and was in so serious a condition that three hospitals in which she became a patient in turn failed to heal her. One day a public health nurse, Gertrude Eckhardt, visited Miss Lyon and showed her something about basket making in the hope of relieving

174

UNION CHURCH AT NIGHT
THIS WAS THE LAST PICTURE MADE IN BEREA, KENTUCKY, BY DORIS ULMANN.
SHE GAVE HER COMPLETE COLLECTION OF PHOTOGRAPHS TO BEREA COLLEGE

both her physical and her mental pain. It was a beginning that developed after her return home into a means of livelihood. Miss Lyon exhibited some of her first baskets at the Upper Potomac Fair at Burlington, West Virginia, where she won a ribbon. She can use her hands, and, lying on her back, with mirrors by which to view her work, she weaves baskets and other articles. This little industry in a home just off the highway has helped to support Miss Lyon, her mother, and her grandmother.

An ideal material for baskets is the native honeysuckle which covers old fences, banks along the roadsides, and countless other places throughout the Highlands. It is tough, pliable, smooth, and durable. Several basket makers use this native vine, but none with more skill than Lena and Flora Dysart who live on the old homeplace, near Rydal, Bartow County, Georgia. In a letter they describe their work:

> We gather the vines from our own farm. They run straight and do not cling to anything. We gather a quantity fifteen and twenty feet long in winter when sap is down, wind them in rolls, fasten securely, and boil four hours. Remove from pot, run each piece through a cloth to remove bark, soak overnight in tub of water, rinse in two waters, and hang in sunshine to dry. Then, we whittle off each little knot with a sharp pocket knife and then they are ready for weaving. We do all the work ourselves from gathering the vine to finished article.

A picture of the Sisters Dysart, as they are known in their home community, at work is shown opposite page 115, and one of their baskets opposite page 209. They will make any kind that can be woven from honeysuckle, and wherever shown their work takes a first prize. Most of their baskets are finished in the clear, natural white of the vine though some are dyed with carefully selected colors. The lids of baskets fit perfectly and are often tied on with pretty cords or ribbons.

A maker of unusual skill and an inventor of several practical forms of honeysuckle trays and baskets is Mrs. Birdie Willis, whose work is marketed through the John and Mary R. Markle School at Higgins, North Carolina. Mrs. Willis also weaves the honeysuckle vine around glasses, bottles, and pottery containers.

The girls at the Tallulah Falls Industrial School have made a number of remarkable baskets, employing, as in their weaving, designs used outside the mountains. They have utilized some of the American Indian technique to work out designs of their own. They sometimes employ a long-leaf pine combined with raffia, and also the native sedge grass which grows so abundantly in the Highlands, in combination also with raffia. One of these sedge baskets is shown opposite page 216.

The Cherokee Indians on their reservation at Cherokee, Swain County, North Carolina, make a wide variety of baskets, using split oak, honeysuckle, but especially split cane, a strong, durable native plant of the bamboo family. The cane is a very difficult fiber to work as it is hard and tough and must be kept wet, but the Cherokees have employed it as far back as memory goes. The shapes made include carrying baskets, arrow quivers, and other forms of value in their own life, also many for general use. Frequently the cane is colored with native dyes and of late commercial dyes have been used. Examples of their baskets are shown opposite page 207.

At Gatlinburg live several pioneer families who carry on old-time traditions in basketry. Besides Mrs. Huskey, who has been referred to in connection with the Aunt Lydia baskets, only one can be mentioned here, Mac McCarter, who earns his living from a small plot of ground and from chair and basket making. He is seventy-five years old and learned the craft from his father, a pioneer of the region. He makes a practical basket out of white oak that grows near his cabin, excellent in color and workmanship. With one of these he is shown opposite page 114.

Allanstand Cottage Industries has from the beginning encouraged basket weaving, and at one time the workers produced about 40 different styles from materials native to the mountains. One of their more recent designs, called the Carolina basket, is shown opposite page 212. This is made with several combinations of natural and dyed woods which give it a very pleasing appearance. Another variant, produced only at this center, is the White Rock basket, named for the locality in which the man who designed the basket lived. It is made of closely woven white oak with a round bottom and a square frame and handle. A decorative design of weaving at the base of the handle adorns the sides.

There is an exceptional basket found at Allanstand Cottage Industries, a small round one of bulrush, once made with oak thongs, but now more frequently with raffia. It is attractive but not widely used. Pine-needle baskets are made in the vicinity of Asheville from needles shipped in from outside the Highlands. They are also made in northern Georgia and northeastern Alabama, whence pine needles are sent for the purpose. While a few of these baskets are made entirely of the long-leaf pine needles, most are combined with raffia, which is an excellent tying material and oftentimes contributes much to the design and color scheme.

MARKETING THE BASKETS

As with every other handicraft, marketing the product is a problem with the mountaineer, and especially so if he lives far from the main avenues of travel. Transporting the article may be by horseback, muleback, wagon, automobile, or on home-made sleds drawn by oxen. This picturesque method may be seen even today far back in the mountains of Tennessee and Georgia. At Pine Mountain, Kentucky, chairs and baskets packed wide and high on the back of a mule are brought to the Settlement School over steep winding trails. At the foot of the mountain near Oldrag, Virginia, a Negro carries all his baskets to market on his back, a means of transportation referred to as his "bone wagon." Tennessee, North Carolina, and Georgia report the same mode of transportation. Few mountain basket makers care to have others take their products to market for them. They are like the Mexican potter who, on the way to the village with his wares piled high on the back of his donkey, refused a buyer offering to purchase his entire stock for more than he could hope to receive at slow retail because he would thus have been robbed of the social experience which would accompany his visit to the village market.

But it is the opportunity to make a sale that gives the maker concern. Assured of that, he is ingenious enough to devise means of getting the article to the buyer. The report on the Rural Industries in Knott County, Kentucky, already referred to, states that basket makers could multiply their output several times if they could sell their products. Yet the report also points out that some farmers receive more income from basket making than from their crops. What is true of Knott County is true of other localities throughout the Highlands. It is therefore obvious that the future of the hand-made product is dependent upon finding new uses outside the mountains for well-made baskets. There is a growing demand for them for carrying, storing, and even shipping farm products. The Farmers Federation, a co-operative with head-quarters at Asheville, North Carolina, is using split-oak baskets in peck and half-bushel sizes made by native people for shipping a high grade of sweet potato raised by mountain farmers, a use that not only will add to the output of the basket maker but will very likely increase the market for any commodity so attractively packed.

Baskets can be made with sufficient uniformity to be satisfactorily sold from samples, and something has been accomplished in this direction; but on the whole, marketing possibilities for the native product are uncertain outside the mountains and at present are inadequate for a healthful development of this home industry. Basketry is a craft that will undoubtedly respond to the stimulation of an increased market. A definite advantage lies in the small outlay for equipment and the method by which one learns it. No other has continued with so little direction or supervision; it is rarely taught in school or community center, but like chairmaking it often descends from father to son, and it is one of the crafts which many of the young generation are interested in learning when there is a market in prospect.

Because basketry is one of the crafts in which handwork can hold its own with machine production, and because it has been so well and widely developed in the Highlands, with materials and skills still available, it is hoped that ways will be found to expand the markets so that the best of the old mountain patterns and traditions can be continued.

CHAPTER XI

WHITTLING AND CARVING IN WOOD

THERE is a modest little tool not mentioned in two learned and delightful treatises on carpenters' tools[1] which cannot be overlooked today by anyone who is watching the progress of handicrafts in the Southern Highlands. That tool is the pocket-knife, and whittling with it in one form or another is definitely taking its place among the arts of that region. Whittling and wood carving find expression in many forms ranging from small boxes made of one piece of wood to finely carved church lecterns worked out after the best Old World traditions. Between the products of the Whittlers' Club at Crab Orchard, Kentucky, one of the youngest groups, and the workers at Tryon, North Carolina, where chisels, gouges, and other tools supplement the pocketknife, there is such a promising diversity of expression that whittling and carving seem to merit a chapter of their own, quite apart from the more comprehensive one on woodwork.

It is not only what has already been accomplished that is encouraging, but of equal importance is the promise that it holds for others who may find opportunity to develop their talents in the same direction. For much of this work a good pocketknife is the only tool required, and the fact that this has long been the stock equipment of the mountaineer explains the widespread skill which pridefully turns up with the least encouragement. There are whittlers of many grades, and like many another mountain skill it seems "to run in families." For instance, Joe Burkett, who lives near Boone in Watauga County, North Carolina, whittles out of oak and hickory a complete latch and handle for a cabin door of the same design which his father and his grandfather made for themselves and for neighbors back in their whittling days.

[1] Mercer, Henry, Ancient Carpenters' Tools, Reprinted from vol. 5 of the Papers of the Bucks County Historical Society, Doylestown, Pa., 1929, pp. 482–497; Hibben, Thomas, The Carpenters' Tool Chest, J. B. Lippincott Co., Philadelphia, 1933.

For the purpose of this chapter three general types of expression in wood will be considered, regardless of the tools or materials employed. One type will be the whittling job with which we are most familiar, such as the door-latch, or the wooden box made of one piece; another the more sophisticated type of carving suggestive of Old World products in method and appearance, although often enlivened by a new motif, as in the adaptation of a local plant in a design; and the third what might be called the folk art type; that is, the expressions of individual carvers who have never known anything about the existence of art schools, but who project their ideas in their own way for the pleasure they derive from them.

WHITTLING

Twenty-five men and boys who live near Crab Orchard and who are whittling out boxes, napkin rings, and other small articles for their own use and for sale, call themselves the Whittlers' Club. To them whittling is a social, an educational, and an economic avocation. It would not be an exaggeration to say that they have determined to whittle themselves out of some of their difficulties. They are all neighbors, with headquarters at the Gilbert Henry Community Center, and they are seeking through whittling in wood to improve themselves and to establish contacts with the outside world. An example of their work is shown opposite page 220.

The IXL brand of pocketknife, familiar to many of us of an earlier generation, has never been put to happier use than by the farm workers, students, and neighbors of the John C. Campbell Folk School of Brasstown, North Carolina. Mrs. Campbell believed that anyone who with his pocketknife could cut a fence rail in two in a short time or cover a board surface with sharply incised mountain hieroglyphics without interrupting his own or anybody else's conversation might, with practice, put that skill and energy to more satisfactory use. Some early experiments were made around the fireplace at Keith House with a goose and a mule as models. Those who cut out their first beasts and birds were able, so the legend goes, to recognize them as such, although in the Craft Museum, where they are preserved today, they bring many smiles from the carvers themselves. But the whittling was interesting and it was decided to confine their efforts for a time to farm animals

THE OLDEST DATED AMERICAN QUILT

This Quilt on the Back Bears the Initials W. T. G., and the Date 1795. It Was Made in West Virginia, Then a Part of Virginia. It Is Described in the Chapter on Quilting and Patchwork

and birds of the countryside. With this limitation established, the whittlers as they worked away thought of other animals and birds they would like to carve. Several of the boys whittled out the familiar mountain mule. A visitor said, "I'm no tame Democrat, I'm a mad one; I want a mad mule." So Floyd Laney whittled out a mad mule for him, and this soon proved to be one of the most popular figures. He also thought he would like to whittle out an old-time logging outfit, and in time appeared the ox, the sled, the logs, maul, wedges, and ax as pictured opposite page 239. Probably in no museum is there a more authentic representation of a typical pioneer logging outfit of the Highlands than this piece of whittling.

In the beginning only the boys practiced whittling. Enthusiasm spilled over into the community, appealing to older men who had been whittling all their lives and who now yearned to put into tangible form some of their own ideas. W. J. Martin, one of the eldest in years but among the youngest in spirit, appeared one day with a wild turkey cut out of apple wood, a bird which the children had never seen but which an old settler of discrimination declared was perfect. One of Mr. Martin's turkeys is illustrated opposite page 209 and his portrait opposite page 122, where, to use his wife's expression, he is shown with "a chance of pigs."

During the six years that whittling and carving have been in progress at the Folk School, boys and girls, farm hands, and neighbors have taken part, among whom are some excellent workers. Nina Bryan, who for several years had charge of the kitchen and dining-room service in the School, worked out several attractive breadboards and other objects in low-relief carving, creating her own designs from wild and domestic plants of the region, a restrained use of wheat, rye, and oats being favorite motifs with her. An illustration of one of her breadboards is shown on page 220.

No scene about the Folk School is more pleasant or characteristic than the young people resting at lunch time or around the fireplace in the evening whittling away at their different figures in all stages from the rough wood to the finished object. A small block from which a mule, a rabbit, a goose, or a rooster is being whittled fits conveniently and safely in the shirt pocket, and a sharp knife in another pocket awaits the free moment when whittling can be resumed. An occasional whittler works his figure out entirely from the block of wood, but much time is saved by first sawing out a rough blank and whittling it down with the knife.

The carvings of the John C. Campbell Folk School are mostly of fruit wood, apple being the commonest, although other close-grained woods, including holly, maple, walnut and cherry, are also used. The finished objects are smooth, waxed, and rubbed by hand, but always retaining the natural appearance of the wood. They are usually naturalistic, but occasionally a little conventional or a bit futuristic.

No attempt can be made here to measure the influence of the whittling done at the Campbell Folk School outside the community itself, but it is very noticeable. On page 197 is shown a carving by Ross Corn, a student at Berea College, who, seeing a friend from the Campbell Folk School whittling out a goose, thought he would like to try his hand at another bird. Recalling a peacock he had seen twelve years before, he whittled one out with his pocketknife as nearly as he could remember it and much as he felt about it. This boy has never had any instruction in drawing or modeling, but he has a fine feeling for form and restrained decoration, which appear in consistent places on the bird, especially on the back of the tail. He has carved peacocks in many sizes, one 10 inches high and one less than one inch.

Quite different from any other whittling or carving carried on in the Highlands, but skilful in execution and full of character, are the animals, human figures, and other work in wood made by the students at Pleasant Hill Academy under the guidance of Margaret B. Campbell, director of the craft industries. Unlike the smooth rubbed surfaces of the Brasstown Folk School pieces, it is rough and angular, having the effect of being done, as in truth it is, by rapid strokes of the knife blade. It thus retains the vitality which is often found in a quick, free sketch, a quality that is sometimes lost in detailed refining. The whittling at Pleasant Hill began with a few animals—a pig, a goat, and a dog—made in the local pine, poplar, and cedar woods without finishing treatment except a little oil for objects made of cedar. In time whittling and also low-relief carving broadened to include several more animals, jointed dolls, bas-reliefs of such rural subjects as haying, hog-killing, and sorghum grinding. Most popular of all at present are the expressive figures of mountain people in characteristic attitudes, such as a man sowing grain, dancing a jig, a preacher in action, a woman splitting wood, picking a chicken, preparing a meal over a cookstove, plowing a hillside with a mule, or the scene of a conversion at a camp meeting. To add realism and charm to these lifelike figures which are from three to five and one-half inches high, a light polychrome wash is used so that they catch the eye through both color and form. These character sketches suggest something of the carvings of the Tyrol, of French-Canada, and of Mexico, but the likeness is only suggestive, for they are original reflections of life in the Tennessee Highlands and add another delightful note to the indigenous crafts of the region. The subjects illustrated opposite page 222 were carved by a native boy, Tom Brown, who also helps to instruct.

At Berea College there is a Whittlers' Club in which are made small objects with the pocketknife—puzzles, bird houses, and many trinkets which boys skilled at whittling can fashion. This work is carried on in connection with the Woodworking Department of the College under the direction of J. Edward Davis, and it has enabled several students to earn part of their expenses.

WOOD CARVING OF A MORE CONVENTIONAL TYPE

The first encouragement in wood carving among the boys and girls of the Highlands was given at Biltmore about thirty-five years ago by Miss Yale and Miss Vance who, as has been said, now direct the Tryon Toy-Makers and Wood-Carvers. In the carving carried on at Tryon they employ only mountain people and use largely native walnut and oak. The finishes of stains and fumes are applied with exceptional care and skill. Small carved pieces such as stools, benches, book troughs, shelves, trays, and paper knives are regularly made, but many commissions for large objects have been carried out for private residences and for churches, pulpits, lecterns, gates, doors, and even pews. An illustration of their wood carving is shown opposite page 228.

While the method of work at Tryon follows Old World traditions with results that would interest and please ancient craftsmen, the carvers have developed motifs from the flora of the Highlands which give their work a distinct local character. The pine cone, galax leaf, dogwood leaves, blossoms, berries, and other native growths are used as patterns for these fine pieces made for homes and churches throughout our country. Similar designs are employed also on smaller objects made for retail trade. Many structural features of the workshops and salesrooms are marked by picturesque and appropriate carving done by mountain pupils.

FOLK ART IN CARVING

It is not possible here to refer to all those engaged in whittling and carving in the Highlands, but this chapter should not be concluded without a brief note on some of those who have worked out their designs largely or entirely unaided, designs that have sometimes resulted in as true expressions of folk art as can be found anywhere. These craftsmen show an interest in nature and a common urge to do creative work without feeling the handicaps which often restrain those conscious of what others do in their fields.

Joe Burkett, referred to before as living near Boone in the mountains of North Carolina, has whittled out many different kinds of articles and animals, working usually in bass or linden wood. However, the subject of his own invention, which has become best known and probably most liked, is his prairie schooner, originally portrayed in the natural wood but now often finished with an application of paint. He uses a bay-red for the oxen, leaving the horns in natural white, and a harmonizing color for the wagon. The wagon might have been done by any experienced whittler, but the oxen are entirely original in design and execution and suggest the primitive carvings of Africa.

Nicodemus Demon Adams, of Banner, in the southwestern corner of Virginia, has long had a compelling interest in small animals and birds, but it is in the carving of these latter that he has attained his best expressions. Two other favorite subjects are miniature coffins and tombstones which he executes with remarkable technique, the coffins being made from one piece of wood with sliding lids which fit perfectly. Mr. Adams does not find these coffins very popular, but he enjoys making them and giving them to friends. His birds, however, are deservedly admired. He carves two types, one the more familiar species such as the bluejay, canary, and cardinal, in the making of which he has observed the birds themselves; the other birds of his fancy provide him with a wider scope for his imagination, with results that please some of his patrons far more than do the authentic birds which can be readily recognized. Adams does one thing which another sculptor probably would not do—he makes the feet and unfeathered part of the legs of his birds with wire which he twists neatly and attaches to the bodies of the birds in a very realistic way. Someone expressed the belief that these legs and feet would be more artistic if carved in wood; Adams "allowed" that they might, but they wouldn't be so strong, and "there is nothing in wood as much like a bird's leg and claw as wire properly twisted," he added, "and they are lasty too."

On the creatures of his own mind which Adams designates as those "I just thought up," he often lavishes great care in the carving. One of his choice ventures is in the treatment of the tail of a bird resembling somewhat the barnyard rooster, which he skilfully splits through the middle, giving it width and quality of lightness that are novel and pleasing.

No wood sculptor has been influenced less by others than has Sam Smith, who lives about six miles from Pittman Community Center, Sevierville, Tennessee. His favorite work is a low-built mountain barn around which are assembled all the farm animals, and he whittles them very much as he feels about each one, regardless of the setting they are to occupy or their proper relative sizes. The illustration opposite page 123 reproduces one of the barns and a few of the many animals that he likes to whittle out of chunks of "popple" (poplar) and other soft woods that grow around his cabin. No attempt is made to produce these beasts and fowl to scale; the chickens may be half as large as the cows, and though appearing incongruous on first sight, one soon shares the delightful spontaneity which this untutored sculptor experiences as he whittles out his creatures, each to its own pattern, each strikingly individual, but all combining pleasantly in a homely rural scene.

It is regretted that the interesting and promising work in whittling and wood carving of other individuals cannot be described here. Some of it, however, is shown on the end papers,[*] the paper knives and other woodwork in relief and in the round, carved

185

usually in walnut by Allen Kilgore of Dante, Virginia; the characteristic Plymouth Rock chickens of Willy Smith of the Allanstand Cottage Industries; and the animals of D. L. Millsaps of Damascus, Virginia, whose bears are as lifelike as though they had walked out of the forest.

As one examines these varied and attractive products of the pocketknife and carving chisel in the hands of heretofore untrained workers, the promise of still further progress in whittling and carving is encouraging. Many a mountain boy and girl have through patience developed aptitudes for whittling and simple carving, and through a long-established mode of living not concerned with urban schedules they have ample time for practice in a craft that may give them great enjoyment and possibly increase of income.

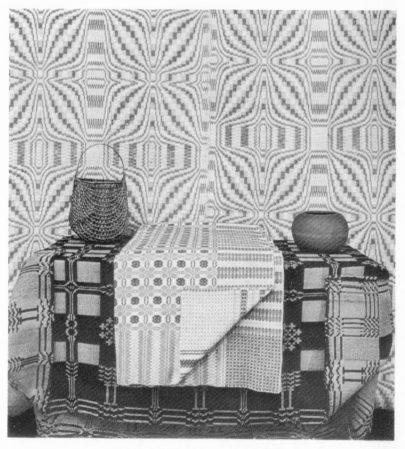

TYPES OF MOUNTAIN COVERLETS

THE THREE TYPES OF COVERLETS WHICH CAN BE WOVEN ON A MOUNTAIN LOOM ARE: THE OVERSHOT OR FLOAT WEAVE, ILLUSTRATED BY THE DOUBLE BOWKNOT PATTERN ON THE WALL, FROM NORTH CAROLINA; THE SUMMER AND WINTER WEAVE BY THE ONE FOLDED, FROM KENTUCKY; THE DOUBLE WEAVE, CONSISTING OF TWO WEBS JOINED TOGETHER, WHICH COVERS THE TABLE, FROM WEST VIRGINIA. BASKET FROM HINDMAN, KENTUCKY; POTTERY FROM CLEVELAND, GEORGIA

CHAPTER XII

DOLLS, TOYS, AND MINIATURE FURNITURE

ONCE at a Christmas tree party at Pine Mountain Settlement School a little boy looking wistfully at some of the decorations, on being asked if he would like to have one, replied, "I don't aim to want anything that I can't hope to get." Doubtless he reflected the philosophy of many of his elders and not a few of the children of the Highlands to whom Christmas gifts were unknown.

In countless mountain families there are no gifts for Christmas such as most city children enjoy, yet parents have always found ways of making playthings from materials at hand, and with their imagination the children have supplied whatever their crude gifts may have lacked. A complete household in miniature and a homestead of many acres is still in existence in a certain fence corner in the mountains of North Carolina near a tiny mountain stream which is a wide rushing river to the children. On this homestead all the household and barnyard equipment consists of sticks, stones, broken bits of iron, glass, pottery, china, pieces of wire and string, and seeds and cones. Out of these materials the rich young owners have created fields of many kinds of grains; herds of livestock, horses, cattle, geese, chickens, turkeys, ducks, guinea fowls, sheep, hogs; and several sets of buildings with gardens, plows, harrows, cultivators, wood and hay sleds, carts, and other possessions limited only by the imagination of this little family who can scarcely await the coming of each spring to get back to work on their estate. They labor all day long during summer in their play world until called to help with the family chores, and on autumn evenings are busy until nightfall gathering in the harvests and getting their beasts and birds housed and under cover before winter sets in. The herds and flocks, including a few wild animals now in captivity, are represented in the main by beans, corn kernels, acorns, and other domestic and wild seeds from the abundance found in the region. Even though the land possessed by their parents comprises only a lean patch of ground, most of it on a steep hillside, yet the children are fabulously rich with their imaginary acres of verdant level land within the fence-row. Such have been the holdings of mountain children for generations, and one seriously wonders if they could be happier with the realistic toys which the world outside possesses in such quantities.

Many parents and grandparents in remote places contribute their part in creating for the children from such materials as are available, dolls, cradles, little settin' and rocking chairs, and other small furniture, miniature coverlets and quilts, tiny clay dishes, gourd fiddles, small spinning wheels, looms, cross-bows, crude wagons, whittled-out animals, and other old-fashioned and sometimes rather modern toys. Some of these occasionally find their way into the small stream of toys coming out of the Highlands.

DOLLS

Among the home-made dolls of the mountains are the poppets, which Mrs. Anne Green Williams near Ary, Kentucky, and her sister, Mrs. Orlenia Ritchie, Viper, Kentucky, made at one time only for their children, but a few of which they now make to sell. Their mother made similar ones for them and their brothers and sisters as far back as they can remember. Kentucky poppets are whittled out of buckeye, a close, fine-grained wood, very light in color, bestowing on the dolls a smooth, pale complexion which is much liked by mountain children. To this attractive skin is added the charm of rosy cheeks by rubbing in a bit of red coloring, poke-berry being a favorite. Then to supply realism to the almost real, the tops of the heads are covered with the soft fur of mole, squirrel, or other wild animal, or the wool of domestic sheep. For the men poppets bear fur is sometimes used. The dress of the women poppets usually is made of homespun or cloth of the type found in mountain stores. Mrs. Orlenia Ritchie's picture is shown opposite page 127. Poppets are perhaps the most primitive dolls of our mountain country, and one family, so far as is known, is the only one making them for market.

Another old type of doll still made in several parts of the Highlands is the corn-husk or corn-shuck doll, an indigenous product of this region where corn has always been the main food crop. The corn-husk dolls probably originated on this continent before the white man came. The corn plant itself is one of the gifts of the Indians to America and the world, and while much of the early record of the use of corn husks for dolls and other purposes is dim, it is definitely known that the Penobscot and other tribes made dolls for their children. It seems unlikely, however, that the Southern Highlander knew of this use of corn plant by the Indians, and probably the making of dolls from corn husks is another instance of the mountain woman's shaping a familiar material to her need.

There are at this time at least five makers of corn-husk dolls and other figures in the region, each quite individual in the character of her product and some showing much originality and taste. They are: a worker for the Allanstand Cottage Industries; Mrs. Mollie Rogers, Mooresburg, Hawkins County, Tennessee; Mrs. A. J. Denton, Concord, Knox County, Tennessee; Mrs. Rosalie Collins Pless, Russellville, Hamblen County, Tennessee; and Mrs. Marshall Counts, Dante, Russell County, Virginia.

The dolls made for the Allanstand Cottage Industries are probably the oldest of this group and hundreds of them have been sold through the salesroom at Asheville. A family of seven members has been developed from corn husks, the faces drawn in ink and the hair of light or dark corn silk. They have been named Cornelius, the father; Maisie, the mother; Millie and Flossie, the girls; the Junior Husk Twins; and Tiny Tot. These figures are from three to eight inches high. A few giant corn-husk dolls have been made as special commissions, but the smaller figures are deservedly the more popular and many purchasers will take all seven rather than break up the household.

The Home Demonstration Agents in Tennessee were once asked to secure a corn-shuck doll to be sent to a little girl in Seattle, Washington. After repeated unsuccessful inquiries at several rural clubs, Mrs. Rogers came forward and said that she had played with dolls her mother had made from corn shucks and would try to make one for the little girl in the far West. Her first efforts were so successful that she experimented further and eventually designed a mother and three daughters. The shop to which these dolls were consigned suggested that the characters be named. The first doll was called Mollie for Mrs. Rogers herself; the tall, thin, red-haired one Agnes, for her daughter; the short one Marion, for another daughter, and the demure dark-haired one Jane, for her oldest daughter. Some 200 groups of this mother and three daughters have been sold in 24 states and three foreign countries.

Mrs. Denton began her work with corn shucks by reproducing a few of her favorite characters from books; now she makes complete sets of figures, the most popular being those from Little Women. She has created Meg, Jo, Beth, Amy, Laurie, John, and other characters as children, and another set of them grown up. The costuming of these characters entirely from corn shucks has been well carried out and they are excellent in craftsmanship, including the delicately braided hats of fine husk fiber which some of them wear.

Most of the corn-husk dolls made by Mrs. Pless are used in combination with other figures for her well-known groups: mountain woman milking, mountain man with oxen and log sled hauling lumber, woman riding horseback on side-saddle, woman churning, and men riding horses, driving cattle, oxen, and sheep. The technique employed by Mrs. Pless is unlike that of other workers with corn shucks, especially in making these animals, which may be likened to the plaiting and braiding method used by the Mexicans. The difficulties encountered in constructing the bulky portions of the bodies of the animals from braided or twisted fiber, and the more delicate parts from the same materials enabling them to stand alone in natural posture, can be best appreciated by one who tries to twist, braid, or plait the corn husk. Yet Mrs. Pless accomplishes this with rare skill and taste. Her achievements, however, are not confined to making corn-husk figures, for she is an experienced basket maker, a woodworker, and also a weaver; but in the work with corn husks she finds one of her best outlets for original expression.

In the corn-husk figures made by Mrs. Counts, some of the husks are dyed before being made up in combination with the attractive natural shade. The array of colors is very pleasing, the husks taking the dyes readily and with evenness and intensity of hue. Mrs. Counts' subjects are both realistic and imaginative: a farmer and his wife in several sizes, and a few other mountain

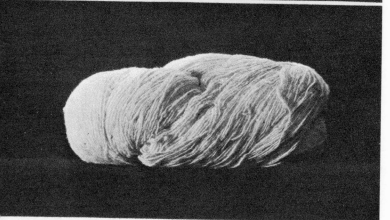

FINGER WEAVING AND HANDSPUN YARN

ABOVE: FINGER WEAVING, SOMETIMES CALLED TAPESTRY WEAVING, "THE COVERED WAGON," DESIGNED AND WOVEN AT THE SPINNING WHEEL. BELOW: WOOLEN YARN CARDED AND SPUN BY GRANNY GREER OF TRADE, TENNESSEE, IN HER HUNDREDTH YEAR

HONEYCOMB SPREAD OR COUNTERPANE

For Counterpanes or "Dimities," as They Are Sometimes Called, the Honeycomb Pattern Is an Old Favorite. This Spread Was Recently Woven for Allanstand Cottage Industries

types, fairies with delicately tinted draperies, clowns in vari-colored raiment, and beasts, both wild and tame. Doubtless her choicest creation is a crèche, a simple and naïve portrayal of the Nativity worked out with deep sincerity in which the manger, the cradle, and all the figures are made of corn husks. An illustration of this scene appears opposite page 270.

In addition to the poppets and the corn-husk dolls of the High-lands are a number of other figures including dolls with heads of hickory nuts, their features drawn with a few light strokes of pen or pencil which, against the tan-colored wrinkled surface of the nut shell, often suggest the hardy mountain types. However, extreme caricatures are also found in the dried-apple and sweet-potato dolls sometimes seen in mountain homes. The colonial dolls made by Mountain Neighbors at Oldrag (now at Kimball), Virginia, have bodies and heads of cloth, painted features and hair, dresses of old-time prints, and quaint slat bonnets. Among the more recently designed dolls are the carved and jointed ones made of cedar wood by students at Pleasant Hill Academy. The heads, faces, and feet are roughly carved, giving them characteristic ruggedness, their joints are movable, permitting elasticity in action, and they are dressed tastefully in old-fashioned mountain costumes.

TOYS

Unlike doll making, which has developed distinct types charac-teristic of the mountain region and of which few are produced in any other part of the country, the trend of toy making has been toward more conventional types, often original in design but in treatment resembling those found in city markets. There are, of course, a few examples of toys bearing individuality in both design and execution, but most of those intended for sale outside the mountains are planned and finished to meet market requirements.

The Tryon Toy-Makers and Wood-Carvers are the best known group in the Highlands, measured by the age of the industry, numbers of toys produced, and variety of design and treatment. Actuated by their earnest desire to develop and promote natural ability, Miss Vance and Miss Yale have labored unceasingly to build up standards for toy making that would assure the workers continued opportunity in this field. From early experiments, through the period of growth and development, when a knowledge of the demands of outside markets was essential to promote a self-sustaining project, this primary objective of providing work in which local people could develop their potential abilities was never subordinated and it is today the guiding motive of this enterprise

The toys made at the Tryon shop are first carefully sawed out of wood obtained from nearby forests, then joined together with great care, usually by hand. The sense of proportion, the taste and feeling for harmonious decoration, and the careful finish of each brightly enameled piece give the toys much animation and a distinction worthy of their source.

A feature that definitely relates the Tryon toys to the Highland is the character of their designs. A Blue Ridge Mountain home comprises a cabin of hewn logs, rough-shingled roof, and a door swinging on wooden hinges; a covered wagon with yoke of oxen; all the members of the family dressed in mountain costume; a home-made tripod and wash pots; rails for fences and pigpens; the mountain mule, cows, ducks, chickens, lean dogs, and the family cat. There are likewise special barnyard sets reminiscent of the mountains, and a series of delightful toys based upon stories that belong to children everywhere: Noah's ark with Mr. and Mrs. Noah, Shem, Ham, and Japhet and their wives, with many pair of beasts, birds, and reptiles; Red Riding Hood; Goldilocks and the Three Bears; Simple Simon; Bo-Peep and her fleecy sheep; and the Old Woman Who Lived in a Shoe and her entire family.

Farther north in the Blue Ridge Mountains of Virginia are the Shenandoah Community Workers of Bird Haven, already mentioned. This group, entering the field of toy making much later than did the workers at Tryon, has featured the designs of John Martin. Many of the animals known as "beasties" to John Martin Book readers, birds and fowls on stands and wheels painted in bright colors with simple stenciled decorations are sold in various parts of the country. Four large sets embrace the Homeyard Friends, Barnyard Friends, Cosy Friends, and Circus Friends, each of which is accompanied by a rhymed booklet by John Martin.

The Shenandoah Community Workers also make attractive building blocks in numerous shapes and sizes. These blocks are cut from solid oak and sandpapered to perfect smoothness. Many ji aw puzzles have been made to appeal to children, especially the Audubon puzzles representing birds—so attractive, well designed, and well finished are they.

In the mountains of Tennessee is a man who makes bears, dogs, and puzzles of wood besides repairing toys and playthings for children. To the question "How did you happen to begin this work?" his reply typifies the spirit of much of mountain toy making. "I don't exactly know unless to please some child." A further symbol of the impulse of this toy maker is revealed in his response to the inquiry as to what prices he received. "None; I usually give them away." In South Carolina originality and versatility are demonstrated by a woman who utilizes cigar and cardboard boxes in constructing toy animals, boats, and houses which she fashions to meet the problem of equipment for a playground that she directs for children. In Kentucky a woman, beginning with the toys she made for herself when a child, has developed a business for which she has trained two helpers. She also writes about the subject for trade magazines and is now engaged on an instructive book called The Art of Making Corn Husk Gifts.

Puzzles, games, and an assortment of novelties are usually to be found in the Highlands in connection with woodworking shops, and some represent a considerable degree of proficiency and artistry. The Jack Knife Shop at Berea College; the Woodcrafters and Carvers at Gatlinburg; the whittlers at the John C. Campbell Folk School; and the whittlers at Pleasant Hill Academy are among such groups.

The Cherokee Indians of North Carolina, makers of the blowgun, a rare survival of the remote past, bows and arrows, Indian ball racquets, and other equipment for their traditional sports and games hold a unique position in the character of the toys and playthings produced. Their bows and arrows are in great favor with children; the output, however, is not large, but they are made by skilful Cherokee craftsmen, some of plain design and others with light carving and painted decorations. Besides the small bows and arrows for children there are others, strong and carefully formed, constructed to serve the discriminating adult archer.

The increasing number of objects whittled from wood has considerably augmented the supply of toys in the mountains. The animals, birds, human figures, and small models of typical scenes can be consistently admitted to the varied collection of indigenous toys that have cheered the little folk and long amused their elders. Since these objects have been referred to in some detail in Chapter XI, Whittling and Carving in Wood, they will not be enumerated.

MINIATURE FURNITURE

Of the great variety of miniature furniture the carefully designed, perfectly joined and finished pieces produced in some of the Highland schools and woodworking shops are as perfectly formed and finished as the full-sized models. In many instances they have a charm exceeding them.

As the mountain chair is predominant in the general field of furniture and woodwork, so it is in that of miniature furniture. Chairs for children, for dolls, and as toys have been reproduced in almost every pattern adopted in making them for adults. Exact likenesses, in both design and construction, are often the end sought in fashioning a miniature chair, whether it be a mountain type or a copy of some more finished style from outside the area.

In the Wee Willie Winkle chair so skilfully made in the woodworking shops of Berea College and put together with the graceful curve in the back as approximate to scale as in the full-sized model, the several parts are joined with wooden pegs as in the antique from which it is copied. This reproduction can be found only at Berea College and is said to be the favorite of several pieces of children's furniture worked out from the larger models. Like other children's chairs, it comes in cherry, walnut, maple, or mahogany. The seat is 8 inches wide, being nearly square, and the total height of the back is 16 inches. The soft finish which brings out the character of the wood marks each piece with distinction. The same group at Berea reproduces a set of children's bedroom furniture with like perfection in construction and finish. This suite consists of bed, straight-back chair, rocking chair, and a three-drawer chest.

At Cumberland Homesteads near Crossville, Tennessee, where many of the community needs are supplied by the settlers themselves, the new school building, erected by the homesteaders, is furnished with chairs made by local chairmakers from material growing on the homestead tract. The impressive fact, however, is that these, like the beds and chairs of the Three Bears of nursery fame, are made in sizes to accommodate respectively the big children, the middle sized, and the least children who attend the Cumberland Community School. These chairs have gone far toward making the school an attractive and unique expression of local initiative and resourcefulness.

Frank Tabor, mountain chairmaker in the Homestead neighborhood, has achieved a pleasing note in a child's rocking chair made with maple posts, hickory rungs, and either oak splint or hickory bark seats, the usual mountain chair specifications. But quite original and entirely appropriate to the background of the natural color of the smooth unpolished wood are the orange-colored rings that adorn the posts and rounds. The color is obtained from bloodroot, sometimes known by its Indian name, puccoon.

Near Pine Mountain Settlement School, miniature chairs are matched with small tables usually of walnut, though frequently of other woods, the chair posts and table legs often carefully turned or tastefully hand carved. Small chairs are also the products of several craftsmen who live in or near Gatlinburg, Tennessee. O. J. Mattil, who through drawings and measurements has revived interest in many of the old pieces of mountain furniture, has also reproduced some of the beds and chests in miniature, finishing them with the same care which he puts into larger pieces.

In every Highland state children's chairs are being made, and no gift for little folk is more appropriate than these small, quaint, sturdy mountain products which serve them not only as settin' chairs, but for tables, ladders, horses, sleds, and other real or imaginary needs. In a home in Wytheville, Virginia, is a child's chair over a hundred years old, which was made during the childhood of the mother of the present owner who is now past seventy, and who recalls that it served her as a coasting sled on more than one occasion, the smooth posts of the back acting well as sleigh runners. The chair has been rebottomed twice, once just before the Civil War and the last time about forty years ago.

The small dainty baskets made by Dolly Greer of Dante, Virginia, and by Mrs. James Herman Jones of Wytheville, Virginia, are faithful copies of the well-known melon-shaped or hip bushel baskets. These tiny baskets are so reduced in capacity as to hold only a fraction of a gill. But in making them every detail in the larger model is observed—careful binding where the handle joins the basket, extra weaving for the slight bulge at the sides, and secure reinforcement on the bottom to take care of the weight.

The work of Fanny Wilson, who lives near Highlands, North Carolina, in making doll clothes, miniature quilts, and furniture, is as perfect in execution as her articles are quaint in appearance. Miss Wilson is a skilful seamstress, which, with her fine feeling for miniature things, places her definitely in the group of those who in England would be known as workers in Tinycraft. She finishes and upholsters minute models of English and American furniture sent to her by a manufacturer in New England, and makes complete wardrobes and house furnishings for both antique and modern dolls.

Toy making is naturally a late development. The Highland culture was marked not by luxuries but by the products of stern necessity. As the making of objects among the people changed from that of things for use to one, in part at least, of making things for sale, toys came to be included. And now that there is a growing interest outside the mountains in poppets, corn-shuck dolls, bows and arrows, and so forth, the toy-making activity is increasing. Contributing to this will be the satisfaction the mountain people will have in making those things which free the spirit to express itself in pleasant ways.

THE McCRARY PATCHWORK QUILT

An Heirloom in Swain County, North Carolina, Said to Have Been Designed in Pennsylvania in 1860. It Was Copied and Pieced by a Mountain Woman in North Carolina in 1932, and Later Quilted in Kentucky

PEACOCK AND MOUNTAIN SETTIN' CHAIR

Left: When Ross Corn of Greenville, South Carolina, Saw a Friend Whittling Out Some Farm Animals He Remembered a Peacock He Had Seen Twelve Years Earlier. This Is His Interpretation of It. Right: A Chair Put Together without Screws, Nails, or Glue, the Parts Being Held Fast by the Natural Shrinking Properties of the Wood

CHAPTER XIII

MOUNTAIN MUSIC AND HAND-MADE INSTRUMENTS

THE element of mountain culture which has found widest acceptance outside the Highlands is its music. These songs, ballads, and carols have been collected and sung in many parts of our country and in Europe, and they appear in numerous compilations. The fact which first gave this music importance to the outside world was the discovery by Cecil J. Sharp of England, Mrs. Olive D. Campbell, and other collectors in our country that in sequestered mountain regions of the South, many of the folk songs of England, Scotland, and Ireland continued to be sung long after they had ceased to be heard in those homelands. And some of the very old ballads and carols of which not a vestige remains in the record or memory of Europe would, but for the Southern Highlanders' love of music, have been lost to the world forever.

The student earnestly concerned with the preservation of this music may not know that an unrecorded wealth of it probably still remains unexplored. At the first meeting of the Mountain Folk Festival at Berea, Kentucky, in April, 1935, both Mrs. Campbell and John Jacob Niles, a collector of mountain music, stated that many counties still possess undiscovered resources. In exploring the southwest section of North Carolina, for instance, several new finds were recently recorded, and among comparatively new accessions is a delightful carol which Mr. Niles first heard in the summer of 1933 from an itinerant girl singer on the street in Murphy, North Carolina. The song entitled I Wonder as I Wander is noted here for its archaic beauty:

> I wonder as I wander, out under the sky,
> How Jesus the Saviour did come for to die,
> For poor on'ry [ordinary] people like you and like I . . .
> I wonder as I wander, out under the sky.

When Mary birthed Jesus, 'twas in a cow's stall,
With wise men and farmers and shepherds and all.
But high from the heavens a star's light did fall,
And the promise of ages it then did recall.

If Jesus had wanted for any wee thing,
A star in the sky or a bird on the wing,
Or all of God's angels in heaven for to sing,
He surely could have had it, 'cause he was the King.[1]

The relation of handicrafts to mountain music is much closer than one might at first think; indeed it is not too much to say that we owe the survival of these ballads and carols largely to the hand-made instruments that accompanied the words. In many instances the instruments were made by the singers themselves, the one most frequently used to accompany the singer being the dulcimer, or, as it is called, the "dulcimore," indigenous to and still made in many parts of the Highlands.

In addition to the songs, for which the dulcimer and other stringed instruments have served as an accompaniment, there is a considerable body of mountain music that is strictly instrumental, some of it, like many of the ballads, carried through a long period of transplantation, and some original, or at least with many local versions and variations to which every fiddlers' contest and music festival bears testimony. So between the need of instruments to accompany the songs and others to render music without words, the mountain people have used a variety of instruments made by them chiefly of native materials. The fiddle, as it is always called, has been made by hand in every state in the region, usually from wood, but sometimes from garden gourds which grow here abundantly. A very crude fiddle is made from corn stalks.

Home-made banjos, flutes, fifes, piccolos, pipes, zithers, horns, and bugles have come down through Highland families to the present time, and there is record of at least one organ and one piano having been made by mountaineers.

[1] Schirmer's American Folk-Song Series. Twelve Ballads from Kentucky, Virginia, and North Carolina. Collected and simply arranged for the piano by John Jacob Niles. By permission of G. Schirmer, Inc., copyright 1934, New York.

MOUNTAIN MUSIC OF TODAY

Encouraging as it is to know that much of this old music is being recorded for permanent use, and that we hear it today in concert halls and over the radio, the most heartening fact is that the people are still singing and playing their ancient tunes, and through their social gatherings are keeping them a part of their life. The old songs and ballads are sung with hearty regularity at many of the mountain schools in the effort to encourage students to take part in the revival of their own music. Berea College, Hindman Settlement School, Pine Mountain Settlement School, and others are centers for ballad singing, and the John C. Campbell Folk School has from the beginning fostered such music. At pioneer meetings, old-timers' day, neighborhood picnics, family reunions, county fairs, fiddling and singing contests, mountain music is invariably a part of the program.

Several public events, planned with the primary object of promoting interest in the music of the mountain people, are observed annually. Among them are the White Top Folk Festival held at White Top, Virginia, usually in August; the American Folk Song Society celebration at Ashland, Kentucky; the Folk Song and Dance Festival at Asheville, North Carolina, during the summer; and the Mountain Folk Festival, already mentioned, which meets at various places in the mountains annually. Among the musical numbers on the programs of the National Folk Festival, held each year in a different city, under the direction of Sarah Gertrude Knott, those of the Southern Highlands have had an important place.

THE DULCIMER

The dulcimer, that quaint, plaintive, oblong instrument with from two to six, and sometimes eight strings but most often three, is the most appropriate accompaniment conceivable for mountain ballads, and never made, so far as is known, in its present form in any other land or in any other part of our country. The dulcimer is often referred to by writers of the Highlands, but by no one with more feeling and appreciation than by Ann Cobb of Hindman, Kentucky, whose devotion to the people among whom she elected to spend her days is wholehearted and understanding. In a book of verses Miss Cobb writes frequently of the "dulcimore."[1] Quotations are made from two of these poems, the first is from A Mountain Seaman:

> Allus-ago I yearned to view the sea.
> Maw had a sight of old song-ballads for
> To sing us young-uns, picking out the tunes
> On her old dulcimore. The one I liked
> Was that that told about the Old Salt Sea,
> And Ships A-Sail, and wonders of the deep.

But it is in the Dulcimer Over the Fireboard that she suggests the mountaineer's deep reverence for the instrument and its true place in his life.

> Dulcimer over the fireboard, hanging sence allus-ago,
> Strangers are wishful to buy you, and make of your music a show;
> Not while the selling a heart for a gold-piece is reckoned a sin,
> Not while the word of old Enoch still stands as a law for his kin.
>
> Grandsir' he made you in Breathitt, the while he was courting a maid.
> Nary a one of his offsprings, right down to the least one, but played,
> Played and passed on to his people, with only the song to abide,
> Long-ago songs of Old England, whose lads we're now fighting beside.
>
> There you'll be hanging to greet him, when Jasper comes home from the fight.
> Nary a letter he's writ us, but he'll be a-coming, all right.
> Jasper's the last of the Logans. Hit's reason to think that he'll beat,
> Beat and beget sons and daughters to sing the old songs at his feet.[2]

The origin of the dulcimer of the Southern Highlands is unknown, although instruments of that name have long been made throughout the world. Research on the subject is rather difficult because the word itself, which can be traced back to ancient times, cannot be relied upon to signify the same instrument in different periods or in different countries. Webster defines the dulcimer as "an instrument having metallic wires stretched over a trapezoidal sound board, with a compass of two or three octaves. It is played with two light hammers held in the hands." This definition clearly

[1] Kinfolks. Houghton Mifflin Co., Boston, 1922, p. 59. Reprinted here by permission of the author.

[2] Ibid., pp. 3-4.

MOUNTAIN CHILD'S ROCKER

Rocking Chair Made at Crossville, Tennessee, by the Traditional Methods of the Mountain Chairmaker. It Is Decorated with Rings Colored by Puccoon or Blood Root

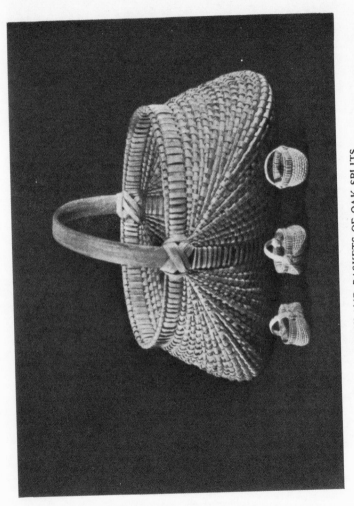

HIGHLAND BASKETS OF OAK SPLITS

Bushel and Three Tiny Baskets, All of Oak Splits, Made by Mrs. James H. Jones, One of the Best Basket Makers in the Mountains, Who Lives Near Wytheville, Virginia

refers to another instrument, much more elaborate in structure and played in a manner differing from any known performance in the Highlands.

The mountain dulcimer is played with a plectrum of wood or a goose quill; in very rare instances with a bow. The best known type was made by James Edward Thomas near Bath, Kentucky. The instrument, of which this is an example, is often referred to as the Kentucky dulcimer and it may have originated in Kentucky, where certainly many more "dulcimores" have been produced in the last half century than anywhere else. But they have also been made and played for many years in Virginia, West Virginia, North Carolina, Tennessee, and Georgia, as well as in Kentucky, and probably in the mountain areas of Alabama, South Carolina, and Maryland.

Reason would seem to uphold the claim that the Kentucky dulcimer originated in the Southern Highlands, and that only the name for it was derived from the instrument of Old World make. It is possible that the Kentucky dulcimer might have grown out of an attempt to fashion with a few crude tools and limited material an instrument after one faintly remembered, rather than to have been a copy of an instrument actually in existence. This would appear to be supported by two facts: first, that no close prototype of the Highland dulcimers is to be found in the instrument collections of Europe or of America; and second, that there are considerable variations in those discovered in different parts of the mountains. When such dissimilarities in form exist among instruments made in the same region, is it not reasonable to suppose that the instrument made for generations in the wilderness of the southern mountains would vary still more from its possible ancestor?

One of the most thorough pieces of research on an American musical instrument that bears a likeness to the dulcimer is that on the Pennsylvania zither by the late Dr. Henry Mercer of the Bucks County Historical Society. After tracing this instrument to sources in Germany, Holland, and France, and indicating the modification that had come through the making of these instruments in America, Dr. Mercer refers to the Kentucky dulcimer as probably having been copied from a similar instrument brought over from England about one hundred and fifty years ago. While this surmise as to the English origin may be correct, it seems to rest rather upon the assumption that the dulcimer came from the Mother Country of many Highland forebears than upon an established fact that there was a similar instrument in England. To England, Ireland, or Scotland would be the obvious directions in which to look, but the obvious direction does not always prove to be the right one; and might it not be possible that the Kentucky dulcimer was influenced directly by the Pennsylvania German instrument, just as some of the spinning wheels found in the Highlands were undoubtedly copied from models originally made in Pennsylvania? Moreover, this theory would be strengthened by the fact that the Germans of Pennsylvania did migrate into the mountains of Virginia and West Virginia and occasionally into other Highland states. There are no dulcimers so old that they could not have been derived from or influenced by the German zither to which it bears such striking resemblance. It is unquestionably true that the dulcimer in the mountains has long been used as an accompaniment to English, Scotch, and Irish songs by the folk of these national strains, but that does not prove its origin. It might reasonably be that the first dulcimer of the Highland type was an adaptation from the German zither; or, as stated before, it may have been an entirely new instrument modeled to meet the need of the Highlander for an accompaniment to his songs, which it does so admirably—the one point about which there is no dispute. Whatever the origin, the dulcimer is now the accredited musical instrument of the Highland region and bids fair to continue in popularity as an accompaniment to old ballads.

Mr. Thomas, the most outstanding dulcimer maker of the Highlands, was born about 1850 in Letcher County, Kentucky. He began making dulcimers when he was twenty-one years old, continuing with considerable regularity until shortly before his death in 1933, a working period of nearly sixty-two years. He is said to have numbered the instruments. It is believed by some of his acquaintances that he may have made as many as 1,500 all told. There is no record showing exactly what disposition was made of all of these, but probably Mr. Thomas' statement that "they went to all lands everywhere" is not too vague if we think of all lands as meaning the United States and England. Most of them, he is reported to have said, were sold in New York because there were "more people there than anywhere else." He sold a considerable number by mail, and these sometimes gave him trouble. His nephew at one time said that "Uncle Eddie" had made a dulcimer for the Prince of Wales, but he had not sent it yet because he did not know his post-office address. The instrument finally went, however, and Mr. Thomas related the agreeable news that "the king" had written him a nice letter "with a lot of gold and purple in it," but one of the children he said burned the letter by mistake, "so he couldn't show it to anyone any more!"

Mr. Thomas made his dulcimers usually of walnut though sometimes of maple or birch, and a few of California redwood which he said came from "far over the seas." His earlier ones were carefully put together, but time and weather have loosened some of the joints and in his late years the craftsmanship did not come up to that in the early ones. His favorite design for the holes in the body of the dulcimer was heart shaped. The decoration around the heart is painted in gold on a few of his instruments.

There are dulcimers in the mountains said to be older than those made by Mr. Thomas. Jean Thomas, founder of the American Folk Song Society, reports two old players, Enos Williams and Tom West, who took part in the first annual meeting of the Society near Ashland, Kentucky, in 1930 as using dulcimers which their grandfathers had made, and she believes that the one belonging to Tom West is the oldest to be found in the mountains.

Jethro Amburgey, who has charge of the woodwork in the shops at Hindman Settlement School, and who is also a proficient player of the dulcimer, is probably the best maker in the mountains today and he learned the craft from Mr. Thomas. Jethro is a descendant of Ambrose Amburgey, who came from Clinch River, Virginia, to what is known as Knott County, Kentucky, in 1825, and bought 10,000 acres of land at the rate of six cents an acre on Carr Creek.

Lewis Hinkle of Volga, Upshur County, West Virginia, who is now seventy-nine years of age, has been making dulcimers for over fifty years. His instruments are about a yard long, often constructed from several kinds of wood. The body of one made recently is of yellow pine, cedar, white oak, poplar, and black walnut. The pegs are carefully carved. During the major part of his life Mr. Hinkie was a teacher and at the noon recreational period he taught some of his pupils to make dulcimers.

Any discussion of the dulcimer of today should include a reference to the experiments of Mr. Niles, an authority on the mountain dulcimer. An accomplished player of that instrument, Mr. Niles has had several made in different parts of the Highlands. These differ in materials used, and somewhat in the form of the body and in other small details. Three of them are made respectively of walnut, maple, and holly wood. After working with these dulcimers and with others in connection with mountain songs, Mr. Niles believes that the original instrument differed from that of today, having possibly fewer frets and probably more than the usual three strings. On this supposition he has worked out with different mountain craftsmen a few models somewhat larger in size and with a number of improvements which give not only a wider range of expression but a much greater volume, so that the tones will carry quite well throughout a concert hall. In the old days the mountain dulcimer was not often required to carry its tones beyond the range of a log-cabin room. It was never used in church although it was used sometimes at a dance. It was essentially a personal instrument. The large dulcimer in the group pictured opposite page 242 was made at the John C. Campbell Folk School by Mr. Niles and Park Fisher.

FIDDLES AND FIDDLERS

While the fiddle is in no way a unique instrument in the mountains, it is one of the most important and is probably played by more people than any other instrument. It is used for entertainment, for dancing, for singing, and occasionally at church. Fiddlers' conventions are still carried on, and fiddling contests are among the popular features of every "old-folks'" day, of pioneer meetings, and family reunions, the competition among players being the keenest of that on any instrument in the South.

Knoxville, Tennessee, is an old-time center for fiddlers' conventions. One is held annually in which there are usually from 20 to 40 entries. The judges are sometimes chosen from the audience, the contestants having the privilege of questioning any candidate for the position and if not found satisfactory of rejecting him. A few years ago one of the candidates was asked by an old-time player which he liked better—the "old-timey" music or the "new fangled" music. The candidate replied that he liked them both, to which the fiddler said with quickness and conviction, "You're out." Other candidates were also rejected by him until one who was positive in his attitude toward old tunes was chosen.

In this fiddlers' convention each contestant had the right to play two tunes of his own choice and there was a great variety of selections, including Grey Eagle, Old Hen and Chickens, Sourwood Mountain, Turkey Buzzard, Old Blue Eagle, and Napoleon Crossing the Rocky Mountains, which several contestants chose to render. This tune seemed to be a favorite and one which it was stated was local to that part of Tennessee. This, however, proved to be an error, for it was found to be also popular in parts of North Carolina and in Kentucky. Dean William Jesse Baird of Berea College heard it in Pine Mountain and tells this story about it: "Uncle John" delighted in playing for visitors and sooner or later he would say, "Now, I want to play you my favorite; I calls hit Napoleon Crossing the Rocky Mountains." One day a teacher at Pine Mountain said, "Uncle John, you mean Napoleon Crossing the Alps." "I don't know, maybe I do," he replied. Sometime later he was playing for a visitor and at his usual point announced, "Now I want to play you my favorite; I calls hit Napoleon Crossing the Rockies. Some folks say Napoleon never crossed the Rockies, that he crossed the Alps, but historians differ on that point."

Fiddler John learned to play on a gourd fiddle and in his time made several of them. These fiddles have no very lasting qualities but serve a need in the absence of any other. Many old people in Tennessee, Kentucky, and the Carolinas can remember when a "fotched on" fiddle was a subject for local wonder. Of course there were home-made instruments in the Highlands, but among many families it was only the gourd fiddle that was to be found, and some are still to be seen at Pine Mountain and in the neighborhood of Hindman today. Miss Cobb, whose verse is always based on facts, in "Ole Bald Eagle" refers to "Gabriel scraping his old gourd fiddle," and in "The Christmas Tree Up Scuddy" as a part of the entertainment someone prophesies that "Granny'll play her old gourd fiddle some." Many an old-time mountain dance has been well and exclusively served with tunes from the old gourd.

OTHER MUSICAL INSTRUMENTS

The gourd, as is known to many, grows in a great variety of sizes and shapes in the South, and when matured and dried the seeds are taken out and the rind hardens into a light-weight shell of almost wooden quality. Its various shapes, which can be partly determined by exterior pressure while the vegetable is growing, lend themselves to several forms suitable for home-made musical instruments some of which undoubtedly do not appear in the catalogues of authentic instruments.

Next to the gourd fiddle in importance is a kind of mandolin or guitar-shaped instrument which is used by the Cherokee Indians both for a rattle and for a drum. The Highlanders at one time made horns out of gourds, and bugles with which to call sheep, or people in to dinner, and one of Miss Cobb's poems entitled The Gourd Horn reads in part:

> Nowadays-folks can't blow that horn;
> Blow and they puff, puff and they blow,
> And swar the dad-busted thing won't go.
> Gee-oh, I've blowed hit sence I was born.
>
> . . . .
>
> Little old Maw could make hit sing,
> Sing of the corn pone and vinegar pie.[1]

Cane, another plant grown in the Highlands, sometimes called wild bamboo and used by the Cherokee Indians for fishing rods and blow-guns, is also made into flutes and pipes by both the Indian and the white mountaineers.

MAKERS OF MUSICAL INSTRUMENTS

There are, according to replies received from inquiries made in several parts of the Highland region, some 30 or 40 craftsmen making musical instruments of one kind or another today. Many of these are obviously amateur workers who say quite candidly that what they do is merely a hobby or side-line. Of the several types

[1] Kinfolks, p. 6.

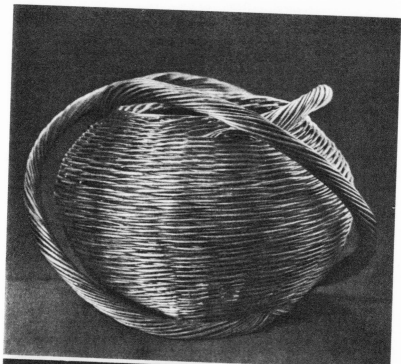

BASKETS FROM KENTUCKY AND VIRGINIA

ABOVE: WILLOW BASKET FROM HINDMAN SETTLEMENT SCHOOL. DESIGNED, MADE, AND DYED BY AUNT CORD RITCHIE, WHOSE PORTRAIT IS SHOWN ELSEWHERE. BELOW: BREAD BASKET, MADE OF GRASS COILS, FROM VIRGINIA

CHEROKEE INDIAN AND HINDMAN BASKETS

UPPER: BASKETS MADE ON THE RESERVATION IN NORTH CAROLINA; TWO ON THE LEFT ARE OF NATIVE CANE, THE OTHER IS OF OAK SPLITS. LOWER LEFT: WILLOW BASKET MADE AT HINDMAN SETTLEMENT. RIGHT: KENTUCKY EGG BASKET OF HICKORY RIBS AND OAK SPLITS

of craftsmen in the Highlands coming under observation in the course of this study, no other group has as large a percentage doing work without any assurance of a market as that making musical instruments. Most of the work is done rather on the principle that there is no probability the product will reach a market. The workers proceed enthusiastically nonetheless, and it is interesting and pertinent to inquire why they employ themselves in producing instruments without a reasonable expectation of money returns.

A maker of violins and guitars, who employs old methods even to making his own tools, states that he does not sell his instruments except to a friend now and then, but he adds, "My guitars win in contests." A rare pride of craftsmanship! Another who makes his violins for local distribution asserts that the pattern is an old Stradivarius dated 1721, which "is easy to copy because it is flat and easy to shave and hollow out." His banjos are old-time instruments with cat-skin heads. A worker of thirty-eight years' experience, making violins of curly maple with ebony trimmings, said he learned "from books and from just working at it." Another in North Carolina constructed a violin from wood taken from an old house built in the year 1837; and a man in Tennessee, who began working in a blacksmith shop at the age of twelve, picked up fiddle making from an "old fellow working there." He plays the fiddle and makes it "just as a hobby." A man who has been a carpenter all his life states: "I made a fiddle in 1924; a guitar in 1926; another one in 1934, just made them for pastime. The fiddle was of poplar, one guitar of black gum and the other of cedar—just experimenting with woods."

The testimony of other instrument makers is interesting:

I am a painter by trade but I have made dulcimers for thirty-eight years.

. . . .

I make my fiddles from start to finish except strings.

. . . .

I have never advertised my violins in any form. I do not make violins for a livelihood but it is entirely a hobby of mine. My age is sixty-five years and I have made 27 violins.

. . . .

I've had a hobby for fiddles and some ten years ago began my first.

I learned by research in the field of the old masters. . . . I have made 20 or 30 violins as good as the best. . . . I do not sell.

. . . .

I have never sold any, but old players say they are good violins. People want them but they have no money to buy, so I make them for pastime.

. . . .

I have always loved the violin above all things else and when I was a little boy I knew I could make one. I always have a buyer for every instrument. I have studied hard for over twenty-eight years. A man's life is too short to learn it all. I am fifty-four years old and feel that I have just begun to learn.

. . . .

Although these expressions from makers of musical instruments are subject to varying interpretations, it is clear that their work is not motivated by market possibilities. The persistent efforts, in the absence of prospective sales, running through many of these reports written in a glowing vein emphasize the close relationship between native music and the making of the instrument that accompanies it. The solitude of the Highlander helped to link two important expressions of mountain culture—its music and its handicrafts.

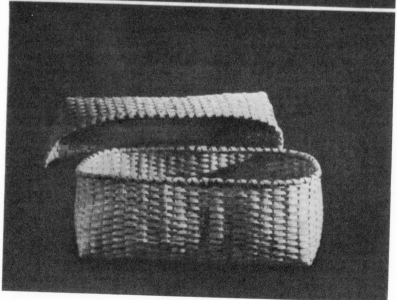

SPLIT OAK BASKETS

ROUND BASKET MADE BY SILAS NICHOLSON OF MOUNTAIN NEIGHBORS, OLDRAG, VIRGINIA;
COVERED BASKET BY A. O. BURTON OF LOCUSTVILLE, VIRGINIA

APPLE WOOD WHITTLING AND TWO FINE BASKETS

Left: Wild Turkey, Made by W. J. Martin Near Murphy, North Carolina. Right: Upper, Basket of Honeysuckle Vine by the Dysart Sisters, Rydal, Georgia; Lower, Finely Cut Oak Split Basket by Nannie Sego of Macon, Kentucky

CHAPTER XIV

POTTERY AND THE USES OF CLAY

THE student of ceramics will find in the Southern Appalachians methods of clay working which go back thousands of years and he will find in the same region commercial potteries of the most modern type. The more primitive end of this remarkable range of ceramic expression is distinguished by the simple gray pottery of the Cherokee Indians of North Carolina, who, using clay from the reservation, shape their pieces by hand, dry them in sun and wind, and harden them in the ovens and fireboxes of their cookstoves, where the gray clay is often smoked brown or burnt black from contact with blazing wood. A piece of the crudest pottery is the result.

The modern end is represented by numerous commercial potteries as, for instance, those at Erwin, Tennessee, where handwork has been largely superseded by power-driven machines, and where chemists and physicists control the product with dependable exactness from beginning to end and the pottery and porcelain become standard articles of world commerce. But interesting and informing as these extreme methods are to the student of ceramics, it is mainly with types which lie between them that this report is concerned—with the old-fashioned hand potteries of the mountain sections, where a few articles of use or beauty are still made by old methods with more or less regularity.

These simple rural potteries, most of them quite primitive, the working force sometimes consisting of only a man and a mule, excite the interest of visitors to the Highlands. In them the nearest approach to a machine is the kick-wheel, a contrivance for throwing clay which was in use in Egypt before the pyramids were built, in China even earlier, and in Europe as far back as written records go. The clay objects are fired with wood, usually in an outdoor arched oven such as was used two centuries ago and longer in the lowlands along the Atlantic seaboard. In these small potteries are made jars, crocks, churns, pots, bowls, cups, saucers, plates, and other household utensils used in many rural homes of the region, besides the vases, candlesticks, door stops, tea and coffee sets, beer mugs, garden pottery, and numerous other articles supplied to buyers both within and outside the Highlands.

PROCESS OF MAKING POTTERY

A rough outline of the main steps employed in pottery making in the Highlands may interest the reader. The clay, whether local or imported (for some potters bring in other clays to mix with the local ones), is washed and ground. Since these potteries use large quantities in making vessels of generous size, the mixing is quite a task and is usually done by mule or horse power. The clay is placèd in a box with the grinding boards or paddles connected with a long shaft to the end of which the mule or horse is attached, and as he makes the circle the boards or paddles slowly grind and mix the earth to workable consistency and proportions. A clay-grinding outfit is illustrated opposite page 139.

The clay is then stored where it is kept wet, and later "wedged" or worked up into small pieces ready to be shaped by hand or turned on the potter's wheel, as are most of the pieces. Throwing the clay on the kick-wheel is one of the most magical processes in the whole field of handicrafts; it cannot be adequately described in words but must be seen to be fully appreciated, and in the unhurried work of the Highlands are excellent opportunities for doing so. After the piece is thrown it is set apart and dried to a point where the glaze can be applied with a brush, or by dipping, and after proper seasoning it is placed in the kiln to fire.

After having been fired and removed, the articles are assorted; some are discarded; a few may require minor operations on an emery-wheel to remove lumps of hardened clay, although not every mountain potter bothers to do this or to level the bases so they will set square. The pieces are then stacked in bins or scattered about on tables and shelves or on the ground for the inspection of the passerby.

POTTERIES OF THE PIEDMONT SECTION

Some of these potteries are in the high mountains, some on the plateaus, and several especially interesting are in the Piedmont section of North Carolina. While the Piedmont section is not, strictly speaking, within the Highlands, as defined and described in the base map of the area, yet there is justification for referring to it briefly in a discussion of the pottery of this region. Reference is sometimes made to the "Southern Highlander and his kin in the Piedmont," for there are many family relationships between these sections and special handicraft practices common to each. Of these the potteries are perhaps the most important link, for frequently in the Highlands one comes across clay products made only in the Piedmont, and in several instances the Piedmont potteries make the jars, bowls, jugs, and other containers used for jams, jellies, preserves, honey, and other foodstuffs prepared by the Highlander for his own markets.

Perhaps the product generally known to the public from the Piedmont section of North Carolina is the Jugtown Pottery, which has been revived and improved under the direction of Mr. and Mrs. Jacques Busbee, near Steeds, Montgomery County, North Carolina. These quaint and attractive articles have been described many times in newspapers and magazines and examples are to be found widely scattered throughout the country. All of the pieces are turned on a primitive kick-wheel by workmen of the neighborhood and usually are in Carolina patterns and glazes. A few forms of exceptional interest to the student of ceramics and to artist and collector, inspired by old Chinese influences, have been developed by the Busbees; but it is the native pottery which is best known, and it is this traditional product which they have conserved, improved, and which they have made available through innumerable outlets the country over.

Other potteries in this region which deserve special mention for form, color, and texture are Cole's Pottery near Seagrove, Randolph County, and the Hilton Pottery at Hickory, Catawba County, both in North Carolina. Some of the most attractive glazes to be found in the South are at Cole's Pottery where all the pieces are shaped by hand, most of them on the kick-wheel, and where they are fired in long, arched kilns of old type. Hilton potters also produce some special glazes including attractive combinations of gray and blue, and they make a good many small containers to hold goods put up by the farm women of the Highlands.

MEADERS' POTTERY

Turning to the potteries within the Highlands, as one gets well over the mountain from Murphy, North Carolina, riding south through northern Georgia in White County, the C. J. Meaders homestead near the small town of Cleveland comes into view. It is situated on a level, grassy spot with a brook running through it, and as one approaches the place he sees between the house and barn, and the road, glistening in the sun, hundreds of pieces of bright, clean ware in brick-reds, browns, blacks, grays, tans, greens, many just out of the kiln.

If one's visit happens fortunately to be in the morning of a day when the kiln is being opened, around the entrance to the arched furnace will be found a lively group of children waiting eagerly to see what is coming out, and each, even the least ones, will now and then claim a piece and, making a bee-line for a certain spot in the grassy yard, will deposit it in the right collection.

Here is a whole family of potters, each child having learned all the operations and never missing the opportunity to shape a few pieces whenever a new kiln is to be fired. There were, when notes were made from which this material was taken, nine brothers and sisters ranging in age from six to eighteen years. It is like Christmas morning at their home whenever a kiln is drawn, and this happens about once every week in the summer.

The family owns a small farm about a mile back from the road on which they get their clay and the wood needed to fire the furnace. The father manages the pottery and gives the children the practical encouragement of making whatever pieces they want for themselves or to sell if buyers should like their wares. One of these pieces, begun as a brown jug, had slumped at some stage in the operation into a candlestick, which the little boy who made it said was just as satisfactory to him as if it had turned out to be a jug. Anyone might well feel the same way; it is not every day that one may see a brown jug turned into a candlestick.

Their kiln is built of brick made from a local clay. Except for some of the glazes, which are now procured from outside by mail this pottery is entirely a local enterprise. Mr. Meaders learned the craft from his father who owned a pottery long ago somewhere in North Carolina. He and the older boys do most of the turning

FOUR EXCELLENT SPLIT OAK BASKETS

The Basket Material Most Used in the Highlands Is Oak Splits. Upper Left, Made in Virginia; Right, in West Virginia. Lower Left, Carolina Basket, in North Carolina; Right, Hamper or Clothes Basket, in Virginia

BASKETS OF DIFFERENT MATERIALS

Mountain Baskets Are Made from Many Materials. Upper Left: Inner Bark of
Hemlock Tree, Called "Spruce Pine"; Right: SmoothedBark of Willow. Lower
Left: White Oak Splits; Right: Buckeye Split So Thin That It Is Pliable

on the old-time kick-wheel, apply the glazes, and do the heavy work of stacking the oven, while the children come in on different operations as they learn how and develop sufficient concentration.

A later visit showed a kiln that four of the smaller children, none older than eleven years, had themselves built of native clay. While in size it was only a small fraction of the family kiln, yet it was so soundly constructed that it drew well and fired the pieces quite satisfactorily. The duty of one of the boys was to go to the forest for the wood needed for firing. Not any kind would do; he must get the same that his father used in the firing of the big furnace, cut it up, dry it out thoroughly, and keep a supply on hand. The children stacked and fired the oven and applied their glazes. A picture of their kiln is shown opposite page 291.

A brother, L. Q. Meaders, conducts another pottery in Leo, White County, Georgia, even more crude in its operation. Most of the work is done by himself and his mule, and there is no great hurry about it. He likes to experiment with local materials and grinds his own glaze between two old millstones. One of these glazes he calls the Shanghai glaze. This he makes partly of the ashes of hardwoods from the fireplace mixed with fine clay which he calls "sedlins." The sedlins he gets only a few hundred yards away, and all the clay he uses comes from within two miles of the pottery. He intends to work up a flint glaze, which melts easily and gives a hard, smooth, dark-greenish finish, from some flint he has seen over in Habersham County about twenty-five miles distant.

The kiln used by L. Q. Meaders is the type employed throughout the mountain region and also in the Piedmont section. It is 15 feet long, 8 feet wide, and 4 feet high. Dimensions of course vary; a kiln is often much longer. It is made of local brick with straight sides and ends and an arched top resembling the tent of a covered wagon. In the front of the kiln is the firebox, a space about five feet deep and running its entire width. This fire space is separated from the rest of the kiln by a low wall. Behind this wall is the oven in which the pottery for firing is stacked. The kiln is opened by removing at one end an oblong section of the wall, about the size of a small door. When the oven is stacked again for firing this small opening is built in once more, brick by brick, and remains closed until the pottery is fired and is ready to be taken out.

After stacking the oven Mr. Meaders builds in the firebox a moderate, slow fire of poplar wood, working up to a hot one of dry pine for finishing. This is the usual formula, sometimes modified in the lowlands and in other parts of the mountains by the woods available. In any case the principle followed is that of beginning with a light fire and gradually building up to a maximum of 3,000 degrees Fahrenheit. The firing requires about twenty-four to thirty-six hours, when the kiln is opened and the objects are taken out as soon as they have cooled enough to handle.

Strong household articles still in use in mountain homes are made in both of the Meaders' potteries. These hard, smooth vessels are especially practical in the milk houses or "mountain spring refrigerators."

OMAR KHAYYAM ART POTTERY

Quite in contrast to the potteries just roughly described, in the mountains of northern Georgia is the Omar Khayyam Art Pottery at Candler, Buncombe County, North Carolina, near Waynesville, which represents the single work of the late O. L. Bachelder, perhaps the oldest potter up to the time of his death in 1935 in the South. Mr. Bachelder had made pottery for more than sixty years and had achieved a high position among American ceramists, receiving a few years ago the award of the Chicago Art Institute craftsmen's prize for his work. His pottery was carefully modeled, was hard, strong, and finished with excellent glazes which he had worked out through long experimentation. He had two kick-wheels and two kilns.

Mr. Bachelder was an individualist and was not concerned with mass production; his attitude toward his work and his feeling as an artist and craftsman is well expressed in a statement which he made upon opening his pottery at Candler:

Here we have come and in the virgin forest and fields of the mountains have builded our home and our shop. Nature has provided at our door a fine clay, richly impregnated with mineral oxides, which produces a pottery of great beauty. The ever-changing and shifting colors of the mountains in this Land of the Sky seem to have found expression in the many-colored shapes produced. Commercial methods of rapid production and duplication are ignored. Each piece produced is a work of loving care. The potter's wheel, ancient of days, the head, a pair of hands, and a small piece of wood for smoothing are the only tools and in our kilns the various shapes are fired.

PISGAH FOREST POTTERY

The Pisgah Forest Pottery made by W. B. Stephens, a friend of Mr. Bachelder, who lives a short distance out of Asheville, North Carolina, is also the work of a single potter. Mr. Stephens' products are not so hard as Mr. Bachelder's, but they often have great beauty of glaze, he preferring as a rule the lighter shades. One of his most successful glazes is turquoise blue, a rare and beautiful color which he applies to both large and small pieces. Sometimes it crackles either in the kiln or later, but it is always very attractive even with the crackle. He has secured some porcelain glazes that rank with the best work of this kind in our country.

Mr. Stephens also does modeling on some of his pieces that results in a type of pottery resembling the old cameo-ware of England, better known as Wedgwood. He is a careful experimenter, building special kilns for his work, and going to great pains to give his product an individual and beautiful appearance.

OTHER MOUNTAIN POTTERIES

Other potteries in the mountain section of North Carolina of the same general character as those already described, which make the receptacles and containers used in that region and some flower pots and other objects for city use, are: the Brown Pottery at Arden, Buncombe County; the Kennedy Pottery, Wilkesboro, Wilkes County; and the Reems Creek Pottery, Weaverville, Buncombe County. D. P. Brown, manager of the Brown Pottery, has made what is said to be the largest single vase ever produced in any southern pottery, measuring 9 feet, 9½ inches around, and 5 feet, 9½ inches high. Mr. Brown's son, aged nine, and his daughter aged seven, model clay pigs, sow and little ones of various sizes, "trying to make every one better and better."

In 1928 the Penland Fireside Industries enlarged the scope of its handicrafts by providing the equipment for ceramics, installing a kick-wheel and a kiln and changing the name to the Penland

Weavers and Potters. They have never produced pottery in large quantities, but have concentrated on both thrown work and tiles and have made many special pieces to harmonize with the textiles for which Penland is noted. In 1935 H. C. Ford, who had helped establish the pottery, assumed full charge and it is now under his able direction.

About 20 miles from Berea College, in Madison County, Kentucky, are two potteries, the Bybee and the Waco, whose products are well known throughout the Southern Highlands and examples of which are often seen as far north as New England. These include a great many forms for all sorts of household and domestic purposes, and each pottery has a large and attractive range of colors in both smooth and semi-mat glazes, although with each the softer finishes predominate. These glazes as a rule are not made of native compounds, but there is a color for nearly every use and the price range for the large variety is very reasonable.

A unique individual product is the work of Mrs. Annie Latham Bartlett of Buckhannon, Upshur County, West Virginia, who took up the study of ceramics after she was well on in years and who has developed a process of hardening the native West Virginia clay without firing by mixing with it certain ingredients of her own discovery. After the pieces have hardened she applies her colors, which are oil paints, then varnishes them, giving the finished object often the appearance of majolica or sometimes almost the quality of colored porcelain. Her figures are all original and include scenes in color and arrangements of local historical or symbolical subjects. Her method makes it possible for her to model the pieces by hand, to secure a wide variety of color, and to sell them at a much lower cost than could be done otherwise.

The most important recent development in the field is the thoroughly equipped and scientifically manned ceramic laboratory installed by the Tennessee Valley Authority at Norris, Tennessee. Here they are carrying out careful experiments with the mineral products of the region, and the prospects are promising for important developments in the ceramics of this area. What this may mean to the hand potters of the Southern Highlands it is not yet possible to say, but it places within their reach unparalleled opportunities for experimentation with their native clays and minerals.

BASKET OF NATIVE SEDGE GRASS AND RAFFIA

Made at Tallulah Falls Industrial School. Sedge Grass, Which Grows Abundantly in Georgia, Is Gathered in Bundles and Bound Together with Some Strong Flat Fiber; It Comes in Many Shades and a Favorite Dye Is Extracted from It

UNCLE WILLIAM AND AUNT SAL CREECH
THEY GAVE THE LAND FOR THE PINE MOUNTAIN SETTLEMENT SCHOOL TO BE USED
FOR SCHOOL PURPOSES, IN UNCLE WILLIAM'S WORDS, "AS LONG AS THE CONSTITUTION OF
THE UNITED STATES STANDS"

FOLK POTTERY

In these rather brief observations on the pottery products of the Highland region, reference has been made mainly to the more usual objects produced for the market. Many of these are in the broad sense examples of folk art, but there are occasional creations that are especially so, instances in which children and grown-ups have made things for the delight of doing them without calculating too carefully how they may be regarded by others or how well they may sell. Among these would be the creations of the younger Meaders children, the pigs made by the Brown children, the chicken salt and pepper shakers of the Jugtown Pottery, as well as the primitive pie plates still made there, the baskets and angels done at Cole's Pottery for the local county fair, the birds and beasts fashioned by Mr. Cole himself and his daughter Nellie just for the fun of doing them, and the odds and ends which one will see at any of these kilns only when it is pretty clear to the timid artist that the visitor would enjoy them.

The pottery of the Cherokee Indians, which though not ranking high as a ceramic product, is expressive of the folk art of this tribe and is evidence of the esthetic feeling of these intelligent and sensitive people who, under the greatest discouragements, have persisted in giving expression to their impulse to creative work through their varied handicrafts. It is a satisfaction to report that steps have recently been taken to give the Cherokees better opportunities to develop their pottery by the installation of a new kiln and some equipment which will enable them to produce a stronger and more varied product.

POTTERY AN OLD CRAFT IN THE HIGHLANDS

It will be noted that some of the most interesting chapters in early American ceramics relate to parts of the Southern Highlands and the neighboring country, including portions of southern Pennsylvania, western Maryland, and Virginia, especially the region of the Shenandoah and that extending into North Carolina through the settlements of the Moravians at Bethabara and Salem, now Winston-Salem. While most of this territory is outside the Highland region, a considerable part is nearby and some entirely within

the area of this study. For those who may be interested in follow
ing up a number of these early leads, a book entitled The Shenan
doah Pottery is recommended, especially its supplement whic
contains excerpts from the Moravian Church Diary of Bethabar
from February, 1756, to September, 1779.[1] These few realistic an
picturesque entries give an exceedingly clear idea of the importanc
of the ware to the early settlers, many of whom had got along wit
little or none of it, and the conditions under which it was produce
and made available to them. Pottery, for a time made exclusivel
in this region by the Moravians, was usually exchanged to th
settlers for butter, "as butter can always be sold for soap makin,
no matter how rancid it becomes."

In these days of creature comforts, when most of us are sur
rounded with more conveniences than we know what to do with
it is worthwhile to turn back the pages of history which revea
what luxuries some of these now common objects of utility wer
to the early settlers of America. Many such glimpses are fur
nished by these records of the Moravians. A part of an entry c
May 18, 1778, reads:

This was a day the like of which had never yet been seen in Salem
Such a crowd had gathered that the street from the tavern to the black
smith shop was so full of people and horses that it was difficult to pas
through. The potter shop was kept closed, and the persons who had
ordered pottery, had paid for it in butter, and had received tickets, were
served through the window. Col. Armstrong did good service, threaten
ing the people with his drawn sword if they did not keep quiet; and for a
wonder they were still; for there were not as many pieces of pottery in the
shop as there were people outside. They realized that it could not be
helped, though many of them got nothing. As many of them were here
for the third day they were hungry, and the bread in the bakery had to be
cut in pieces in order to help the largest number. On this occasion the
store bought about 400 lbs. of butter from those who had come the long
est distance, paying for it 8 d. in silver, or 2 sh. new money. Those who
lived near by took their butter home with them. Soon after noon our
town was clear, and we thanked the Saviour heartily that all had gone so
well.[2]

[1] Rice, A. H., and Stoudt, John Baer, The Shenandoah Pottery. Shenandoah
Publishing House, Inc., Strasburg, Va., 1929.

[2] Ibid., pp. 276–277.

In the limitations of this study it has not been possible to pursue he many fascinating leads which the region and neighboring country hold for the student of clay products, but if one is encouraged to follow out his own lines of research it can be safely predicted that he will find in the Highland states one of the most noteworthy chapters in American ceramics.

CHAPTER XV

MISCELLANEOUS HANDICRAFTS

THE term "miscellaneous handicrafts" as used here wil embrace roughly the types practiced in the Highlands whicl have not been considered in other chapters. Some of th crafts included are important because of the large number of peopl engaged in them, as the candlewick bedspread industry, which ha had a concentrated development in northern Georgia, and hooked rug making carried on in almost every part of the Highlands Others, although they employ only a few people, are worth men tion, as tanning and working of leather or the use of corn husks ir a variety of ways, because with other small industries they have possibilities of future expansion. Some are indigenous, a numbe have been brought in, but all are a part of that ever increasing lis which characterizes the handwork of the region.

Among the types of work taken up in this chapter are rugs candlewick and knotted spreads; needlework, crocheting, anc knitting; metal work; objects made from the corn plant, barks seeds, and gourds; leather work; candles; feather fans; semi precious stone cutting; and food containers. Among these handi crafts, hooked rugs and candlewick spreads have been extensively commercialized and have developed production to meet both whole sale and retail outlets, sometimes having wide business relations with department stores. They are made by individuals, many of whom sell their products to tourists or through schools and handi craft centers to buyers outside the region. Since some work part of the time for commercial organizations and in part independently there will be no attempt to separate or segregate them, simply to indicate some of the best products with an occasional observatior on the worker.

RUG MAKING

There are three general types of rug making—the hooked rug the braided rug, and the woven rug. In the hooked rug, narrow

220

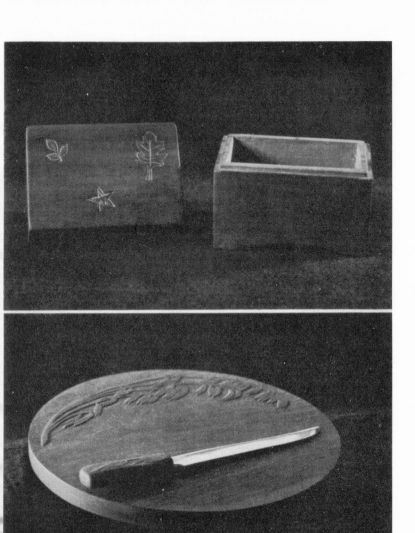

EXAMPLES OF WHITTLING AND CARVING
THE CEDAR BOX WAS DESIGNED AND WHITTLED OUT OF ONE PIECE OF WOOD BY ORBIN
CRANK OF CRAB ORCHARD, KENTUCKY. THE BREAD BOARD WAS DESIGNED AND CARVED
BY NINA BRYAN OF BRASSTOWN, NORTH CAROLINA

CHIP CARVING FROM NATIVE WOODS

At Pleasant Hill Academy Students Are Encouraged to Whittle and Carve.
This Fox Is a Good Example of the Quick Technique They Sometimes Acquire

cloth strips or heavy yarn are pushed and pulled with a metal hook through a cloth base, usually of burlap. The braided rug is made from narrow cloth strips, usually wider than those in hooked rugs, braided into a kind of rope or cord and these are sewed together or interlaced to form a flat mat, usually round or oblong, sometimes small, sometimes large. Practically the same technique is employed in making small table mats and runners. The woven rug is done on a loom, and the old-time heavy frame is especially good for this type of weaving. The loom is usually strung up with a cotton warp and strips of cloth or heavy yarn are used for the weft. The best known form of the woven rug is called rag carpet and is frequently woven in long widths, as a rule through a straight weaving process. Some rugs, however, are inlaid, that is, a part of the design is put in by hand similar to finger weaving, or it may be worked out by laying in strips of weft as the weaving proceeds.

Of these three methods the hooked rug is by far the most common in the region. It is probably not indigenous; since in our country it seems to have had its beginning in New England, where it reached great perfection in the nineteenth century. It has also been long made and used in the Province of Quebec and the maritime provinces, and of recent years hooked rugs of high standard have been made by the Grenfell Industries of Labrador. Throughout the Highlands rug making has come to be one of the more widely practiced handicrafts. In some instances temporary factories have been established by commercial organizations which supply all the materials, select the designs, and supervise the work usually handled on a piece basis; in others the work is taken into the homes where it is always done on a piece basis. But there are hundreds of people throughout the region who work independently of commercial agencies, making their own rugs, either from original designs or from patterns stamped on canvas obtained from the local store, the mail-order houses, or through magazines and pattern books.

The technique of the hooked rug is not difficult to master, but there is considerable variation of workmanship in the finished product. The same is of course true of the patterns and color combinations; one traveling through the region will see great numbers of uninteresting and mediocre rugs, just as he will in sections of rural

Canada. But there are many skilful workers in the Highlands, and when leaders develop good patterns and harmonious color schemes the results are often worthy of the hooked-rug craft.

The rugs around which was grouped the traveling exhibition of the Southern Highland Handicraft Guild in 1933 were products of the Spinning Wheel. Of these the central and largest rug was a good example of freedom in design, the workers having used their discretion and pleasure in much of the detail. The Anderson family, who live in the hills near Beaver Lake, make many of the Spinning Wheel rugs. The family consists of five members, all of whom often work together around the rug frame, deciding among themselves just how to fill in certain parts of the pattern which had been left for them to "cipher out." The quality of their hooking is excellent. Mrs. Anderson and her son are shown at work in the illustration opposite page 158.

Rag-rug making has been one of the principal activities at the Crossnore School since the founding of the school industries, the other being hand-loom weaving. Some of the designs are already stamped on the canvas, but others, especially for the picture rugs, are originated at the School. In this section of the mountains this craft is carried on extensively; one journeying from Asheville to Crossnore passes many homes where rugs are hanging out on clotheslines and porches with signs reading "hand-made by the natives of the Blue Ridge Mountains." Along the route Mrs. Mark Hill of Bat Cave, Henderson County, specializes in rugs which she supplies to many stores and shops in the North. Some are made in her own home, but most in the homes of her neighbors. In either case Mrs. Hill exercises careful control over the design, color, and workmanship.

The Rosemont Industries at Marion, Virginia, as already mentioned,[1] have developed an important hooked-rug department under the direction of Mrs. Laura Copenhaver. A recent design by Mrs. Copenhaver called The Sampler is shown on the end papers. Some of the pictorial subjects such as Mount Vernon, Wakefield, and others of historical interest are original with these workers.

Eastern Tennessee has two rural communities which have developed important and successful hooked-rug industries through

[1] See p. 76.

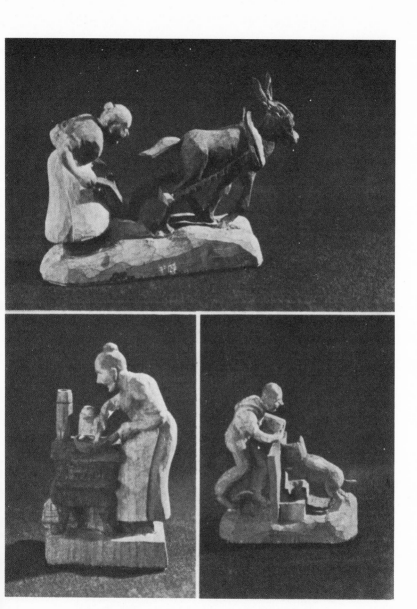

CHIP CARVINGS OF HIGHLAND CHARACTERS

FIGURES WHITTLED OUT OF BUCKEYE OR POPLAR BY TOM BROWN OF PLEASANT HILL
ACADEMY, WHO ALONG WITH HIS SKILL DEVELOPED A SURPRISING SPEED. MOST OF HIS
FIGURES ARE SLIGHTLY COLORED

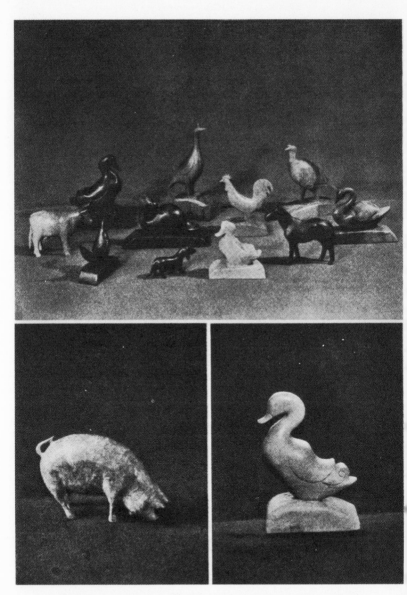

WHITTLING FROM THE JOHN C. CAMPBELL FOLK SCHOOL
THIS SCHOOL WAS THE PIONEER MOUNTAIN GROUP IN WHITTLING. THROUGH NEIGHBORS
ITS INFLUENCE HAS TRAVELED FAR. FARM ANIMALS AND BIRDS ARE FAVORITE SUBJECTS

the persistent experimentation of local women in co-operation with the Extension Division of the Agricultural Department of the University of Tennessee. In 1921 at a community fair in Apison, a few women of Hamilton County exhibited some carefully made braided rugs. They were so well liked that Mrs. Elizabeth Louderback, home demonstration agent, arranged to have them shown at the next session of the Chattanooga district fair. The exhibition was organized by Mrs. F. D. Huckabee of Apison, who, to the surprise of the rug makers, sold out the exhibit while on display at the fair. Following this success the women made both braided and hooked rugs for the Harvest Market held at the Hamilton County Court House. Here more were sold and orders came in from outside until, in 1930, the Apison community rug makers had made and sold about 500 rugs for $5,000, and 10,000 mats at 50 cents each. More than 100 people were engaged in the work during that year.

A similar community industry was developed at Asbury, Knox County, not far from Knoxville, largely through the encouragement of Inez Lovelace, home demonstration agent for Knox County. The work of instruction here has been largely in charge of Mrs. Huckabee, who organized the work, and these rugs and mats find a market in many states. Some of the designing is done by workers themselves, some by Mrs. Huckabee; others are standard designs procured from commercial sources. All the work is very carefully executed and the effort to improve its quality is constant. The hooked rugs here and elsewhere are usually made of cotton rags, though wool and other materials are often combined. Occasionally old silk stockings are used, especially for the small mats and table runners.

Quite the most unusual example of the hooked-rug technique in the Highlands is that displayed in the wall decorations of Mrs. Joy Kime Benton of Hendersonville, Henderson County, North Carolina, whose work is not only exceptional in technique and beauty but whose experience is a fine illustration of the therapeutic value of a handicraft. Mrs. Benton had experienced a nervous breakdown, and her physician told her that hope for recovery lay in a life in the open with some interesting and not too strenuous work to do with her hands. She acquired a small tract of land in the

Blue Ridge Mountains, went there to live, and then addressed herself to the question of what she could learn to do with her hands to follow out her physician's instructions. In the neighborhood she had seen people making hooked rugs, some of which she thought could be improved. She began work in a most primitive way. Making herself a hook with a bent nail and obtaining some canvas and rags she determined to make a rug. But what should the design be? Looking out the window of her cabin was a view which she felt the impulse to interpret in this new medium. Getting some dyes for her rug palette she painstakingly worked out the picture. It was a slow job for she was both weak and ill, and when finished, it seemed too delicate to place on the floor, so she hung it on the wall. Someone came in and wanted to buy it for a wall decoration.

In time Mrs. Benton found that she had developed a unique home art. She prepared the rags, dyed them with special attention to the color needs, hooked them with care, and when completed clipped the loops of the rug and brushed out the ends to make the colors blend more effectively; the result was a picture of interest and charm. These rugs are frequently called rag paintings, or tapestries. To earn something meant a great deal to Mrs. Benton after she had thought her earning days had passed, but an even deeper satisfaction came from doing creative work, for it helped as nothing else could in those long days of the rebuilding of her strength. In May, 1934, Mrs. Benton's work won the award at the Chapel Hill Dogwood Festival for the most outstanding artistic achievement during the year in the state of North Carolina.

Braided rugs are not nearly so common in the Highlands as hooked rugs. Those made by the women of Apison, Tennessee, have already been mentioned. They still make them, of superior quality, although the demand for them is quite limited. The small mats are also made in the mountains of Georgia and South Carolina.

The Highland rag rugs and carpets that are woven on old looms are not so much for market as for home use. However, in the neighborhood of Staunton and Harrisonburg, Virginia, a considerable amount of rag carpeting is made for sale mainly by descendants of the Germans from Pennsylvania who settled in that section.

CANDLEWICK AND OTHER BEDSPREADS

The most concentrated home industry and the one employing the largest number of workers in the Southern Highlands is the candlewick bedspread industry, which, as said earlier, has experienced a remarkable development in northern Georgia where innumerable families are engaged, some members working at it continuously. The ride from Dalton through Calhoun to Cartersville, Georgia, is a most picturesque one with hundreds of bright tufted bedspreads flying from farmhouse clotheslines on both sides of the highway like banners of many colors. They have foundations of white, cream, yellow, green, tan, blue, red, pink, rose, and peach, and are tufted in harmonizing colors, often with an occasional crude design in many hues. But even these at a distance are attractive in the breeze. The countless spreads displayed are but a fraction of the output of the rural homes, for many of the occupants are under contract with commercial firms to supply them on a wholesale basis, and these in turn are sold in department stores throughout the United States. A large firm with headquarters at Dalton, it is said, at one time shipped out 1,000 spreads each morning.

J. Cooper Morcock, Jr., county agent of Gordon County, which is the center of this picturesque district, writes:

There are more than 2,000 farm families in this county. In 90 per cent you will find some member of the family doing bedspread work which they call tufting. It consists of working designs on sheeting with tufting yarn, which is coarsely spun cotton of many strands, about one-quarter inch in diameter. The sheeting on which a design is stamped is obtained from local dealers or bedspread companies. The women and girls, and in many instances the men when they are not otherwise occupied, tuft the design with the various colored yarns.

In addition to the rural families, there are scores of people in town at work. The completed bedspreads are disposed of through bedspread companies, and many hundreds of articles including bath mats, spreads, curtains, etc., are displayed along the highway and sold at what you might call a curb market to the tourists who travel this road.

While the tufting is done in a large variety of patterns, some very attractive designs are "made up" by members of the family and these occasionally prove to be the best sellers on the clothesline. Recently the pattern of an attractive candlewick spread of white tufting on a white background was designed by the grand-mother of the household and executed by her daughter. The grandson also liked to work things out his way, and he drew a small peacock in a few simple lines to use as decoration for a child's apron.

Incidentally the peacock seems to be a favorite motif, usually two birds facing each other, with all their natural colors portrayed by the tufting yarns and often many more. Where the design originated no one seems to know, but almost everyone uses it and presumably sells it. It seems perhaps the least tasteful of any of the designs, because of its elaborate form and its variegated colors.

Another kind of bed covering belonging to the same classification is the knotted spread, one in which the base may be the same as or similar to that used in the candlewick spread, but the design is put on in knots or loops and remains so. It is often spoken of as a tufted spread, but the material is not cut and frayed as in the candlewick. Bird in the Tree is a favorite design and a good example of a knotted spread.

The tufted, or "turfed" as some of the old-timers call the operation, and the knotted spreads are not new to the Southern Highlands, nor do all those being made at the present time come from the northern section of Georgia. The industry is located there but the craft is carried on in the homes of North Carolina, Kentucky, and Tennessee, and in some instances these spreads are made for sale. It is an old occupation, the origin of which is perhaps unknown, but it is referred to in Mountain Homespun[1] as one of those which marked the early days of the revival of handicrafts in North Carolina, and today near Allanstand a few women still practice it. At the salesroom of the Southern Highland Handicraft Guild in Asheville, both candlewick and knotted spreads are to be had, some survivals of the old-time designs, Wreaths of Roses, Bird in the Tree, Bowknots, Flowers, and Napoleon's Wreath.

A visit to the home of Mrs. W. B. Thompson, who made the candlewick spreads for Fryemont Inn, Bryson City, North Carolina, which is furnished largely by mountain-made things, revealed the naïve way in which she worked out most of her patterns. The

[1] Goodrich, Frances Louisa, Mountain Homespun. Yale University Press, New Haven, 1931.

design was founded on an old method of play once common with country children. A large sheet of paper was folded over and over again into small squares, and then some simple forms were cut through the several thicknesses which, when opened out, would yield circles, squares, or other repeated geometric motifs. This unique way of getting designs has in it a delightful element of surprise. Although most of Mrs. Thompson's are very simple in order that the spreads which sell for $2.00 and $3.00 each may be done quickly, she has devised for herself and family other figures which were quite elaborate and very attractive.

A report[1] made in 1935 goes quite extensively into the candlewick spread industry as carried on in northern Georgia. In the opinion of the investigators it should be possible so to organize it as to increase considerably the earning power of those engaged in it, many of whom receive at present less than a subsistence wage.

In passing, it may be stated that the industry is one about which the business interests are enthusiastic. It is one of the few handicrafts that have been commercially standardized. As one sees the great quantity of spreads in department stores throughout the country one would like to feel that it denotes prosperity at the source of supply, but when the low retail prices which have helped to make them so popular are traced back to their origins, it is too often discovered that the makers' share is pitifully small. The profits are first to the department store, which will usually average about 100 per cent on the sales; then to the jobbers, whose firms showed sufficient returns even in depression times to open several new establishments; and finally comes the worker who in most cases is very much underpaid.

Meager as the wage is, however, there are hundreds of homes in northern Georgia which depend upon it for cash incomes, and when working and living conditions are considered the small returns are more important than the figures would indicate. There is little doubt that the situation could be improved through co-operation and with results beneficial to the entire industry. The various

[1] Nienburg, Bertha M., Potential Earning Power of Southern Mountaineer Handicrafts. U. S. Dept. of Labor, Women's Bureau, Bulletin 128, Washington, 1935.

interests concerned should take up these problems and gradually work them out, rather than wait until a quick adjustment is forced that might injure or even destroy the industry which is flourishing at the present time because it supplies an acceptable article at a very low price. The adjustment should not result in raising the price of the product so high that it will no longer seem a bargain to the consumer, for once this is done the industry will suffer, perhaps irretrievably. The problem must therefore be approached in the interest of all those who are engaged in it.

NEEDLEWORK, CROCHETING, AND KNITTING

There are many forms of needlework practiced in the mountains, including embroidery, appliqué, cross-stitching, sampler making, and a good deal of ordinary sewing. It would be possible to mention a great number of examples of work with the sewing needle, the knitting needle, and the crochet hook in every Highland state, but such a list once begun would never end. Therefore only an occasional example will be referred to and that perhaps for a special reason. For instance, Granny Donaldson's blanket, which is a combination of crocheting and appliqué, is noted because it is a good expression of folk art and reflects a delightfully refreshing spirit. Granny Donaldson, who lives near Brasstown, North Carolina, saw an Italian cow blanket, a beautiful covering with decorations of crocheted flowers sewed on a linen base. The blanket had been used in Italy to drape over the back of the family cow on festival occasions, and a fine, colorful decoration it was. Granny Donaldson became interested in the purpose of the blanket and the way it had been made and she set about to create a blanket of her own. The work illustrated opposite page 272 is the result. She is glad to make any article that she can sell, for her income is very meager, but she hardly expected that anyone would be interested in purchasing her cow blanket, for she made it to satisfy her desire. Someone admired it and asked her if she would be willing to make another just like it. No, she was not interested in duplicating anything. In fact she would not do two things alike for any amount of money, but she would be glad "to do something else, maybe better," for a very reasonable price. The order was placed and the result was even more satisfactory to the purchaser than the

DOOR TO A HOME IN WASHINGTON, D. C.
THE TRYON TOY-MAKERS AND WOOD-CARVERS OF TRYON, NORTH CAROLINA, WHO
CARVED THIS DOOR ARE MOUNTAIN BOYS AND GIRLS TRAINED BY ELEANOR VANCE AND
CHARLOTTE YALE, PIONEERS IN HIGHLAND HANDICRAFTS

WORK OF A NATIVE MOUNTAINEER

PRAIRIE SCHOONER AND OXEN WHITTLED OUT BY JOE BURKETT OF BOONE, NORTH CAROLINA

first blanket, without having done violence to the maker's artistic convictions.

A wide variety of crocheted, knitted, and braided articles is made in the Highlands, most of it for personal or family use, but a few centers make special articles for sale; for instance, members of the Mountaineer Craftsmen's Cooperative Association of Morgantown, West Virginia, in addition to other novelties crochet some interesting toy animals. The students of Berea also make stuffed animals, dolls, and a variety of novelties.

METAL WORK

In pioneer days the blacksmith was an important figure, and in the more remote places a mountaineer had to be his own blacksmith. In certain regions similar conditions prevail today, and there are instances in which practically everything that is constructed of iron about the home is done on the place. Some of the shops in the towns and villages and along the roads where they once repaired wagons, buggies, machinery, and so forth, have branched out into wrought-iron work and in a few instances have found quite a demand for it.

Such an experience came to the Boone family. There were four brothers, descendants of Daniel Boone, who worked as blacksmiths in the mountains near Burnsville, North Carolina. As automobiles came in, both horse shoeing and wagon repairing decreased until only two of the brothers continued to work at the old trade. Finally three sons of one of them succeeded to the business, where they made principally wrought-iron objects for household use. Their products included andirons, fireplace sets, candlesticks, door knockers, lanterns, weather vanes, and other articles in both sheet and solid metal. Now they are working separately in different parts of the Highlands.

At Berea College iron work has long been one of the handicrafts which have appealed to mountain boys, giving them the double opportunity of developing their skill and of making objects to help defray their school expenses. The work includes an excellent range of objects.

A unique business has been built up by a Highland family in the neighborhood of Hendersonville, North Carolina, which collects old iron from the countryside and works it up into attractive objects for fireplace fixtures and other home furnishings, the craftsmen usually making their own designs. Frank Gayhart, who runs the sawmill at Wooton, Leslie County, Kentucky, where he makes furniture for himself and neighbors, also does iron work. The lanterns at the entrance to the crafts building of the John and Mary R. Markle School were made by Mr. Gayhart.

Several schools make candlesticks, candelabra, trays, fire sets, and sometimes articles in which wood and metal are combined. Among the latest to develop objects from scrap-iron is the John C. Campbell Folk School. The workers also combine copper and brass with wood, one of their best efforts being a small fireplace bellows.

A new departure in metal work was inaugurated by the Penland Weavers and Potters when several of the boys and men were instructed in the hammering of pewter. Most of this work is plain and on simple lines but well done, and the objects are often very attractive when used with the excellent Penland weaving as a background.

ARTICLES MADE FROM THE CORN PLANT

Some of the most interesting handicrafts of the region are made from its basic food plant, corn. The little patches on the steep hillsides or in the pocket valleys of the Blue Ridge, the Smokies, or the Nantahala ranges would seem to the farmer of the broad and rich lands of Iowa or Kansas, or the fertile valleys of New York and Pennsylvania, as of little consequence, but to many a Highlander they are the foundation of his existence. The corn patch furnishes food for man and beast. It is the main and dependable crop of the mountains, and as winter sets in the poorest settler will look to his corn-crib and his pigpen to carry him through.

The attitude toward the corn crop does not take the form of a beautiful ceremonial as with some of our Indian tribes; but the mountaineer, if you visit him after harvest time, will show you with eagerness and feeling his supply of corn for the winter stored away under the best shelter he can devise. Even to those who have more than corn and pork in prospect for the winter, corn is still the staff of life, and many families able to purchase a variety of table supplies from the market will make water-ground cornmeal the main item in their larder. There are many places where better corn is grown than in the Highlands, but surely there is no place where it means more to those who raise it. And probably no people in our country have developed so many handicraft expressions from the plant as they have.

Among some of the uses to which this great food plant has been put are the following: the stuffing of mattresses, the twisted and woven fibers for chair and stool bottoms, and for screens and other pieces of furniture. The making of chair bottoms of corn husks is shown opposite page 99. Corn husks are woven into door mats for both house and barn, and light-weight mats are made for lamps, hot dishes, and teapots. The husks are sometimes twisted into ropes and used as bed cords, and both horse and mule collars are made from them. They are also pressed out and made into lamp shades, trays, work baskets, shopping bags, handbags, and pocket-books, also plaited and braided into attractive hats for girls and women. A great number of other objects both ornamental and useful are now fashioned out of the husks, stalks, cobs, silk, and kernels. A very light-weight fan is made of husks, and necklaces are made by stringing together some of the nicely colored grains of corn. Picture and mirror frames are sometimes made of corn stalks, usually with a wooden framework, except with very small frames when no wood is required. A woman in Tennessee makes napkin rings, bracelets, hatbands, flowers, and small fruits and vegetables, all in color from corn husks.

The common uses for the corn-stalk and the corn-cob in home and farm are infinite, that of the corn-cob pipe being a familiar feature of the mountain scene. But the most pleasing sight of all undoubtedly is that of the rows and rows of beautiful strings of field and popcorn hanging in the kitchen or chimney corner of mountain homes to be used when snow lies on the hillsides and the fire on the hearth is bright. Combined with strings of shucky beans and red and yellow peppers they make the most appropriate decoration for the mountain cabin that could be devised.

The use of corn husks in the making of dolls and other figures has been described in some detail in Chapter XII, Toys, Dolls, and Miniature Furniture.

ARTICLES MADE FROM BARK, SEEDS, PLANTS, AND GOURDS

There are numerous instances of the use of native barks, cones, grasses, seeds, and so forth, for home use or decoration that may be worthwhile to note. Chestnut, poplar, and other barks are employed quite extensively for covering houses in the vicinity of Crossnore and Linville, Avery County, North Carolina. The bark is carefully cut in strips from about six to 15 inches wide, and from two to four feet long, then flattened out by piling one strip on top of the other out in the woods. When shaped and cured the bark is nailed over the log or board frame of the house, usually vertically, which gives an outside finish that resists the weather, never requires paint or stain, and the color and texture of which are in perfect harmony with the surroundings.

Sometimes these natural barks are effectively used for interior finishing, a notable instance being in the community church at Crossnore. This church is a good example of the adaptation of native materials to the construction of a building, much of the wood and all the stone coming from the community. The work was directed by a pioneer Highlander, Uncle Will Franklin, father of the well-known mountain minister, McCoy Franklin. Uncle Will did not begin the church, but reluctantly took the work over in the early stages and finished it. Some "outlanders" had begun by building a foundation which, when the concrete forms were taken off, on measurement proved to be from a foot to a foot and a half in error. Preacher Franklin discovered the mistake and asked his father if he would come in and take charge of the work. The father finally consented, and although he could neither read nor write, there having been no schools in the section where he grew up, he was a practical woodsman and carpenter and he finished the job according to his best ideas. The result is one of the most interesting and attractive churches in the mountains.

The rafters in the construction of the roof were left exposed and the ceiling open. Instead of finished lumber to fill in between the beams, which would have been quite expensive, Uncle Will thought to use native bark, which he cut into random widths and fastened to the sheathing in a simple but attractive herringbone pattern. When asked how he came to employ that pattern, he explained that he had put some pieces of bark up longways and then some

ORIGINAL DESIGN BY A MOUNTAIN WHITTLER
Rooster Carved and Decorated by Nicodemus Demon Adams of Banner, Virginia.
Body of Maple Wood and Legs of Twisted Wire

BEAR BY A MOUNTAIN CARVER

Carved Out of Native Holly Wood by D. L. Millsaps of Damascus, Virginia. The Tooling, Which Gives an Interesting Texture, Is Done with a Small Sharp Gouge Held in the Hand "Used Much as You Use a Pen When Writing"

sideways, and neither of them looked just right to him, but by joining them up into something that was "kind of between" he thought they looked nice, and so continued that way. This section of North Carolina seems to be the only part of the Highlands where bark is extensively used for both exterior and interior finishing.

The use of pine cones for making birds is not a new idea nor one native to these regions, but it is likely that the little turkeys made in a number of places in North Carolina are original with mountain people. The wild turkey is sometimes still to be seen in the Highlands. The cones which form the body of the miniature bird are usually moist and quite smooth when made, but later the warm temperature of the house causes them to "ruffle up" much as the turkey does. The color of some of the dry cones is not unlike that of the turkey's feathers, so that altogether they are quite realistic little toys.

In wandering through the mountains it is not uncommon to come across women and children gathering the seeds, pods, berries, acorns, leaves, and cones in which the Highlands abound and arranging them in attractive and interesting forms. The natives call these "wood pretties." Much of this work is not especially artistic in arrangement but it affords much pleasure. Particularly in parts of Virginia and West Virginia are to be seen well-made wreaths and decorations, and some miniature gardens to be kept under glass which find their way into many homes and to a few markets outside the mountains, especially at Christmas time. The skill and taste required in the arrangement of these attractive plants bring them into the realm of handicrafts. One of these craftswomen is Mrs. W. H. Blauvelt of Asheville, who makes compositions of seeds, stems, and grasses for Allanstand Industries, utilizing both wild plants and those from her own garden.

The wild sedge grass growing in many parts of the Southern Highlands is interesting from a handicraft point of view for two reasons: first, it yields very good dye and was in the old days used quite generally in the mountain home for coloring wool; and second, it is suitable for basket making, the most attractive creations of which have come from the Tallulah Falls Industrial School. These have been noted in Chapter X, Mountain Baskets.

Perhaps more gourds are grown and wider use found for them in the Southern Highlands than in any other part of our country. The plants thrive there, and from pioneer days gourd receptacles have been in daily use in the mountain home, the proverbial gourd dipper being a good example. Gourds have, as already mentioned, long been used as sounding boxes for home-made fiddles and banjos. At the present time small gourds are grown quite extensively because of their decorative value, and middle-sized ones are used widely for bird houses. Very little up to this time has been accomplished in the way of decorating gourds, as is the custom in Mexico and other countries, but this practice is likely to come with more intensive handicraft development.

LEATHER WORK

One of the pioneer industries which has disappeared from most rural sections of our country but is still carried on in parts of the Southern Highlands in the same way as it was a hundred years ago in New England, is the tanning and working of leather. The Highlands are particularly rich in trees producing tannic acid, and by old-time tanning methods excellent leather is made there. One of the tanners and leather workers of the region is Covey Odom, living at Luther, Hamblen County, Tennessee, who produces a fine leather, tanned entirely with materials from his own homeplace. He makes the leather up into saddle-bags, harness, and other practical articles used in the region. A study of him at his one-man tannery appears opposite page 154. William Isaac Wimpey of Hayesville, Clay County, North Carolina, also has a tannery which he operates alone. Probably no better job of tanning could be done than that undertaken in this spot where nature has furnished the materials needed.

In addition to the saddle-bags, harness, horse equipment, and purses made in the Highlands the leather for bellows used by blacksmiths and metal workers is prepared in such a way as to insure long service. It seems reasonable that some leather work will continue on a small scale where conditions are so favorable and natural tanning acids are to be found in such abundance.

CANDLE MAKING

Candle making is still carried on in a few homes in the Southern Highlands. Two types are made for the market—one the bayberry, the other the honeywax candle. Bayberry candles are made at Penland, North Carolina. The Penland Weavers and Potters prepare these to harmonize with the pottery and pewter candlesticks which they produce.

The honeywax or beeswax candle, which was very common in the old days, is made now by Leonard Lamb of the Wayside Mountain Products Company, Knoxville, Tennessee. Mr. Lamb, who has made a special study of candles, has developed several artistic forms and a variety of colors. The core is standard with a very thick beeswax covering which gives a pleasant fragrance when burning. The flame of the candle makes a cup for itself, which holds the melted wax, and it thus burns much longer than an ordinary candle and without any smoke.

FEATHER FANS

An old-time home industry practiced quite widely throughout the United States and now carried on in parts of North Carolina, Georgia, Tennessee, and Kentucky is the making of fans from the feathers of geese, turkeys, guinea fowls, and peacocks. The use of the turkey wing for the mountain hearth is proverbial, but the fashioning of the white and gray feathers of the domestic goose or peacock into a carefully designed and made fan for personal use is a much more refined article.

In addition to this type of fan, a "fly bush" of peacock feathers is made; a gorgeous object which was used before the day of mosquito netting and wire screens to shoo the flies away from the dining table. The feathers, sometimes a hundred of them, are held together by braiding the quills into a strong, firm, handsome handle, the completed object being usually about three or four feet long.

STONE CUTTING

Stone cutting or lapidary work in the Highlands has not developed far as a handicraft, although a number of men and boys throughout the country are very much interested in the native mineral products. Roby Buchanan in Cane Creek Valley near

Hawk, Mitchell County, collects the stones in the rough and uses his water wheel for the power to grind them into shape when it is not needed for the regular work of grinding local grain and corn.

Another lapidary, Rev. R. B. Owens, of Charlotte, North Carolina, has brought together a very attractive group of semi-precious stones of the state which he himself grinds and polishes.

DECORATED FOODS AND CONTAINERS

Handicrafts are now being used increasingly in connection with the preservation of foods for home and market. Among the outstanding accomplishments so far in this respect have been the making and use of different pottery receptacles for jams, jellies, and preserves, and other confections mentioned in the chapter on mountain pottery. Because of the abundance of pottery produced in the South, it is possible for mountain people to obtain excellent small containers and receptacles at low prices which they can sell at a profit and which in many instances help to dispose of the food as well. Wild strawberries grow in abundance in parts of North Carolina and Kentucky; blueberries and dewberries also grow wild and there are cultivated berries and other fruits which can be sold much more readily when packed in artistic containers.

Probably the most popular food confection in the Highlands is the attractively decorated tea sugars from Berea College of which over a million boxes are reported to have been sold in the past two or three years. Berea students began by decorating the sugar cube with native wild flowers, a motif that is still the most popular perhaps of all they produce, but now they make special designs for Christmas, Hallowe'en, Easter, Fourth of July, and other seasons thus multiplying the output of the candy kitchen of the school.

Food does not ordinarily come within the scope of handicrafts but when in the preparation thought is given to the form, color and texture, or special attention given to the receptacles in which it is packed, then it becomes a handicraft within the definition of the term as used in this report. The proper packaging of rural foodstuffs is in its infancy, and there is no question that as country people become more experienced and artistic in the way they process their foods and in the choice of containers for them, the demand will be much greater and higher prices will be the result.

CHAPTER XVI

THE SOUTHERN HIGHLAND HANDICRAFT GUILD

NOT until more than thirty years after the revival of handicrafts had begun in the Southern Highlands, did the producing centers unite in a co-operative effort to improve their products and work out their common problems. The first meeting for this purpose was held at Penland, North Carolina, in late December, 1928, and out of this came plans leading to the formation of the Southern Mountain Handicraft Guild, later changed to the Southern Highland Handicraft Guild, an organization now comprising the leading handicraft centers and many individual workers of the region.

The founding of the Guild marks one of the most important developments in the handicrafts of the Highlands and of the entire country. Through it the standard of design and workmanship has been improved, variety of products enlarged, individuality of expression encouraged, use of native materials increased, better exhibitions held, markets expanded, and co-operation both within and outside the mountains greatly augmented. Inasmuch as the Guild has come to be widely recognized as a source of information and its co-operation has extended to interests outside the region, a brief sketch of its development and activities would seem in place here.

BEGINNING OF THE GUILD

Two days after Christmas, in 1928, a small group of people, mainly from the mountain sections of North Carolina, Tennessee, and Kentucky, came together in the Weavers' Cabin on the top of Conley's Ridge at Penland, North Carolina, to talk over the handicraft situation in the mountains and to take what proved to be the first steps toward the formation of the Southern Highland Handicraft Guild. The Guild itself was not formally launched until some time later, but here were developed the ideas and principles which have guided the organization from its beginning to the present time.

In all the Highlands there seemed no more fitting place for this pioneer meeting than the Weavers' Cabin on the summit of this mountain ridge. The cabin had been built by the weavers and their husbands, whose homes were scattered about in coves and hollows and on mountainsides within a radius of about 20 miles, as a central place to assemble for weaving instructions, receiving supplies, shipping out products, and discussing problems connected with their work. The significance to those who were gathered within its walls was that in this remote section, far from the sources usually looked to for help in such instances, these neighbors, all poor in money and goods, had through an inspiring experience in co-operation growing out of their handicraft activities built a cabin of native materials with their own hands and equipped it for their use. Tacked to a log in an obscure place on the wall behind one of the looms was a sheet of paper on which was written in that brevity of expression characteristic of mountain people the legend of the cabin. A part of it ran about like this:

> 3 logs by Henry Willis
> 1 log by Doc Hoppas
> 2 days work by Dave Hoyle
> 2 loads of stone for fireplace by John Maughn
> 4 logs by Sally Sparks

Some of the logs had been snaked long distances from several mountain homes, and the "boards" for the roof were rived out of white oak, all materials in the cabin except the nails, glass, and hardware coming from the country around. The labor was of course local, and the frame, including the roof, was shaped up and put together in a day by country folk at "a house raisin'."

The surroundings of that evening meeting in late December were of great natural beauty which those who were there can never forget. It had been a green Christmas in that part of North Carolina, but early in the day of the meeting the first snowstorm of the winter had set in and there were many misgivings as to whether or not the guests would be able to get through, for long before nightfall a heavy blanket of white covered what from the mountain top looked like the whole world. When, however, in the light of the blazing fireplace the evening discussion began, all who had started

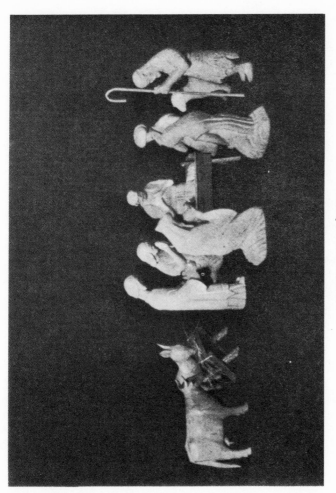

MOUNTAIN CRÈCHE

This Was Carved at the John C. Campbell Folk School

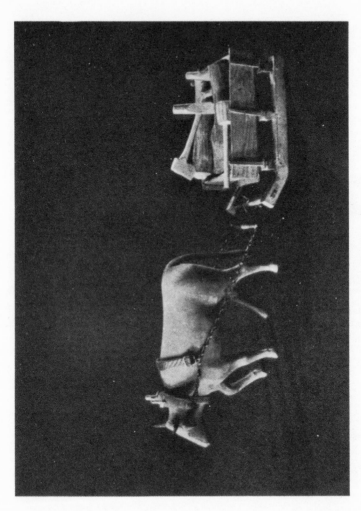

MOUNTAIN LOGGING OUTFIT

Ox, Home-Made Sled, Tools, and Logs, Whittled Out by a Mountain Man to Show
the Old Way of Logging in North Carolina

that day were safely there, eleven in all, with the following handicraft centers represented: Allanstand Cottage Industries, Asheville, North Carolina; Berea College, Fireside and Student Industries, Berea, Kentucky; Brasstown Handicraft Association, Brasstown, North Carolina; Cedar Creek Community Center, Greeneville, Tennessee; Crossnore School, Crossnore, North Carolina; The Spinning Wheel, Asheville, North Carolina; Penland Weavers and Potters, Penland, North Carolina.

Discussion continued until late when, in spite of the heavy snow which was still falling, part of the group went to the little town of Spruce Pine about six miles away to spend the night. By morning the storm was over and the sun shone on a beautiful world. The guests from Spruce Pine were at the meeting early, some of the Penland neighbors dropped in, and at noon the weavers served a chicken lunch of proverbial mountain quality and abundance.

At lunch time Dr. Mary Sloop of Crossnore School, the nearest handicraft neighbor to Penland, read some extracts from a local document, an Anthology of Death on Three Mile Creek, written by Jake Carpenter, an old settler. Literary records are rare among the mountain folk, and this was exceptionally interesting because it was part of the history of that section. Uncle Jake had lived for eighty-seven years down on Three Mile Creek in the heart of the Blue Ridge Mountains. He knew every family in the region, and for about seventy-five years, from 1845 to the time of his death, March 10, 1920; he kept a notebook, recording each death in the community, with brief annotations, reflecting his opinion of the departed. Although the spelling is faulty and the grammar crude, this self-taught woodsman of a community without schools has made his limited knowledge of writing serve his purpose well. The original journal is now in the hands of Alberta Pierson Hannum, of Moundsville, West Virginia, who is planning to publish it in the near future. With her permission, a few of the entries, some of which include references to the hand skills of the mountain people, appear here, exactly as written by Uncle Jake.

Alen Wiseman age 80 dide March 10 1877 ware a farmer and stild never had no dronken boys never had no dock in hos for sick he had 12 in famely

Frankey Burleson age 86 july 3 dide 1896 she spon cloth by 5000 [yards]

Wm Davis age 100.8 dide oct 5 1841 ware old soldier in rev war and got his thi broke in last fite at Kings mountain he ware a farmer and made brandy and never had no dronkers in famely

Joe Frank age 72 july 8 dide 1899 ware fin man he sed what he thot

Charles McKiney age 72 dide May 10 1852 ware farmer live in blew rige had 4 womin cors marid to 1 live at Mckiney Gap all went to fields to work to mak grane all went to the crib for corn all to smok hos for mete he cild 75 to 80 hogs a yer and wimen never had no words bout his havin so many wimin if it ware thes times thar wold be hare puld thar ware 42 children belong to him they all went to prechin together nothin sed Thady ware a very bad girl he mad brandy all his life never had no foes got alon fin with everbodi i nod him

Samel Frank age 94 dide july 2 1857 he ware farmer he hewed logs for hoses no man cod bete him

Tiliam Black age 73 dide oc 10 1896 ware mason for bildin chimleys

Kim Hone age 73 oc 15 1888 ware black smith had 6 gals that cod work in shop he ware 6 feet hi

Wm Austin age 80 dide jun 6 1912 ware fine man ware tenor

Sady Wise age 95 dide ap 1895 she wov spon cloth

Liley Wise age 82 feb 23 1875 did spon wov cloth mad all they wore

Loney Ollis age 84 dide jun 10 1871 grates dere honter wreked bee trees for hony cild ratell snak by 100 cild dere by thousen i nod him well

Lege Carpenter age 99 march 18 dide 1859 it snode that nite 14 inch hi

Lib Wise age 80 dide june 20 1846 ware greates womin for contrary

Turner Carpenter age 23 dide nov 20 1862 fite for his contery lost life

Samel Hugkin age 18 dide aug 18 1882 ware farmer he ware a grate lier

Lib Franklin age 72 dide aug 22 1889 ware fin lady to anybody she lik

Loner Whitman age 18 1914 dide shot hisself cos his gal went back on him dec 25

Frank James age 74 feb 28 1900 he ware grate bank rober him and Jesse James and Bob Ford

At the evening meeting Mrs. Campbell of the John C. Campbell Folk School opened the discussion and President William J. Hutchins of Berea College spoke of the part played by the handicrafts in the educational and economic life of the college. Dr. Sloop told of what they had done for both children and adults at Crossnore, adding "But it is their character building qualities which concern us most at the school." It was, however, the vital place of handicrafts in the homes of the mountains which seemed to the group of the greatest importance. There was abundant testimony that the whole aspect of life had been changed by bringing into the lonely mountain cabins a loom or a work bench through which one or more members of the family found both economic and social contact with the outside world.

The gathering held three sessions; there were no formal addresses, no committee meetings, no telephone interruptions, no hurrying away to other engagements, but a satisfactory sticking by the subject until all had asked the questions in their minds or had made their contributions to the discussion. The following topics were among those considered: the economic significance of handicrafts in homes and schools; influence of the crafts upon the character of the workers; necessity of keeping standards of craftsmanship high; disposing of work not up to standard; protection of designs originated by others; use of native materials; use of attractive and permanent colors in weaving; methods of marketing employed in other countries such as Canada, Norway, Sweden, and Denmark; creation of new objects and new designs to meet market requirements; methods of financing these industries and of paying workers; cost of production and its relation to selling price; partial use of machinery in hand-made articles; commissions allowed to dealers and consignment plans; extent of output in the industries represented at this meeting; and possibilities of extending markets.

What might be accomplished by a co-operating organization was considered. It was unanimously agreed that, although there were many problems that could best be worked out through such a body, each center should be left a maximum freedom to work out its own methods of production and marketing, and that none should be deprived of any outlet it had already developed. A point especially stressed was the high value of creative work and individual expression, and the desire to avoid as far as possible the duplication of objects by different centers. Because most of the centers in the mountains had long been identified with the Conference of Southern Mountain Workers,[1] and because of the wish

[1] The Conference of Southern Mountain Workers was organized by John C. Campbell and the first meeting was held in the spring of 1912. It meets annually at Knoxville and includes a three days' program. Mountain Life and Work, published quarterly at Berea, Kentucky, is the organ of the Conference.

to share with the Conference the satisfactions which would grow out of an association concerned entirely with handicrafts, it was resolved to bring the matter before the Conference at its next meeting.

The following formal motion was passed unanimously:

That we organize ourselves into an informal association whose function may be described by some such name as the Southern Mountain Handicraft Guild; that a committee be appointed by the chair to present to the Russell Sage Foundation the urgent desire of this group that the Foundation advise them with reference to the best form of organization; and further, that the Foundation conduct an early survey of the handicrafts in the schools and homes of the Southern Mountains as a fact basis for the association's wisest development; that the Committee be empowered to take such steps between now and the Conference of Southern Mountain Workers in Knoxville, April 2–4 [1929], as seem best to advance the development of the Guild and its work.

Helen Dingman of Berea reporting as chairman of the meeting later said:

We met on a mountain hilltop literally and the freedom and friendship of the group as they talked over the mountain handicraft situation—the hopes and fears and practical problems—made it a real mountain top experience.

ORGANIZING THE GUILD

At the Seventeenth Annual Conference of Southern Mountain Workers, held on April 2–4, 1929, at Knoxville, Tennessee, there was considerable discussion among the members concerning the possibility of forming the Handicraft Guild that had been proposed at Penland, but it was not until December 28, 1929, just one year after the Penland meeting, that a slightly larger group gathered at the Spinning Wheel at Asheville, North Carolina, for the purpose of organizing the Guild. It included Frances L. Goodrich of the Allanstand Cottage Industries, Asheville; Mrs. Campbell of the John C. Campbell Folk School at Brasstown; Dr. Mary Sloop of the Crossnore School; Lucy Morgan of the Penland Weavers and Potters; Wilmer Stone of the Weave Shop, Saluda; Clementine Douglas of the Spinning Wheel; Evelyn Bishop of Pi Beta Phi Settlement School, Gatlinburg; Helen H. Dingman of Berea, who

MOUNTAIN DULCIMERS

The Large Modern Dulcimer on the Left Is Referred to on Page 204. The Other Instruments by Various Makers Show a Few of the Wide Variety of Forms the Dulcimer Takes in the Southern Highlands

J. E. THOMAS OF BATH, KENTUCKY

Uncle Eddy Was Probably the Most Widely Known "Dulcimore" Maker in the Highlands. Part of His Story Is Given in the Chapter on Mountain Music and Hand-made Instruments

was chairman of the meeting; and Allen H. Eaton of Russell Sage Foundation, New York City. This group worked out the foundation for the organization of the Guild, based upon the recommendations made at the earlier Penland meeting.

The meeting at the Spinning Wheel was held in the sturdy old log cabin which Miss Douglas had found at Democrat and had rebuilt log for log, with an excellent stone fireplace at one end. This house of one great room was very comfortable in spite of winter weather, with an old-fashioned iron stove in the center, around which the guests sat in a circle on mountain chairs. Hand-hooked rugs and gay-colored weavings gave comfort and cheer to the meeting place. It was a pleasant and appropriate place for handicraft deliberations, and visits were made to the weaving room nearby where scores of skeins of beautifully colored yarns were hanging on loom frames or being woven into webs.

Three types of membership were agreed upon: $1.00 for individual craftsmen; $5.00 for friends wishing to advance the purpose of the Guild; and $10 for producing centers. Representatives from the producing centers were to constitute the voting members, each center to have one vote. Those represented at the meeting and those that should join before the next were admitted as charter members. After that date all applicants would require approval of the admissions committee and be voted on by the entire Guild membership.

The officers of the Guild were to consist of a president, vice president, secretary-treasurer, and a board of directors of five members. There were to be semi-annual meetings, one in the spring at the time of the annual Conference of Southern Mountain Workers at Knoxville, and the other in the autumn at a place to be chosen by members. An exhibit of articles made by Guild members was planned for the Knoxville Conference in 1930.

FIRST CO-OPERATIVE EXHIBITION OF MOUNTAIN HANDICRAFTS

The exhibit of the Southern Mountain Handicraft Guild at the 1930 spring meeting of the Conference of Southern Mountain Workers brought together for the first time a really comprehensive and representative collection of the handicrafts of the region. Notices had been sent to some 24 centers, but when the shipments were unpacked in the old Presbyterian Church, not only the centers invited but eight previously unknown groups had sent in their work, making in all 32 centers represented. This was not only proof of a wide interest in handicrafts but also a good illustration of the way news travels in the mountains without the aid of letter writing or newspapers.

The exhibition was held in a semicircular room completely lined with beaverboard, making a suitable background for the many exhibits of furniture of mountain design and construction, as well as carefully styled pieces from some of the schools and better work shops of the region. There was a large collection of baskets, brooms, elaborate and beautiful examples of hand weaving, hooked rugs, and of modern adaptations of mountain handicrafts. For the first time these various objects were arranged, not as separate displays from different centers, but in a way to assure the greatest harmony for them as a whole. At the entrance to the hall was a special group consisting of one object from each center represented, part of which is illustrated opposite page 286. This arrangement not only presented a striking group of mountain handicrafts but expressed the principle for which the Guild stood—a co-operative effort of all the centers to advance the work of the entire region.

This first comprehensive exhibition was a surprise to members of the Guild as well as to visitors, for with a few exceptions the centers themselves had little idea what others were producing.

At the meeting of the Guild held at this time its constitution and by-laws were adopted. Serving on the first Board of Directors were Marguerite Butler of the Campbell Folk School; Miss Stone of the Hindman Settlement School; Miss Douglas of the Spinning Wheel; Miss Morgan of Penland Weavers and Potters; and O. J. Mattil of the Woodcrafters and Carvers. Miss Butler was chosen president, Miss Stone vice president, and Miss Dingman secretary-treasurer.

AUTUMN MEETING OF THE GUILD, 1930

The autumn meeting of the Guild in 1930 was held at Berea College, which afforded visiting members an opportunity to see the activities carried on at this important center. These included the Fireside Industries, the Woodworking Shop, the Mountain Boy

Weavers at the College, the Matheny Weavers, Mrs. Mary Anderson, and the Churchill Weavers. Headquarters were established at Boone Tavern, an excellent stopping place in which the service is provided mainly by college students.

Among other matters discussed was the establishment of museums in the region to preserve good examples of pioneer mountain handicrafts. The Guild decided to hold during the following year an exhibition of these old-time handicrafts. The discovery of the madder bed near Berea, with plants still vigorous, was reported on and provision made to protect it. A committee on marketing was appointed to study the comparative prices being asked by different centers and the possibilities of getting co-operation from outside in an effort to style some of the goods. A lending library of books on handicrafts was also proposed and a directory of Guild members planned.

MEETINGS OF THE GUILD DURING 1931 AND 1932

At the 1931 spring meeting, held in connection with the Conference of Southern Mountain Workers, the exhibit of old-time handicrafts which had been planned at Berea was shown. In this collection were very early hand-made tools, cooking utensils, looms of massive proportions, coverlets, patchwork quilts, and so forth. The exhibition also included a collection of coverlets exhibited by Jean Montgomery of Galax, Virginia. In addition to the old handicrafts, and in a separate room, was a fine exhibit of modern weaving from the St. Louis Handicraft Guild which had been brought to the meeting by Emile Bernat, editor of The Handicrafter. It was of great interest to the weaving members of the Guild.

The business meeting of the Guild which followed the close of the exhibition held at Mountain View Hotel, Gatlinburg, was marked by the generous offer of Miss Goodrich to turn over to the Guild the right and title to the Allanstand Cottage Industries, which she had over a period of nearly forty years developed into a salesroom and supervising center at Asheville. Miss Goodrich had refused opportunities to sell the Industries because it was not a commercial organization in the sense that some of those who wished to buy the enterprise might like to make it, and her desire was to have it continue under auspices that would as nearly as possible uphold the original ideals. Later, in writing of the transfer, Miss Goodrich said: "It was given to the agency which offered the greatest promise of carrying on our purpose, the Southern Mountain Handicraft Guild, then newly formed. It has amply fulfilled my hopes."

After Miss Douglas who had been appointed trustee for the Guild had fulfilled her task, making this service a contribution to the Guild, she resumed her own work at the Spinning Wheel. The management of the Industries was later taken over by Mrs. Agnes Loeffler, who had been associated with Miss Goodrich in building up the center, and through Mrs. Loeffler's thrift, energy, and tact and Mr. Loeffler's loyal support, the Guild exhibit and salesroom has grown and its business shown a steady increase each year.

The autumn meeting of 1931 was held on October 16–17 at the John C. Campbell Folk School, Brasstown, when the members had an opportunity to visit the weaving room in Keith House where an exhibition of local handicrafts was on display; also the Mill House where the wood and metal work are carried on. The new cow barn with its unique decorations of farm animals, tools, bundles of grain, and other symbols of country work, both modeled and incised in the cement facings, had just been completed and gave the visitors much enjoyment. Sixty persons representing 17 handicraft centers were present.

At this meeting an invitation was extended to the American Federation of Arts and the American Country Life Association to co-operate with the Guild in the formation and circulation of a representative exhibition of the handicrafts of the entire mountain region. So well did this plan for an exhibition of handicrafts fit into the program of the American Country Life Association, that the Association agreed to arrange for the initial showing of the exhibition at its annual meeting to be held at Blacksburg, Virginia, in August, 1933. The Russell Sage Foundation agreed to assist in assembling the articles on display, and the American Federation of Arts offered to take charge of the exhibition after the Blacksburg meeting and circulate it throughout the country. Thus through co-operation this important plan was carried out which none of the organizations could have handled separately.

The 1932 spring meeting of the Handicraft Guild was held

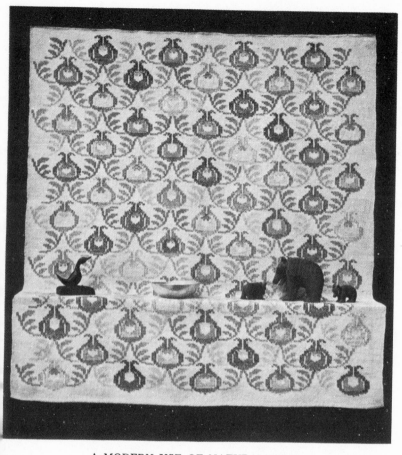

A MODERN USE OF NATURAL DYES

THIS FINGER-WOVEN TEXTILE WAS MADE WITH NATURAL DYES DEVELOPED BY
WILMER STONE VINER. OF TWENTY-SEVEN COLORS USED ALL ARE VEGETABLE
DYES EXCEPT ONE RED MADE FROM THE INSECT COCHINEAL

on April 1 also in the Mountain View Hotel at Gatlinburg. By this time 25 producing centers had come into membership. At this meeting the Library Committee assembled some 20 volumes on handicrafts, the nucleus of a Guild library, which placed within reach of members for the first time some of the best books on the technique and traditions of handicrafts. These books are available to Guild members through the secretary's office. One of the features of the meeting was the admission of the Cherokee Indians to membership. They had already submitted examples of their work, including basketry, pottery, bows and arrows, blow-guns, and Indian game materials which had been approved by the Admissions Committee.

The 1932 autumn meeting of the Guild convened on October 11 at Pine Mountain Settlement School, Kentucky, the most remotely situated of any of the handicraft centers, yet one of the most interesting and picturesque. In spite of the difficulty in reaching it, attendance was good.

Pine Mountain is about four or five miles by trail from what is now a main highway, and is generally reached from Laden by going over the mountain on foot or by muleback. The question of transporting delegates to the meeting was finally solved by an arrangement with the local logging train, which operates out of Laden and into the Pine Mountain country, to carry them around the mountain in a box car. This little logging railroad journey required about seven or eight miles of traveling to reach Pine Mountain Settlement School instead of the four miles of climbing over the mountain if one used the trail. The road-bed of the railway is hardly up to standard, and the engine, and the box car which had been hooked on to accommodate the passengers, ran off the track three times during the trip. This experience furnished plenty of excitement, but most of the members remained in the car until safely delivered at the School. A few, however, on the occasion of the second jumping off the track got out, and sighting a cabin down in a mountain valley made for it, finally securing horses on which they rode into Pine Mountain, arriving late that evening after some of the delegates had spent several hours in search of the lost members.

Thirteen producing centers were represented at the conference which, among other matters, approved an expenditure for printing a catalogue of the circulating handicraft exhibit to be arranged by the Educational Committee in collaboration with the American Federation of Arts. Business at the salesroom of the Guild at Asheville had improved, and four additional producing centers had been admitted to membership. Doris Ulmann of New York City presented the Guild with 50 photographic portraits which she had made of mountain people in Virginia and Kentucky.

It should be added that when at the close of the meeting the logging train came to take its passengers back to Laden, it was discovered that a considerable number had left early to walk over the mountain. Those who remained boarded the train. In the journey around the mountain, although the engine again left the track three times, the mechanics soon jacked it back and the seven-mile run was made in the record time of two hours.

MEETINGS OF THE GUILD DURING 1933 AND 1934

At the 1933 spring meeting of the Guild held on March 31 at Hotel Farragut, Knoxville, the word "Highland" was substituted for "Mountain," making the name Southern Highland Handicraft Guild.

At the autumn meeting there were two sessions, one at Weld House, Altamont, Avery County, North Carolina, on the evening of October 10, where the delegates had supper and spent the night; the other in the Weaving Cabin at Crossnore School on October 11. At the latter meeting Miss Morgan reported on the exhibit of the Penland Weavers and Potters at the Century of Progress in Chicago. The Guild had made a real effort, backed by organizations interested in rural life, to hold an exhibit of mountain handicrafts at the Century of Progress, but charges for space and lack of sympathetic interest on the part of the Fair management had made the undertaking impossible. However, the citizens of Penland encouraged the Penland Weavers and Potters to build a small log cabin on a truck, and with it as a background and showroom, an effective display was made, the business secured in Chicago keeping 34 weavers employed during one of the slackest handicraft seasons the workers in the mountains had known. The cabin and other equipment were designed and built by H. C. Ford of Penland. A report was also made on the Guild exhibition which had been held in August at Blacksburg, Virginia. The closing meeting at Crossnore was held in the spacious weaving rooms which consist of two historic log cabins joined together to serve the handicraft needs of the School.

The 1934 spring meeting of the Guild opened at Ferris Hall, the University of Tennessee, Knoxville, on the morning of March 23, with luncheon served by the Co-operative Extension Workers in Agriculture and Home Economics.

The experience of Miss Morgan at the Century of Progress in Chicago, where there had been many calls for inexpensive articles, was discussed, together with the problems incident to supplying the national parks of the Appalachians with suitable souvenirs at low prices. This brought to a focus a discussion of the possibilities of producing inexpensive handicrafts. The matter of low-cost objects the Guild felt to be distinctively one of its own because of the promise by the National Park Service that handicrafts will be featured in the eastern parks for their educational and cultural value, and that the cheap souvenirs manufactured in cities and sold in other parks will be discouraged in those of the Appalachians.

In the autumn of 1934 the Guild met at the invitation of the Shuttle-Crafters at Russellville. The opening meeting was held in the Old Mill House on the evening of October 16. No more appropriate or beautiful place for a meeting could have been chosen than this old mill preserved for years by the Dougherty family and now occupied as a home by Mrs. Z. C. Patten, who was hostess to the Guild for supper and the evening session. Many of the original features of the mill have been preserved—the floors, steps, water wheel, grain hopper, flour bins—and the quaint interior was beautifully decorated with autumn fruits, flowers, vegetables, and handicrafts from many lands. The guests were housed during the conference at the home of Mr. and Mrs. Robert Blair in Hayslope just outside Russellville.

At the evening meeting Bertha M. Nienburg, economic consultant of the Women's Bureau, United States Department of Labor, reported on a study, which the Bureau had conducted, of employment opportunities for rural women of the Highlands, particularly in handicraft developments, and asked for the co-operation of the members of the Guild in carrying out the recommendations based on their findings. At the same session a tentative plan developed by L. L. Campbell of the Tennessee Valley Authority, involving a determination of the economic feasibility of a number of small co-operative enterprises throughout the region, was presented for consideration. The discussion of both reports was taken up at the morning session and a committee, with President Hutchins of Berea as chairman, was appointed to confer with both the Women's Bureau and the Tennessee Valley Authority.

In the afternoon of the second day the Guild members attended a reception and exhibit of the work of the Shuttle-Crafters at the Dougherty home and at the log cabin work and exhibit rooms. Among the exhibits were shown examples of the weavings of five generations of the Dougherty family, the first being a bed sheet of linen spun and woven by Elizabeth Cable Mart, great-grandmother of Sarah Dougherty, and examples of coverlets woven by her grandmother, Betsy Flannery Adams, and her mother, Leah Adams Dougherty, one by herself and one by her niece, Mary Dougherty.

Outside the cabin had been arranged a demonstration of the complete process of flax growing and the preparation of linen thread, the flaxseed, the grown plant, the fiber broken on the "break," the scutching of the fiber, the separation of the fine fiber from the tow by hackling, the placing of the fiber on the distaff, the spinning of the fiber, and the twisting of it into heavier thread.

MEETINGS OF THE GUILD DURING 1935

The spring meeting in April, 1935, held on the campus of the University of Tennessee at Knoxville, was characterized by three encouraging facts reported: the Guild salesroom at Asheville had had the best sales in its history; the exhibition of handicrafts under the sponsorship of the Guild, which had been circulated by the American Federation of Arts, had developed a wide interest in handicrafts outside the Highlands; and the Tennessee Valley Authority had, after several conferences with the Guild Committee appointed to confer with it, decided on a co-operative plan for handicrafts with those already engaged in the work as a basis of organization. The outstanding feature of the business meeting was, therefore, the new plan of co-operation between the Guild and

MOUNTAIN PEOPLE AND THEIR HANDICRAFTS

Levi Eye of Pendleton County, West Virginia, Estimated in His Eightieth Year That He Had Made Over 7,000 Baskets. Babe Caldwell, Youngest Ballad Singer in the American Song Festival, Plays a "Gourd Banjer" Made by His "Grandsir." Grandma Rice with Her Home-Made Things. The Oak Broom Was Given to Her Husband, A Doctor, for Services to a Neighbor at Her "First Birthin'." Last Two Photographs Lent by Jean Thomas

A FEW MOUNTAIN DOLLS

Among the Many Kinds Made in the Southern Highlands Are Rag Dolls, Corn Husk Dolls, Kentucky Poppets, Jointed Wooden Dolls, and Others Described in the Chapter on Dolls, Toys, and Miniature Furniture

the Tennessee Valley Authority for the advancement of handicrafts in the region. As already indicated, the territory which the Tennessee Valley Authority occupies includes a large part of the Southern Highlands.

In making up the advisory committee for the Tennessee Valley Authority, several members from the Guild were selected and Miss Douglas was chosen to direct the work of the new handicraft cooperative known as the Southern Highlanders, Inc.

The autumn meeting of the Guild was held on October 2, 1935, at Ashland Farm, St. Elmo, near Chattanooga, Tennessee, with Mrs. Patten, owner of the farm, as hostess. The principal subject for consideration was the report on the Southern Highlanders, Inc., and the opening of the handicraft shop at Norris Dam, Tennessee. The need for determining the requirements of a new consuming public was discussed, and the advisability of engaging a designer and a production manager to assist in solving the numerous problems growing out of the demands of this public in handicrafts production and marketing. One of the farm houses was made available for an exhibition of the latest handicrafts of the Guild and a collection of Tennessee articles.

MEETINGS OF THE GUILD DURING 1936 AND SPRING OF 1937

The seventh semi-annual meeting of the Guild took place on March 27 at the University of Tennessee in Knoxville. At this session the by-laws were amended to permit individual craftsmen not connected with handicraft centers to serve on committees; this change also applying to friends of the Guild. The Board of Directors was increased from five to seven. Paul Johnson, acting general manager of the Southern Highlanders, Inc., stressed the advisability of an information service that would serve all members of the Guild and the Southern Highlanders, Inc., as well as unaffiliated persons in the field of handicrafts.

The autumn meeting on October 13 and 14 was held at Cashiers, Jackson County, North Carolina, at the home of Dr. and Mrs. J. K. Stoddard. In the living room where the delegates gathered were arranged many interesting and beautiful articles which Dr. and Mrs. Stoddard had collected in different parts of the world. To this setting was added an exhibit of oriental crafts which Miss

Dingman had recently secured in China. O. J. Mattil reported for the Old Crafts Committee the plans of the Tennessee Park Committee for a museum of old crafts for the Great Smoky Mountains Park. It was thought advisable for the Guild to co-operate with the Tennessee Park Commission for a museum in the Park. Mrs. Patten offered her collection in The Mill at Russellville, and others offered articles or collections, for this purpose. An invitation from the Mint Museum at Charlotte, North Carolina, for members of the Guild to display their handicrafts at the museum from October to December was accepted.

The first session of the 1937 spring meeting of the Guild was held on March 11, at Knoxville, in connection with the Twenty-fifth Anniversary of the Conference of Southern Mountain Workers. This session was devoted to an address and the discussion that followed on Handicrafts in Mountain Life, by Allen H. Eaton, who gave an outline of conclusions drawn from the present study which he had just completed on the subject for the Russell Sage Foundation. Important points relating to handicrafts were taken up by the whole Conference.

The second session was marked by encouraging reports from both the Allanstand salesroom in Asheville and the Southern Highlanders, Inc. The latter now maintains salesrooms at Norris Dam, at the Patten Hotel in Chattanooga, Chickamauga Dam, Tennessee, and at International Building, Rockefeller Center, New York City. The Guild expressed its desire to join with workers from other parts of the country in mapping out a plan by which the handicrafts in general could be improved and advanced. It also expressed itself as willing to co-operate with the Department of Agriculture in the preparation of an exhibition of rural arts to be held in Washington, D. C., in November, 1937, in connection with the Seventy-fifth Anniversary celebration of the Department.

EXHIBITIONS OF THE GUILD

Up to the time of the organization of the Guild, little concerted thought had been given to acquainting the country generally with the various types of handicrafts produced in the Highlands. Contacts had been made largely through mountain schools with individuals in different parts of the country, some of whom helped support the schools, and others who were eager to promote enthusiasm for the continuance of handwork among the mountain people. Coincident with the development of the Guild, a plan for exhibiting at one time examples of the best of the handicrafts produced in the mountains was agreed upon as the most satisfactory way of bringing them before the whole country.

The first general exhibition held at the Conference of Southern Mountain Workers in Knoxville in 1930 confirmed the belief that not even the Highland people themselves realized the extent to which handwork was carried on in the region. The collection of examples of old crafts shown at the Conference the following year likewise held many surprises, even for those who had been acquainted with the work for a long time. The old tools, rough hand looms, and other articles were of especial interest to those who wished to study the pioneer implements of the mountain country.

The assembling, and financing in part, of a comprehensive exhibition of handicrafts for circulation through museums and other art organizations is thus far one of the major achievements of the Guild. The response in interest and purchases has far exceeded any estimate that had been made in anticipation of the development of the project. While the main objective was its educational value, the many sales that have resulted have given substantial encouragement to the workers.

This exhibition known as The Exhibition of the Southern Highland Handicraft Guild, which was first shown at Blacksburg, Virginia, in 1933 at the annual convention of the American Country Life Association, consisted of 586 pieces of handicraft representing 33 handicraft centers. No more fitting event could have been chosen for its initial presentation than this meeting of the outstanding rural organization in our country. In the same hall was a collection of color reproductions on Rural Scenes and Country Life arranged to harmonize with the display of handwork by rural people. The effect upon leaders in the country life movement was highly encouraging, and county and home demonstration agents were unanimous in their feeling that similar exhibitions should be brought before other rural groups throughout the country.

At the close of the meeting the American Federation of Arts took charge of the circulation of the handicraft exhibition and booked it at museums throughout the country. From Blacksburg it was taken to Washington, D. C., and for some weeks was on display at the Corcoran Art Gallery. A constant stream of visitors viewed it each day, and the newspapers carried many interesting articles about the work. Any doubt that may have been evident before as to the advisability of including exhibitions in the program of the Guild was entirely dispelled by the cordial reception given to the display by government officials and other residents, and by art, social, and educational groups.

After the Corcoran Gallery at Washington, the circuit included the Brooklyn Museum of New York City; the Decatur (Illinois) Art Institute; the Joslyn Memorial at Omaha, Nebraska; the New Municipal Auditorium in St. Louis in connection with the National Folk Festival; the Everhart Museum, Scranton, Pennsylvania; the Milwaukee Art Institute; the Norfolk (Virginia) Museum; and the Art Museum of Berea College at Berea, Kentucky, at the time of the dedication of this Museum.

This exhibition was sponsored by Mrs. Herbert Hoover, Mrs. Calvin Coolidge, and Mrs. Franklin D. Roosevelt, each of whom has had a special interest in the Southern Highland people and their handicrafts.

A TYPICAL HILLSIDE CORN PATCH

This "Uptilted" Corn Patch Might Be Seen in Any Mountain State. Corn Is the Plant upon Which Man and Beast Depend and from Its Stalks, Leaves, Cobs, and Kernels Many Useful and Some Very Attractive Handicrafts Are Made. Photograph by Cline Studios, Chattanooga, Tennessee

FIGURES MADE FROM CORN HUSKS
Corn Is the Principal Domestic Plant in the Highlands and from Its Husks Mrs.
Rosalie Pless of Russellville, Tennessee, Fashions a Large Variety of Figures
in Smoothed, Braided, and Plaited Forms

CHAPTER XVII

MUSEUMS AND COLLECTIONS OF HANDICRAFTS

SCATTERED throughout the Southern Highlands, and increasing in number, are small log cabin museums, important to the student of handicrafts and also to the people of the several communities because of their social and educational potentialities. These cabins with their assortments of crude pioneer objects are folk museums in a true sense, although the meagerness of both buildings and exhibits and the absence of a staff or any plan of administration might make it difficult for the American Association of Museums to give them recognition. In addition to brief descriptions of some of these museums, reference will be made in this chapter to a number of the collections situated a little outside the Highland boundaries, where objects similar to those found in the mountains may be seen. It is, however, the small local museum within the Highlands with which we are mainly concerned.

The building is usually an old log cabin, a folk house, that has been lived in sometimes for several generations. It may have belonged to a well-known family or in other ways be associated with the history of the community; or it may be only a typical cabin of early days. Its contents comprise mainly the things that have been used by those who once lived in the house or in similar ones in that part of the country, and reflect quite faithfully the pioneer life of the region.

These small museums have been established usually as local projects without money cost to anyone. No contributions have been sought, no taxes imposed for either equipment or maintenance. They have come in response to a desire to preserve the records of a life now passing. A museum that represents the habits and customs of local people brings about a marked change in the attitude of the community, and the mountaineer, after visiting one, usually attaches more importance to his own hand-made possessions; he is also sometimes influenced to contribute to their collection.

MUSEUM OF THE JOHN C. CAMPBELL FOLK SCHOOL

One of the early activities in which the John C. Campbell Folk School family and the people of the Brasstown neighborhood united was in building a local museum in a natural grove between the farm house, then in process of restoration and development, and the site of Keith House, the new school building and community gathering place for which plans were being made. In enlarging and restoring the farm house, which was done by local labor, the furnishings consisted, as far as possible, of furniture, coverlets, and other handwork that could be secured in the neighborhood. Many old tools, implements, and locally made furniture came to light which aroused keen interest. Neighbors told of other old hand-made objects that had been burned or otherwise destroyed which might have been saved for the community. These facts suggested that a place be provided at the school where some of the remaining old-time things could be cared for.

Among the hills near Brasstown were several abandoned log cabins, and the possibility of selecting the best logs, stone, and other material from them for constructing a shelter for these rural treasures was discussed with the neighbors. Men, women, and children joined enthusiastically in the venture, which culminated in the building of a typical mountain cabin for which many objects had already been contributed.

It contains two rooms approximately equal in dimensions, with a dog-trot running between. The dog-trot is covered with the same roof that shelters the two rooms, and in this particular case it is about eight feet wide. At the outer or gable end of each room is a fireplace, one of stone and mud, the other of sticks and mud, the two types of outside chimneys characteristic of the Highland country. The stone type is more common in the Brasstown section because stone is to be had in most places and is much more durable. Many of the stick-and-mud chimneys burned down in the early days, often setting fire to the whole cabin; therefore, in thoughtful households, a long pole always stood in the chimney corner outside the cabin ready to be used, in case the chimney did catch fire, to push it away from the house and to the ground so that the remainder of the cabin could be saved.

Men were found in the neighborhood who could build fireplaces with both kinds of chimneys and others who could lay puncheon floors, hew and notch logs, rive boards for shingles, and perform all the kinds of work required in building a cabin. This work brought out many of the skills of the community and aroused great enthusiasm among the old people who recalled their own, their parents', and grandparents' unforgettable experiences here and in other parts of the Highlands in home building and pioneer living. In accordance with the old custom there was a neighborhood log raising, one of the most enjoyable social events the community had experienced. One of the donors of land to the Folk School, who also did considerable work on the museum, told of how the local lodge had met for several years in the loft of a log cabin where it was necessary in going through the ritual to bend over when standing in order to avoid striking the ceiling.

The logs of the cabin were skilfully cut, smoothed with the broadax, and put together in the old-time way. Gradually the museum collection grew through the interest and the generosity of neighbors, some of whom were always on the lookout for new accessions. It now includes the few articles of furniture characteristic of a pioneer home, benches, bedsteads, quilts, rugs, and so forth, traps for catching animals and fish, and the greatest gift of all, a beautiful old blue Conestoga prairie schooner, the like of which had conveyed many a family from the mountains of North Carolina, Tennessee, and Kentucky across the plains to the Oregon country or to California.

Building a museum for the sole purpose of preserving the old things of the community brought about a marked change, especially among the younger people. Those who had been anxious to replace their hand-made native walnut bedsteads with factory-made iron ones, and their comfortable light-weight wooden chairs of mountain make for upholstered chairs from the store, now came to place a new value on the old furniture.

Every Fourth of July when the Highland woods and fields are beautiful with blooming flowers, an old folks' reunion is held at the Folk School Museum. Mountain ballads and other songs are sung to the accompaniment of the dulcimer or often without accompaniment at all; fiddles and banjos are played, simple country food in abundance is served, neighbors bring new objects for the Museum, others a favorite plant or shrub for the Museum grounds, local history is recalled, while everyone has an enjoyable time and the Museum starts on another year of growth and experience.

MUSEUM AT THE PINE MOUNTAIN SETTLEMENT SCHOOL

At Pine Mountain, Kentucky, is a slightly different type of museum, one dedicated to the memory of Uncle William Creech, a fine old mountaineer who gave the land upon which the school was built. The Museum building is the picturesque old log cabin in which Uncle William and Aunt Sal had reared their family. When Uncle William died in 1918 and Aunt Sal went to live with one of her children, it was moved down to the School grounds with as many of their possessions as could be spared and made into a memorial. This is probably the most personal of any of the Highland museums. Here are Uncle William's guns, his ax, and several pieces of furniture he had made, Aunt Sal's loom, blankets, coverlets, and linsey-woolseys she had woven, and the fireplace, an unusually refined one of cut stone both inside and to the top of the chimney on the outside. On the porch is the handmill, a quern of two grinding stones set in a hollowed-out upright section of a sycamore tree, which was used to grind corn into meal for years before water mills were established in that part of the mountains.

Every child in the School and every neighbor who visits it feels the significance of this simple memorial, although probably no one has ever before given it that name. It is to them just Uncle William's and Aunt Sal's cabin. When Doris Ulmann went to Pine Mountain to procure the photographs for this book, several of the grandchildren and other members of the Creech family dressed in old costumes and were photographed at work as in pioneer days. One grandchild spun woolen yarn on Aunt Sal's old wheel, and another wove blankets on the loom that stands by the fireplace. Others turned the grinding stones of the home-made mill. Two of these pictures are shown opposite pages 68 and 53. In the summer relatives visit on the porch of the little cabin, and occasionally there are gatherings of the Creech clan before blazing logs in the old fireplace.

MUSEUM OF MRS. EDNA LYNN SIMMS

Only one other of the mountain museums will be described, one in process rather than completed. It contains hand-made objects gathered in Tennessee in the region of Gatlinburg by Mrs. Edna Lynn Simms of Knoxville, and it is known as the Mountaineer Museum located near the entrance of the Great Smoky Mountains National Park in Gatlinburg, Tennessee.

Ten years ago Mrs. Simms began her collection of handicrafts with a bread tray made by Wiley Oakley, a well-known Smoky Mountains Park guide who had won the prize for the oldest bread tray at the Gatlinburg Fair. The collection now contains beds, chairs, tables, benches, baskets, iron and brass kettles, brooms, churns, lamps, spinning wheels, looms, shuttles, reels, cards, pottery, hoes, rakes, pipes, guns, mouse traps, whetstones, fishing tackle, forest tools, powderhorns, and many other articles once used in the Smoky Mountains region. In addition to gathering these objects, Mrs. Simms has secured all the information available concerning them and the people who once used them. Of these she has written quite extensively, and wherever possible has related each piece in the Museum to its maker or user. The following extracts are taken from a record made of a small part of the collection.[1]

A sifter made by old Aunt Lydia Whaley, grand old woman of the Smokies, who died only a few years ago. Its sides are constructed of a thin strip of bass wood, bent into a circle and firmly sewed together with the aid of Aunt Lydia's shoemaker's awl, needle, and heavy waxed thread. The bottom is woven from black and white hairs of horses' tails.

A bed which Joel Kear (Carr), father of Lydia Whaley, had cut out of the wilderness with only a crude ax and drawer knife and polished only by use. Trundle beds carved out of white walnut. Spool beds and button beds made by Napoleon Cardwell, long since dead.

A giant spinning wheel. A reel equipped with a cog that still clicks with mathematical accuracy after a given number of yards have been "reeled off."

Aunt Lydia Whaley was the most versatile woman I ever heard of. She spun and wove and ran her own grist mill up on Holy Branch, plowed and went hunting, made medicine for the surrounding country, and

[1] Perry, Jo Ruth. The Knoxville News-Sentinel, Knoxville, Tenn., March 23, 1930.

"raised" her children and her crops. She was nurse, preacher, under-taker, doctor, tailor and dressmaker, tanner and shoemaker to the entire community.

Aunt Lydia spun all her clothes and her children's clothes from wool and cotton that she grew. . . . I have heard Aunt Lydia's daughter say that one of her earliest memories was hearing her mother tell the children they'd have to be good to the little calf because it was their winter's shoes.

Aunt Lydia did all her shoemaking. And . . . there is only one last for both feet. In those days Aunt Lydia and everybody else made both shoes as if for the same foot, saying that "the foot would wear them into shape." After they wore the shoes a few months they would change them around and put each shoe on the opposite foot . . . so they wouldn't wear their shoes out on any one side.

The importance of gathering and recording facts, as Mrs. Simms has done, cannot be overestimated, because written records are not common with the Southern Highlanders. For generations they have trusted to word of mouth to preserve the local record, and while this method is unquestionably good training for the memory much of accuracy is lost in transmission. The minds of many people still living are replete with the history and folklore of their communities and nothing is more likely to tap these springs of memory than the treasures in a mountain museum.

OTHER MOUNTAIN MUSEUMS

Among other log cabins in which mountain handicrafts are pre-served are: the Uncle Solomon Everidge cabin at Hindman Settle-ment School; Homeplace, a new log house built by Lula M. Hale at Ary, Kentucky, on lines of her father's old cabin a few miles away; the cabin museum called the Traipsin' Woman, that Jean Thomas established near Ashland, Kentucky, which furnishes the setting for the American Folk Festival each year; the log cabin from Democrat, North Carolina, now a part of the Spinning Wheel, Asheville; the Dougherty cabin, once an inn, and the Old Mill at Russellville; an old cabin at Pi Beta Phi Settlement School, Gatlin-burg, filled with local relics; the Weaving Cabin of two log houses at Crossnore; the Friendly House, Canton, Haywood County, North Carolina, a pioneer cabin over a hundred years old which

OLD VEGETABLE DYEING AND NEW

THE OLD COVERLET LENT BY D. F. FOLGER CAME FROM SOUTH CAROLINA. THE FINELY WOVEN SHAWL, WORN CONTINUOUSLY FOR SIXTY YEARS, WAS LENT BY MRS. FANNIE BIBBEE OF WEST VIRGINIA. THE CAROLINA BLANKET WAS MADE AT THE WEAVE SHOP. THE YARNS WERE COLORED BY LOUISE PITMAN OF THE CAMPBELL FOLK SCHOOL

was known as Collins House and has been restored by Rev. Hannah J. Powell; the old Mast cabin at Valle Crucis, North Carolina, built in 1828, in which Mrs. Finley Mast wove until her death in February, 1936, and where her sister still weaves on the old family looms; the McWhirter cabin on the Stonewall Jackson homeplace at Jackson's Mill, West Virginia.

Among other museums and collections in or close to the Highland region which contain examples of mountain handicraft are: the Governor's House at Knoxville, Tennessee; the Harrodsburg Fort and Museum at Harrodsburg, Kentucky; the State Museum at Raleigh, North Carolina; the private collection of weaving, hearth brooms, baskets, costumes, and so forth, assembled by Mrs. Jacques Busbee near Steeds, North Carolina. There are undoubtedly several others not mentioned in connection with this study.

It is gratifying to note the encouragement from the federal government which the National Park Service, the Resettlement Administration, and the Tennessee Valley Authority are extending to local museums in the region. As time goes on, appreciation of mountain handicrafts, particularly the crude implements and furnishings fashioned by our pioneers, is certain to increase; and it is fortunate that many communities in the Highlands are already sensitive to this fact even though they may not be trained in present-day museum methods of carrying out their desires.

CHAPTER XVIII

HANDICRAFT TRAINING, PRODUCTION, AND MARKETING

IN CONTEMPLATING the variety of handicrafts produced in the Southern Highlands one wonders how this large volume of handwork came into being, what training and aptitudes lie behind the continuation of these expressions of rural life. Many of these craftsmen were unschooled and unlettered; they had little opportunity to observe the work of others and no access to pictorial reproductions of good handwork. Unfortunately there is only meager record of the life of the Highland pioneers, but tradition confirms the belief that a driving incentive behind the building of the cabin, the shaping of crude furniture, the weaving of cloth, and the fashioning of wooden and gourd dishes was the hope of being able to make still more useful and beautiful articles.

TRAINING

Much of the handwork of the Southern Highlands is indigenous —it had grown out of the needs and aspirations of the people of the region. In the beginning the craftsman was as near self-taught as a man can be; his shop was his place of abode, his materials what nature had provided, the tools were his own hands and a few simple implements brought on or made by his forebears; his teacher was the urgent necessity for the object he created.

His skill often found expression in a particular craft, one for which there was need or that he liked to practice best. While thus engaged, younger members of the family picked up from observation some of the processes and in turn sometimes exceeded in ability those from whom they had learned. There came forth, therefore, in the Highland homes what may be called family crafts: good basket makers from one family, chairmakers from another, outstanding weavers from this household, and fine quilters from that, all self-taught or family trained.

There were instances, however, where the craft did not immediately follow down the family line. Of scores of chairmakers, basket makers, and weavers reporting on their training, a surprising number learned from their grandparents. This sometimes indicates the break of a generation in practice of the craft or it throws light on the family economy in which the grandparents had a definite part in the preservation and progress of the group. On the other hand the skill was sometimes handed down without a lapse in any generation.

A remarkable feature of this individual or family training is the number of excellent craftsmen it developed, some as expert and meticulous as those trained elsewhere by accredited teachers. Today throughout the Highlands are self-taught woodworkers who pride themselves on the special turn they can give to a hickory post or weavers who can produce a textile so even that only an authority could detect it from a machine-made product.

Many of the young mountaineers through the use of their imagination from early childhood have developed an inventiveness which enables them to do things that children in other sections are taught to do. Therefore their skill may be partly inherited and partly derived from the ability to work their own way over difficult problems. Edward F. Worst of the Chicago Public Schools, who directs the summer Weaving Institute at Penland, points out that native mountain people have often helped him in the solution of a technical difficulty encountered in the course of his instruction; or they would indicate some other than the usual way of making an adjustment in the use of a loom. William Bernard Clark of the Shenandoah Community Workers, Bird Haven, Virginia, where woodworking is the principal industry, states that a number of excellent suggestions have come from the native men and boys engaged in the logging, lumbering, or manufacturing operations.

As most of the handicraft objects of today are styled to meet changing fashions, it would be difficult to determine how many designs are original. But sufficient evidence is available about weaving, for instance, to make certain that many of the old designs came through the desire of mountain workers to create something definitely their own. What is true of weaving applies to other handicrafts. Numerous types of baskets were inventions of the makers, some of which still bear their names. The pattern of one of the most famed and best made mountain chairs, the Godlove chair, originated with an old mountain family and is still used. Originality in design was a characteristic of the handicrafts of pioneer days.

The second stage of training emerged during the early part of the revival of handicrafts when supervision first entered into the process. Up to this time when few had to be satisfied, practically everything had been made for home use, but now in order to maintain the quality expected by outside purchasers and to guarantee the filling of orders, it has been necessary to subject the work to a degree of regulation by those sponsoring the revival. These leaders, however, were not usually craftsmen themselves, and they were compelled to seek aid from experts who were brought to the producing centers to improve methods of work and to establish standards both with their own handwork as examples and by appraising the products of others.

Following these first efforts at teaching and supervision, as the revival progressed came training in groups or classes. This took place in schools, settlements, and in individual homes and centers. Stimulated by the opportunity to sell their products, the desire among workers for guidance grew and the leaders co-ordinated their teaching with the activities carried on in mountain homes. Direction given to group training did not come as a rule from professional designers or craftsmen, but from instructors who had gained a practical knowledge about the character and work of the Highlanders and who knew enough about the craft to guide beginners, to advise those already skilled, and to meet sales requirements.

Too much cannot be said of the understanding these leaders showed for the nature of the people of the Highland country, their individualism, their eccentricities, and their strong traits of character. The schools and other agencies nourished the relationship between themselves and the independent handicraft workers, and established a foundation of confidence that has been strengthened with the succeeding years. It was during this period that the greatest expansion in mountain handicrafts took place, and this method of individual and group training is practiced in the region today. Under this form which encourages and preserves the old skills by assisting in the regulation of output, a considerable number of centers have been established where workers gather to receive instruction, materials, and assistance in difficult problems of technique or the working out of new designs. A practical and happy accompaniment of the system is that neighbors who are able to go to the centers often carry the lessons they receive to those who cannot leave their homes.

Outstanding in its contribution to training in handicrafts is Berea College where the Fireside Industries and the Wood Craft shop, as well as other branches of the student industries, have afforded hundreds of mountain boys and girls opportunity to earn a part or all of their way through school. In addition scores of students have gone out into the mountains and to communities far outside the region to teach the skills learned. Berea has probably furnished more weaving teachers for the Highlands than all other schools in our country combined, and for many years has supplemented this service by making looms which have been widely used both in the area and outside it.

The Penland Weaving Institute held at Penland, North Carolina, each summer under the auspices of Penland Weavers and Potters has a record of drawing widely distributed exponents of handwork from many parts of the country. Established in 1930 by Lucy Morgan for the purpose of giving to the large group of mountain weavers which she had developed in the neighborhood the benefit of instruction from Mr. Worst, the Institute each succeeding year has drawn new applicants, many of whom could not be accommodated. In 1936, 116 students enrolled, representing 22 states, the District of Columbia, and Alaska. These included occupational therapists, home demonstration agents, relief workers in handicrafts, social service workers, registered nurses, leaders in government work, and other teachers and weavers. The course occupies two weeks and preceding it is a preliminary week in which the Penland Weavers give instruction to those not especially advanced in craft but who wish to learn how to set up a loom, warping, beaming, threading, and the weaving of simple designs. Then follows the regular course under Mr. Worst's personal direction which comprises instruction in weaving with many harnesses, crackle weave, summer-and-winter, double weaving, and a large variety of work in which any student having a good working knowledge of hand weaving can participate. Courses in basketry, pottery, and other crafts for both beginners and teachers are offered at the Institute, but it is weaving that draws attendance from many distant states.

In addition to Berea College and the Weaving Institute at Penland other schools and centers in the Highlands which offer instruction in weaving are referred to in Chapter V, Spinning and Weaving for Home and Market.

The most recent undertaking in supervision is that of the Southern Highlanders, Inc., the co-operative organization of handicraft workers formed through the encouragement of the Tennessee Valley Associated Co-operatives, to secure competent designers of textiles and other products whose services will be available to many of the workers throughout the Highlands. These designers will act also as stylists, being familiar with the types of products for which there is a demand outside the region. The work will be closely co-ordinated with production and marketing.

PRODUCTION

Production, like training, was originally a process based almost entirely on individual effort and, as a rule, the purpose of producing was for individual use rather than to promote sales. Therefore the idea of bringing forth commodities to be sold in quantities to create a wider margin of profit did not enter into the calculations of the pioneer worker. Neither was he very accurate in figuring the cost of producing an article, for costs to him were considered largely in terms of materials which he already had at hand, in time of which he had an abundance, and in labor which he himself supplied.

From the first stages in producing entirely for family consumption, and later occasionally for exchange with neighbors for other commodities, or for barter at a country store, the evolution of production was carried along similar routes to those of training. The several agencies coming into the field for group training under supervision introduced the incentive to produce for market. With this a new element appeared, namely, careful duplication of the article. The Highlander had heretofore felt free to change slightly or as much as he wished each article that he produced, a privilege

266

that gives some craftsmen particular satisfaction, and relieves others of an irksome task. Therefore when leaders in the revival received orders for exact duplicates, the worker if he wished to market his product was compelled to accept this new requirement and he sometimes found it difficult. He did not always want to repeat; he could not see any sense in it anyway.

Occasionally one finds in the mountains today an older worker who still refuses to duplicate any design exactly, insisting that to do so would be distasteful. Granny Donaldson, whose crocheted and appliquéd blanket is illustrated opposite page 272, holds tenaciously to her conviction against duplication. The feeling for individuality in production is indicated forcefully by the mountain chairmaker who refused politely but firmly to make a hundred chairs that would "match exactly alike." His story is similar to the one told by Mrs. Dwight W. Morrow in her delightful article[1] on Cuernavaca, in which a Mexican craftsman who had given a price on one chair was asked what he would charge for making a dozen just like it. He replied graciously that if he could be persuaded, as he was not sure he could be, to make several chairs without any variation in the design he would certainly ask a considerably higher price, because the work of duplicating a piece would be both tiresome and uninteresting.

Producing for market introduced still another element into the worker's program. Until now time had been an elastic feature with him, and he was not accustomed to placing a limit on completing his work. For instance, if a drought or other caprice of nature affected a flower or shrub from which coloring was to be extracted he, rather than sacrifice the desired color, was quite willing to wait for a more favorable season to finish his basket, or anyone else's basket for that matter. When the new supervision attempted to set up a time framework into which workers should fit in the making of objects ordered, this was considered an invasion of personal rights, and some workers will not even now promise when delivery can be made.

A recent example of antagonism to time pressure is reported of a potter in one of the towns of the Highlands who closed his shop

---

[1] Morrow, Elizabeth, Our Street in Cuernavaca. *In* American Mercury, August, 1931, p. 411.

quite unexpectedly a week before Christmas. A customer, disappointed in not being able to purchase several articles for the holiday season, asked him about the closed business. He replied that so many orders had come in that to fill them would have hurried him, and he therefore decided to close up and start over after Christmas.

In spite of some of the eccentricities, both trying and refreshing, which the Highlander disclosed when he was brought into trade channels, he accepted the new demands with a reasonable response, and a fairly satisfactory system of production has evolved.

While production is still largely an individual process under partial supervision, yet a number of crafts have been brought entirely under the guidance of commercial producers. Probably the candlewick spread industry, already described, carries on the most extensive operations in the form of complete regulation of mountain workers. All the materials are factory made and are brought to the door of the worker by whom the tufting is done usually on a piece basis of compensation. Similar conditions obtain in the hooked-rug industry, where temporary factories are set up, materials and designs provided, and workers paid per square foot for hooking. In this type of product, although performed by hand, the merest suggestion of the creative element, so pronounced in the indigenous handicrafts, is entirely lacking and work becomes a process by rote.

Methods of production therefore fall into four general classes: first, that process without any supervision whatsoever where the article is shaped entirely by hand or maybe even partly by machinery, but its character is determined wholly by the individual who makes it, as in the case of basket makers and some of the older weavers; second, that under moderate supervision particularly as to craftsmanship and assistance given in design but the article is primarily individual; third, that where designs and workmanship are both supervised and the article conforms to standards, but where the worker is encouraged to originate designs and to keep up a high quality as in schools and handicraft centers; and fourth, that where there is exclusive commercial supervision and management, and no regard is paid to individual aptitudes, as in factories and communities concerned with getting out products for commercial houses.

MARKETING THE HANDICRAFTS

Selling or marketing handicrafts is now, as always, one of the most pressing problems in the Highlands, and nearly every known method has at one time or another been employed. The worker living in remote parts of the mountains usually peddles his handwork in the neighborhood; others are fortunate enough to have their wares called for and taken to nearby markets; some have roadside stands or salesrooms; the largest group of producers sell through the handicraft centers of the region or through gift shops and other agencies outside; some have special exhibits and sales; some sell to department and other stores while a few sell by mail.

Peddling by the maker of the articles, on foot, or muleback, began with the country store as the place of exchange where the products were given for provisions needed in the household. At the same time exchanges were made with neighbors for other articles or for materials to go into the objects made, and sometimes for money. Products are often peddled by car or by truck hundreds of miles from where they were made, as far north as New England and south to Florida. Usually the trips to the far distant places are made by other than the makers of the wares and the method of marketing becomes more complicated.

Sometimes a craftsman will sell all his output at home, that is, people will come and get it as the objects are finished. In some places, as in parts of Virginia, North Carolina, and Georgia, dealers in baskets, small furniture, and pottery will go to the source of supplies and purchase these commodities as reasonably as possible, transporting them to the main highways, where they resell them in shops or roadside stands to tourists and travelers.

The holding of exhibitions of mountain handicrafts has been a fruitful method of making sales outside the Highland country. The exhibition is often accompanied by a representative of the center identified with the work. An annual exhibition is held in Washington under the auspices of the Daughters of the American Revolution; the Pi Beta Phi Settlement School at Gatlinburg exhibits its products through chapters in every part of the country; Penland Weavers and Potters and other centers connected with church schools hold exhibits among the churches; the Campbell Folk School has annual exhibits and sales in New York City and other places; and the exhibitions of the Southern Highland Handicraft Guild bring before many different groups the best handwork of the region. From time to time handicraft centers conduct special exhibits in connection with meetings where opportunity is given for purchasing their products.

Among the most reliable and satisfactory sources of marketing have been the agencies established to encourage a continuation of handicraft production. Through schools, settlements, and training centers the products flow to the outside region in various ways, and these groups are ever eager to take advantage of any new opening for the benefit of the workers. Connected with several of the producing centers is a salesroom where articles are displayed and from which purchases may be made at reasonable prices. This method provides an effective opportunity for acquainting tourists and other visitors to the South with the kinds of handicrafts available. The salesroom of the Southern Highland Handicraft Guild at Asheville is the largest single outlet as it serves the majority of the centers in the Highlands.

The newest developments in marketing are being worked out by the Southern Highlanders, Inc. A salesroom has been opened at Norris Dam, Tennessee, to serve the immediate region, and a plan is in process to establish marketing outlets in other cities. In November and December, 1935, a very successful sale was conducted by the Southern Highlanders, Inc., at Rockefeller Center, New York City, with the result that a most attractive permanent exhibit and salesroom has been opened in the Concourse of the International Building, where both wholesale and retail business relationships are being developed. Salesrooms have recently been opened at the Patten Hotel, Chattanooga, and at Chickamauga Dam, Tennessee.

In connection with most of the plans for selling referred to, the goods are sent out on a consignment basis. This is not a very satisfactory arrangement for the producer as it puts upon him a part of the burden of selling, and in some of the gift shops his wares are not pushed as are others in which the shop has made an investment; however, at present it seems that a considerable amount of consignment business must continue, although buying outright is slightly on the increase.

CRÈCHE OF CORN HUSKS

Many Corn Husk Objects Are Made by Members of the Handicraft Guild of the Diocese of Southwestern Virginia at Dante. This crèche Is a Favorite

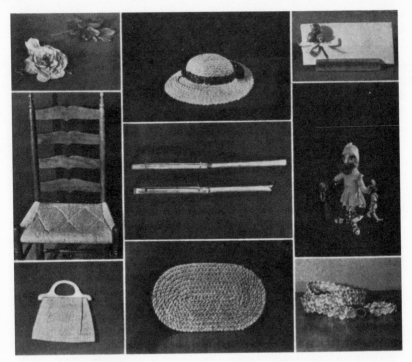

OBJECTS FASHIONED FROM THE CORN PLANT

From Left to Right. Upper Row: Flowers, Hat, Place Card. Middle Row: Chair Seat, Corn Stalk Fiddle, Blue Beard and Two of His Wives. Third Row: Knitting Bag of Woven Husks, Braided Door Mat, Bracelet, and Hat Band

Prophecies as to future methods of marketing must, of course, be speculative. The gradual growth from purely individual efforts to those embracing co-operation among the workers themselves and with the agencies to which they are related has moved forward with encouraging signs and results. But while these experiments have contained many practical elements none has reached anything like its full possibilities. What can be accomplished by greater co-operation is the most important question engaging the minds of those interested in the people and products of the mountains; as suggested more fully in the following chapter marketing is not an isolated problem, but a vital part of the whole problem of the home and school industries of the Highlands in which training, design, and production are also component factors.

CHAPTER XIX

FUTURE OF THE HANDICRAFTS IN THE HIGHLANDS

ONE who has followed the development of handicrafts in the Southern Highlands from the revival up to the present time is impressed with the changes that have taken place in their character and variety. If he tries to visualize what the situation may be in ten, twenty, or fifty years he is likely to feel both hope and fear: hope because of prospective co-operation to improve their quality and to extend their markets, and fear that in the processes of standardization and adaptation to commercial requirements some of their best uses and values may be lost. Also there is the possibility that a number of the worthy old mountain crafts may disappear with the passing of the present generation, particularly the making of musical instruments, a considerable part of basketry, old methods of wood turning, coverlet weaving, ancient forms of pottery making, and primitive chairmaking. Unless new and conscious effort is made to encourage the continuance of these crafts they will go, and once gone they are not likely to return.

The whole situation presents a strong challenge to everyone concerned with handicrafts or with the general welfare of the mountain people. These home, community, and school industries, together with small agriculture, will form the economic base upon which countless families can build; they now constitute the base upon which many of them are building. In the proportion that they are supported will public relief with its unwanted and undermining influences be reduced.

But the handicrafts have much more than an economic significance; they are, as it is hoped this report has shown, an integral part of Highland life and culture. Hence the challenge is not only to increase the income they supply but so to utilize them in their development that they will yield a large measure of satisfaction to those who practice them and to the greater number who in one way

MOUNTAIN COW BLANKET

Someone Showed Granny Donaldson an Italian Cow Blanket of Homespun with Crocheted Decorations Appliquéd on It. Using the Same Technique She Made Several Blankets of Her Own, No Two Alike

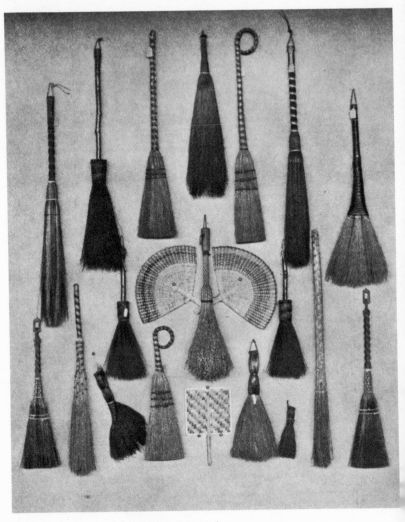

HIGHLAND BROOMS AND FANS

These Brooms from North Carolina, Tennessee, Kentucky, and Georgia Are
Made from Home Grown Broom Straw. The Fans Are of Oak Splits, Dyed in
Bright Colors. The Fan at the Bottom Is of Flattened Wheat Straw

or another come within the sphere of their influence. That is to say, we must think of the handicrafts not only as a means of making a living but as a way of life.

Once we have accepted this larger point of view we shall be on the road to make of this region not only a great source of handwork for our country and the world but to build for our people of the Highlands a handicraft culture, for here exist in an unusual degree and mixture the elements essential to such a culture. What some of these elements are, as well as some of the forces which threaten them, will be discussed briefly in this chapter.

This does not mean that all people in the Highlands shall be urged to practice the handicrafts, nor that the use of machinery and modern methods should be opposed when common sense will approve them, or that other opportunities for improving social and living conditions be disregarded; quite the opposite. It means that the people of the region, whether or not they practice the handicrafts, shall be conscious of their importance as a great economic and cultural resource around which long-time plans can be made; that in addition to encouragement for the isolated worker, local co-operatives should be formed, as is now being done in a few instances, to bring into the region social, educational, and economic benefits, and that a sound basis be laid for that wider co-ordination of community, state, and federal agencies needed to insure an outstanding development of the handicrafts.

HELPFUL FORCES

Among the strong and hopeful influences favoring such a development which may well be considered here are the following:

1. There is a continuous economic pressure on the Highlander to make things for himself and to earn in his home or neighborhood some money to support his standard of life; this need provides a stable basis for home industries which does not exist in places where a worker can turn to other means of income.

2. The life of the average Highland family is simple, and cash needs are so small that a good standard of life can be supported on what they can raise, plus small earnings from handicraft or other work which they can perform without leaving home.

3. Most Highlanders own their own homes, an encouragement to the development of these fireside industries.

4. The Highlanders are by circumstances and tradition accustomed to work with their hands and often acquire unusual skill and taste.

5. The tempo of life gives time and opportunity to encourage creative work.

6. There is throughout the region an abundance of materials and climatic and soil conditions favorable to growing many plants for handicraft purposes.

7. Instruction and training are steadily improving and mountain people like to help one another to advance in the work.

8. Handicrafts are being encouraged through the Southern Highland Handicraft Guild, the Southern Highlanders, Inc., the Tennessee Valley Authority, the Extension Division of the U. S. Department of Agriculture, the Vocational Division of the Office of Education, the National Park Service, the Resettlement Administration, the Relief Administration, and a large number of schools, settlements, and voluntary agencies.

9. Increasing numbers of possible purchasers are being brought into the region through the building of many fine highways, the establishing of the Great Smoky Mountains and the Shenandoah National Parks, the Tennessee Valley Authority developments, and other influences.

10. There is already, outside the mountain area, a wide and sympathetic interest in the Highlander and his work and a clientele which has been built up gradually by schools and settlements since about 1900. Moreover, handicrafts have proved such valuable interpreters of the mountain people and mountain problems for schools and settlements that these latter will, in their own interest, continue to encourage this work.

11. And finally there is throughout our country a great body of consumers with a high average buying power, who can be counted upon to sustain a considerable output of handicrafts if they are of good standard and have meaning for the people who buy them.

This enumeration does not exhaust all the elements that mark the Southern Highlands as a favored region for development of handicrafts in connection with small agriculture, but it probably includes the important ones.

OPPOSING FORCES

A clear recognition of the forces that operate against such a development is also important. Therefore in looking into the future something should be said about them. Among the first of these opposing forces is the attitude of many people toward the handicrafts. They are likely to judge them in terms of their income only. Also many people feel that the handicrafts are out of date, a step backward in the march of progress. And far too many think of them, not as requiring the skill, taste, and judgment that come from training and experience, but something which anyone can do if he is told how, and that he should do only if there is nothing else. These and other prejudices are strong in the public mind, and they are not easily broken down.

In addition to the prejudices just mentioned there are other forces, more definite and more positive, operating against the development of handicrafts in the Highlands. They are of two kinds: first, those that by their nature are antagonistic, or at least competitive; and second, those that are urged ostensibly to help but which actually defeat their avowed purpose. These latter forces are not so easily recognized. The difference between the two kinds may be made clearer by illustrations.

When a factory-made article duplicates one made by hand, and it is sold in the market at a much lower price, the case is clearly one of competition before which the hand-made article will disappear unless its price can be lowered or its quality, design, or appearance made more acceptable to buyers than is that of the factory product. This may be called deliberate or conscious competition in which it is quite possible to foresee the result.

An instance of a force intended to help the Highland craftsman but which worked the opposite way was that of a basket maker who as a matter of fact did not sell nearly all the baskets he could make by hand, but yielded to the advice to put in a machine which would saw out his oak and hickory splints much more quickly than they could be split out with ax and knife. In the process of sawing, the splints were cut into the cross grain of the wood and were not only weakened and their pliability lessened, but were made splintery and difficult to weave. The completed baskets were so inferior that it was necessary to sell them at prices much lower than the hand-made ones and at the expense of the reputation of the craftsman. If they had been widely marketed they would have injured the reputation of the craftsmen of the Highlands who supply baskets of high grade.

Thus, suggestions to speed up production, to standardize, to use machines for the wrong operations, should be carefully examined and checked lest they produce the opposite result from what is intended. To lower prices, to save time, or to make articles in quantity are not the first needs of these workers. There is no reason to speed up production when what is already being made cannot be marketed. It is much better to improve quality, design, color, and serviceability. Moreover, the slower pace of the mountain worker is often a distinct asset in both conception and execution.

The gigantic and ever increasing competition of machine-made and mass-produced goods is clearly demonstrated to the layman by the standardized merchandise in chain stores, especially the former "five and ten" stores which are expanding so that they will soon offer most of the smaller-cost necessities and even a great number of the luxuries of life.

While one should rejoice to see so many useful and attractive objects within reach of the consumer who has only a few cents to spend, yet it must not blind one to the fact that this mass production affects the worker in handicrafts everywhere in two ways: it competes with him directly on like objects which he offers in the market, and it restricts the variety which he can make for the market by supplying cheaper substitutes.

COMPETITION OF FOREIGN HANDWORK

Next to machine-made products perhaps the most serious competition is some of the cheaper handwork from other lands. Many of these latter objects fill the market, and in comparison the small group of articles from a mountain school or center is not always impressive. This fact is a strong argument for comprehensive displays where a wide variety of Highland products may be offered for sale.

There are instances in which foreign competition is direct and keen. At the time of a recent meeting of the Southern Highland

Handicraft Guild at Knoxville, Tennessee, hand-loom rag rugs, "made in Japan," were on sale in an American chain store for 15 cents each, in sizes for which the mountain weaver usually received from 40 to 70 cents. These rugs were well woven and the patterns and color combinations were better than those usually made in the mountains. With them no American hand weaver can compete. But the rugs were made in only one or two set patterns, in three color combinations, and in two sizes—a typical formula for mass production by hand and by extremely cheap labor. The Highland weaver, however, can make rugs of many patterns, of any number of original color combinations, and in a variety of sizes, which, except on standardized articles, helps to lift him out of this competition with the foreigner.

The competition of Japan, Germany, Czechoslovakia, and other highly industrialized countries is not, however, through like objects only, but through the large variety of articles supplied to attract the American consumer's dollar. These hand-made articles are in wood, metal, textiles, glass, clay, paper, fabricated and other materials; and while they are actually competitive they also stimulate interest in handwork generally and are full of suggestions for the Highlander when he has opportunity to see them. He does not often imitate but works out something that the imported object suggests. And they are helping to teach him what he needs most to know, that the only advance for handicrafts is in continuous improvement of quality of design, materials, and workmanship.

COMPETITION OF AMERICAN HANDWORK

Something should perhaps be said about the competition in handwork from other parts of the United States, from Canada, and from Mexico, and how the Southern Highlander feels about this. The League of New Hampshire Arts and Crafts[1] is a keen competitor in the state of New Hampshire, while the Grenfell Labrador Industries and the Province of Quebec are very active in hand-woven textiles, hooked and woven rugs, some types of wood carving, and a considerable number of small objects. Mexico has a greater variety of handicrafts than any of our near neighbors, with

[1] For description see Chapter XX, The Handicraft Movement in Rural America, p. 291.

perhaps a larger volume of sales. It is probably accurate to say that the Highlander does not feel this competition keenly, since it is quite widely distributed, but when he is aware of it there is a frank and hospitable realization on his part of a mutual interest which may some day promote co-operation for handwork that will benefit all concerned. There is an especially friendly relationship between the Southern Highland Handicraft Guild and the League of New Hampshire Arts and Crafts which promises mutual benefits to both organizations in the future.

PROPOSALS OFFERED THAT CREATE DIFFICULTIES

While in his particular field competition is one of the most persistent factors with which the Highlander has to contend, it is by no means the only obstacle he must overcome. There are, as has been said, proposals ostensibly made to forward his interests which result quite differently from what has been intended. These touch all the steps involved—training, production, and marketing.

They usually begin with the ever pressing problem of markets and reach back into planning and designing. A few of the more common proposals are: (1) speed up production by installing modern machinery already alluded to briefly; (2) take the work out of homes and establish centers where producing and working conditions can be controlled; (3) sell in quantity through department and other commercial stores; (4) install efficiency cost systems and make only articles that can be sold at a profit; (5) employ expert designers and use only their designs; (6) and above all produce a standard article and eliminate sentiment about the Highlander from the work.

Speed Up Production with Modern Machinery

The advice to apply power to hand looms and to use other machines is natural and grows out of the age-old desire to save time for other things, and in recent years, by saving time, to cut down the cost of production. But time is a relative matter and is quite a different thing in parts of the Highlands where the tempo of living and working differs from anything that modern industry and urban life know. Good tools, simple machinery, cheap and practical power will be a boon to the Highlander if gradually

VEGETABLE DYED EASTER EGGS

These Eggs Were Dyed with Colors Native to the Region by Sarah Dougherty of Shuttle-Crafters. The Rooster and Duck Were Whittled at the Campbell Folk School; Pewter Candlestick Was Made by the Mountaineer Craftsmen; Honeywax Candle by Leonard Lamb

introduced on a basis that he can afford and become accustomed to, and if they shall not lessen his skill or undermine the quality of his product; but, as has been explained, speed is neither his first nor in most cases a very pressing need. To utilize time for good work is better than to save it for something less important.

There are instances in certain community undertakings where power-driven machinery has immense advantages for land clearing, plowing, seeding, cultivating, and harvesting, also in the preparation of materials for building, and in community activities where several neighbors can afford to join in the use of one machine and where its repair and upkeep can be provided for. All the subsistence homesteads in the region of the study have utilized successfully a considerable amount of machinery in their community work. Machinery planned to meet simple needs, of types which can easily be kept in working order, will become more and more used by Highlanders, and with the advent of cheap power, which seems an early prospect, it is hoped that small home and neighborhood industries can be developed. But the handwork that insures a product of high grade is usually preferable to entering into the large field of machine competition.

ESTABLISHMENT OF WORKING CENTERS

To take the work out of the home and to establish centers where production and working conditions can be controlled is a comparatively new suggestion. There are, as has been indicated, a few centers in the Highlands, in addition to the schools, where workers, especially weavers, come together to get their supplies or instructions and sometimes to work, even though they have their own looms or other facilities at home. The advocates of supervised working centers believe that it would be possible to control working conditions and gradually to raise wages, which they claim cannot be done when work is carried on at home. Moreover, it is held that the product could be standardized to meet continuing demands. These plans are predicated upon rather extensive financing for both production and marketing through government loans to be retired within a reasonable time.

The principle of striving for a uniform product is in many cases desirable, but the bringing of the workers together into a common center would be impossible for those who live from five to 30 miles apart, sometimes with only mountain trails leading out. In addition to these physical difficulties there is a strong feeling among those who have pioneered in the handicraft revival that the fireside industries must remain in the home and not be turned into small mountain factories. Moreover, as good hand weaving as has ever been done in the mountains has been done on home looms, and it is contended that there is no work so difficult that it cannot be produced as well there as in a weaving center, and at a lower cost. This would also apply to other crafts than weaving.

Whatever is done to finance and develop new and special industries should not take away from the mountain people the advantages which the slow building up of homework has brought to them. There is also strong feeling that the handicrafts of the Highlands cannot be safely financed on a large scale until more progress has been made in establishing local co-operatives.

Selling through Department Stores

A department store must as a rule have a uniform product, a requirement which producers generally should strive to achieve; but it ordinarily requires a mark-up of approximately 80 to 100 per cent on merchandise of the handicraft type, a mark-up which few of the Highland handicrafts will at the present time support. There are some standardized objects which will carry the necessary margin of profit, but these have usually been made in what are practically small mountain factories, organized by outside concerns which conduct all the work on a piece basis. Often these factories are temporary and are practically sweated industries, run mainly to get the cheapest labor possible to fill their contracts. Not many mountain products will stand a profit of more than 50 per cent, some not that, and this margin does not interest the city department store. Under present circumstances it seems very doubtful whether the regular channels of trade organized to respond to mass production can be utilized to market handicrafts to any great extent. Progress is, however, being made in larger production of some articles heretofore made in very limited quantity, and this will continue, but great care must be exercised to maintain the quality already established.

Efficient Cost Systems; Selling Only at a Profit

All will wish the Highlander to have some profit on the objects which he makes, but to determine what it may be is not always easy. If one has to buy the materials and sell the finished article for less than these cost, the financial loss could not be approved unless there happened to be a compensating satisfaction of some kind which justified the sacrifice. But normally it is not easy to evaluate the Highlander's time because there are few standards by which it can be measured, and also because urban time schedules are not operative in the mountains. Many handicrafts have been developed under what would seem to be any but efficient methods, and had they been subjected to efficiency systems of measurement they would probably have been discontinued. The way in which the handicrafts of the mountains have been pushed forward by apparently haphazard methods until out of unpromising beginnings some small industry would get to a point where it was established has been noteworthy. Could this have been achieved if efficient cost systems had been applied?

Employ Only the Designs of Experts

One of the reasons which make the marketing of certain handicrafts of the Highlands difficult, especially some of the weaving, is that the designs, color schemes, and styles are often not in the vogue. It is sometimes urged that Highlanders are not qualified to meet this demand and that all designs should be prepared by professionals and then carefully carried out by mountain and other craftspeople. Undoubtedly gains will come through co-ordination between trained designers, who know market needs, and workers who execute them. This is an essential service which the Southern Highlanders, Inc., is now endeavoring to make available to its members. It is intended to offer this designing and styling service to all handicrafts, but weaving is one they hope to reach early.

It should be pointed out, however, that this service is not simple to work out. Obviously it requires knowledge of what will sell, also a knowledge of the types of hand looms throughout the mountains. Most of the textile designers have been trained for modern factory looms and find it difficult to adapt themselves to the simple hand looms with their limited yarn and thread supplies. The problem, therefore, is to secure those who know the capacities and limitations of these looms and who are thus able to prepare patterns which can be produced advantageously.

Often the preparation of detailed designs is not as much needed as an advisory service on styles, colors, and trends. This is true where there are good teachers and able weavers who can carry out ideas if given suggestions. If an advisory service could be made available to these teachers, they could continue to develop their own ideas and encourage the workers to do likewise and thus adapt their wares to the market. This would encourage originality upon which the advancement of handicrafts must always depend. The environment and temperament of the Highland people combine to encourage new expressions in various kinds of work, and a little good teaching leads to much independence and inventiveness.

Standardize the Product and Cut Out Sentiment

One often hears that all Highland handicrafts should be standardized, sold on their merits, and all sentiment abandoned concerning the people who make them. With the advice to make the products so well that they will sell on their merits, there will be general agreement. Every object of handicraft that goes out of the Highlands affects the sale of others for years to come. One poor article will often damage the handicrafts of a home or school because it will create a general prejudice against the source which later a superior article cannot repair.

There is, however, no work so good but that some knowledge of the person who is doing it and the attendant circumstances will help to make it more significant. The ethical significance of an object of handicraft cannot always be determined by its esthetic appearance or by its conformity to the standards of the day. To appraise it fully one must know something of the maker, his environment and his opportunities, or lack of opportunities, and this knowledge will oftentimes raise a commonplace object to a plane of interest where it will be much enjoyed. Or even if the quality of the work is not the best the human interest attached to it may influence the appreciator to suggest or help toward a better product. The deep interest that many people feel in the Highlanders clusters about the true and quaint stories of them which have been captured by social workers, writers, and visitors to the region. To discard this element of appeal would be to throw away what is often a strong bond relating the possessor of an example of Highland handicraft to some mountain character, family, or group of neighbors.

The above proposals which have been made to help solve the handicraft problems of the Highlands are, as has been said, a mixture of very good and sometimes very bad advice; the task is to choose between the two and apply that choice at the place where and the time when it is most needed.

It is obviously easier to criticize suggestions made than to formulate workable substitutes. And it is far better that those who have ideas about improving the handicrafts should be encouraged to test them, for often to try out new ideas will be the only way to prove whether or not they are practical and feasible. Therefore if this report permitted the printing of but one recommendation to those seeking to influence the future of this work, that recommendation would be to leave wide open the doors of experimentation for all who participate. Through the freedom of a trying-out process will come the only way short of regimentation to promote production, and it is assuredly the only way to build up a body of rural arts that will have the vitality to endure. The co-operation of planners, designers, stylists, from both within and without the mountain area, is indispensable to the continuation of the handicrafts; but co-operation from the outside will avail little if the people themselves are not encouraged to experiment continuously. Experimentation and experience will alone engender that vitality of interest and expression upon which the sturdy growth of these small industries depends.

SOME GENERAL OBSERVATIONS

As has been said, there will continue to be differences of opinion on what will best advance the handicrafts in the Highlands; and that is as it should be. An effort has been made here to sum up the advantages which the region possesses for their development, and to recognize difficulties that must be surmounted. Some observations that may help those who are directly or indirectly concerned with this development may now be added. These observations are based on the results of the experience of the past forty years in the Highlands, and are to a considerable degree supported by experience in the practice of handicrafts elsewhere. Among them are the following:

1. That everyone cannot do handicrafts well;
2. That three distinct elements are involved—design, production, and distribution—and all must be worked out together;
3. The key to the solution of the problem is a greatly widened co-operation;
4. A new type of business technique may have to be worked out for production and distribution;
5. The handicrafts must be utilized as a social, educational, and general cultural force for the Highlands as a whole if they are to have complete development.

Not Everyone Can Do Handicrafts

A considerable number of people seem to cling to the idea that anyone, especially if he is unemployed, can take up a handicraft and that a ready market awaits his product. That many individuals could make with their own hands objects of use and often beauty, which would serve their own or family purposes, is true; but that is quite a different thing from making objects for the market. Handicrafts for the market require taste, skill, which come only from practice, perseverance, and at least some originality. Although a good craftsman is the exception rather than the rule, it is the testimony of those who have worked with mountain people that a surprisingly large number of women and girls learn to sew, weave, quilt, knit, and to do other types of work very well; and that many men and boys are especially skilful in woodworking, in whittling, and in other forms of manual expression. The testimony of those who have charge of labor in the spinning mills, the rayon factories, and other mechanized industries of the South, as well as those engaged in printing and other crafts, furnishes abundant proof of the resourcefulness of the Highlanders and their skills and general abilities. There would seem to be hardly any limit to the number of people in the mountains who might do good handicraft work in their homes and working centers if the demand for products

BROOMS OF VARIOUS TYPES

Left and Right, Made at Berea College; First from Left, at Gatlinburg by "Broom Tying Richard"; Middle, Dyed Striped Handle at Higgins, North Carolina; Next, with the Seeds Left on the Broom Corn, at Campbell Folk School

COMPOSITION OF HIGHLAND WOOD PRETTIES

Plants Found in the Forest Whether Green or Dry Are Called "Wood Pretties."
They Are Sometimes Arranged in Decorative Masses or Flat, as Above, Designed
by Mrs. W. H. Blauvelt of Asheville, North Carolina

could be provided and reasonable support in training and production given.

Design, Production, and Marketing Must Be Correlated

Design is the preliminary step in production, and the close interdependence of production and marketing is brought home to the centers engaged in the work through many practical transactions. While most of these centers now have some outlets in which selling the products to the public is carried on by others, yet much of the marketing is still done directly by the centers themselves, so that they receive the whole gamut of experience from the inception of the object to its disposal to the consumer. The time may come when more of the marketing will be done through other agencies, but any such arrangement will not change the dependence of these two basic operations upon each other, and it seems certain that the plans now in process for building up the handicrafts can be carried out successfully only through this correlation.

There were instances during the so-called prosperous years preceding the late depression when a considerable quantity of handicrafts was bought at their source by traders and dealers who had their own methods of distribution; but when the depression came these connections were discontinued and the producing centers thrown back "on their own." All through those trying years most of the centers managed to keep some roads to market open, and though the stream of distribution often ran low, there was a continuation of service to handicraft workers which commercial interests did not and presumably could not extend. During this period the salesroom of the Southern Highland Handicraft Guild was able to provide a steadily increasing outlet for most of the products of its members.

Handicrafts Dependent upon Co-operation

The key to the working out of the handicrafts in the Highlands, as has been said, is co-operation, but it must be widespread and elastic. It will not only take the form of local and regional legal co-operatives but it will include a wide variety of co-operation which for one reason and another should not be so limited; but this looser association will be nonetheless effective. It has already begun, but it will include many more people than formerly and involve many agencies both voluntary and governmental in many states and perhaps in other countries. The roots of this new and growing plant will be in the Highlands wherever a few are working together, and these workers in turn will form their district, state, or perhaps regional co-operatives. Especially should the government become concerned, from the local school district to the federal departments at Washington.

Reference has already been made to the present activities or potential interests of the Tennessee Valley Authority, of the Extension Division of the Department of Agriculture, the Vocational Division of the Office of Education, the Women's Bureau of the Department of Labor, the National Park Service of the Department of the Interior, and others. These services need to be strengthened and correlated and others added to make a more effective part of the co-operating program which should include all the relief and social service agencies, private and public, that operate in the Highlands.

The co-operation between agencies in the mountains with individuals and agencies outside will be a long continuous trial and error process. This does not necessarily mean the formation of new agencies, especially in the Highlands; what seems in that region to be a practical and in many ways an ideal set-up is being evolved through the Handicraft Guild, the Southern Highlanders, Inc., and other co-operators. These agencies, and others yet to be formed outside the mountains will co-ordinate their activities in both educational and business programs, for the development of the handicrafts is at base educational. Many persons and organizations throughout the country will give valuable support to the movement as they come to understand its significance to the mountains and to the country as a whole. Indeed already many whose interest could not have been elicited by the commercial aspect alone are giving invaluable co-operation.

The Highland people are to be commended for developing their own potentialities and forms of co-operation before they seek outside grants and government appropriations; but it is to be expected that such support will be forthcoming, not necessarily in the form of subsidies for business, but for educational and promotional work.

286

FIRST EXHIBITION, 1930, OF THE HANDICRAFT GUILD

Handicraft Objects Which Formed the Center of an Exhibition of the Southern Highland Handicraft Guild, in the Sunday School Room of the Second Presbyterian Church in Knoxville, Tennessee. Below: Cedar Pail of Red and White Natural Color from Pendleton County, West Virginia. Basket, Double Weave, to Hold Clover Seed, from Sevier County, Tennessee. In Center a Photograph Showing Initials and Date of Quilt Illustrated Opposite Page 180

HIGHLAND TASTE, SKILL, AND INGENUITY

Hat Made of Buckeye Wood Which Can Be Split into Strips as Fine as Paper. Boutonnieres Made from Seed, Seed-Pods, and Other Plant Forms. Knives Made from Discarded Saw Blades by Boys in the Highland Counties of Maryland

It is this latter policy, exercised in a limited way by the Tennessee Valley Authority, which is one of the strongest and most promising factors in the present development of the handicrafts. There is excellent reason for further federal, state, and private co-operation.

A New Type of Business Technique

It seems certain that a special business technique must be applied to handicrafts in contrast to those employed in mass production and distribution. The conditions in the two fields are essentially different. In factory production all workers are concentrated in one place, where the work is so divided that each person performs a definite part of the process; in the mountains much of the work is carried on in separate homes where success is dependent upon the initiative, skill, and industry of the worker. In factory organization, work is done on a time schedule and wages are paid accordingly; in the mountains it is usually done "between times" and there is no set-up for carrying out a wage system. In the factory the objective is a uniform product which can be multiplied, usually by machinery, in great numbers with unvarying results; in the mountains there is little exact repetition, and no great quantities can be produced at such low cost per unit that they will allow large profits for subsequent distribution.

From these brief comparisons it must be clear that it is not possible to apply as fully as some have advocated the techniques of factory production and distribution to handicrafts. The basic requirement in the mountains is that the craftsman shall receive for his product enough to meet his simple needs. Yet he must sell at a reasonable price or demand will cease. Thus a reasonable return at a price that will be satisfactory to the purchaser is the economic base upon which the continuance of the handicrafts depends. There are a few articles made in the Highlands which could stand considerable advance in price, but it is better to sell an object for less than it is worth than for more. There is no appeal to the American public which the Highlander can devise that will be more helpful in building up trade than to maintain prices that will make their products seem to be bargains.

In working out these problems every proposed experiment should be referred back to the all important question, "Will this help the

Southern Highlanders to help themselves?" The handicrafts depend more than anything else upon the measure of vitality that can be engendered in the people to go on. To repeat, it must be kept ever in mind that this is a social problem with social objectives, which must not be cut off and treated as a separate and distinct experiment in economic efficiency. There is ample opportunity for the application of sound business principles within the larger circle of general welfare and social progress. It seems certain that the great hope for handicrafts lies more in the co-operative than in the competitive way.

HANDICRAFTS A CULTURAL FORCE FOR ALL

In looking toward the future, thought should be given not only to the producers of handicrafts but also to the many people of the region who have little or no part in production. They as a part of a population in which this type of work prevails may take satisfaction in the achievements of their neighbors, and partake of the experiences growing out of this mountain activity and expression in culture. There is a great opportunity to utilize the co-operation which a well-rounded handicraft program will call forth to increase general growth and inspiration. The average Highlander is eager for education. The teaching, the exhibitions, the demonstrations of a comprehensive handicraft program, and the working out of personal, family, and community expressions in dignified handwork can be made to contribute to the happiness and welfare and inspiration of many individuals and many mountain neighborhoods hungry for the best things of life.

PART III

THE RURAL HANDICRAFT MOVEMENT AND
THE WIDER USE OF HANDICRAFTS

MOUNTAIN HANDICRAFTS AT BERRY SCHOOLS

Student at Work on a Tufted or "Candlewick Spread" in the Weaving Room of Sunshine Cottage at the Martha Berry Schools Near Rome, Georgia. Native Handicrafts Are Especially Encouraged at These Schools

CHILDREN'S POTTERY KILN

THIS KILN WAS BUILT AND IS OPERATED BY FOUR MOUNTAIN CHILDREN OF GEORGIA,
THREE BOYS AND A GIRL, WHO CARRY OUT ALL THE PROCESSES OF POTTERY MAKING

CHAPTER XX

THE HANDICRAFT MOVEMENT IN RURAL
AMERICA

ANYONE making inquiry about handicrafts in the United States in the early years of this century would have found his paths of investigation leading toward the cities, for many had developed handicraft societies, or, as they were more frequently called, arts and crafts societies—organizations of artists and craftsmen who were devoting themselves to the idea of bringing beauty into everyday life through the making and using of fine handwork. They were consciously or unconsciously responding to the influence of the philosophy of work and life developed by Carlyle, Ruskin, and Morris of England, especially Morris, who put these principles into fine and tangible expression in houses, furniture, woodwork, metal work, textiles, and beautiful books, in addition to preaching a gospel of beauty that was heard around the world.

Leaders from other lands were drawn into this movement, and its effect upon the improvement in American taste was profound and continues so to be, because while the names of these leaders may be forgotten, their principles still pervade not only the work of individual craftsmen but much of the enormously developed machine industries. It was, however, in the cities and in villages related to cities that one found the movement best expressed; there was little evidence of it in the rural sections except the work of an occasional craftsman who sent his product to the city for display and sale.

During this time country people did make by hand many things which they used, but few objects to sell. Sometime the threads of the movement in America may be gathered into a book and it will prove an important chapter in our development. Much of what was in progress then was recorded in Handicraft, a small but purposeful publication edited by Frederic A. Whiting, director of the Boston Arts and Crafts Society, published monthly by the Society from 1902 to 1904, and distributed among those especially active in these pursuits. In 1901 Gustav Stickley, maker of some excellent furniture, founded The Craftsman, a magazine that had great influence upon American taste and thought. In time other publications accepted material similar to that appearing in The Craftsman, and today articles about arts and crafts may be found in several magazines and newspapers, and a great grist of books has been published on these subjects.

But the handicraft movement once associated with our cities now marks many of our rural areas. Today handicrafts in the cities are practiced for recreational and therapeutic purposes, and the results are not so noticeable as if the objects were made for sale. Since there is a distinct rural movement in which the people of the Southern Highlands have in a sense been pioneers, and of which they are destined to remain an important part, it seems fitting that some aspects of this country-wide movement should be mentioned here.

FEDERAL AGENCIES CONTRIBUTING TO RURAL HANDICRAFTS

The Extension Division of the United States Department of Agriculture, operating through state agencies, was the first of the federal groups to initiate a program for improving opportunities for country people and thus increasing their satisfactions in rural life. Extension agents—the county agents promoting work with men and the home demonstration agents assisting with the problems of women—have brought to great numbers of country folk not only means to improve their crops and augment their income but to add a greater measure of convenience, efficiency, and attractiveness to the farm home. They have helped the country dweller to realize that many conveniences for home and family may be acquired through his own handiwork from resources already within his reach, and their counsel and co-operation have contributed much to the improvements that have taken place in country life in recent years.

Plans for houses, barns, chicken houses, animal shelters, fencing units, septic tanks, tools, simple machinery, which the farmer can build or make, constitute some of these conveniences. Refinishing furniture, chair seating, home-made fireless cookers and refrigerators, interior decoration, and landscaping of the home grounds are other features of economy and beautification that have come through this co-operation. In the cotton-growing states of the South the making of cotton mattresses has become a significant home industry. After cultivating, harvesting, and preparing the cotton for filling, the farmers are able to make the mattresses entirely by hand at home, thus providing an excellent article for use, the equivalent of which they could not afford to buy.

The marketing of butter, eggs, and other farm produce has long been an important enterprise of rural people, and the carefully detailed information regularly furnished by the Extension Division on the preparation and processing of many varieties of food has not only improved the home supply but has materially increased the income from the sale of goods in many farm districts. The constant demand for such products at roadside stands and other market places has stimulated the use of attractive receptacles, and many country people have turned to handicraft containers for processed foods.

At meetings of granges, garden clubs, and county and state fairs different types of handwork made in farm homes have been exhibited from time to time. This participation has given rise to a new interest in which enthusiasm for original ideas has been shown. Although much of this phase of the movement is in its initial stage the possibilities are encouraging, and the need for leadership in the field is country wide.

Connected with the Extension Division are young people's organizations known as 4-H Clubs,[1] organized in every state in which boys and girls and young men and young women among other activities carry out well-defined programs for improved methods in farming and homemaking, and among many projects stress is placed on handicraft activities. For instance, at Jackson's Mill, West Virginia, where the 4-H Clubs of the state hold their annual conventions, exhibits of the work of the young people are shown and study courses for handicrafts and related work are offered. In many county, district, and state fairs recognition is given the country arts, and the county and home demonstration agents often provide valuable assistance in these projects.

[1] The initial H stands for Heart, Head, Hand, Health. Membership in these clubs is large.

The Extension Division has not confined its interest to promoting hand-made objects, but has made several studies relating to handicrafts and has issued reports on them. Among these publications of the federal Department of Agriculture are Home Dyeing with Natural Dyes;[1] References on the Handicrafts of the Southern Highlanders;[2] and Rural Industries in Knott County, Kentucky.[3]

The increasing interest and activity in handicrafts throughout the rural areas of the United States by the Extension Division are worthy of special note. It seems safe to predict that the greatest development of handicrafts in the rural areas of this country will come through the encouragement and direction of this large and far-reaching branch of the federal government, which is realizing more and more the importance of creative work for rural people.

The Division of Subsistence Homesteads, created by the Department of the Interior during the early part of the recent economic depression, furnished a good opportunity for introducing handicraft work both as an individual activity and as a partial solution of problems growing out of unstable industry in areas where large numbers of workers were displaced, especially in coal mining. While the utilization of land as a basis for a degree of economic security was the strongest motive behind the efforts of the Homestead Division, the plan to establish small shops and home industries as part of some of these developments was a determining factor; and therefore in the selection of families for residence, consideration was sometimes given those that possessed skills or could do some work in handicrafts.

The success of the Cumberland Homesteads project near Crossville, Tennessee, an undertaking within the area of this study, demonstrates the practicability of accompanying rural living with handicraft activities. Settlers without homes and out of work, beginning on uncleared land with government guidance and cooperation, have undertaken to rebuild their family and community

---

[1] Furry, Margaret S., and Viemont, Bess M., Home Dyeing with Natural Dyes. Bureau of Home Economics, Washington, 1934. (Mimeographed.)

[2] Edwards, Everett E., References on the Handicrafts of the Southern Highlanders. Bureau of Agricultural Economics, Washington, 1934. (Mimeographed.)

[3] Nason, Wayne C., Rural Industries in Knott County, Kentucky. U. S. Bureau of Agricultural Economics in Cooperation with Kentucky Agricultural Experiment Station, Washington, 1932. (Mimeographed.)

life after new and unexpected patterns. The clearing of land, the constructing of houses and barns from rock underlying the soil and from lumber cut from trees growing on the land, the making of a large portion of the furniture and furnishings for the houses and the local school, all present achievements of distinction. Here is an example that should be studied by everyone interested in what may be accomplished through co-operation among rural people and the government to extract from their own land and with their own labor materials, crops, and products to meet their needs, which they did not have the money to buy. An admirable feature of the Cumberland Homesteads development is the good taste in the houses and furnishings which provide examples of individual preference and charm.

With the single exception of the Southern Highland Handicraft Guild, the group of co-operatives represented by the Southern Highlanders, Inc., has done most to stimulate the recent development in handwork in the mountain section. The Southern Highlanders, Inc., was organized in 1935 to encourage small rural industries and handicrafts throughout a large area of the Southern Appalachians. Its activities will undoubtedly increase because of the breadth of its operations and its policy of improving the quality of Highland products. The handicraft salesroom, opened in 1935 at Norris Dam, is well situated for the convenience of innumerable visitors, and with the permanent exhibit and salesroom at International Building, Rockefeller Center, New York City, at the Patten Hotel, Chattanooga, and at Chickamauga Dam, Tennessee, it forms an important sales outlet.

The Tennessee Valley Authority has also encouraged handicraft work as a part of the training and educational program in the town of Norris, where well-equipped shops give excellent opportunity for residents to carry on work in wood, metal, and other materials as they cannot do in their own homes where equipment is more limited. A number of newly built homes, however, have some facilities for such work, and as a result several residents have made their own furniture and others have developed unusual skill in iron and woodworking. These shops mark the beginning of a social experiment which it is hoped will be emulated in other communities.

The Vocational Division of the Office of Education in the Department of the Interior has aided the various states in carrying out undertakings in the field of handicrafts. Under the Smith-Hughes Act operating through the Vocational Division, financial assistance is granted. A regional Agent for Trade and Industrial Education is empowered to co-operate with each state in promoting approved courses in these fields. Some handicraft centers in the confines of this study have benefited appreciably from this support.

Other divisions of the Department of the Interior giving attention to handicrafts are the National Park Service and the Office of Indian Affairs. As indicated in Chapter XVI, the National Park Service is developing a plan for utilizing handicrafts in the Great Smoky Mountains and the Shenandoah National Parks as part of their educational program, and also to take the place of the more ordinary type of souvenirs sold in other parks throughout the country.

A major purpose of the Office of Indian Affairs is to promote the best in native Indian life including their indigenous handicraft work. Through the Division of Extension and Industry of this Office efforts have been made to interest the Indians on reservations in constructing simple furniture to improve their homes, and exhibitions of such furniture are held periodically as a means of presenting patterns to guide them and otherwise encourage handwork. Indians constantly appeal to the Extension Agent to find support for their tribal arts and crafts through which to increase their income, and this contact affords agents the opportunity to urge the importance of continuing the work by well-established standards and by the use of the designs of their ancestors. These crafts embrace silver and shell work, blankets and other textiles, pottery, basketry, painting, beading, bone and stone work, leather work, and woodwork.

Both the Department of Labor and the Department of Commerce have lent support to this movement in studying particular phases of their own interests which are directly related to production and upon which they have issued reports.[1] That published by the

[1] Nienburg, Bertha M., Potential Earning Power of Southern Mountaineer Handicrafts. U. S. Dept. of Labor, Women's Bureau, Bulletin 128, Washington, 1935.

Bureau of Labor in 1904 is the only extended account of handicrafts as practiced in the rural regions of our country at that time. It contains some valuable material on the early stages of the revival in the Southern Highlands.[1]

In 1933 the Bureau of Foreign and Domestic Commerce of the Department of Commerce made a valuable study of woods.[2] The Division of Self-Help Cooperatives of the Federal Emergency Relief Administration has included considerable handicraft work in some of its relief programs and has given much thought and study to the subject. It has also issued a report.[3]

STATE AGENCIES SPONSORING HANDICRAFTS

The League of New Hampshire Arts and Crafts is the only handicraft organization yet created by state authority. It was founded in 1931 to develop "the educational and economic values in arts and crafts" and is one of the first rural groups outside the Southern Highlands established to foster handwork. It is directed by a State Commission appointed by Governor John G. Winant, of which Mrs. J. Randolph Coolidge is president, Jessie Doe, vice president, and A. Cooper Ballantine, secretary-treasurer. Frank Staples was selected to be the first director of the League and continued until 1936, when he became director of arts and crafts for the National Recreation Association. He was succeeded by Edgar Keen. There are 34 group members and a total membership of 1,500 persons. The objective, as stated by the League, is

. . . to help the people of New Hampshire to spend their leisure time in a profitable way by means of home industries. The League has worked with individuals and groups of people interested in supplementing their incomes and bettering their standards. It has helped them to do this by developing in them co-operative effort and a cultural and artistic appreciation of beauty in whatever they create, stressing originality, individuality of expression, and artistic form.

[1] West, Max, The Revival of Handicrafts in America. U. S. Dept. of Commerce and Labor, Bulletin 55, Washington, 1904.

[2] Oxholm, Axel H., Utilization of Wood in the Mill Creek Region. (Typewritten.)

[3] Fairbank, Nathaniel K., Handcraft: An Investigation of the Present and Potential Market for Non-competitive Handcraft in the United States. Division of Self-Help Cooperatives, Federal Emergency Relief Administration, Washington, 1934. (Mimeographed.)

The League was based on a careful survey of the resources of the state, and no other body has proceeded as cautiously and with such gratifying results in a comparatively short time in the effort to meet the demand for "single articles and for small quantities of articles of certain form, sizes and designs which can be worked out more economically by hand than by factory methods."[1]

The faith of the Commission in the economic possibilities of handicrafts for New Hampshire was voiced in its first report of September 4, 1931: "While there is a certain amount of competition between factory and handwork, yet the carefully planned small industry and handicraft center has its distinctive place in our economic system." The maintenance of a chain of attractive sales places in several towns and cities along the highways of the state, continually increasing in number, with strict supervision by a jury of standards and constant alertness for new talent to increase the range of articles produced, are contributing factors to the progress of the League. Each shop carries near the entrance a sign in the form of a white New England cottage suspended from an iron bracket, and each article is marked with an artistic tag bearing the League emblem. A manager and several volunteer workers of the community assist with the handling of consignments. This reduces overhead expense, cost of marketing, and increases the number of citizens directly interested.

In addition to the training of workers the League undertakes to educate customers to the superiority of good hand-made articles over low-priced, poorly made products. This is done in part through demonstrations carried on by craftsmen at work in the various shops. Travelers from many sections of the country driving through the scenic state of New Hampshire are attracted to the white cottage sign outside the shops and buy objects to take away with them. A few shops remain open during the winter months. The League confines its selling to the state of New Hampshire, and the sales have increased gradually each year, as have the number of workers.

If those who have contributed to the success of this undertaking were asked to name one person to whom the League is most in-

[1] Commission of New Hampshire Arts and Crafts Report to Governor Winant, September 4, 1931.

THE HIGHLANDS GO TO THE WORLD FAIR

The Penland Weavers and Potters Built This "Travel-log" and Hauled Their Handicrafts to the Century of Progress, Chicago, Where, from Sales and Orders, They Supplied Folk Back in the Mountains with Work during Two Hard Seasons

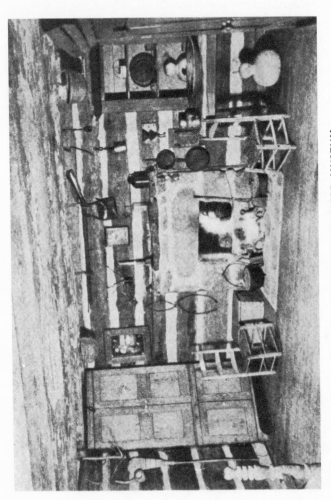

FIREPLACE IN THE MOUNTAINEER MUSEUM

Near the Entrance to the Great Smoky Mountains National Park, Gatlinburg, Tennessee, Mrs. Edna Lynn Simms Has Established and Completely Furnished This Museum with Original Mountain Things

debted the vote would be unanimous for Mrs. Coolidge, who, before a state organization was ever dreamed of, pioneered this field in her home and neighborhood at Center Sandwich and kept her faith and her work going until their influence spread and Governor Winant created the Commission.

The Home Crafts League of New York State was for a time one of the agencies promoting the handicraft movement. Organized by the State Bureau of Industrial Education in 1933 as the result of an initial gift by Mrs. Franklin D. Roosevelt through the state Temporary Emergency Relief Administration, a program of rural home craft work for the state was set up. In the plan was included the training of unemployed adults living in both city and country to help design, produce, and sell various home crafts.

The classes held throughout the state included training in basketry, sewing and embroidery, wood carving, woodworking and carpentry, crochet and knit goods, hooking and braiding, metal craft, pottery, and weaving. Classes open to unemployed adults were conducted during the day free of charge. Several exhibitions of work were shown to the public to indicate what could be accomplished through such a program. The work is now carried on under the direction of the Works Progress Administration of the federal government.

PRIVATE AGENCIES INTERESTED IN HANDICRAFTS

The Southern Highland Handicraft Guild, described in Chapter XVI, is the oldest and, measured by the number of centers and individuals represented and the amount of business passing through its salesrooms, the most outstanding handicraft organization in the country. Members of the Guild represent a background of years of effective and continuous work in many types of handicrafts.

The American Friends Service Committee with offices in Philadelphia, under the direction of Clarence E. Pickett, introduced handicrafts into their relief work among the stranded families in the coal regions of West Virginia and Kentucky about 1931, when the Committee responded to the invitation to help issued by President Hoover. While engaged in relief, rehabilitation became a very pressing need and, beginning with the simple operation of converting cast-off clothing for impoverished families, the work grew and broadened into what is now a well-developed handicraft industry, the Mountaineer Craftsmen's Cooperative Association, with headquarters at Morgantown. This organization is one of the active members of the Southern Highland Handicraft Guild, and its work, especially in furniture making, is described elsewhere in this report.

Ever ready to assume responsibility for providing guidance for those seeking release from the demands of daily routine, the National Recreation Association has for some time included arts and crafts in its list of free-time occupations. As is its custom, it has conducted studies in several communities in the effort to determine the choice of activities among a representative group experiencing an increase in the amount of their free time. From the deductions that were made, a pamphlet[1] of suggestions for adult education community programs was prepared by the Association, in which it gave a variety of examples of the effective use of arts and crafts. And now a handicraft division or department has been organized within the Association to supplement this work.

The American Country Life Association, striving to encourage better educational and cultural opportunities for country people, selected a committee several years ago to study the rural cultural arts in America. This study has furnished a basis for discussions at the annual meetings of the Association and also has stimulated members to introduce handicrafts into their local and state programs. The Association also sponsored the first showing of the traveling Exhibition of Handicrafts of the Southern Highland Handicraft Guild at their annual meeting at Blacksburg, Virginia, in 1933, described in Chapter XVI, The Southern Highland Handicraft Guild.

It is obviously not possible to include here all the agencies throughout the country engaged in some form of handicrafts or otherwise encouraging their conservation or development, particularly in rural areas. To obtain such information would be difficult at any time, for the movement has run quite ahead of any attempt to record it adequately; moreover, the present study has

---

[1] Program Suggestions for the Enrichment of Adult Life. The National Commission on the Enrichment of Adult Life, National Education Association, Washington, 1932.

been mainly concerned with the Highland country. There are a number of museums in which collections are being built, many private collections, and dealers throughout the country who are stimulating an interest in hand-made things. Supplementing those agencies already noted in this chapter are many others, only a few of which can be mentioned here; the activities of some of these apply to both urban and rural areas. Among them are the National Committee on Folk Arts, established to "assemble, record, and protect the folk arts before they perish at their source, and to make them available for study and use"; the Boy Scouts, Girl Scouts, Camp Fire Girls, Young Women's Christian Associations, all of whose interest in American handicrafts finds expression in their club programs; Junior Achievement, Inc., a national organization of clubs whose activities are based partly on craftwork and the development of definite skills; the Ozark Colony, which embraces areas in Arkansas, Missouri, and Oklahoma, whose members work independently and develop several types of furniture and furnishings characteristic of the area; the School of Living at Suffern, New York, sponsored by Ralph Borsodi and Associates, which both teaches and produces handwork for home use; and the several groups and organizations working in the Southwest and other places to preserve the native Indian arts of America. The Early American Industries Association is a significant group in the scope of its purpose which is "to encourage the study and better understanding of early American industry, in the home, in the shop, on the farm, and on the sea, and especially to discover, identify, classify, preserve and exhibit obsolete tools, implements, utensils, instruments, vehicles, appliances and mechanical devices used by American craftsmen, farmers, housewives, mariners, professional men and other workers."

While there is unmistakable evidence of a handicraft movement throughout our country areas based largely upon the making of things by hand for use or for sale, there are also indications that the handicrafts are destined to play an increasingly important role in some of the activities which cut across both rural and urban life, where the accent is upon the other values referred to throughout the foregoing report—the subjective values. There are at this time two rapidly expanding fields of popular activity in which handwork has such definite potentialities that something specific may well be said concerning them; these are the field of adult education and the field of recreation. They both present already quite widely organized backgrounds for handicraft programs, and for this reason the two chapters immediately following will suggest some of the opportunities which each has in utilizing the handicrafts in its sphere.

WEAVERS' CABIN AT PENLAND

This Cabin on the Crest of Conley's Ridge, at Penland, North Carolina, Was Built by Families of the Vicinity and Is an Important Center for That Widely Scattered Community. It Was in This Cabin That the Meeting Was Held, Out of Which the Southern Highland Handicraft Guild Grew

FEATHER FANS
MADE OF FEATHERS FROM VARIOUS FOWLS; THOSE ABOVE, MADE FOR ALLANSTAND
COTTAGE INDUSTRIES, ARE OF GOOSE FEATHERS

CHAPTER XXI

ADULT EDUCATION THROUGH HANDICRAFTS

UNDOUBTEDLY the most important contribution made to adult education in our generation was the convincing proof offered by Edward L. Thorndike and associates of Columbia University that adults could learn on the average as readily as children. In an illuminating report on the subject Dr. Thorndike writes: "In general nobody under forty-five should restrain himself from trying to learn anything because of a belief or fear that he is too old to be able to learn it."[1]

While there have always been many who have not accepted any limitations on learning, and some of America's great leaders, including one President of the United States, Andrew Johnson, could not read or write until after maturity, the idea that everyone may continue education throughout life has only recently been generally accepted. When Dorothy Canfield Fisher made her challenging and inspiring plea in support of this idea, one thing which gave it irresistible force was the long citation of individuals and groups in our country who had been continuing their learning before the movement for adult education got under way.[2] Now these numbers have been multiplied many times.

But the fact that adults can learn carries with it no assurance that they will, and so the search continues with new zest for those things that stimulate learning. From this search have emerged two definite schools, with variants between—the old school which would teach all the facts to children while they are young; and the newer school which would give them the tools of learning while young but would provide the facts and techniques as near as possible to the time when they will need to use them. The significance of these developments is that the future is bound to bring

[1] Thorndike, Edward L., and others, Adult Learning. By permission of The Macmillan Co., publishers, New York, 1928, p. 177.

[2] Fisher, Dorothy Canfield, Why Stop Learning? Harcourt, Brace and Co., New York, 1927.

radical changes in our system of education, and the doctrine of John Dewey, "First the need, then the knowledge or technique to satisfy the need,"[1] seems certain to find a wider application as adult education develops and is more closely co-ordinated with formal schooling.

Adult education in the United States is the inevitable outcome of the great experiment embarked upon a century or so ago, when we adopted the inspiring principle that education should be within the reach of the children of all classes. The extension of this idea to include adults rests upon the conviction that we should try to supply them with what they need when in their judgment they need it.

The modest claim which this chapter is intended to support is that handicrafts offer to many adults an excellent basis for study and development, a prospect so important that it seems justifiable to call attention to it here, and to give some of the reasons why it is so.

By adult education is here meant continuation of the process of learning among men and women regardless of age or previous experience in school. The term comprises more than learning; it connotes growth, as Eduard C. Lindeman wrote in his early but ever fresh monograph on the subject. "Adult education presumes that the creative spark may be kept alive throughout life, and moreover that it may be rekindled in those adults who are willing to devote a portion of their energies to the process of becoming intelligent."[2]

THOSE WHO MAY USE HANDICRAFTS IN ADULT EDUCATION

One of the advantages of handicrafts in the process of adult learning is that they can be used as a starting point, as a center of interest for a large number of individuals regardless of their level of intelligence or experience. That is, they hold potentialities for the doctor of philosophy on one end of our educational procession and for the man who does not read or write on the other end, and of course for the far larger number in between.

[1] Thorndike, Edward L., and others, Adult Learning, p. 190. By permission of The Macmillan Co., publishers.

[2] The Meaning of Adult Education. New Republic, Inc., New York, 1926, p. 87.

OLD WAYS CONTINUED IN VIRGINIA MOUNTAINS

MRS. BYRD PAYNE OF CARROLL COUNTY, VIRGINIA, PREPARES HER YARN, WINDS HER
WARP, WEAVES HER CLOTH TODAY AS HER PEOPLE HAVE DONE FOR GENERATIONS.
SHE TAUGHT HER DAUGHTERS ON THE LOOM MADE BY HER FATHER NINETY-TWO YEARS
AGO. SHE IS WINDING THE WARP ON AN OLD FRAME WITH CORN-COBS FOR BOBBINS

HANDICRAFTS FOR USE

This Excellent Cottage of Wood and Stone, Taken from the Land, Was Built by a Homesteader and His Neighbors at Crossville, Tennessee, after Plans of His Own Choice. Although a Coal Miner and Untrained in Masonry He Did Most of the Stonework on His Own House and Helped Neighbors with Theirs

To state it roughly the handicrafts may be used for advancement in learning and enrichment in experience by at least the following classes or grades of people: (1) the graduate of college, university, or professional school; (2) the adult who may have had only a grammar or high school training; (3) the grown-up who has not gone to school much, but who has learned to read and write after a fashion; (4) the immigrant who cannot read or write the English language, but who may have had schooling in his homeland; (5) the adult who because of lack of opportunity has never learned to read or write; (6) the mentally handicapped who as a retarded child was unable to take a normal place in school and who grows up without learning to read or write. Space will not permit the inclusion of case records to illustrate all the grades mentioned above, but reference will be made to some.

We will instance the debt which a highly educated man, whose life has been enriched by intellectual experiences, pays to the emotional and spiritual growth induced by the practice of handicrafts. Such an illustration will perhaps indicate the contribution the pursuit may make to lives less endowed. For this purpose the story of Sir Esme Howard, British Ambassador to the United States from 1924 to 1930, is chosen. To Ambassador Howard the binding of books by hand provided a needed outlet for the creative instinct, and on more than one occasion he admitted that he eagerly looked forward to the time when he could retire from public life and work at his favorite occupation in his little bookbindery at home in England. What he felt about the importance of all persons taking some part in creative work, and how a handicraft no matter how modest would often supply that need, he indicated in a rather intimate address to the literary and political societies of Princeton University just before leaving for England in 1930. He said in closing:

What I would like to impress on my audience today is the great loss of happiness they will undoubtedly suffer if they do not try to learn and to understand something of the arts of architecture, of music, of painting. There are, no doubt, some unfortunate individuals who cannot distinguish one note from another. I remember one old General who used to say he knew two tunes: "God Save the King and the rest." Such persons have only half their hearing and are as much to be pitied as the very shortsighted. But they can find pleasure in other arts such as painting and architecture.

There are, however, very few mortals who can create anything worth mentioning in any of the major arts. We can learn to enjoy them and so to add to our stock of happiness. We may even join with enthusiasm, intelligence and pleasure in conversation on these subjects without becoming either creators ourselves, or professional art critics—a career I should always be inclined to avoid.

But the actual joy of creating great things which are a source of happiness to ourselves as well as to others will always remain the privilege of the elect.

There is nevertheless a smaller part in the creation of beautiful things in which we can all share. There is, I imagine, scarcely one here present who could not if he or she tried become a first class craftsman in some branch or other. Any of us taking up as a hobby, as a pastime, carving in wood or stone, iron work, pottery making, stained glass making, bookbinding, tapestry making, carpet weaving and the like, would if he tried hard enough and learnt enough to choose or make for himself good designs and combinations of colours—any of us doing these things might become really good craftsmen and leave behind us something whereby we might be remembered.

The moral of all the foregoing is that you young people of America and also our young people in England can add much to your own happiness and also the happiness of the world generally if you will learn not only to appreciate beautiful things but also to create them within the measure of your capacity.

An illustration of the educational value of practicing a handicraft to one who, unlike Sir Esme Howard, had never experienced the privilege of schooling or the cultural advantages which the British Ambassador had enjoyed, is that of a man whose forebears lived for generations in the mountains of Kentucky isolated from the influences of formal education. He has a good mind, is a close observer of nature and an excellent gardener, and knew well the properties of the many native woods of Kentucky. But in his youth there were no schools within walking distance of his home and he grew up without learning to read or write. He liked to whittle out figures in wood, and a short while ago carved some puzzles which drew admiration from others in the neighborhood. Later a whittling club was formed and the subject of this sketch was made its instructor and its president. Feeling more strongly than ever before the need for learning to read and write he attended the Opportunity School, a short term held each year at Berea College for those without formal education. "A person can get along without an education while young," he says, "but as he grows older he feels the need for learning more and more." With the co-operation of the members of a community house in the neighborhood this man is continuing his learning along with the craft that has meant so much to him. A letter dictated by him recently stated that a neighbor had given the Whittlers' Club a cedar tree which it could have sold for 50 cents for fence posts. Under his direction the members decided to whittle it up, and from the objects made they received $40. One of the boxes carved from a single block of the cedar is illustrated on page 220.

Evidence of the effective use of a handicraft in strengthening the dull memory of a girl whose family had failed to guide her in combating retarded development and who, through the process of weaving, has not only recovered her memory but has achieved a normal and satisfying position in the life of her mountain community is recounted in Chapter V, Spinning and Weaving for Home and Market, page 109.

An excellent example of the educational potentialities of handicrafts is furnished by a group of weavers at the Spinning Wheel, already briefly referred to in the same chapter. Here several mountain women, acting upon the suggestion of two of their companions that they try to learn something about weaving as done in other places and in other times, soon found themselves engaged in a study embracing all the basic processes of textile making. Their quest for knowledge carried them into the beginnings of history and in their studies they traveled around the globe, making contacts with every continent and seeing interesting and sometimes rare examples of weaving from the hand looms of many countries. The majority of these examples, it is true, came through books, but the workers were able to secure actual samples of textiles as they made their needs known. For more than three years they have been on this quest, and one of the outgrowths has been a collection of prints, including color reproductions of several masterpieces of painting in which distaffs, spinning wheels, or weaving looms appear. Theirs is an ever widening search which has opened up the fields of history, literature, geography, anthropology, agriculture, and art, with glimpses into botany, chemistry, and other branches of learning, until, as one of the number said recently, "It appears like if you knew all there is to know about spinning and weaving you would know about all there is to know about everything."

The experiences of these weavers support one of the basic principles of adult education, stressed by Robert M. Lester of the Carnegie Corporation in an address before the Conference of Southern Mountain Workers at Knoxville, Tennessee, in March, 1930. Adult education, declared Mr. Lester, should begin with an established interest.

Equally satisfying as the experiences of these weavers could be the quest by craftsmen in any other handicraft—basketry, woodworking, pottery, and many others—for it is not alone the importance of the product but quite as much the significance of the craft to those engaged in it which counts. The place of any handicraft in the march of the race, the distribution of the product in its interesting variety among the nations of today, the study of materials, of tools used from the beginning until now, the part performed by machinery, the problems of transporting the materials used and the finished products, the place of the work and the product in literature, in music, in the other arts; what possibilities in adult education these handicrafts suggest, especially for those who know them intimately through practice and association.

HANDICRAFTS OF SLOW GROWTH IN ADULT EDUCATION

"Why," it may be asked, "if handicrafts can be employed to stimulate intellectual and emotional progress among men and women on so many levels of learning, has not adult education made more of this important aid?" Some of the answers are easy to find. In the first place it should be remembered, as Morse Adams Cartwright has pointed out in an excellent summary of the movement, that this new development is largely a realization of the last decade; it is just getting under way.[1]

[1] Cartwright, Morse Adams, Ten Years of Adult Education. By permission of The Macmillan Co., publishers, New York, 1935.

Again, in its development adult education has naturally followed the more or less formal lines which we have set up in our public school system for children and young people. This system in the main puts the accent on reading, writing, the learning and correlation of facts and processes that are mainly mental. Also the first concern of this new movement has quite properly been to provide educational opportunities for the masses, for the large numbers of persons who could be reached through audiences, classes, study circles, and so forth. Handicraft is largely an individual activity, and obviously adult education leaders have not yet reached a point where they can give much attention to the individual. But as its advantages are more widely recognized, some means of utilizing it in group work will undoubtedly be devised.

Another reason for the slow acceptance of handicrafts in relation to adult education is that many people think of them only for the money they will bring. The money economy which we have developed so thoroughly has tended to put the emphasis on the price an object will bring rather than on the quality of the work itself or its effect upon the person doing it. Also the tremendous rate at which machine production has supplanted handwork, for urban people especially, has crowded out much of our appreciation of good craftsmanship and in many instances even a knowledge of handicrafts. The old magic processes of wood turning, glass blowing, bobbin lace making, and hand throwing on a potter's wheel have given place generally to mechanized methods in which much of the skill and wonder of work seems to have disappeared.

Aside entirely from our school and teaching patterns which undoubtedly reflect our attitude toward life and work, we as a people have been educating ourselves away from manual labor, away from work with the hands, into what has come to be regarded as more refined effort, and which has with some few exceptions also been more remunerative. Thus we have been emerging out of a handicraft culture into another type, where work with the hands is not popular. These are among the reasons which help to explain the comparatively slow recognition of handicrafts in this new adult educational movement and why adequate teachers and leaders in this field have not been developed.

HOW TO USE HANDICRAFTS IN AN ADULT EDUCATION PROGRAM

There are three ways in which handicrafts may be utilized in a program for adult education: (1) they may be studied, (2) examples of them may be collected, and (3) they may be practiced. These activities may be kept entirely separate, or, two or all may be merged.

Much can be said for the study of handicrafts; they mark the growth of the race from before the dawn of history to our own times; all peoples are distinguished by the record of their handwork. Especially have agriculture and handicrafts gone along together through the ages; but even the traveling tribes, the gypsies, the hunters, the warriors, all have had handwork distinguishing their people one from another, and yet providing through it a kind of universal language which everyone may understand.

In our own country the first days of discovery and settlement through the years of colonial development were marked by such records. The struggles of the new nation, in the pilgrimages to the Middle West and out over the Oregon and the Santa Fé Trails, in life on the frontier before the coming of railroads, were all characterized by a handicraft culture, the study of which is fascinating. Turning to the homelands of Europe from which so many of our citizens have come, or to other continents, one will find the same significant indications of the characters, skills, and cultures of their peoples. So whether one's reading and research cut vertically through the accumulations of time, or horizontally across the handicrafts of the earth as we know them today, the field is unparalleled for inspiring study.

To some, however, study alone will not prove as engaging as the collecting of specimens of handicraft; the value of this latter interest is not limited to the objects actually acquired, but extends to collections that exist elsewhere. One advantage in such a pursuit is that these specimens are often inexpensive, probably no form of creative work being so universally available at low prices. It is encouraging to note that in addition to amateur searchers in these arts are dealers everywhere, and several museums are building up their collections.

Often more important from an educational point of view than study or collecting, is working in a handicraft. Practice vitalizes

A VARIETY OF HANDICRAFT PRODUCTS

Fine Damask Table Cloth by Penland Weavers; Wooden Cheese Bowl, Knife, and Pewter Salt Bowls by Mountaineer Craftsmen; Copper Candlestick, Lees-McRae College; Candle, Leonard Lamb; Jellies and Jams in Native Pottery Containers, John and Mary R. Markle School; Wooden Salt Bowl and Spoon, Woodcrafters and Carvers; Decorated Sugars, Berea College; Pewter Plate, Penland; Covered Pitchers, Waco Pottery; Tea Set, Hilton Pottery; Home-spun Blanket, Pine Mountain

both study and collecting, and in addition affords an outlet for the creative impulse. Fortunately it is not always necessary to limit the interest in handicrafts to one form of activity, that is, to study, collecting, or practicing; the ideal is to combine all in the proportion which meets best the needs and circumstances of the craftsman or the group, as the case may be. But the practice of the handicrafts may have two distinct functions in adult education: one as an incentive to participation in the generally accepted forms of learning; the other as having strong potentialities for learning within itself. In the former a handicraft may encourage reading, writing, inquiry, analysis, discussion and other activities associated with formal education as illustrated in some of the cases cited; but a handicraft in its practice also provides training in estimating, measuring, in judging the yielding and resisting qualities of materials, the powers and limitations of tools, and it affords exercise in the choosing of color, form, texture and other qualities both practical and esthetic.

Thus we may experience through a handicraft the cultural satisfaction which comes through knowing, and also that which comes through doing. This double advantage cannot be too highly esteemed. In our systems of formal schooling and in our general attitude toward education we have overemphasized intellectuality, the thinking of things, and have neglected the educational importance of the doing of things. In life the two cannot be entirely separated, nor should they be; it is through their happy and constructive blending that we grow, experience, and advance. As Ernst Harms has so well expressed it, "Human life and human culture as well consist not only of thoughts but also of feelings and impulses that spring from esthetic and moral sources."[1] And from wide observation and experience he has concluded that "of all the means by which we can educate the whole personality none seems more effective than the home crafts and other types of handicraft."

In addition to the study, collecting, and practice of handicrafts there is another potentiality that it is hoped adult education will help develop, which is referred to also in Chapter XXII, Recrea-

[1] The Cultural Values of Handicraft. *In* Journal of Adult Education, January, 1937.

tion through Handicrafts. That is the employing of good workmen who may have had little formal schooling to teach a handicraft, as has often been done in the Highlands. The recruiting of such leaders and teachers from unexpected sources is both a quantitative and a qualitative gain to leadership in adult education. As has been pointed out in this report, most of the old crafts in the mountains have been handed down from father to son, mother to daughter, or neighbor to neighbor; and many are the instances in which old and untutored women have, with distinction, passed on to the young and the schooled the skills and secrets of the textile and other arts.

There is a feeling, too prevalent in our sophisticated centers of culture, that only those who have had school advantages are capable of instructing others. It is wholesome for anyone to find that an illiterate person may teach well a craft which he has learned not in school but through long and arduous experience. Professor Worst, who directs the Weaving Institute at Penland, North Carolina, has called mountain women to help when his classes have been large. They are always thorough and are sometimes very amusing in their criticisms. Recently one of these native women after inspecting the work of a new spinner of flax, a graduate teacher who was at the Institute for a few days, said, "Now you've spun a halter, see if you can spin some thread."

RELATION OF HANDICRAFTS TO THE OTHER ARTS

What has been said of handicrafts in the field of adult education has been predicated upon their intrinsic qualities; but something should be said concerning their relation to the fine arts. There is much talk these days about the need for giving more attention to the arts in our scheme of education and living. And many new courses are springing up in schools and colleges, special stress being laid upon their place in the new education for adults. Not very satisfactory progress, however, is reported in this field, and yet here seems to be a place where handicrafts can be of immediate and great assistance. The need and the difficulties attending this problem of relating the arts to adult education are well stated by Mr. Cartwright in the study already referred to. "One prefers to think of two movements," he writes, "one in art and one in adult education, moving forward systematically and wisely toward a cultural goal for the United States." But he finds that "the difficulties of translating art concepts into terms readily understood and enthusiastically accepted by the mythical 'man in the street' are obstacles similar to those confronting adult education generally at every hand." Nevertheless, he believes that "the growing partnership between the arts and adult education ought to mean increasing progress toward that solution which will herald the arrival of a national culture."[1]

This "growing partnership between the arts and adult education" is, as Mr. Cartwright indicates, a good sign, but much remains to be done to make it strong and lasting. For one thing there must be an agreement between the two as to what art means, and perhaps what education means also. The definition of art must be understandable to the man in the street, regardless of whether or not he agrees with it; and it must make a place for a much wider range of beautiful expression than has usually been admitted to the rather exclusive art circle which has too often limited its interest to the old conventional fine arts concept. Adult education therefore can, by broadening its own concept of art to include the handicrafts, help greatly to simplify and clarify and so strengthen the good partnership.

The first and most important step in strengthening the partnership is to think of art and adult education not as two movements paralleling each other, which means that they will never touch, but to think of art as a great integrating force in this new movement, a force that will vivify education from the kindergarten through college into mature life. Such a definition of art will shift the emphasis from the kind of work done to the manner of doing it. It will not limit the concept to painting, sculpture, and architecture of certain styles or periods, but it will include all these and much more; it will include a carefully built log cabin, a well-printed and bound book, a beautifully wrought patchwork quilt, or any other object which has been done better than is necessary to serve its utilitarian purpose. The great masters have always had this inclusive concept of art, but the critics, the dealers, too many mu-

[1] Cartwright, Morse Adams, Ten Years of Adult Education, pp. 128–129. By permission of The Macmillan Co., publishers.

313

seums, and we laymen ourselves have made it complex, difficult, and confusing. If art is to be an influence in adult education it must touch the lives of people as a whole; for the foundation of adult education in the United States rests upon the democratic intention of making the best available to all; and if we can agree that art is doing well something that ought to be done, then we have made way for an appreciation of all the arts with their infinite variety of expression. And among these, handicrafts will have an important place.

If therefore we can make this simple though fundamental shift in the definition of art, we will find it and adult education running in the same channel; art as we have known it will be humanized, education will be enriched. If we regard handicrafts as among the arts, we will turn into the stream of world culture many forms of plastic expression and thus bring within the circle countless people who through lack of opportunity or through choice would never practice what we call the fine arts. Of the several good reasons for giving handicrafts an important place in adult education not the least is because they will usher into this vital field a new and fuller measure of beauty.

We are accustomed to associate learning or education with books, classes, and schools. What has been achieved with these helps is beyond human calculation to measure or express; but is it not possible that we often overlook the great amount of learning that comes through doing; and especially doing work with the hands which calls for skill, thought, and artistry? Learning through books and the wide use of reading and writing are for the masses of our people comparatively recent achievements; making things with the hands has been an everyday practice for ages.

It seems reasonable to hope that some day American communities will come to regard a public workshop as indispensable to their cultural equipment as a library. Such a shop would reach many people whose interest in investigation, experimentation, and expression could not be served by the library alone. It would give opportunity for learning new crafts and advance interest in old ones. Men and women who had done only the crudest work could become proficient in the use of tools, learn about the qualities of materials, and make acceptable things for home and personal use.

The shop could have its reference library or be co-ordinated with the local library. Any community, through a little co-operation, could have a better workshop than most of its members could afford alone. A new type of leadership and service would thus be developed to meet the demands of a broader educational concept.

CHAPTER XXII

RECREATION THROUGH HANDICRAFTS

AT NO time in history has so much emphasis been put upon the importance of recreation for everyone. The Standard Dictionary defines recreation as the "refreshment of body and mind." Its value for children has long been recognized, but for adults the idea has been of much slower acceptance. However, three facts among others, all of comparatively recent growth, have forced upon us an increasing realization of the necessity of recreation for our adult population. First is the strenuous, concentrated, and sometimes deadly monotonous character of much of the work connected with mill, factory, and office, from which some relief is necessary. Second is the rapid rate at which the hours of labor in practically all occupations have been shortened, giving workers more spare time than they had ever known, thus creating a considerable margin of leisure. Third is the unprecedented unemployment in almost every field of labor, resulting in idle time for millions of our people.

Many have called this margin of spare time, whether voluntary or enforced, "leisure time," but that term seems highly inappropriate when applied to persons out of work and exerting every effort to find it. Nor does it fit those who are employed at less than a living wage, of whom there are now many. Leisure time is a term which can fairly be applied only to those who have incomes sufficient to secure at least the essentials of life for themselves and their dependents, with the unoccupied hours to be used as they please. It is the freedom from pressure which gives leisure to an individual, and to apply the term indiscriminately to all people out of work is misuse of the word. These several conditions present us with the problem of encouraging wholesome recreation for those who have work with or without leisure and those who have no work but much spare time thrust upon them. What makes the problem difficult is that it is not only quantitative, involving vast

THE ARTISANS' SHOP, BILTMORE FOREST

ONE OF A GROUP OF PICTURESQUE WORKSHOPS IN BILTMORE FOREST NEAR ASHEVILLE, NORTH CAROLINA. THE CYPRESS PANELS AND BEAMS WERE CARVED BY THE CRAFTSMEN WHO WORK THERE

HAND-MADE PRODUCTS OF ROSEMONT
CANOPY-BED, ITS EQUIPMENT, AND OTHER FURNISHINGS MADE BY WORKERS AT MARION,
VIRGINIA, UNDER THE DIRECTION OF MRS. LAURA COPENHAVER

numbers of people, but also qualitative, for what is recreation for one may not be recreation for another. It is a wider application of the old saying that "What is one man's meat is another man's poison."

It is therefore of the greatest importance that we know as many as possible of the resources upon which we can draw for our recreation. It is hoped that this report on handicrafts, although dealing largely with their economic aspects, may encourage wider experiments in work with the hands for those everywhere who are in need of "refreshment of body and mind." It is believed that there are instances, perhaps many, where the thing that will best bring this refreshment is work with the hands in the soil or with materials intimately related to the earth. A vital service may thus be rendered in helping individuals to discover what their interests and abilities are. In the great variety of handicrafts something can be found which almost anyone can do well, or well enough to become a recreation.

The main purpose of this chapter is to note some of the more important recreational values which handicrafts possess and to suggest reasons for these potentialities. Perhaps the most basic reason for the potentialities of handicrafts is to be found in the philosophy of play as developed by students in the field of recreation.

In several theories of play expounded by sociologists, psychologists, and other students of human interests and activities, one basic point upon which they are in substantial agreement is that in recreation, both child and adult repeat over and over those things which for long periods of time have been characteristic achievements of the race. That is to say, when children, and grownups too, have an opportunity to play or do what they wish, they will often hunt, fish, hike, garden, and engage in other occupations which were once the work upon which their ancestors depended to sustain life. Hunting and fishing are today the favorite recreations of countless adults whose prospects of catching fish or bagging any game may be very remote. The practice of many of the handicrafts is so long established in man's experience that they too have some of the qualities of recreation that hunting and fishing possess.

Upon this basic point of the persistence of motor habits and the spirit of the past of the race, Professor G. Stanley Hall said:

Thus, in play, we rehearse the activity of our ancestry back we know not how far, and repeat their life work in summative and adumbrated ways. The pleasure is always in direct proportion to the directness and force of the current of heredity. The pain of toil died with our forbears; its vestige in our play gives pure delight.[1]

If the theories of scholars are correct, and common observation seems to confirm them, is it not true that the recreational values of handicrafts rest upon the same broad foundation as hunting, fishing, and other life-sustaining practices which reach back to ancient times, shorn of their original pain but, as Dr. Hall says, "with that vestige in our play which gives pure delight"?[2]

It is difficult for us, born in a machine age, to realize how much we owe to the handwork of all time, or even to that of our own. When our nation was at its beginning, as has been pointed out elsewhere, practically 90 per cent of the necessities of life were raised or manufactured on the farm, and then, of course, it was possible for everyone to see achievements in handwork. Now on most American farms the proportion of hand and home manufactures is reversed; but even with this radical change the average family in the country has an opportunity to do a considerable amount of handwork. And if we take the long view of handicrafts we realize what an overwhelming part they have played in the development not only of civilization and cultures but of man the individual, and it is back to the individual that all our plans for recreation, education, and other social considerations are referred.

The outstanding importance of handicrafts in the development of man is revealed nowhere more convincingly than through the study of archaeology. We of this day have clear glimpses of it, made possible through the aids of modern science, such as have never been vouchsafed to the people of a former period. Through archaeology we are today getting quite a clear perspective of how man has progressed from his beginning, now set at a million or more years ago, rather than at a few thousand as we had long

[1] Playground and Recreation Association of America, The Normal Course in Play. A. S. Barnes and Co., New York, 1926, p. 92.

[2] *Ibid.*

supposed. We are seeing how he first used his hands alone to procure and prepare those things upon which his life depended; then how a few crude natural objects such as a stone, a stick, or a vine or fiber, he made serve as tools or other helps; then, for possibly a million years, says Dr. Breasted,[1] who has given us such amazingly clear glimpses of the past, man labored to shape natural objects into less crude tools that would enable him to achieve his ends, then into better tools, both stronger and finer, until he could make objects of utility and beauty which will stand for all time as flowers of civilizations. All this came through his handicrafts, for it was only yesterday that he developed machines and harnessed them with power and ushered in the marvelous mechanical age in which we live, an age which with all its magic and its creature comforts is separating many of us so far from the sources of life that we are often confused. In order to find our way back we must retrace some of the long-lost paths over which man has made his slow but ever upward way.

In considering the advantages of handicrafts in general as a means of recreation, one often finds the fields of education and recreation overlapping. It should be a matter for congratulation when any field of learning is lightened by a subject, or the treatment of a subject, which makes study as fascinating as play. And reciprocally there should be satisfaction when any recreational activity is discovered to have as important an educational content as handicrafts have.

It is not possible here to go into detail as to the advantage of certain handicrafts over others as a source of recreation. The important thing is to have one that is interesting, and there are any number from the simplest tinkering job to carrying out large construction, from the formation of the plainest utilitarian object to its most thorough elaboration. Many games and sports contain values other than the recreation which they afford. If space permitted, it would be interesting to compare certain handicrafts with other forms of recreation to find their common denominators. It may suffice here to refer to a few of the qualities possessed by many handicrafts which give them special recreational value.

---

[1] Breasted, James H., Dawn of Conscience. Charles Scribner's Sons, New York, 1934.

One of these is their educational value, which is suggested more fully in the chapter on Adult Education through Handicrafts, where it is pointed out that learning by doing is an educational process; that this is open to some who could not, or do not want to, pursue the more widely accepted book learning processes; that it is a means of learning which can apply at many levels of progress and degrees of mentality; and that it establishes or promotes a continuation of interest sometimes lifelong. In this connection the encouragement a handicraft gives to research through observation, conference, and books deserves emphasis, for research is undoubtedly to many one of the most satisfying recreational experiences. It is a great loss to recreation that research, the finding out of things through various methods of inquiry, has been regarded generally as hard work and its quality of refreshment overlooked. Perhaps when the recreational value of work is better recognized and distinction between drudgery and work (which may be play, and so often is) is made clearer, the fascination and refreshment of research will become more widely recognized, and more of it will be voluntarily done. A handicraft opens up avenues of inquiry which may become in themselves new sources of recreation.

The development of recreation in our country has naturally followed one of the lines of formal education, the well-established teacher-pupil method as known in school, camp, and social center, by first placing emphasis on those types of activity by which large numbers could be reached. Recreation therefore has been largely a group movement, partly because the demand has been for greater service than could be given. But as the movement has grown and experiments have multiplied, there has been an increasing concern about its meaning to the individual. This concern has developed beyond an interest in the moment of participation and now includes the question, what does the experience give the individual to carry into the future? Thus has come the idea of encouraging a more permanent interest, one which would enable him to go out and work or play unaided, to become more resourceful, and when possible to develop into another recruit for advancing recreation in his own community. It was in part at least this critical inquiry into the effect on the person himself of engaging in certain activities that led to a recognition of some forms of recreation that were more individual than collective. It was found that when an enthusiasm could be aroused in a handicraft which could be carried on at home, independent of the group or the occasion where it was first learned, there would sometimes be established a vital interest of high recreational value, sometimes a life interest. The worth of such an experiment did not end with the individual worker for he became an influence upon others, a contributor not only to the recreation of the community but to its cultural growth.

Some of the practical advantages of handicrafts through the stimulation of both mind and body, stated without any plan as to their order of importance, are as follows: (1) they develop skill; (2) they provide a creative outlet; (3) they are an inexpensive form of recreation; (4) they increase sensitiveness to surroundings and give dignity to common things; (5) they bring out unsuspected abilities; (6) they furnish esthetic satisfaction and are pathways to wonder and beauty that form a link between nature and art; (7) they explain and help rationalize the machine; (8) they bring the handicapped into better adjustments. A little elaboration of some of these points may help to make them clearer.

The exercise and development of skill is one of the great compensations to the craftsman; but lack of skill should not deter anyone from taking up a handicraft for recreation. One of the most encouraging and stimulating experiences is to feel the growth of skill. The worthwhile measurement, however, is not to compare the beginner or the amateur with the expert in the same craft, but to note the improvement from time to time of the individual himself. In a handicraft this improvement, this progression in skill, is often a large part of the satisfaction which comes to the individual, and one should note that it does not necessarily cease when advancement has reached its high point; it simply changes. By then, in the case of a handicraft, the worker will usually find that he can achieve such satisfactory expression with skill already acquired that he gets his recreation through the release of his creative power; and the more skill he has the greater will be the ease with which he can perform his work.

Here then is the great value of a handicraft over certain other kinds of recreation; as, for instance, a game or sport in which skill is the great objective. When in a sport like tennis one's skill begins to decline, the player's satisfaction is likely to decline also, unless he develops a philosophy by which he gets his reward through other things than his prowess. But in a handicraft, the avenues for creative expression which are open to one of moderate attainment are so many and varied that it makes this form of recreation a very choice one. This fact is testified to by a man of unusual intellectual insight and pedagogical experience:

I have tasted many sorts of pleasure in my life, and I will tell you what my experience has been—not because I think it unique or peculiar, but because I believe it to be very common. The pleasures that have given me most satisfaction, the times when I enjoyed myself most completely, were the times when I was exercising some kind of intelligent skill. I am far from counting myself a skilful man, but I have just enough skill to know the enjoyment that comes from it.[1]

If it were desirable to limit the claims of handicrafts in recreation to a single argument it would probably be that they furnish an outlet for the creative impulse. Fortunately that need is coming to be widely recognized and with it the appreciation of those activities that provide opportunity for self-expression. Handicrafts stand in the forefront of such occupations.

One of their important advantages is that most of the handicrafts are comparatively inexpensive, and sometimes to keep them within reasonable limits brings the greatest satisfaction. In this changing economic world in which the tendency is to take a man's simple tools from him and put him to work on expensive machines, or on complicated or elaborate equipment which he cannot own, house, or care for, it is a real privilege for him to have something which he can call his own and which to a certain degree he can control. Moreover, much fun, much recreational value, come from doing things simply, with meager equipment and from utilizing materials that might otherwise be wasted. Nearly everyone likes a bargain, and the craftsman who gets his material cheap or for nothing and makes some acceptable object from it experiences a peculiar satisfaction. A woodworker is delighted when he can fashion a useful or attractive object from wood salvaged from a

[1] Jacks, L. P., The Education of the Whole Man. University of London Press, London, 1931, p. 215.

discarded piece of furniture, as is the amateur seamstress who makes a pleasing garment from stuff which might under other circumstances be thrown away. However, it must be borne in mind that some people derive great enjoyment from elaborate and even showy equipment. This flair may be just what is needed to furnish the maximum recreation. These activities are forms of play, and if the individual prefers expensive equipment no exception need be taken to it.

He who works at a handicraft as a recreation becomes sensitive to materials so that they have a special meaning for him. For instance, the woodworker in passing a pile of lumber is likely to stop and examine it, and whenever wood is exposed in buildings, sidewalks, bridges, or even packing cases, he becomes more observant of it. He is interested in all the ways woodworkers use wood and the tools employed. Every stool, bench, chair, comes to be more and more a possession of his watchful eye. He finally realizes from observing these how really beautiful many everyday objects are. He goes through a museum noting as he had not done before some of the common things of beauty, but still better he finds them on his way to work or at home.

There is probably no experience that affords more personal satisfaction to an adult than to learn to do something which always had seemed a little beyond the reach of his abilities. The enthusiasm engendered by such an experience is expressed by an outstanding exemplar of the potency of handicrafts, both in recreation and in adult education, who said:

There is something about tools that fascinates the normal man. Christopher Morley tells in one of his essays how men stand enthralled in front of windows where the instruments of precision, micrometers, compasses, calipers and protractors, are displayed in concentric patterns. The thrill of owning and using them is even greater. I achieved something of the rapture of a poet who has written a sonnet when I found I could use a tap and die and make a perfectly practicable bolt and nut.[1]

Napoleon is credited with having declared that the thing worth doing is the thing a man believes he cannot do. Handicrafts taken up as recreation often provide such opportunity. Fitting illustra-

[1] Calkins, Earnest Elmo, Care and Feeding of Hobby Horses. Leisure League of America, New York, 1934, p. 18.

tions of this fact are furnished by several of the best whittlers in the Highlands, which have been referred to in this report, who are today making attractive animals in wood sculpture. Many of these are grown men who from an ordinary knack for cutting up wood aimlessly with a pocketknife have developed sufficient skill and taste to create a demand for their products; to others it has become a very satisfying pastime, and to all it has revealed a new and unsuspected individual resource.

One of the greatest values of most games and sports is that they bring people together in congenial relationships, but one should also cultivate habits of being congenial with himself. A handicraft will often foster the development of such resourcefulness and encourage one to become good company for himself.

The esthetic satisfaction which comes through exercise in one of the fine arts is widely acknowledged, but there has not been an adequate recognition of the similar quality of enjoyment that is experienced by a worker in handicrafts who designs and carries out an embroidery in threads on canvas or some other textile, or the weaver who works out the pattern, lays in the carefully blended threads, and produces the woven fabric. After all it is the conception of the pattern, the building up of a structure, which expresses the idea of the worker—whether it be a painted picture, a piece of sculpture, a coverlet, or a mountain basket—that brings to the creator that esthetic satisfaction which accompanies any new creation.

But a handicraft does more than relate one's work to that of other artists. It develops, through a feeling for the materials employed, an interest in the source of all materials, nature. The craftsman, whether he works with raw materials such as plant, animal, or mineral substances, or those forms which science has prepared to make them more suitable for his use, has found a link between art, the realm of man's expression, and the great field of nature of which he is a part.

Whatever reason there may be in the contention that since we are no longer living in a handicraft age no one need feel concerned about handicrafts, the same course of reasoning certainly cannot apply to the machine that has so widely supplanted them. Everyone desires to have some knowledge of machines, and countless

PIONEER CABIN WITH TWO ANCIENT LOOMS

IN THIS LOG HOUSE BUILT IN 1812, MRS. FINLEY MAST AND HER SISTER, MRS. ROBERT
MAST, WOVE TEXTILES FOR THEMSELVES AND OTHERS UNTIL MRS. FINLEY MAST DIED
IN 1936. HER SISTER STILL CONTINUES THE WORK. THIS PHOTOGRAPH WAS TAKEN AND
LENT BY BAYARD WOOTTEN OF CHAPEL HILL, NORTH CAROLINA

FORM AND TEXTURE FROM THE HIGHLANDS

Woolen Shawl Designed and Woven by Mrs. John Rorex; Pewter Candlestick by Mountaineer Craftsmen; Candle by Leonard Lamb; Corn Husk Figure by Mrs. Rosalie Pless; Crystalline Vase by W. B. Stephen; Feather Flowers by Anna Lee Morrison and Lily McThetridge; Carved Sheep by Campbell Folk School; Kentucky Egg Basket by Unknown Craftsman

young and old find much wholesome recreation in studying and manipulating machines, but the point to be made here is that handicrafts do often assist in explaining machines. Every machine before it is standardized and the forms for its parts prepared is a hand-made mechanism. The model is a handicraft product, and he who shapes these parts and assembles them so that they will function smoothly knows better than any other what they signify. But next in appreciation to the individual who makes the model is one who makes some other object entirely by hand which must also be very accurate, and who by this experience gains some knowledge of and feeling for the elementary principles of machines. For instance, one who has not sawed a board with a hand-saw, taking great pains to do it true to line, cannot fully appreciate a gang of saws in a mill which have a hundred times the efficiency of a hand-saw in accuracy and in speed. Who can feel the wonder of the thousand spindles in a modern spinning mill as well as she who has spun yarn by hand? These are educational considerations, but they are recreational as well for they open up avenues of perception, understanding, and refreshment to the human mind.

Much of the most valuable and convincing evidence that has been developed concerning handwork for the "refreshment of body and mind" has come through a specialized field not yet well known to the public, that of occupational therapy. It is not possible within the bounds of this volume to give attention to the remarkable record that has been achieved through the use of handicrafts in this branch of therapy, but for those who may be especially interested a reference to a bibliography on Occupational Therapy, issued by the American Occupational Therapy Association, is listed in the Bibliography at the end of the book. There are now a great number of documented cases, some of the most serious nature, both physical and mental, which prove clearly the therapeutic efficacy of handicrafts where other measures have failed. They have come to be an indispensable feature of treatment in our best hospitals, particularly in mental hospitals and among the feebleminded.

All the therapeutic cases touch in a significant way the principles at the root of recreation. When the practice of a handicraft becomes the main factor in restoring to mental or physical health a patient who has fallen desperately ill, does the case not suggest its power to prevent such ailments if taken up as a recreation in time? Specialists in recreation may not think of themselves as directly concerned with handicrafts as preventives of illness, but it will strengthen them in pressing for their wider use to know of the great significance of these constructive activities as demonstrated in the field of medicine.

And finally it will be remembered that the pursuit of a handicraft is a strong influence in establishing pride in all work which, if there were no other argument, would place this form of recreation high in the list of refreshments for mind and body.

CHAPTER XXIII

IN CONCLUSION

THE two preceding chapters on the handicrafts in Adult Education and Recreation do not pretend to outline completely the applications of handwork to these two particular fields, nor does the author wish to imply that they are the only ones in which handicrafts play an important part. These two fields have been chosen, as has been said, because they represent two nationally extensive groups that are fairly well organized, both actively seeking ways to strengthen, extend, and improve their programs. Perhaps their inclusion will suggest the potentialities of the handicrafts in other present-day activities.

It is to be regretted that there has not been space to say something about the handicrafts, or the arts and crafts as they are often called, in the schools, especially in primary education, of which progressive schools, public and private, are wisely taking advantage to prove the value of learning by doing, a process which makes partners of joy and achievement and has the important advantage of bringing esthetic influences into the work and play of children.

To be regretted too is the omission of a chapter on the handicrafts in the field of health, a comparatively new therapeutic aid in both corrective and preventive medicine, in which our country has made great advancement in recent years, with some outstanding contributions to both its theory and practice. But partly because of the exigencies of space and partly because the field is a highly specialized one, this omission seems justified.

The foregoing pages have been mainly concerned with the producers of handicrafts, with those who rely upon them for their economic return, for their contribution to social life, to education, to esthetic enjoyment, and sometimes to mental and physical rehabilitation. But the benefits from such work are not limited to the producers alone, and something may well be said about their significance to those who use them, the ultimate consumers, for it is they upon whom the continuation of the handicrafts and their flowering in the future will so largely depend.

It is not, however, as the purchaser of handicrafts that the consumer is brought in here, for the importance of this support has been suggested throughout the foregoing report; it is rather as an individual who needs the handicrafts for interest, inspiration, and satisfaction, as others, and perhaps he, need books. It is this personal appraisal of the handicrafts, this subjective relation, which in the final analysis is so vital to the movement of which he is an indispensable part. For instance, one who buys an occasional article solely to help the one who makes it may improve the immediate situation, but he will be contributing little to the growth and permanency of the handicrafts as a whole. But if one buys with discrimination and the object purchased brings personal satisfaction, that is a far more important thing; then a reciprocal relation is established between maker and user, which is the soundest foundation upon which to build.

Too much emphasis cannot be placed upon the importance of this feeling of the user or consumer for the article produced, this subjective value; it lies at the base of discrimination and accounts for many of life's little enjoyments. Most people have their own special catalogue of pleasant things; the list given by Rupert Brooke, in his poem, The Great Lover, is a delightful one, not only for the intimate items included but because through it he confers upon our own choices, whether they include his or not, a true measure of dignity and worth. His list in part reads:

> White plates and cups, clean-gleaming,
> Ringed with blue lines; and feathery, faery dust;
> Wet roofs, beneath the lamp-light; the strong crust
> Of friendly bread; and many-tasting food;
> Rainbows; and the blue bitter smoke of wood;
> And radiant raindrops couching in cool flowers;
> And flowers themselves, that sway through sunny hours,
> Dreaming of moths that drink them under the moon;
> Then the cool kindliness of sheets, that soon
> Smooth away trouble; and the rough male kiss
> Of blankets; grainy wood; live hair that is

Shining and free; blue-massing clouds; the keen
Unpassioned beauty of a great machine;
The benison of hot water; furs to touch;
The good smell of old clothes; and other such—
The comfortable smell of friendly fingers,
Hair's fragrance, and the musty reek that lingers
About dead leaves and last year's ferns.   .   .   .[1]

The catalogue of handicrafts, the long, long list stretching from before the beginning of history down the ages, is filled with objects about which people have felt much as the poet has expressed himself. It is no great wonder that some should feel so strongly and so sensitively about the objects which men and women and children are making with their hands today.

It is not intended to suggest here that all handwork be substituted for machine work, or that we abandon already established methods of mass production which have brought comforts and blessings within the reach of so many. The only point claimed is an indispensable place for handicrafts in our economy and in our culture. Moreover, there is nothing in the appreciation of handwork which lessens one's enjoyment of the many fine products of the machine; indeed, as has been said, the highest appreciation of our industrial arts, now so hopefully advancing, is through an understanding of the handicrafts out of which they all have come.

While education will help greatly to increase our interest in and enjoyment of handicrafts, yet their significance as esthetic expressions is grounded in experiences more strongly rooted than in any schooling of recent days. They lie deeper than all the advanced cultures; the enjoyment of beauty in its broad sense is a primal instinct. No words have been said on the subject more cogent than these by Dr. Alexis Carrel,[2] a scientist famous alike in his native France and in his adopted America:

Esthetic sense exists in the most primitive human beings as in the most civilized. It even survives the disappearance of intelligence.   .   .   .
The creation of forms, or of series of sounds, capable of awakening an esthetic emotion, is an elementary need of our nature.   .   .   .

[1] Brooke, Rupert, Collected Poems. Used by permission of Sidgwick and Jackson, Ltd., London, for the British Empire, and Dodd, Mead and Co., Inc., New York, for the United States. Copyright, 1915, by Dodd, Mead and Co., Inc.

[2] Man the Unknown. Harper and Bros., New York, 1935, pp. 131–132.

Esthetic activity manifests itself in both the creation and the contemplation of beauty. . . . Beauty is an inexhaustible source of happiness for those who discover its abode.

That interest in handicrafts throughout our country is growing and that there are definite developments contributing to appreciation of them there are many signs; only a few can be noted here, and those briefly. Among the first is the increasing interest in the folk arts, first stimulated through the peasant arts of Europe. The local, provincial, and state museums of these lands into which the objects of everyday life, especially of rural life, have been gathered have formed a basis for much of this appreciation. But probably the beautiful and popularly priced English Studio Supplements issued by John Lane of London on the Peasant Arts of several European countries and widely circulated in America have stimulated our appreciation most for these folk arts. Following the Studio Supplements have come other attractive publications on similar subjects which have found their way into public, school, and private libraries, until now one can hardly find a town with a good library in our country where there are not some books on these arts.

An outstanding contribution to this interest in the United States has been the increasing recognition of the rich mine of artistic skills, traditions, and cultural achievements associated with our immigrant citizens through public and private events held to bring out their gifts to American life and to foster better understanding among all our citizens. These events, in which both native and foreign-born citizens have joined, have included special exhibitions of the arts and crafts of the many different groups which make up our population. All such projects have increased enthusiasm for these simple objects of use and beauty. A number of American museums and societies are building up permanent collections of the folk arts, and others include them in their special exhibitions. If persons who are caught by the general enthusiasm for folk art become half as sensitive to the present as to the past, and can learn to recognize in the handicrafts of today the antiques of tomorrow, these present-day products will flow in a small but steady stream out of the mountains toward homes where people have the means of buying them and where they are wanted.

Another enthusiasm to which many people are happily responding is the growth of what might be called the American tradition in handicrafts. This tradition is expressed in the things made by our own people in colonial days, during the early periods of the republic, and in later years. Interest in these American handicrafts has been heightened by several art museums, historical and educational organizations, writers and publishers of books and magazines on the subject, and by no means least or last the collectors and the antique dealers who have helped to make us conscious of the value of these old-time things.

Another and very considerable influence toward increasing our sensitivity to the esthetic qualities of articles of everyday use which still include many items of handicraft is the remarkable improvement in form, color, and texture of countless industrial art objects. These fill our stores and find their way into our homes. One of the most hopeful influences toward this wider appreciation is coming through improvement in the taste of school children, where emphasis is placed upon the esthetic as well as upon the technical side of handicraft work. These efforts are augmented later by courses in art appreciation in high schools and colleges, in clubs and societies, and finally by books, magazines, and newspapers that carry the printed word and the printed picture relating to handicrafts into every section of our country.

No experience can advance the cause of the handicrafts more than the cultivation of the habit of seeing beauty all along the way of life. An increasing number of our people are cultivating that habit and are practicing in their homes the sound and satisfying principle expressed by the great craftsman, teacher, and philosopher of art, William Morris, who said, "Have nothing in your house which you do not know to be useful, or believe to be beautiful."

It is the homemakers of America scattered throughout all the states, in cities, towns, villages, and open country who are, as has been said, the hope for the fireside industries of the Southern Highlanders, and, it may be added, for the handicrafts of all the other rural areas of our country. These homes are more than temporary markets, more than recipients of whatever may be offered for sale to them; they are in a very real sense partners with the makers in conserving and developing the extraordinary range of handwork with which the United States is so richly endowed.

Probably no country contains more potentialities for the development of a great handicraft movement than our own, certainly none has such a variety of skills and traditions as we have. Beginning with the original inhabitants, the American Indians, who still practice some of the finest of their ancient arts, it includes also people from every continent who are pouring their contributions into the stream of American culture; and to these we have added traditions and patterns which may rightly be called American, because they represent the reactions of our people, both native and foreign born, to the New World environment. Nothing just like it has ever been known before; there is more to conserve and encourage than we have had time to recognize. But we must not leave this conservation of human energy and talent to chance. The quality of our civilization will be largely determined by our recognition of the values that lie in the great variety of our differences and in the encouragement which we give them to develop and to flower.

One reason why the building up of the handicrafts is a task for all, as well as a privilege, is that their possibilities are as dependent upon attitudes as upon markets. For example, referring once more to the Southern Highlands, it is not enough that we develop efficient methods of production and distribution for the handicrafts of the mountain people; our interest and our concern must extend beyond these symbols of a culture to the other elements which make up their life. We must try first to find the qualities of excellence which these people have developed before insisting that they accept our formula for living, thinking, and expression, a formula worked out under very different circumstances from theirs and not necessarily perfect even from our own point of view. It should not require a detailed knowledge of these elements of mountain culture to enable us to respect them; here, as in so many instances, a little imagination is the need. Better certainly, if we know, as those who have worked and lived in the Highlands have had a chance to know, what are the standards and the ideals to which the people cling. But even that experience should not be necessary for us to understand and to cherish the spirit of the young Highlander who, after expressing gratitude to the missionary who had come in to help build a school, said with characteristic mountain frankness, "Bring us your civilization, but leave us our own culture." As for the old, they do not want their children to suffer the privations they have borne, but they want them above all to hold onto the things of the past that have made for the better life. To bring these people our civilization and yet save their culture is the task in which we should all have some part.

There is but one approach to this task; that is the ethical approach which seeks, before imposing its own ideals on any person or group, to draw from them the best they have to give.

APPENDICES

APPENDIX I

SELECTED LIST OF NAMES OF COVERLETS AND COUNTER-PANES GATHERED FROM MANY SOURCES

Acres of Diamonds
Alabama Beauty
American Beauty

Bachelor's Buttons
Bachelor's Delight
Bachelor's Fancy
Baltimore Beauty
Battle of Richmond
Beauty of Kaintuck
Big Works of Tennessee
Blazing Star
Bonaparte's March
Boston Beauty

Catch Me If You Can
Charity Wheel
Church Windows
Cornwallis' Victory
Cuckoo's Nest

Daniel Boone
Democratic Victory
Dogwood Blossom
Doors and Windows
Double Bowknot
Double Chariot Wheel
Double Muscadine Hulls
Downfall of Paris

Eight Ways of Contrariness
Everybody's Beauty

Farmer's Fancy
Federal City
Flower of the Mountain
Flowers of Edinboro
Forty-Niners
Four Square Beauty
Freedom's Home
Freemason's Walk
Friendship

Gentleman's Fancy
Governor's Garden
Granny's Garden

Hickory Leaf
High Cricks Delight by Day and
    Night
Huckleberry

Irish Chain
Isaac's Favorite
Isle of Patmos

Jackson's Army
Job's Trouble

Kentucky Garden
Kentucky Snowflakes
King's Flower
King's Garden

Lady's Fancy
Lasting Beauty
Lee's Surrender
Liberty
Lilies of the Valley and of the
    Meadows
Lily of the Valley
Little Blazing Star
Little Girl's Fancy
Lonely Heart

Magnolia
Maiden's Fancy
Maid of Orleans
Maple Leaf
Mary Lincoln
Missouri Beauty
Missouri Trouble
Morning Star
Mother's Favorite
Mountain Rose
Murphy's Legacy

337

Nameless Wonder
Noah's Wonder
North Carolina Beauty

Ocean Wave
Olive Leaf
Owsley Forks

Parson's Beauty
Petersburg Beauty
Pine Bloom
Pine Burr
Pomegranate
President's View
Primrose and Diamonds

Queen Anne's Lace
Queen of England

Rich Man's Fancy
Richmond Beauty
Rising Sun
Road to California and Back
Rocky Mountain Beauty
Rose in the Blossom
Rose in the Garden
Rose in the Wilderness
Rose of Sharon
Rose of the Valley
Roses and Pinies in the Wilderness
Royal Beauty

St. Ann's Robe
Sea Shell
Sea Star
Single Chariot Wheel

Sixteen Chariot Wheels
Sixteen Snowballs
Snail Trail and Cat Track
Snowball and Dewdrop
Snowball and Pine Tree Border
Snow Drop
Snow Storm
Soldier's Return
Solomon's Delight
Spider Web
Steps to the Altar
Sunrise on the Walls of Troy

Tennessee Trouble in North
Carolina
Thistles and Lilies
Troy's Beauty
True Lover's Knot

Virginia Beauty

Washington's Diment Ring
Washington's Victory
Weaver's Choice
Weaver's Pleasure
Whig Rose
Wide World's Wonder
Wind Flower
Wonder of the Forest
Work Complete
Wreaths and Roses

Young Lady's Perplexity
Young Man's Fancy

Zion Rose

APPENDIX II

THE COLONIAL COVERLET GUILD

The Year Book of the Colonial Coverlet Guild, 1934–1935, states that

The Colonial Coverlet Guild of America was organized in Chicago in 1924 by a group of women interested in the study and collection of hand-woven coverlets and American textiles in general. . . . The object of the Guild is the study and preservation of early American weaving and all objects of historic interest connected with the growth and development of our country. . . . As a part of its program the Guild has commenced the formation of a collection of coverlets . . . which includes many unusual and rare examples of early American weaving.

The work of the Colonial Coverlet Guild is the study and collecting of hand-woven coverlets. A Study Department specializes in the study of quilts, counterpanes, samplers, and American antiques in general. A photographic record of coverlets owned by Guild members is kept and samples of hand weaving and dye recipes are collected. The Guild owns about 40 coverlets.

A memorial library of reference books on weaving and American antiques has been established as well as a collection of Guild papers that have been presented at regular meetings or at meetings of the Study Department. Photographs of coverlets owned by members of the Guild and detailed information concerning them are a part of the resources of the Study Department.

A Year Book is issued giving full account of the activities of the Guild. The official address is 428 North Michigan Avenue, Chicago, Illinois.

APPENDIX III

COLORS DERIVED FROM PLANTS GROWING IN THE SOUTHERN HIGHLANDS

This list has been compiled from various sources, including a considerable number of letters from experimenters with natural dyes.

BLACK . . . . Logwood chips
Oak bark
Red maple bark
White walnut or butternut bark and root
Willow bark and hulls

BLUE . . . . Indigo

BROWN . . . . Black walnut bark
Chestnut oak bark
Cutch
Pecan hulls
Spruce pine bark
White walnut or butternut, bark, roots, and hulls

Dark brown . . . . Black walnut bark and hulls

Dark yellow brown . . Black walnut bark
Hickory bark

Dark yellow tan . . . . Apple bark
Black walnut bark
Tupelo bark

Drab . . . . Black walnut hulls
Maple bark

Golden brown . . . . . . Chestnut oak bark

Greenish tan . . . . Maple bark
Northern red oak bark
Tupelo bark

Khaki . . . . Juniper berries
Maple bark

Light brown . . . . Northern red oak bark
Norway maple bark
Sweet gum bark
Willow bark

Reddish brown . . . . . Black walnut hulls
Hemlock bark
Sassafras bark

340

Rose tan...........Northern red oak bark
                     Norway maple bark
                     Pecan and shellbark hulls
                     Willow bark

Yellow brown......Alder catkins
                     Birch bark
                     Black walnut bark
                     White oak bark

Yellow tan ....Apple bark
                     Birch bark
                     Black oak bark
                     Chestnut oak bark
                     Mountain laurel leaves
                     Northern red oak bark
                     Osage orange wood
                     Tupelo bark

CRIMSON............Poppy petals

GRAY..............Mountain laurel leaf
                     Pecan hulls
                     Rhododendron leaf
                     Sumac berries

GREEN.............Hickory bark

Yellow green.......Lily-of-the-valley leaves

ORANGE............Bloodroot root
                     Yellow dye flower blossom

Bright orange ......Madder

Dull orange........Onion skins

Terra cotta ....Coreopsis flowers

PURPLE-RED.........Red poppy flowers

RED................Birch, inner bark
                     Hemlock bark
                     Potentil roots
                     Red oak bark
                     St. John's wort leaves
                     Sorrel roots and stalk

Henna............Madder

Lacquer red........Madder

ROSE...............Poke berries

SLATE..............Sycamore bark

YELLOW............Ash, fresh inner bark
                     Bay leaf
                     Birch leaves

YELLOW (*continued*)... Black-eyed Susan flower
Bog myrtle
Bramble
Broom-sedge stalk and leaf
Buckthorn berries and bark
Burdock
Clematis leaves and branches
Cockle burrs
Common dock root
Crab apple bark
Golden rod head and stalks
Golden seal
Gorse bark, flowers, and young shoots
Hickory inner bark
Iron wood
Kidney vetch
Marsh potentil
Meadow rue
Nettle flower
Pignut hickory inner bark
Pear leaves
Plum leaves
Poplar leaves
Rye
St. John's wort flowers
Saw-wort
Sassafras flower
Stone crottle
Sundew
Sweet laurel leaves
Sweet leaf (horse sugar or dye bush) leaves
Teasle
Tomato vines
Weld (wild mignonette) leaves, stalk, and flowers
Wild sunflower
Willow leaves
Yellow camomile
Yellowroot root

Brass.............Apple bark
Marigold flowers
Onion skins

Bright...........Peach leaf

Deep yellow.......Hickory bark

Dull.............Touch-me-not or Jewelweed stem, leaf, and flower

Gold.............Black oak bark
Fustic
Privet leaves
Tulip leaves

APPENDIX IV

EXTRACTS FROM REPORT ON INDIGO EXPERIMENTS, PINE MOUNTAIN, KENTUCKY, SEPTEMBER 15–OCTOBER 1, 1925

By

EDNA H. FAWCETT

THE author became interested in indigo during a visit to the Pine Mountain Settlement School in Harlan County, Kentucky, in the fall of 1922. Here, as in other mountain schools, the old native hand industries, including the art of vegetable dyeing, are being revived and taught.

At that time considerable success had been attained with the native bark and root dyes from which the workers got their various shades of brown and yellow and green. Their reds they obtained with madder, which is on the market in the form of a coarse powder made from the dried ground root of the madder plant. Vegetable indigo they were able to buy also, in lump form, but they had not learned how to use it successfully.

The author felt a desire to help them with their blues if possible, and since it is the policy of those industrial centers in the mountains which are fostering the old hand industries to go back as far as possible to the beginnings of things, it occurred to her that it would be of historical and educational value to the school even if not practical economically to learn to raise indigo and extract the dye from the plants.

This met with the approval and enthusiasm of the executive committee at Pine Mountain, and through the interest and cooperation of Doctor Stockberger, of the Bureau of Plant Industry, seed was obtained from Vilmorin-Andrieux, France, in the spring of 1923, some of which was sent to Kentucky, and the remainder planted at Arlington Farm, Va. By the middle of September the plants at Arlington were from three to four feet high and just coming into flower. They were cut and brought into the laboratory where a small quantity of indigo was successfully extracted by a hot water steeping process.[1]

The dried powder thus obtained was made into dye-extract by mixing it with sulphuric acid, and some preliminary dyeing experiments were tried with wool sent from Pine Mountain.

[1] Marsden, F., Indigo Manufacture in Madras. Dept. of Agriculture, Madras, India, vol. 4, no. 74, 1918.

The seed planted in Kentucky also made a good stand, but those in charge of the work had neither sufficient time nor knowledge to make a success of the extraction process, although an attempt was made.

In the spring of 1924 more seed was sent to Pine Mountain by the Bureau, but too late to be planted. This seed, also from Vilmorin-Andrieux, was saved and planted in April, 1925. Due to a phenomenally dry season, the growth of the plants was very slow, and for some unknown reason very uneven. The stand was not nearly so good as in 1923.

On my arrival at Pine Mountain September 1, 1925, I found a plot of indigo about 30 feet square containing twelve rows of plants. The soil had been well manured and cultivated. The plants looked thrifty, but the average height was only about 16 inches. A few of them had reached the height of 2 to 2½ feet and showed flower buds.

EXTRACTION EXPERIMENT, PINE MOUNTAIN, KENTUCKY

On September 16 all the plants which were in bud were cut. These ranged in height from 2 to 3 feet and comprised about one-fourth of the plants in the plot.

They were cut early in the morning and the leaves and tender tips were stripped from them immediately. The total weight of plant material after discarding the stems was 12 pounds.

The leaves were distributed in four large cans, capacity 6 gallons, covered with water and placed on a coal range. Since there was some doubt as to whether the limestone water of the region would be efficacious in the extraction process, filtered rain-water was used in three of the cans and limestone water in the remaining one for comparison. The proportion of water to leaves was 1 gallon of water to 1 pound of leaves, an amount just sufficient to cover them well when pushed down.

The steeping was carried on for 1½ hours, taking care to keep the leaves under water. About one hour was required to raise the temperature of the water to 50° or 55° C. During the next half hour it rose gradually to 60°. At this stage the leaves had become well wilted, the water was colored a greenish amber, and was beginning to turn blue at the surface. A little was removed from time to time during the last half hour, aerated by pouring rapidly from one cup to another, and tested by adding a little lime water. When the blue precipitate seemed to be forming abundantly and the temperature was about 60°, the cans were removed from the stove in turn, and the liquid was strained into a clean barrel by pouring it through a colander in which a piece of coarse cheese-cloth had been laid. The leaves in each can were rinsed with an additional gallon of cold water to save more of the indigo if possible and this was added to the liquid already in the barrel. When the straining was completed the barrel was a little over half full.

The next step in the process is aeration by means of which a colorless substance (indoxyl) present in the liquid at this stage is oxidized to indigotin—the dye principle which gives indigo its blue color.

This was accomplished by churning the juice as follows: Two little girls stood on either side of the barrel and carefully agitated the liquid by raising and lowering in it (as if churning butter) two coarse mountain brooms made of oak splits fastened to the end of rude handles (new clean brooms were used). This was continued for a half hour. One quart of limewater was then added, churning was continued for another 5 minutes and the liquid was allowed to settle.

Three holes had been bored in the barrel, one about 6 inches from the bottom, the other two directly above and about 12 inches apart. These were closed with tight-fitting wooden plugs which were removed in turn to facilitate decantation of the upper layers of clear liquid. The middle plug was removed about 5 hours after completing the churning and all the liquid was poured off which could be reached through the bung-hole by carefully tipping the barrel. The lowest plug was removed the following morning, more clear liquid was decanted, and the remainder, containing the indigo, was transferred to a pail from which it was poured into a bag of fine cotton cloth and allowed to drain as in making cheese. The moist cake of indigo collected in this way was spread out on a saucer to dry.

The total dry weight of the indigo collected from 12 pounds of leaves was 26 and a fraction grams (just a little short of one ounce). This was a fair yield, since an ounce from 10 pounds of leaves is considered good, but at this rate our 30 ft. plot could not have produced over four or five ounces of indigo—possibly one-half pound in a good year.

Taking into consideration the cheapness of Madras vegetable indigo which is obtained by Pine Mountain School and Berea at $2.00 per pound, it would not be practical from the point of view of time and expense for the school to extract the dye from the plants, though it would be entirely possible to do so in case of emergency provided the seed were available.

.   .   .   .   .   .

[The report also contains a section on The Mountain "Blue Pot" Method, The Sulphuric Acid Method, and a comparison of the two, concluding the last section as follows:]

It is possible that the mountain blue pot method accomplishes by natural means the same kind of chemical action which takes place in the vat dye process, used commercially. In both cases the wool is green when first taken from the dye, becoming blue on exposure to air.[1]

The disadvantages of the mountain method are the very disagreeable odor, and the fact that the "yeast" may not be available when wanted or may have become contaminated with some deleterious organism.

(I have been told that sometimes the pot "foams" when being started, but that the dye is not so good when this happens.) It is possible, however, that with a little standardization from a biological as well as a chemical standpoint, this very interesting old process is the best simple method available for country use.

[1] Mairet, Ethel, A Book on Vegetable Dyes. 3d ed., 1920, pp. 62–64.

SELECTED BIBLIOGRAPHY

SELECTED BIBLIOGRAPHY

THE purpose of this Bibliography is to give the student of the Southern Highlands references to books and articles bearing upon the life of the region and upon
its handicrafts. For the student of handicrafts in general a few selected works
on specific subjects referred to in the text have been included; these have been
limited to publications that are difficult to find listed elsewhere and to a few
subjects of special importance to the Highlands. Therefore the list includes
references to baskets, coverlets, dyes (natural), quilting and patchwork, rug
making, spinning and weaving, and whittling and woodcarving. The Russell
Sage Foundation Library is considering the publication in the near future of a
Bulletin to contain a fuller bibliography on the handicrafts.

BIBLIOGRAPHIES ON THE SOUTHERN HIGHLANDS

Badcock, Mabel A. The Southern Highlander. Russell Sage Foundation
Library, Bulletin No. 115, New York. 1932. 3 pp.

Campbell, John C. Bibliography. *In* The Southern Highlander and His Homeland. Russell Sage Foundation, New York. 1921. pp. 375–389.

Campbell, Mrs. John C. The Southern Highlands. Russell Sage Foundation
Library, Bulletin No. 39, New York. 1920. 3 pp.

Edwards, Everett E. References on the Mountaineers of the Southern Ap-
palachians. Bibliographical Contributions No. 28. Bureau of Agricultural
Economics, U. S. Department of Agriculture, Washington. 1935. 148 pp.
(Mimeographed)

Meyer, H. H. B. List of References on the Mountain Whites. Division of
Bibliography, Library of Congress, Washington. 1922. 14 pp. (Typewritten)

BIBLIOGRAPHY ON THE HANDICRAFTS OF THE SOUTHERN
HIGHLANDS

Edwards, Everett E. References on the Handicrafts of the Southern Highlanders.
Bureau of Agricultural Economics, U. S. Department of Agriculture, Washington. 1934. 22 pp. (Mimeographed)
Although issued separately, this material is included in the Bibliography
entitled References on the Mountaineers of the Southern Appalachians noted
above.

BIBLIOGRAPHIES ON HANDICRAFTS

American Occupational Therapy Association, Special Committee. Bibliography
on Occupational Therapy. Occupational Therapy Print Shop, Kings Park
State Hospital, Kings Park, New York.

Calkins, Earnest Elmo. Bibliography. *In* Care and Feeding of Hobby Horses.
Little Book No. 1. Leisure League of America, New York. 1934. 105 pp.
This bibliography comprises the following subjects: Arts and Crafts; Bas-
ketry; Chair Caning; Metal Work; Model Making; Book Binding and

Ornamentation; Textile Crafts; Woodworking Methods; Dyeing; Leather Work; Pottery Making and Glazing; Furniture; Pewter Ware; Coverlets, Bedspreads, and Quilts.

Edward Pease Public Library. A Select List of Books on Handicrafts. Public Library and Museum Committee, Darlington, England. 1928. 8 pp.

This list comprises the following subjects: Handicrafts, General and Miscellaneous; Basket Making and Raffia; Bookbinding; Embroidery; Fret-Work; Knitting and Crocheting; Lace-Making; Leather Work; Lettering; Metal Work and Jewelry; Modeling; Model Making; Needlework; Printing; Rug Making; Stenciling and Design; Toy Making; Weaving; Woodcarving; and Woodworking.

Gamble, William Burt. Bibliography. Hand-Spinning and Hand-Weaving. New York Public Library. 1922. 41 pp.

Lovell, Eleanor Cook, and Hall, Ruth Mason. Index to Handicrafts, Model-making, and Workshop Projects. F. W. Faxon Co., Boston. 1936. 476 pp.

Schibsby, Marian. Bibliographies on the Songs, Dances, Festivals, and Handicrafts of Certain Immigrant Groups. Foreign Language Information Service, New York. 1929. 23 pp. (Mimeographed)

Slade, William Adams. Handicraft: A Bibliographical List. Division of Bibliography, Library of Congress, Washington. 1930. 22 pp. (Typewritten)

This bibliography comprises the following subjects: General; Basket Making, Raffia Work, Chair Caning, etc.; Bird Houses; Carpentry, Cabinet Work, and Woodcarving; Coverlets; Hand-Loom Weaving; Lace and Lace Making; Leather Work; Metal Work and Jewelry; Model Making; Needlework, Crocheting, Knitting, Tapestry, etc.; Pottery; Rugs; Stencil Work; and Toys.

Viemont, Bess M. A Partial List of References on Handicraft. Miscellaneous Extension Publication No. 25. U. S. Department of Agriculture, Washington. 1932. 11 pp. (Mimeographed)

This bibliography comprises the following subjects: General; Basketry; Crocheting and Knitting; Dyeing; Hand Spinning and Weaving; Hand-Made Rugs; Leathercraft; Quilts and Quilting.

GENERAL WORKS ON THE SOUTHERN HIGHLANDS

Bureau of Agricultural Economics, Bureau of Home Economics, and Forest Service, in cooperation with the Office of Education, United States Department of Interior and the Agricultural Experiment Stations of Tennessee, Virginia, West Virginia, and Kentucky. Economic and Social Problems and Conditions of the Southern Appalachians. Miscellaneous Publication No. 205. U. S. Department of Agriculture. Government Printing Office, Washington. 1935. 184 pp.

Campbell, John C. The Southern Highlander and His Homeland. Russell Sage Foundation, New York. 1921. 405 pp.

Cobb, Ann. Kinfolks: Kentucky Mountain Rhymes. Houghton Mifflin Co., Boston. 1922. 81 pp.

Cushman, Rebecca. Swing Your Mountain Gal. (Verse) Houghton Mifflin Co., Boston. 1934. 151 pp.

Douglass, Harlan Paul. Christian Reconstruction in the South. Pilgrim Press, Boston. 1909. 407 pp.

SELECTED BIBLIOGRAPHY

Furman, Lucy. The Quare Women: A Story of the Kentucky Mountains. Atlantic Monthly Press, Boston. 1923. 219 pp.

Kephart, Horace. Our Southern Highlanders. Macmillan Co., New York. 1929. 469 pp.

Raine, James Watt. The Land of Saddle-Bags: Study of the Mountain People of Appalachia. Published jointly by the Council of Women for Home Missions and the Missionary Education Movement of the United States and Canada, New York. 1924. 260 pp.

Ross, Malcolm. Machine Age in the Hills. Macmillan Co., New York. 1933. 248 pp.

Sheppard, Muriel Earley. Cabins in the Laurel. Illustrations by Bayard Wootten. University of North Carolina Press, Chapel Hill. 1935. 313 pp.

Spaulding, Arthur W. The Men of the Mountains: The Story of the Southern Mountaineer and His Kin of the Piedmont, with an Account of Some of the Agencies of Progress among Them. Southern Publishing Association, Nashville. 1915. 320 pp.

Stuart, Jesse. Man with a Bull-Tongue Plow. (Verse) E. P. Dutton and Co., New York. 1934. 361 pp.

Vance, Rupert B. Human Geography of the South. University of North Carolina Press, Chapel Hill. 1932. 506 pp.

Wilson, Samuel Tyndale. The Southern Mountaineers. Literature Department of the Presbyterian Home Missions, New York. 1906. 202 pp.

GENERAL WORKS ON THE HANDICRAFTS OF THE SOUTHERN HIGHLANDS

American Federation of Arts. A Catalogue of Mountain Handicrafts. Southern Highland Handicraft Guild, Berea, Kentucky. 1933. 132 pp.

Ames, Marjorie B., Editor. Looking at the Crafts: Crafts of the Southern Mountains. *In* The Handicrafter, November–December, 1930. 5 pp.

Beck, Minna McLeod. The Crafts of the Southern Mountain People. *In* Kentucky High School Quarterly, July, 1919. 4 pp.

Berryman, Florence Seville. Southern Mountain Handicrafts Touring the United States. *In* Daughters of American Revolution Magazine, February, 1934. 7 pp.

Burt, Amy M. The Appalachian School. Department of Fireside Industries. Appalachian School, Penland, N. C. (No date) 16 pp.

Eaton, Allen H. The Handicrafts. *In* Culture in the South. University of North Carolina Press, Chapel Hill. 1934. pp. 299–318.

Erskine, Ralph. The Handicraftsmen of the Blue Ridge. *In* The Craftsman, November, 1907. 9 pp.

Ford, Bonnie Willis. The Story of the Penland Weavers. Appalachian School, Penland, N. C. 1936. 23 pp.

Goodrich, Frances Louisa. Mountain Homespun. Yale University Press, New Haven. 1931. 91 pp.

Hannah, Paul F. The Shenandoah Community Workers. *In* Nature Magazine, November, 1929. 3 pp.

Harris, Mrs. Julian. A Revival of Handicrafts in Rural Georgia. *In* Art and Progress, April, 1912. 3 pp.

Hill, Jennie Lester. Fireside Industries in the Kentucky Mountains. *In* The Southern Workman, April, 1903. 4 pp.

McCabe, Lida Rose. Regenerating Handicrafts in the Carolinas. *In* Art World, November, 1917. 3 pp.

McGarvey, G. A. Home-Made and Hand-Made Fireside Occupations in a Machine Age. *In* School Life, February, 1934. 3 pp.

Morgan, A. Rufus. Reviving the Art of the Mountains. *In* Spirit of Missions, April, 1930. 3 pp.

Mountain Life and Work, published quarterly at Berea College, Berea, Kentucky. It contains many articles on the handicrafts of the Highlands. Among them are: A Dream Come True, by Marguerite Butler, October, 1931; The Spinning Wheel, by Helen H. Dingman, January, 1928; Mountain Handicrafts: What They Mean to Our Home Life and to the Life of Our Country, by Allen H. Eaton, July, 1926.

Nason, Wayne C. Rural Industries in Knott County, Kentucky. Bureau of Agricultural Economics, U. S. Department of Agriculture, in cooperation with the Kentucky Agricultural Experiment Station. Washington. 1932. 24 pp. (Mimeographed)

Nienburg, Bertha M. Potential Earning Power of Southern Mountaineer Handicrafts. Bulletin of the Women's Bureau, No. 128. U. S. Department of Labor. Government Printing Office, Washington. 1935. 56 pp.

Palmer, Estelle. Mountain Industries in the South. *In* Country Life in America, December, 1914. 2 pp.

Redding, Winogene B. An Old Art Modernized. *In* The Handicrafter, August–September, 1929. 3 pp.

Remington, C. Swapping Coverlets for Shingles. *In* Mentor, June, 1929. 3 pp.

Sims, Anne Ruffin. Rosemont Workers. *In* The Commonwealth, February, 1937. 2 pp.

West, Max. Revival of Handicrafts in America. Bulletin of the Bureau of Labor, No. 55. U. S. Department of Commerce and Labor. Government Printing Office, Washington, 1904. 49 pp.

Whiting, Frederic Allen. Native Craftsmanship Will Come into Its Own in the Southern Appalachians. *In* American Magazine of Art, October, 1933. 3 pp.

WORKS ON SPECIAL HANDICRAFTS

Baskets

Gill, Anna A. Practical Basketry. David McKay Co., Philadelphia. 1916. 167 pp.

James, George Wharton. Practical Basket Making. J. L. Hammett Co., Cambridge. 1932. 132 pp.

Lang, Minnie (McAfee). Basketry: Weaving and Design; Reed Weaving, the Use of Wood Beads with Reeds, Reed and Raffia Basketry, Pine-Needle Basketry. Charles Scribner's Sons, New York. 1925. 93 pp.

White, Mary. How to Make Baskets. Doubleday, Page and Co., Garden City, New York. 1928. 194 pp.

SELECTED BIBLIOGRAPHY

COVERLETS AND COUNTERPANES

Goodrich, Frances Louisa. Coverlets. *In* Mountain Homespun. Yale University Press, New Haven. 1931. pp. 61–64.

Hall, Eliza Calvert. A Book of Hand-Woven Coverlets. Little, Brown, and Co., Boston. 1931. 279 pp.

Worst, Edward F. Old Kentucky Drafts. *In* How to Weave Linens. Bruce Publishing Co., Milwaukee. 1926. pp. 154–163.

DYES—NATURAL

Beriau, Oscar A. La Teinturerie Domestique (Home Dyeing). Province of Quebec, Canada. 1933. 188 pp.

Furry, Margaret S., and Viemont, Bess M. Home Dyeing with Natural Dyes. Bureau of Home Economics, U. S. Department of Agriculture, Washington. 1934. 26 pp. (Mimeographed)

Goodrich, Frances Louisa. Dye Plants, Appendix II. *In* Mountain Homespun. Yale University Press, New Haven. 1931. pp. 84–88.

Hall, Eliza Calvert. Coverlet Colors. *In* A Book of Hand-Woven Coverlets. Little, Brown, and Co., Boston. 1931. pp. 129–168.

Mairet, Ethel. A Book of Vegetable Dyes. Chaucer Head Book Shop, New York. 1931. 89 pp.

Pellew, Charles E. Dyes and Dyeing. Robert M. McBride and Co., New York. 1928. 362 pp.

Peyre-Porcher, Francis. Resources of Southern Fields and Forests. By Order of Surgeon-General, C. S., Charleston, S. C. 1863. 733 pp.

Thurston, Violetta. The Use of Vegetable Dyes for Beginners. Dryad Press, Leicester, England, 1930. 55 pp.

——— Vegetable Dyeing. Dryad Press, Leicester, England, 1929. 65 pp.

Viner, Wilmer Stone. The Katherine Pettit Book of Vegetable Dyes. Excelsior Press, Saluda, North Carolina. In press.

QUILTING AND PATCHWORK

Beyer, Alice. Quilting. Recreation Department, South Park Commissioners, Chicago. 1934. 78 pp. (Contains a Bibliography.)

Finley, Ruth E. Old Patchwork Quilts and the Women Who Made Them. J. B. Lippincott Co., Philadelphia. 1929. 202 pp.

Heynes, Anne. Quilting and Patchwork. Dryad Press, Leicester, England. 1930. 16 pp.

King, Elizabeth. Quilting. Little Book No. 8. Leisure League of America, New York. 1934. 91 pp.

Webster, Marie D. Quilts: Their Story and How to Make Them. Doubleday, Page and Co., Garden City, New York. 1926. 178 pp.

Rug Making

Bowles, Ella Shannon. Handmade Rugs. Little, Brown, and Co., Boston. 1927. 205 pp.

Hicks, Ami Mali. The Craft of Hand-Made Rugs. McBride, Nast and Co., New York. 1914. 250 pp.

Kent, W. W. Hooked Rug. Dodd, Mead, and Co., New York. 1930. 210 pp.

Macbeth, Ann. The Country Woman's Rug Book. Dryad Press, Leicester, England. 1928. 48 pp.

Phillips, Anna M. Laise. Hooked Rugs and How to Make Them. Macmillan Co., New York. 1925. 154 pp.

Taylor, Mary Perkins. How to Make Hooked Rugs. David McKay Co., Philadelphia. 1930. 154 pp.

Walker, Lydia Le Baron. Homecraft Rugs: Their Historic Background, Romance of Stitchery and Method of Making. Frederick A. Stokes Co., New York. 1929. 421 pp.

Pamphlets on rug making are published by the Extension Division of the following schools: Utah Agricultural College, Logan; Michigan State College, East Lansing; Texas Agricultural College, College Station; Oklahoma Agricultural College, Stillwater; University of Missouri, Columbia.

Spinning and Weaving

Atwater, Mary Meigs. The Shuttle-Craft Book of American Handweaving. Macmillan Co., New York. 1933. 275 pp.

Beriau, Oscar A. Tissage Domestique (Home-Made Textiles). Minister of Agriculture, Quebec, Canada. 1933. 216 pp.

Crawford, Morris De Camp. The Heritage of Cotton: The Fibre of Two Worlds and Many Ages. G. P. Putnam's Sons, New York. 1931. 244 pp.

Hooper, Luther. Hand-Loom Weaving, Plain and Ornamental: With Line Drawings by the Author and Noel Rooke. Sir I. Pitman and Sons, Ltd., London. 1920. 341 pp.

———— Weaving for Beginners: With Plain Directions for Making a Hand Loom, Mounting It, and Starting the Work. Sir I. Pitman and Sons, Ltd., London. 1920. 113 pp.

Landes, John. A Book of Patterns for Hand-Weaving. Shuttlecraft Guild, Cambridge. 1925. 100 pp.

Oelsner, Gustaf H. Handbook of Weaves. Macmillan Co., New York. 1915. 402 pp. (Dover reprint)

Orman, P. Handloom Weaving. Isaac Pitman and Sons, New York. 1930. 100 pp.

Reath, Nancy Andrews. The Weaves of Hand-Loom Fabrics: A Classification with Historical Notes. Pennsylvania Museum, Philadelphia. 1927. 64 pp.

Shook, Anna Nott. A Book of Weaving. John Day Co., New York. 1932. 190 pp.

Simpson, Lilian Eva. The Weavers' Craft.. Dryad Press, Leicester, England. 1932. 137 pp.

Todd, Mattie Phipps. Hand-Loom Weaving: A Manual for School and Home. Rand, McNally and Co., New York. 1902. 160 pp.

Worst, Edward F. Foot-Power Loom Weaving. Bruce Publishing Co., Milwaukee. 1933. 275 pp.

——— How to Weave Linens. Bruce Publishing Co., Milwaukee. 1926. 166 pp.

WHITTLING AND WOODCARVING

Faulkner, Herbert W. Woodcarving as a Hobby. Harper and Bros., New York. 1935. 140 pp.

Faurot, Walter L. The Art of Whittling. Manual Arts Press, Peoria, Ill. 1930. 91 pp.

Jackson, James. The Handicraft of Woodcarving. Sir I. Pitman and Sons, Ltd., London. 1921. 63 pp.

Maskell, Alfred. Wood Sculpture. G. P. Putnam's Sons, New York. 1911. 425 pp.

Moore, Harris W. Chip Carving. Manual Arts Press, Peoria, Ill. 1922. 46 pp.

Tangerman, E. J. Whittling and Woodcarving. McGraw-Hill Book Co., New York. 1937. 293 pp. (Dover reprint)

INDEX

INDEX

359

J- 344